Effective Elementary
Social Studies

Effective Elementary Social Studies

JOHN DOUGLAS HOGE

The University of Georgia

WADSWORTH PUBLISHING COMPANY

I(T)P® An International Thomson Publishing Company

Belmont • Albany • Bonn • Boston • Cincinnati • Detroit • London • Madrid • Melbourne
Mexico City • New York • Paris • San Francisco • Singapore • Tokyo • Toronto • Washington

♦ ♦ ♦ ♦ ♦

Education Editor:	Sabra Horne
Assistant Editor:	Claire Masson
Editorial Assistant:	Louise Mendelson
Production Services Coordinator:	Debby Kramer
Production:	Cecile Joyner/The Cooper Company
Print Buyer:	Karen Hunt
Permissions Editor:	Jeanne Bosschart
Copy Editor:	Lura Harrison
Illustration:	John and Judy Waller
Interior Designer:	Janet Bollow
Cover Designer:	Tom Kane/Bay Graphics Design
Photographs:	© Elizabeth Crews
Compositor:	Patricia Bonn
Printer:	Quebecor Printing Book Group/Fairfield
Cover Printer:	Phoenix Color Corporation

 This book is printed on acid-free recycled paper.

I(T)P The ITP logo is a registered trademark under license.

Printed in the United States of America

1 2 3 4 5 6 7 8 9 10

For more information, contact Wadsworth Publishing Company:

Wadsworth Publishing Company
10 Davis Drive
Belmont, California 94002, USA

International Thomson Editores
Campos Eliseos 385, Piso 7
Col. Polanco
11560 México D.F. México

International Thomson Publishing Europe
Berkshire House 168-173
High Holborn
London, WC1V 7AA, England

International Thomson Publishing GmbH
Königswinterer Strasse 418
53227 Bonn, Germany

Thomas Nelson Australia
102 Dodds Street
South Melbourne 3205
Victoria, Australia

International Thomson Publishing Asia
221 Henderson Road
#05-10 Henderson Building
Singapore 0315

Nelson Canada
1120 Birchmount Road
Scarborough, Ontario
Canada M1K 5G4

International Thomson Publishing Japan
Hirakawacho Kyowa Building, 3F
2-2-1 Hirakawacho
Chiyoda-ku, Tokyo 102, Japan

Library of Congress Cataloging-in-Publication Data

Hoge, John Douglas
   Effective elementary social studies / by John Douglas Hoge.
      p.   cm.
   Includes bibliographical references and index.
   ISBN 0-534-22908-5
   1. Social sciences—Study and teaching (Elementary)—United States. I. Title.
LB1584.H64   1996
372.83044—dc20   95-42388

CONTENTS

CHAPTER 5
◆ ◆ ◆ ◆ ◆
Fostering Learner Involvement   82

CHAPTER 15
◆ ◆ ◆ ◆ ◆
Multicultural Education 265

CHAPTER 16
◆ ◆ ◆ ◆ ◆
Global Education 288

P R E F A C E

Welcome readers! I hope you enjoy—yes, I said enjoy—reading this textbook! I hope it builds your interest in teaching social studies to young children. I hope it tickles your curiosity and at times challenges your social thinking.

Before we begin the first few chapters, read and consider the statements that follow. They argue the need for teaching elementary social studies and may help you make a personal commitment to learning the content offered in this book. As you read, consider whether you agree or disagree with the ideas presented.

BASIC BELIEFS

The nature of today's world demands improved social studies education for all of our nation's children. Ours is an increasingly complex and global society. Immense opportunities lie in stark contrast to other realities that fill the world. Shadows of persistent national, international, and global problems, such as racism, homelessness, famine, violent ethnic conflicts, and abrupt emergence of refugees, dim the landscape. The failures of local, state, and national governments; funding shortfalls; and corrupted political processes block solutions to these problems.

Many people believe that high-quality universal education is essential to our nation's progress. Indeed, America's educational record is clear: we have achieved basic reading, writing, and arithmetic skills for the vast majority of our population.[1] What our schools lack is effective programs for citizenship preparation.

Preparing productive and responsible citizens requires education directed at that goal. Such education imparts knowledge about our history and our political and economic systems. It develops the skills, attitudes, and values that support motivated citizen involvement. It shows students that accurately informed and directly involved citizens are important to our national well-being.

---

[1]Estimates of functional illiteracy in the United States vary greatly. Many leading scholars contend that educators and politicians exaggerate America's illiteracy problem. The most recent government survey I could find showed that 97 percent of young adults can read well enough to understand a newspaper story. However, national adult functional illiteracy is often estimated at about 15 percent and may go as high as 30 percent in areas of the rural South.

Educating citizens so they might control their own government was a fundamentally radical ideal at the birth of our nation. A citizen-based government required a citizenry that could read, write, and calculate. Merely tools, however, these subjects existed to aid learning about the citizenship subjects of government, politics, economics, and law so that future citizens could shape and control their shared lives. Knowledge of these essential citizenship subjects—and current events—armed common people so they could defend their community, state, and nation from foolishness and corruption.

To the community, state, and nation we must today add the world. Included with this sphere of concern comes knowledge of the many other nations and cultures so closely connected to us. Knowledge from geography, religion, sociology, anthropology, and psychology are essential too if we seek to direct our nation's course in the swirl of world events. Gaining useful command of this knowledge is no small task, so it is little wonder that our schools have struggled to provide adequate citizenship preparation.

Thoughtful government leaders, prominent educators, and highly respected national organizations have long advocated effective citizenship education in our public and private schools. Common sense and mounting research evidence suggest this effort must begin in children's earliest school contacts. Carefully planned learning experiences in these early years can develop the knowledge, skills, attitudes, and values needed to act intelligently and humanely in social groups. Children learn to expect and value community involvement by functioning as citizens in their classrooms, schools, and communities. America's children must learn to care for one another and their communities. They must experience lessons that teach them to defend their rights and fulfill their responsibilities. A high-quality social studies program is essential if we expect children to become the future citizens our nation needs to thrive and exert leadership in the world.

ABOUT THIS BOOK
♦ ♦ ♦ ♦ ♦

This book advocates providing high-quality kindergarten through sixth-grade social studies. *Social studies* is the area of the school curriculum that combines the accumulated facts, concepts, generalizations, skills, processes, and values of the social sciences and humanities. Students use this knowledge to examine themes or topics of study considered important to the development of citizenship, making social studies an essential ingredient of basic education for all of our nation's children.

A fundamental belief underlying this book is that the explanatory power of the social sciences and humanities is basic to citizenship literacy. For example, knowledge of women's successful struggle for voting rights in the United States may help today's children take a stand on the equal treatment of girls in their own classroom. Or, as another example, knowledge gained from a field trip to the police station may spur actions to report crimes occurring in the neighborhood. Many other examples could be cited. The point is that it is impossible to be a good citizen without learning content gained from the social studies. This content does more than open students' eyes to the world; it gives them the thoughtful perspectives they need to become productive, caring citizens.

This book provides practical information on how K–6 teachers can carry out high-quality social studies programs in their classrooms. Beginning teachers will learn how to plan engaging activities for the wide range of students met in public and private school classrooms. The unique aspects of planning and teaching social studies are a central focus.

Part One of the book provides an overview of the formal and informal social studies curriculum, its history, current status, and content. It explains in detail the unique aspects of lesson and unit planning for social studies instruction. Readers are introduced to using textbooks and trade books intelligently and fostering increased learner involvement through a variety of approaches. Sample dialogues, exercises, discussion questions, scenarios, and activity ideas illustrate the key points. Part One helps you understand not only what social studies is and how social studies fits into the K–6 curriculum, but also how to plan effective social studies lessons.

Part Two provides a broad overview of the social science and humanities disciplines that form the foundation of social studies. Readers see sample K–6 lesson plans based on all areas of the social sciences and humanities. Part Two offers a discrete view of each discipline as a convenience to the reader who is attempting to gain a global understanding of the important content of the social studies. These chapters may be used as a future resource for identifying potential new topics of study and analyzing the adequacy of textbooks and district curriculum documents. But a word of warning: This "separate discipline" exposition of elementary social studies content should not be taken as an endorsement of offering social studies to children in the form of separate disciplines. I wholeheartedly support an integrated disciplines approach to teaching elementary social studies. Discipline-focused instruction is only appropriate in specific situations where it is clearly necessary.

Part Three develops an understanding of special social studies topics and methods including: inquiry instruction, handling differences of opinion, teaching positive attitudes and values, multicultural education, and global education. A recurring theme of this section is the tie between these topics, the academic disciplines covered in Part Two, and the demands of citizenship in the twenty-first century.

I wish to express my gratitude and acknowledge my intellectual debt to colleagues at Florida State University; the Social Science Education Consortium in Boulder, Colorado; Boise State University; the Social Studies Development Center at Indiana University; and the University of Georgia; as well as to the following people who reviewed the manuscript: Gerald Barkholz,

University of South Florida; Frederick Isele, Indiana State University; Rod Janzen, Fresno Pacific College; Saundra McKee, Clarion University; Carolyn Schluck, Florida State University; Ben Smith, Kansas State University; and Terry Whealon, Northern Illinois University. Most important, many thanks go to the kindergarten through sixth-grade and college students who helped me improve my understanding of elementary social studies and inspired me to remain positive about the future.

John D. Hoge

An Overview of Elementary Social Studies

INTRODUCTION

Part One provides an overview of elementary social studies. Individual chapters focus on the nature and mission of social studies, the past and present status of the social studies curriculum, strategies for teaching social studies content, planning in social studies, and ways to foster learner involvement.

As you plunge into these chapters, I ask that you give serious consideration to the discussion questions and suggested exercises. Think about what you are reading and attempt to relate your own background of experience to the ideas being presented. Please consider what is being offered, but above all, make up your own mind about the ideas being presented.

The figures contained in Part One are often models of teaching or sets of guidelines for practice. I recommend that you read these figures carefully, for it is these models and guidelines that you will later use to develop successful social studies instruction for young children. It is my hope that you'll leave Part One ready to explore the rich intellectual content of social studies presented in Part Two.

The Nature and Mission of Social Studies

Ring . . . Ring . . . Ring . . . (The school bell sounds the start of the day. Ms. Tyner's second-grade class has already assembled.)

MS. TYNER: Okay, it's time for reading.

SONJA: Ms. T., my mommy had a new baby last night.

MS. TYNER: That's nice. Maybe we can talk about it at recess. Group A, you should be on workbook page 47. Group C, you'll need to finish reading the story about Ted.

ERIC: I got a new Halloween costume! I'm going to be a dragon!

TERRANCE: I'm gonna get lots of candy this year.

MS. TYNER: *(ignoring the comment)* Group B, I'll meet you at the reading circle.

ERIC: Will we decorate the room and have a Halloween party?

MS. TYNER: The school board decided we can't have Halloween parties. Anyway, Halloween is not a part of the curriculum. We don't test it.

PRINCIPAL: *(over the intercom)* Teachers, remember that the canned food drive ends Friday. If your class is participating, remind the students to get in their donations.

SONJA: Ms. T., how come we didn't participate? My big sister's fourth-grade class did.

MS. TYNER: I'd like to, but we have to focus on basic skills in reading, writing, and math. And remember, you all are behind! Now let's get down to work. I want group B at the reading circle.

Fade . . . (Ms. Tyner moves toward the reading circle.)

INTRODUCTION
• • • •

What did you think as you read the opening scenario? Did you think, "Wow! Ms. Tyner is a real drudge," when you considered the way she acted? Did you feel sorry for the children?

Unfortunately, the imaginary dialogue that opens this chapter is not far from the reality some students face at the hands of misguided primary grade level teachers. Unwittingly perhaps, this teacher has removed humanity from her classroom. She has disassociated education from the daily social reality that the children experience. Further, she has most likely turned schoolwork into pure misery!

Ms. Tyner was right in saying that many of the children's interests aren't tested. But she was wrong in assuming that such content wasn't important enough for her consideration or class time. In fact, early childhood content area experts in math and reading would urge Ms. Tyner to recognize and make good instructional use of the children's interests.

A key point here is that much of what interests children, much of what adds meaning to their lives, is obviously social studies in nature. But even more important, while it is fundamentally correct to capitalize on these interests to support the learning of reading, writing, and arithmetic, it is not enough to use children's social studies interests simply as icing to sugarcoat the rather dry substance of reading and math.[1] Insight into real-life events develops best with direct and extended attention to such matters for their own sake, not just for satisfying the development of basic skills.

In this chapter, you'll learn about the nature of the social studies curriculum, inspect a rationale for young children's social studies, and briefly view your role as a teacher in this important area of the school curriculum.

WHAT IS SOCIAL STUDIES?
• • • •

The answer is surprisingly complex. Authorities recognize that social studies encompasses a diverse formal curriculum in addition to a powerful set of informal experiences. The social sciences and humanities compose the formal curriculum. The informal curriculum includes naturally arising experiences such as holiday celebrations, current events, and a host of other important learnings conveyed to students through the "hidden curriculum."

---

[1] I am not trying to restrict the use of social science or humanities content as a substantive vehicle for building reading, writing, and math skills. After all, these areas must make use of either science or social studies in order to have the real-world meanings they need. When (or if) reading, writing, and math instruction claim to be achieving the content goals and objectives of social studies (that is, for example, a reading lesson is offered that seeks to teach children something about history), then I want that instruction to be good social studies instruction, offered for its own value.

The Formal Curriculum

The formal curriculum may be thought of as the purposefully taught lessons that students experience in schools. State-adopted textbooks and curriculum guides support the formal curriculum. The formal curriculum is open to public review and frequently tested to document students' learning and teacher performance. In the subject area of social studies, the intellectual foundation of the formal curriculum comes from the social sciences and the humanities.

The Social Sciences and Humanities   The subjects that most educators group under the label of social studies are history, geography, political science, economics, sociology, anthropology, and psychology. Included along with the social sciences are areas of the humanities such as philosophy, religion, and aspects of art history and literature.

These subjects are often thought of as academic disciplines and represented on college campuses as departments. Research and writing by the scholars in these disciplines provides the content that, in a simplified form, gets taught to young children.

Topics or themes structure elementary social studies instruction, making use of all applicable social sciences and humanities. For example, a first-grade unit on the contemporary family would involve elements of sociology, economics, psychology, and perhaps religion. Alternatively, a unit on a specific Native-American culture in the early 1800s would primarily involve information from history, anthropology, and geography.

Occasionally, teachers in the elementary school will devote some special instructional time to a specific discipline, such as a unit focusing on one or more concepts from economics, or a week of geography instruction on map skills. But such discipline-focused study is the exception rather than the rule in most elementary classrooms. The predominant approach to teaching elementary social studies is an integrated disciplines approach and this approach is likely to remain popular in the future.

So one very common answer to the question of what is social studies is that it is the content of the social sciences and certain humanities simplified and applied to themes or topics studied by young children. Yet social studies involves more; it also includes an informal curriculum.

DISCUSSION QUESTIONS
◆ ◆ ◆ ◆ ◆

1. What are the benefits of instruction that is discipline focused?

2. What are the benefits of the integrated approach to social studies?

3. How might knowledge from the social sciences and humanities benefit young children?

The Informal Curriculum

Many authors refer to the informal curriculum simply as the "hidden curriculum." Calling the entire informal curriculum hidden, however, is not appropriate. The meanings associated with the word *hidden* are not typically positive and much of what happens in the informal curriculum exerts a positive influence on children. More important, much of the informal curriculum is not hidden at all! Instead, it is a highly visible, yet unwritten, aspect of schooling. This highly visible, yet unwritten, aspect of the school experience may be thought of as a natural social studies curriculum.

The Natural Curriculum Returning to the theme of the opening scenario, imagine how dull a young child's school year would be in a classroom where the teacher refused to consider the influence of holidays, important current events, and events in the children's homes. What view of school would children have if they experienced the same routine "Three Rs" instruction over and over? The standard school day would involve reading out of the basal, completing reading skills workbooks, doing math worksheets, polishing handwriting skills, and learning spelling words. Each day would repeat in a similar manner—day after day, week after week, all year long.

Quite obviously, an effective early childhood teacher must use the powerful natural curriculum for its motivational value within the Three Rs. Beyond this, however, she must also use it to positively influence the citizenship development of her young students. To use the opening classroom scenario as an example, the teacher might offer lessons on how a family's life is influenced by the arrival of a new child, what the real history of Halloween is, and why some people need food donations. Accurate, age-appropriate answers to these questions demand knowledge from the social sciences and humanities. Such answers are a legitimate focus of thoughtfully developed early childhood social studies instruction. As your knowledge of this area develops, you'll see how to design lessons that develop citizenship skills, knowledge, and positive attitudes based on the natural curriculum.

The Hidden Curriculum While the natural curriculum is visible, the hidden curriculum is less so. Tucked down under the daily routines, slipped into the mutually shared understandings of the teacher's gestures and words, and buried between the lines of the school's formal curriculum, are an assortment of unspoken and largely unchallenged beliefs, attitudes, values, and assumptions about the social world.

To illustrate the importance of the hidden cultural knowledge we all typically command, stop for a moment and think about how you might offer your hand in greeting another person. Would you grip the person's hand fully and shake with considerable motion? Or would you offer mainly your fingers and make only the lightest touch? Would you look the person in the eyes and say "How nice to meet you"?

Your answers to these questions clearly show the significance of the "hidden" social knowledge that influences our perceptions of what is correct to do in interactions with other people. You probably found yourself saying, "Well it depends on who I'm meeting! I would shake hands one way if it was the president and I was getting the opportunity to greet her on the White House lawn. I would shake hands quite another way—or perhaps not at all—if I was meeting my new academic advisor for the first time."

The factors that could potentially influence the way in which you might shake hands include: the person's age, sex, appearance, social status, the occasion or social setting, and even your own mood. Quite obviously, failing to have such important socio-cultural knowledge could produce disastrous results! Clearly, adequate socialization is essential to the individual and to society.

The hidden curriculum serves as a medium for passing along the implicit cultural and social knowledge we all need in order to function effectively. This hidden knowledge is either assumed or purposefully transmitted, but seldom analyzed. For example, expectations related to traditional classroom teaching dictate that teachers typically stand, talk, move, and command while students remain seated, silent, stationary, and submissive. Obviously, certain beliefs, attitudes, values, and assumptions have formed such expected behaviors. Thinking about, and sharing with students, the reasons why we behave as we do is an important part of the social studies learning teachers must offer.

You may be wondering what all this has to do with social studies. The answer is twofold. First, it is the social sciences and humanities that have systematically studied and expanded our understanding of such cultural and social phenomena. This taken-for-granted aspect of all schooling is a part of every lesson regardless of whether it is social studies, science, math, or reading. However, it is the disciplines of social studies that contain the knowledge needed to examine the hidden curriculum. Second, since schools must function as our society's primary means of socializing the young for citizenship, it is important that teachers be keenly aware of this instructional responsibility and be capable of explaining the reasons for the knowledge, beliefs, attitudes, and values students must gain. This is an especially important task of elementary grade level teachers since they bear the brunt of such endless questions as: "Does every state have a president?" "Is there really an Easter bunny?" "How long is a half hour?" and "Why do I have to share?"

DISCUSSION QUESTIONS

1. How important is the informal social studies curriculum compared to the formal social studies curriculum?
2. What message does it send to a child when a teacher ignores a child's question or provides a flippant or incorrect response?
3. Should the hidden curriculum be openly taught and thoughtfully examined?
4. What are the hidden beliefs, attitudes, values, and assumptions that underlie the stereotypical teacher and student behaviors previously described?

WHY TEACH SOCIAL STUDIES?

There are two basic answers to this question. A frequent answer, commonly cited in statements of the National Council for the Social Studies, stems from the need for informed civic participation in a democracy. A second response stresses the importance of social studies as an aid to understanding the activities of people as they organize their society, evolve culture, and individually go about the daily business of living.

Social Studies Is Fundamental to Democratic Citizenship

Preparation for citizenship is often identified as the central mission of social studies. While all areas of the curriculum make important contributions to citizenship preparation (for example, language arts and reading contribute to the future citizen's ability to read and write), social studies focuses the development of the knowledge, attitudes, values, and skills that we would want all citizens to share. The essential role social studies plays in the development of citizens may be illustrated by asking some rhetorical questions such as: Wouldn't you expect all citizens to know something about the geography, government, and history of their country? Wouldn't you hope that all citizens stood up for their legal rights and fulfilled their responsibilities? Wouldn't you be pleased if all citizens used their literacy skills to keep informed of current events and to participate in civic life?

Of course, it is hard to answer "no" to these questions. We want to do our very best to form all of our nation's young people into the best possible citizens. But this task is complex. It involves more than what the individual teacher and school can do; it involves the family, the church, the community, and even such relatively uncontrollable influences as the media. As we shall see in future chapters, social studies can play a role in reinforcing the positive messages of all of these powerful influences. Social studies can also provide children with the knowledge, attitudes, values, and skills needed to overcome deficits and handicaps associated with limited family, church, and community experiences.

Citizenship Attitudes Form Early   It has been shown that political and social attitudes important to citizenship develop early in the life of a child. For this reason alone, schools must provide young students with positive experiences in these areas. Teachers must show children how to participate responsibly in the many decisions that affect their lives in school. In doing so, schools implant the expectation that citizens make the governmental decisions of their communities. Examples of this type of experience in the primary grades include involving students in questions about: aspects of their daily schedule *(Should we continue working on our projects into the next period and then make up the time tomorrow?)*; the method of instruction *(Would you rather work in small groups or alone?)*; the organization of the room *(I've been thinking* *about placing the desks in a different arrangement, but I'd like to know what you think . . .)*; and even the standards and rewards provided in the room *(How well should a student be able to do this in order to get a satisfactory grade?)*.

Experiences such as these show how a teacher might share the governance of the room with her students to build the important democratic citizenship expectation that we all must have a say in governing our communities. Equally important to this democratic ideal is the role that the teacher plays in promoting positive citizenship attitudes and values. For example, the teacher should create a warm accepting climate and provide experiences that promote dignity and self-respect regardless of a child's level of intelligence, physical appearance, wealth, religion, or other personal characteristics. Lessons that build the knowledge—and attitudes—required to promote genuine caring are basic to social studies.

Participatory Citizenship Requires Practice   Why do some individuals rise to community service and leadership? Why are so many other people disengaged, uninformed, and apathetic? Social studies educators contend that an important difference is the kinds of citizenship preparation experiences individuals have during their school years.

People become involved in their communities when they have self-confidence in their ability to contribute, feel a desire to improve their community, and have positive experiences that build the knowledge and skills needed to succeed. The traits typically associated with these people are average or higher grades, membership in school clubs and athletics, participation in school governance, and youth service activities. By establishing classrooms and schools with a variety and number of opportunities for participation in service and governance capacities, and by clearly showing the desirability of such activities, teachers can do much to increase the chance that students leaving their classrooms will continue to be good citizens.

DISCUSSION QUESTIONS

1. The school is not the only source of learning directed at good citizenship. What role do families, churches, and youth groups also play?

2. Does the school have a special responsibility or unique role to play in citizenship preparation? If so, what? If not, why?

3. Students have academic and personality traits that vary as widely as their physical appearance. Should the teacher play a role in assuring that all children experience leadership opportunities despite such differences?

4. What is a good citizen? Are certain kinds of knowledge, skills, and abilities needed for good citizenship?

Social Studies Aids in Constructing Social Meaning

The second answer to the question of why we teach social studies reflects the role that the social sciences and humanities play as tools for constructing social meaning. The meaning that each individual makes of his or her experiences is unique. Yet some portion of that individual meaning must be shared in order for individuals to function collectively in a social setting. Social studies plays a role in helping children construct shared meanings out of their experiences.

Informal learning in the home or preschool may do much that is positive to prepare the child for entry into kindergarten. Available evidence shows, however, that many children enter kindergarten unprepared. The difference is often the presence of a caring adult—or older sibling—who took the time required to teach basic information and focus the child's mind on the meaning of the life events he or she experienced. Young students need carefully developed instruction on the informal learnings they gain. Carefully developed social studies instruction can aid students in developing an improved understanding of their lives. The following example illustrates the significance of this statement. As you read the story, think of the openings in Seth's life for lessons that might improve his understanding and self-esteem.

S E T H
· · · · ·

At the tender age of two Seth had already learned that when the rest of the day-care children were gone it wouldn't be much longer before his own mom showed up. He clung to Ms. Abercrombie's arm sucking hard on his pacifier as she quietly read "The Tawny Scrawney Lion."

By three, Seth had visited his mother's place of work. He understood that there were other children like him who lived with their grandparents. Mom said it was only "temporary," whatever that meant. To him it meant Grammy's good cooking and games with Grandad.

Taking a bubble bath with Mom in the big claw-foot tub was a nightly treat. After she got out there was always time for water play with his collection of bath toys.

By four, Seth and his mom had moved to a new town. Day care changed some. There were more children and the teachers seemed less fun. They were always watching, giving orders, and breaking up fights. Seth was really anxious to go home each day when his mother arrived. Mom's cooking just wasn't as good as Grammy's, but there were more snack foods that he liked. Bath time meant bathing on his own since Mom said he was getting bigger and could handle it.

Seth's fifth year brought him the first father he had ever known. Grammy and Grandad came for the wedding. Seth and his parents moved to a new house, and once again, he changed day-care settings. Life bumped along as the threesome adjusted to each other.

That summer Seth had his sixth birthday. His mother told him that in the fall he would start kindergarten, and she took him to visit the school. It was bigger than he ever imagined. There were lots and lots of children running everywhere. Seth thought this place could be fun, but at the same time he wanted to stay home and he hoped that summer would never end. . . . .

Upon entering kindergarten or first grade, most children have had five or six years of first-hand experiential knowledge of their mother. Yet each child bases his or her conception of Mother only on the example he or she experienced. The ways in which women—and some men—execute the role of mother vary as greatly as the individuals who fill this important place in child rearing. Yet commonalities exist in the way this role is fulfilled and there are many culturally defined expectations concerning the rights and responsibilities of this role. Children inevitably make informal comparisons with other schoolmates' parents. Most educators would prefer, however, that some careful attention be directed at helping children understand the diversity in how mothers fulfill their role.

For example, mothers cook, draw the bath, buy the groceries, and go to work. Or do they? Some children's fathers may do all of the cooking and cleaning. Some children may draw their own bath. Grandparents living in the home may do the grocery shopping. What do such differences tell us about our own experiences? What do they tell us about our classmates' experiences?

Classroom activities aimed at informing children about the natural diversity of their own families may be a child's first lessons in social studies. Such lessons will naturally involve the collection and examination of information. Children will generalize about what they have found and each child will be able to put his or her own experience in a richer context that builds a deeper understanding of what it means to be human. These are the first experiences a child will have with the methods and content of the social sciences and humanities. In addition, these may well be the first noncommercial glimpses that a child gains of the larger social world. This type of basic cultural learning is just as important as learning to read, write, and calculate.

The Formation of Social Knowledge Must Not Be Left to Chance

You might be thinking that this type of learning could wait until children are in the fourth, fifth, or sixth grade. Or perhaps you are thinking that such learning occurs naturally, that it is simply unnecessary to involve children in carefully constructed lessons designed to enhance understanding of their everyday lives. Logic and experience suggest otherwise.

First, gaining the important social knowledge we all need to function well within society must not be left to chance. Some children have expert parent-teachers who carefully answer questions about the world. Other children may come from homes where there is a significant lack of such education-oriented parenting. Children coming from such families are likely to have difficulty in school and other areas of life. Society entrusts the school to develop a common base of knowledge, attitudes, values, and skills citizens need. When the focus of learning turns to the real-world experiences of daily life, children gain social tolerance and self-control, in addition to the knowledge they need to add meaning to their lives.

Beyond the personal knowledge gained when the focus of classroom learning turns to real life, there is the undeniable fact that schooling itself demands more than a little socialization. A large and varied collection of social knowledge, attitudes, values, beliefs, and skills are needed to attend school. In fact, skillful teachers deliver some excellent social studies lessons at the start of each year. Typical lessons focus on school rules (an aspect of political science), classroom manners (an aspect of sociology), the plan of the school building (an aspect of geography), and the chronological sequence of events in the day and week (an aspect of history). A student's failure to gain this essential information can mean instant trouble! Exhibiting an openly antisocial disregard for this information could result in a trip to the principal or even suspension. Such is the essential nature of social studies content.

THE ROLE OF THE TEACHER

The teacher is the central figure in the classroom. She rightfully assumes responsibility for determining what content is most appropriate for individual learners, she works hard to employ engaging methods that will be used to convey the content, and her personality shines through all aspects of the child's classroom experience. Is the teacher autocratic and authoritarian? Is she "hard-nosed" and cold? Does she exude contempt for her young learners' ignorance? Or is the teacher a democratic leader; a person who shows warmth and humor when working with children; an individual who treats children as colearners on a quest of importance, intrigue, and excitement? The answer depends, at least in part, on how the teacher views herself and her students as decision makers.

The Teacher and Students as Decision Makers

Decisions about what to learn, when to learn it, and how to go about it are the essence of teaching. Curriculum coordinators, school boards, principals, textbook authors, editors, and teachers typically make such decisions. In subject areas such as math where there is a relatively restricted body of content and a well-established sequence of instruction, there is relatively little controversy or debate over the what, when, and how of teaching. But in social studies, where the content body is huge and the skill-learning sequence more arbitrary, decisions about the what, when, and how of teaching are problematic. In addition, because the content of social studies deals with all aspects of social life, we have the added responsibility to consider what is appropriate for students in regard to family and community values.

Participatory citizenship is a desired outcome of social studies instruction. In addition, social studies plays a key role in helping individuals construct and interpret social meaning. To achieve these two ends teachers must pay attention to the interests of children and give them some say in determining the what, when, and how of their social studies lessons. Children should influence decisions about the formal and natural social studies curriculum.

Controlling the Formal Curriculum

The formal curriculum in social studies often becomes, by default, the officially adopted textbook. Research tells us that a high percentage of the elementary social studies lessons experienced by children are textbook-based. If the principal tells the teacher to "cover the book," and enforces a rigid daily schedule, then teacher and student decisions concerning the what, when, and how of social studies learning are drastically narrowed. Experience suggests that this is not an effective way to teach social studies. In addition, it is an ineffective way to use a textbook.

Teachers and students must have some say over the what, when, and how of social studies instruction. Parent involvement is important too. Sharing power and addressing students' interests are keys to effective social studies instruction. When the explanatory power of the social sciences and humanities are brought to bare on students' real interests and when this learning takes place in a cooperative, self-determined manner, meaningful social studies learning is likely to result.

Using the Informal Curriculum

Shaping the formal social studies curriculum to meet the interests of students requires conscious effort on the part of the teacher. Perhaps even more challenging and rewarding is the opportunity to use aspects of the informal curriculum (both the natural and the hidden curriculums) as a basis for meaningful social studies lessons.

For example, few elementary schoolteachers allow Thanksgiving to slip past without making a special bulletin board, preparing children for a school program, or using the motivation of the celebration for special projects in art and music. Language arts may feature stories with a Thanksgiving theme and turkey feathers may appear printed on mathbook pages for addition and subtraction exercises.

Yet what do students (and teachers!) know about the real history of Thanksgiving? (Chapter 15 features a multicultural primary grade level lesson on Thanksgiving.) For example, how much do you know about the first Thanksgiving feast or the struggle to have Thanksgiving recognized as an official national holiday? In addition, how much thought have you given to what our current Thanksgiving customs imply about us as a society or how our current Thanksgiving celebration could be improved?

Teachers who focus the reflection of the twin mirrors of the social sciences and humanities on our daily activities give children valuable insight into their lives. Deciding to use the natural and hidden curriculums as the focus of social studies is yet another key to effective social studies lessons.

DISCUSSION QUESTIONS
♦ ♦ ♦ ♦ ♦

1. What are the benefits and drawbacks of sharing power over social studies curriculum decisions?

2. How can a teacher make better use of a social studies textbook than simply using it as a reader?

3. Could lessons on aspects of the natural and hidden curriculums ever backfire and cause trouble for the teacher?

REFERENCES AND SELECTED READINGS
♦ ♦ ♦ ♦ ♦

Alleman, J. E., and Rosaen, C. L. 1991. The cognitive, social-emotional, and moral development characteristics of students: Basis for elementary and middle school social studies. In *Handbook of research on social studies teaching and learning*, ed. J. P. Shaver, 121–133. New York: Macmillan.

Angell, A. V. 1991. Democratic climates in elementary classrooms: A review of theory and research. *Theory and Research in Social Education*. 19:241–266.

Atwood, V. A., ed. 1986. *Elementary school social studies: Research as a guide to practice*. Bulletin no. 79. Washington, D.C.: National Council for the Social Studies.

Benninga, J. S. 1991. *Moral, character, and civic education in the elementary school*. New York: Teacher's College Press.

Berman, S., and La Farge, P. 1993. *Promising practices in teaching social responsibility*. Albany, NY: State University of New York Press.

Callahan, W. T., Jr., and Banaszak, R. A., eds. N.d. *Citizenship for the 21st century*. Bloomington, IN: Social Studies Development Center.

Dewey, J. 1916. *Democracy and education*. New York: Macmillan.

Engle, S. H., and Ochoa, A. S. 1988. *Education for democratic citizenship. Decision making in the social studies*. New York: Teacher's College Press.

Ferguson, P. 1991. Impacts on social and political participation. In *Handbook of research on social studies teaching and learning*, ed. J. P. Shaver, 385–399. New York: Macmillan.

Goodman, J. 1992. *Elementary schooling for critical democracy*. Albany, NY: State University of New York Press.

Haladyna, T., Shaughnessy, J., and Redsun, A. 1982. Correlates of attitudes toward social studies. *Theory and Research in Social Education* 10:1–26.

Hepburn, M. A., ed. 1983. *Democratic education in schools and classrooms*. Bulletin no. 70. Washington, D.C.: National Council for the Social Studies.

Joyce, W. W., Alleman-Brooks, J. E., and Orimoloye, P. S. 1982. Teachers', supervisors', and teacher educators' perceptions of social studies. *Social Education* 46(5):357–360.

Knight, S. L., and Waxman, H. C. 1990. Investigating the effects of the classroom learning environment on students' motivation in social studies. *Journal of Social Studies Research* 14(1):1–7.

McGowan, T. M., Sutton, A. M., and Smith, P. G. 1990. Instructional elements influencing elementary student attitudes toward social studies. *Theory and Research in Social Education* 18:37–52.

President's message. 1993. *The Social Studies Professional* 116 (May/June):2.

Schug, M. C., Todd, R. J., and Beery, R. 1984. Why kids don't like social studies. *Social Education* 48(5):382–387.

Shug, M. C. 1989. Why teach social studies? Interviews with elementary teachers. *The Social Studies* 80(2):73–77.

Social studies for early childhood and elementary school children preparing for the 21st century. 1989. *Social Education* 53(1):14–23.

Who needs the social studies? The case for social studies in the elementary school curriculum. 1990. *Instructor* 99(6):37–44.

Wronski, S. P., and Bragaw, D. H., eds. 1986. *Social studies and social sciences: A fifty-year perspective.* Bulletin no. 78. Washington, D.C.: National Council for the Social Studies.

Wyner, N. B., and Farquhar, E. 1991. Cognitive, emotional, and social development: Early childhood social studies. In *Handbook of research on social studies teaching and learning,* ed. J. P. Shaver, 109–120. New York: Macmillan.

The Social Studies Curriculum:
Past and Present

A BRIEF HISTORY OF ELEMENTARY SOCIAL STUDIES

In the early colonial days of our nation formal education opportunities were quite limited. The education of slaves was forbidden. Boys and girls from poor families often did not attend school. Middle- and upper-class families routinely denied young women access to education beyond the first few years of grammar school.

Each community's "common school," forerunner of our present public elementary school, offered instruction in reading, writing, arithmetic, and quite frequently, religion. Corporal punishment controlled student misbehavior and lessons were commonly taught by the recitation method.

With the overthrow of British colonial rule in 1776, opinion in our nation gradually shifted toward the view that universal education for all children was necessary to a self-governing nation. Benjamin Franklin, Thomas Jefferson, and Noah Webster, among others, developed plans for furthering the education of all citizens. These individuals argued for adding civic education, composed primarily of lessons on our history and government, to the common school curriculum. Of particular importance was Jefferson's belief that education was a civic necessity in a democracy.

Public sentiment in favor of tax-supported common schools gained momentum in the early 1800s. Horace Mann, a Massachusetts legislator, did much to sway opinion in favor of this new and uniquely American approach to education. Ornstein and Levine (1989) state:

> Although the major thrust of the American common school movement of the first half of the nineteenth century was to win popular support for publicly financed elementary education, it also had broad social, political, intellectual, and economic ramifications. The common school may be defined as an institution devoted to elementary education in the basic tools of reading, writing, and arithmetic. It was common in that it was open to the children of all social and economic classes. Through a common or a shared program of civic education, it was to cultivate a sense of American identity and loyalty. Its major social purpose was to integrate children of various social, economic, and ethnic backgrounds into the broad American community. The political objective of common school had been enunciated earlier by such leaders as Jefferson. It was to educate the future citizens of a country with self-governing political institutions. (pp. 169–170)

The curriculum of the common school grew and changed throughout the 1800s. By the last quarter of the century, history and government were taught in many urban elementary schools as a means of preparing students for the demands of citizenship in our diverse immigrant-based and rapidly industrializing society. The growth during the late 1800s of geography, sociology, anthropology, and psychology as legitimate academic disciplines in their own right laid the foundation for a diversification of social studies education.

Opportunities for education beyond elementary school were rapidly developing throughout our nation during the early 1900s. High schools sought to expand and strengthen the history and government lessons students had learned in elementary education. Lybarger (1991) notes that the 1916 Committee on Social Studies of the National Education Association's Commission on the Reorganization of Secondary Education popularized the term *social studies* and planted the seeds of many present-day, high-school social studies practices.

The work of the 1916 NEA commission was quickly followed by the formation of the National Council for the Social Studies (NCSS) in 1921. The NCSS vowed to bring together teachers and others interested in education for citizenship through social studies. In response to the turmoil in high-school social studies, the American Historical Association published a sixteen-volume commission report that secured a role for history as a unifying subject at the very core of the social studies.

As a result of this brief review of curriculum history, we can see that formal elementary schooling from our earliest days included social studies, first as instruction in religion and next as lessons celebrating our history and government. It was not until the early 1900s that the social sciences were formally added into the mix. This happened first at the secondary level and later at the elementary level as a part of the birth of the "expanding environments scope and sequence."

DISCUSSION QUESTIONS

1. Is social studies more, less, or equally necessary today compared to the past? On what would you base your arguments?

2. The content and place of social studies in the curriculum has changed over time. What factors account for such changes and are such changes in the curriculum necessary?

3. If children from low-income families cannot receive a high-quality education in our tax-supported public schools, is it right to require their attendance? Argue both sides of this issue.

ALTERNATIVE STRUCTURES FOR K-6 SOCIAL STUDIES

As you might imagine from the title to this section, there is no single correct answer to the question of what social studies content should be taught and when it should be learned. Individuals, professional organizations, and states have advocated alternative plans for the K–6 social studies curriculum.[1] These alternatives to the K–6 social studies scope and sequence have been the subject

---

[1] *The Instructor's Resource Manual* contains the NCSS twenty-first-century scope and sequence model and California's history social science framework. The three history-focused curriculum models proposed by the Bradley Commission are presented in Chapter 6.

of persistent debates, featured prominently in professional journals and reports of official commissions (Mehlinger, 1992; Epstein and Evans, 1990; Finn and Ravitch, 1988; LeRiche, 1987; Akenson, 1987; Ravitch, 1984).

Although there are many scope and sequence models, the dominant pattern for elementary social studies remains the *expanding environments* approach. Originating in the early 1900s, this approach to organizing the social learning experiences of young children is based upon the presumption that a typical child's sphere of awareness and readiness to learn expands grade by grade. The focus of social learning should, then, expand to increasingly distant and complex environments as the child becomes capable of such study. Figure 2-1 shows the typical progression of topics in the expanding environments approach. These topics still provide the thematic focus for elementary social studies textbooks from major publishers.

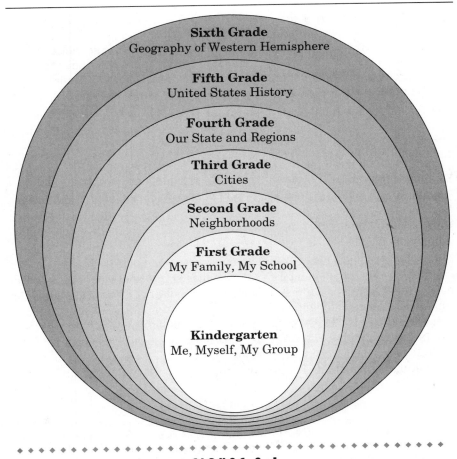

FIGURE 2-1

The Expanding Environments Scope and Sequence

Despite the availability of many scope and sequence models, in actual practice the individual classroom teacher may have little say over a school's elementary social studies curriculum. True, a small group of teachers may periodically serve on a curriculum committee that considers state and national guidelines, reviews new curriculum material, and attempts to update the district's social studies program. Most elementary teachers, however, work with whatever textbook is provided and follow the existing district-approved curriculum guide.[2]

Since it is highly likely that you will—at least initially—teach the curriculum you are given, it is less important for you to become acquainted with the alternative scope and sequence patterns than it is for you to understand the reasons different patterns will always exist and the factors that you should consider in determining whether to favor one alternative over another for your particular teaching situation.

DISCUSSION QUESTIONS
● ● ● ● ●

1. If you were given an opportunity to plan your own K–6 social studies scope and sequence, what topics or themes would you include? What factors, other than the developmental characteristics of children, would you take into account in determining your topics and themes?

2. Does the old age of the expanding environments scope and sequence invalidate it? What technological and social changes have occurred since it was first proposed in the early 1900s? How, if at all, do these changes influence the social studies knowledge of K–6 children?

3. How do you feel about being left out of the scope and sequence decisions regarding social studies? Are you willing to teach what others determine should be taught, or do you feel like you should have some say over the what, when, and how of social studies instruction? Explain your position.

Figure 2-2 shows a list of five factors that help account for the existence of so many alternative elementary social studies scope and sequence arrangements. The first factor addresses the huge amount of content available in the social sciences and humanities. The second factor reminds us that the freedom of speech and conscience that we enjoy in our diverse, multicultural society results in a continuing dialog on the content of the social studies curriculum. The third factor emphasizes that state, not federal, governments make decisions about curriculum. Factor four recognizes the influences of special

---

[2]Many curriculum guides are written in a way that allows individual teachers the freedom to add an occasional unit. Teachers may also be able to speed up or skip and return to prescribed units in the district's curriculum guide. If you attempt to insert your own unit into an existing program, it's a good idea to check with teachers in later grades to make sure you aren't addressing a topic that has been assigned to them.

1. Amount of social science and humanities content

2. Our diverse, multicultural society

3. State and local (not national) control over school curriculum

4. Pressure from special interest groups

5. Limitations of research

FIGURE 2-2

Factors Affecting Diversity in the Social Studies Scope and Sequence

interest groups who seek to have their particular interest represented. And factor five reminds us that research seldom dictates teaching practices.

The factors listed in Figure 2-2 help account for the presence of many competing scope and sequence designs for elementary social studies. They remind us that the immense amount of social studies content available dictates that arguments for teaching any particular item must be made in comparison to alternative content that others would doubtlessly argue to be of equal or greater importance. Yet the factors do not aid you, the individual teacher, in determining whether to favor one alternative over another for your particular teaching situation. Practical considerations such as having several high-quality textbook series to choose from and the amount and quality of supplementary material available are paramount in most teachers' minds. Teachers might also be concerned if a proposed alteration of the curriculum would have them addressing topics they felt were inappropriate or if it relied on teaching methods that demanded time or other resources that were unavailable. Finally, teachers should be alert to how well any proposed scope and sequence addresses the characteristics and qualities put forth by the National Council for the Social Studies. These guidelines are shown in Figure 2-3. But stop a moment. Before you read the guidelines, do the following exercise.

EXERCISE 2.1

Imagine you are a district curriculum coordinator—the administrator in charge of monitoring and improving the school district's curriculum—and you are walking down the hallway of the best elementary school in your district. You can hear the children happily talking and answering questions in the classrooms. The walls are covered with children's work—much of it social studies. You stop for a moment to talk with the school's principal who asks your help in submitting an application for the annual NCSS awards program for outstanding elementary social studies programs. She wants your help listing the characteristics that make her school's program noteworthy. Close your eyes for a minute and mentally walk back through the school, noting the outstanding social studies learning that is going on. Now jot down at least five items present in the school's program that you think would impress the NCSS judges. Compare what you've written with the standards presented in Figure 2-3.

CULTURE

Social Studies programs should include experiences that provide for the study of *culture and cultural diversity,* so that the learner can:

a. explore and describe similarities and differences in the ways groups, societies, and cultures address similar human needs and concerns;

b. give examples of how experiences may be interpreted differently by people from diverse cultural perspectives and frames of reference;

c. describe ways in which language, stories, folktales, music, and artistic creations serve as expressions of culture and influence behavior of people living in a particular culture;

d. compare ways in which people from different cultures think about and deal with their physical environment and social conditions;

e. give examples and describe the importance of cultural unity and diversity within and across groups.

TIME, CONTINUITY, AND CHANGE

Social Studies programs should include experiences that provide for the study of the *ways human beings view themselves in and over time,* so that the learner can:

a. demonstrate an understanding that different people may describe the same event or situation in diverse ways, citing reasons for the differences in views;

b. demonstrate an ability to use correctly vocabulary associated with time such as past, present, future, and long ago; read and construct simple timelines; identify examples of change; and recognize examples of cause and effect relationships;

c. compare and contrast different stories or accounts about past events, people, places, or situations, identifying how they contribute to our understanding of the past;

d. identify and use various sources for reconstructing the past, such as documents, letters, diaries, maps, textbooks, photos, and others;

e. demonstrate an understanding that people in different times and places view the world differently;

f. use knowledge of facts and concepts, drawn from history, along with elements of historical inquiry, to inform decision making about and action taking on public issues.

PEOPLE, PLACES, AND ENVIRONMENTS

Social Studies programs should include experiences that provide for the study of *people, places, and environments,* so that the learner can:

a. construct and use mental maps of locales, regions, and the world that demonstrate understanding of relative location, direction, size, and shape;

b. interpret, use, and distinguish various representations of the earth, such as maps, globes, and photographs;

c. use appropriate resources, data sources, and geographic tools such as atlases, data bases, grid systems, charts, graphs, and maps to generate, manipulate, and interpret information;

d. estimate distance and calculate scale;

e. locate and distinguish among varying landforms and features, such as mountains, plateaus, islands, and oceans;

f. describe and speculate about physical system changes such as seasons, climate and weather, and the water cycle;

(continued on next page)

FIGURE 2-3
NCSS Early Grades Standards[3]

[3]From *Expectations of Excellence: Curriculum Standards for Social Studies.* 1994. © National Council for the Social Studies. Reprinted by permission. The term *early grades* was left undefined in the document, but, according to the chairman of the commission, it means grades K through 4. Middle-grades standards apply to grades 5 through 7.

PEOPLE, PLACES, AND ENVIRONMENTS (continued)

g. describe how people create places that reflect ideas, personality, culture, and wants and needs as they design homes, playgrounds, classrooms, and the like;

h. examine the interaction of human beings and their physical environment, the use of land, building of cities, and ecosystem changes in selected locales and regions;

i. explore ways that the earth's physical features have changed over time in the local region and beyond and how these changes may be connected to one another;

j. observe and speculate about social and economic effects of environmental changes and crises resulting from phenomena such as floods, storms, and drought;

k. consider existing uses and propose and evaluate alternative uses of resources and land in the home, the school, the community, the region, and beyond.

INDIVIDUAL DEVELOPMENT AND IDENTITY

Social Studies programs should include experiences that provide for the study of *individual development and identity*, so that the learner can:

a. describe personal changes over time such as those related to physical development and personal interests;

b. describe personal connections to place—especially place as associated with immediate surroundings;

c. describe the unique features of one's nuclear and extended families;

d. show how learning and physical development affect behavior;

e. identify and describe ways family, groups, and community influence the individual's daily life and personal choices;

f. explore factors that contribute to one's personal identity such as interests, capabilities, and perceptions;

g. analyze a particular event to identify reasons individuals might respond to it in different ways;

h. work independently and cooperatively to accomplish goals.

INDIVIDUALS, GROUPS, AND INSTITUTIONS

Social Studies programs should include experiences that provide for the study of *interactions among individuals, groups, and institutions*, so that the learner can:

a. identify roles as learned behavior patterns in group situations such as student, family member, peer play group member, or club member;

b. give examples of and explain group and institutional influences such as religious beliefs, laws, and peer pressure, on people, events, and elements of culture;

c. identify examples of institutions and describe the interactions of people with institutions;

d. identify and describe examples of tensions between and among individuals, groups, or institutions, and how belonging to more than one group can cause internal conflicts;

e. identify and describe examples of tension between an individual's beliefs and government policies and laws;

f. give examples of the role of institutions in furthering both continuity and change;

g. show how groups and institutions work to meet individual needs and promote the common good and identify examples where they fail to do so.

(continued on next page)

◆ ◆

FIGURE 2-3, continued
NCSS Early Grades Standards

**POWER,
AUTHORITY, AND
GOVERNANCE**
Social Studies programs
should include experi-
ences that provide for
the study of *how people
create and change struc-
tures of power, author-
ity, and governance,* so
that the learner can:

a. examine the rights and responsibilities of the individual in relation to his/her
    social group such as family, peer group, and school class;
b. explain the purpose of government;
c. give examples of how government does or does not provide for needs and
    wants of people, establish order and security, and manage conflict;
d. recognize how groups and organizations encourage unity and deal with
    diversity to maintain order and security;
e. distinguish among local, state, and national governments and identify
    representative leaders at these levels such as mayor, governor, and president;
f. identify and describe factors that contribute to cooperation and cause
    disputes within and among groups and nations;
g. explore the role of technology in communications, transportation,
    information processing, weapons development, or other areas as it
    contributes to or helps resolve conflicts;
h. recognize and give examples of the tensions between the wants and needs
    of individuals and groups, and concepts such as fairness, equity, and justice.

**PRODUCTION,
DISTRIBUTION,
AND CONSUMPTION**
Social Studies programs
should include experi-
ences that provide for
the study of *how people
organize for the produc-
tion, distribution, and
consumption of goods
and services,* so that the
learner can:

a. give examples that show how scarcity and choice govern our economic
    decisions;
b. distinguish between needs and wants;
c. identify examples of private and public goods and services;
d. give examples of the various institutions that make up economic systems
    such as families, workers, banks, labor unions, government agencies, small
    businesses, and large corporations;
e. describe how we depend upon workers with specialized jobs and the ways
    in which they contribute to the production and exchange of goods and
    services;
f. describe the influence of incentives, values, traditions, and habits on
    economic decisions;
g. explain and demonstrate the role of money in everyday life;
h. describe the relationship of price to supply and demand;
i. use economic concepts such as supply, demand, and price to help explain
    events in the community and nation;
j. apply knowledge of economic concepts in developing a response to a
    current local economic issue such as how to reduce the flow of trash into a
    rapidly filling landfill.

**SCIENCE,
TECHNOLOGY,
AND SOCIETY**
Social Studies programs
should include experi-
ences that provide for
the study of *relation-
ships among science,
technology, and society,*
so that the learner can:

a. identify and describe examples in which science and technology have
    changed the lives of people such as in homemaking, childcare, work,
    transportation, and communication;
b. identify and describe examples in which science and technology have led to
    changes in the physical environment such as the building of dams and levees,
    offshore oil drilling, medicine from rain forests, and loss of rain forests due to
    extraction of resources or alternative uses;

(continued on next page)

FIGURE 2-3, continued
NCSS Early Grades Standards

SCIENCE, TECHNOLOGY, AND SOCIETY (continued)

c. describe instances in which changes in values, beliefs, and attitudes have resulted from new scientific and technological knowledge such as conservation of resources and awareness of chemicals harmful to life and the environment;

d. identify examples of laws and policies that govern scientific and technological applications such as the Endangered Species Act and environmental protection policies;

e. suggest ways to monitor science and technology in order to protect the physical environment, individual rights, and the common good.

GLOBAL CONNECTIONS

Social Studies programs should include experiences that provide for the study of *global connections and interdependence,* so that the learner can:

a. explore ways that language, art, music, belief systems, and other cultural elements may facilitate global understanding or lead to misunderstanding;

b. give examples of conflict, cooperation, and interdependence among individuals, groups, and nations;

c. examine the effects of changing technologies on the global community;

d. explore causes, consequences, and possible solutions to persistent, contemporary, and emerging global issues such as pollution and endangered species;

e. examine the relationships and tensions between personal wants and needs and various global concerns such as use of imported oil, land use, and environmental protection;

f. investigate concerns, issues, standards, and conflicts related to universal human rights, such as the treatment of children and religious groups and the effects of war.

CIVIC IDEALS AND PRACTICES

Social Studies programs should include experiences that provide for the study of *the ideals, principles, and practices of citizenship in a democratic republic,* so that the learner can:

a. identify key ideals of the United States' democratic republican form of government such as individual human dignity, liberty, justice, equality, and the rule of law, and discuss their application in specific situations;

b. identify examples of rights and responsibilities of citizens;

c. locate, access, organize, and apply information about an issue of public concern from multiple points of view;

d. identify and practice selected forms of civic discussion and participation consistent with the ideals of citizens in a democratic republic;

e. explain actions citizens can take to influence public policy decisions;

f. recognize that a variety of formal and informal actors influence and shape public policy;

g. examine the influence of public opinion on personal decision making and government policy on public issues;

h. explain how public policies and citizen behaviors may or may not reflect the stated ideals of a democratic republican form of government

i. describe how public policies are used to address issues of public concern;

j. recognize and interpret how the "common good" can be strengthened through various forms of citizen action.

FIGURE 2-3, continued
NCSS Early Grades Standards

OFFICIAL POSITION STATEMENTS
◆ ◆ ◆ ◆ ◆

The National Council for the Social Studies recently released its National Standards for K–12 social studies. The standards (1) serve as an overarching framework for K–12 social studies program design based on ten essential instructional themes, (2) guide curriculum decision making by providing expectations of knowledge, processes, and dispositions essential for all students, and (3) guide teachers in making decisions about classroom practice by providing examples of instruction designed to achieve the performance expectations. Figure 2-3 lists the ten essential social education themes and sample performance expectations for early grade level students. As you explore the content of this figure attempt to decide whether you feel some of the themes are more important than others. As a further exercise, see if you can apply traditional labels associated with the social science disciplines (for example, history, geography, political science) to the themes.

THE STATUS OF K-6 SOCIAL STUDIES INSTRUCTION IN PUBLIC SCHOOLS
◆ ◆ ◆ ◆ ◆

In this section, you'll learn about the status of formal and informal curriculums and issues in selecting and implementing content. Having knowledge of these two aspects of the social studies curriculum will help prepare you for the conditions you will meet in schools and provide you with a portion of the knowledge needed to plan effective social studies lessons.

The Formal Curriculum

Schooling in the primary grades quite often emphasizes learning to read, write, and calculate. Because of this, the K–3 curriculum may sometimes neglect formal instruction in social studies. Many primary grade level teachers openly state that they "don't do social studies." What these teachers often mean is that they don't have a specific period of time each day or week set aside for social studies. They may also mean that they don't have a textbook or curriculum guide that directs such teaching. Such teachers may, in fact, do excellent social studies lessons centered on the development of classroom rules, learning appropriate interpersonal behaviors, and developing cultural knowledge through the celebration of popular holidays.

Research confirms that formal social studies instruction is often a low curricular priority in the early primary grades. A recent survey of 3000 early childhood teachers in seven midwestern states (Finkelstein, Nielsen, and Switzer, 1990) showed that only half of the respondents knew that their school district required a period of instructional time devoted to social studies. Most of these teachers (almost 68 percent actually taught social studies for less than 2 hours each week) generally based their instruction on a textbook. Teachers in this study perceived the high priority assigned to reading, writing, and arithmetic as being the chief reason they did not provide a greater amount of formal social studies instruction.

Starting in the fourth grade, social studies instruction begins to receive equal treatment with other subjects (Hahn, 1985; Morrisette, Superka, and Hawke, 1980). The typical fourth-grade teacher devotes an average of 40 minutes a day to social studies. Often this instruction is on the home state and geographic regions. Some state departments of education mandate a study of the home state in the fourth-grade. Local districts may add requirements. Publishers often tailor their fourth-grade books to the existing curriculum requirements and some even "custom publish" editions of their textbooks to accommodate each state's mandate.

The fifth-grade social studies curriculum has typically focused on U.S. history. Offered as a survey from prehistoric times to the present, this offering has come under frequent attack for being superficial and needlessly dull. Suggestions for improving history instruction abound. Educational improvement and change are slow processes, however, depending as much or more on the actions of individual teachers as they do on new curriculum ideas.

Sixth-grade students traditionally devote their attention to the Western Hemisphere. Students often learn the history and physical and cultural geography of South and Latin American countries as well as Canada. The scope of the sixth-grade curriculum also invites a superficiality that is difficult to overcome.

The Informal Curriculum

The status of the informal curriculum is much less documented than the formal curriculum. School-district curriculum guides, policy manuals, textbooks, and other instructional materials help document the prevailing practices in the formal curriculum. Similar materials do not exist to help show changes in the natural and hidden curriculums. Despite the lack of a clear paper trail, some generalizations concerning the status of these areas are possible.

The natural curriculum, as defined in Chapter 1, consists of holiday celebrations, teaching devoted to current events, and attention devoted to children's immediate social needs and interests. The most significant change in the natural curriculum has come in the way in which Christian holidays are recognized in public schools. While there were always exceptions, up until the 1970s many schools called their winter break "Christmas break," and their spring break "Easter break." Public school functions associated with these religious holidays often included musical programs that predominately used Christian hymns and skits with Biblical origins. Lawsuits filed by parents of children with different religious backgrounds brought an end to these practices. Public schools still schedule their winter and spring breaks to coincide with the religious celebrations for Christmas and Easter, but school programs are no longer allowed to be primarily religious, and classroom decorations, parties, and instruction have abandoned practices that were indoctrinative.

During this same time period many public schools began to allow students of Jewish, Islamic, and other faiths excused absences for the celebration of their religious holidays. Thus, recognition of holidays in public schools has changed to include a more accurate representation of the religious diversity present in our nation. Public schools have stopped practices that were forms of religious indoctrination and have begun providing instruction about (*about* is the key word) all religions as a part of their regular social studies curriculum.[4] There is little evidence to suggest that schools have altered their treatment of current events or that teachers have begun to give greater attention to the interests of children. Natural disasters, wars that have an effect on our national self-interest, and elections all tend to increase current events instruction. It might also be argued that whole-language reading instruction has helped center instruction more on the interests of children.

The hidden curriculum was defined in Chapter 1 as an assortment of unspoken and largely unchallenged beliefs, attitudes, values, and assumptions about the social world that are conveyed to children through daily routines, the teacher's gestures, and the hidden content of the formal curriculum that lies between the lines. To my mind, little has changed in this realm of schooling. Few students or teachers question the wisdom of giving rewards to our best-performing students, challenge the prevailing foreshortened versions of history offered in textbooks, or ask whether it might be more important to study Haiti than Hawaii. It seems too difficult to question whether reciting the pledge of allegiance really builds patriotism and even more difficult—perhaps danger-ous—to allow children to investigate the meaning of patriotism.

In sum, the status of the informal social studies curriculum is little changed with the exception of the public school celebration of holidays. Your task as a thoughtful K–6 social studies teacher will be to use the informal curriculum to foster social thinking. The ideas presented in this book should help you accomplish this goal.

The Influence of Special Interest Groups and Societal Trends

Special interest groups and societal trends influence the school curriculum. Special interest groups include teachers, administrators, teacher educators, and their professional associations. Parents, too, are a powerful special interest group that may urge curriculum change. Other groups also seek to influence the curriculum. Among them are such groups as the American Bar Association, Educators for Social Responsibility, B'nai B'rith, the National Council on Economic Education, the National Council for History Education, and the National Geographic Society. Each of these groups promotes different aspects of social studies education through newsletters, workshops, and curriculum materials.

---

[4]Chapter 13 includes additional information on teaching about religion.

Social trends also influence the social studies curriculum. For example, the civil rights movement of the 1960s and feminist movement have brought calls to correct history instruction that focused exclusively on white males. The end of the Cold War and the disintegration of the former Soviet Union have added a new chapter to international relations and changed the face of the globe that students study. A final example, less dramatic perhaps, but still exerting influence on the social studies curriculum, is the widespread use of day care as more and more U.S. families found it necessary for both parents to work outside the home. This last societal change doubtlessly has added to demands for more challenging and appropriate content than typically provided in elementary social studies (Larkins, Hawkins, and Gilmore, 1987).

ISSUES IN SELECTING AND IMPLEMENTING CONTENT

With so much content to select and teach, it is important to consider the guidelines typically used to determine what is appropriate to teach. The major factors to consider are the developmental level of the child, experiential readiness, community concerns, district guidelines, and the special needs of children.

Developmental Level

I assume that you have already taken a course in child development and that, as a result, you understand that children grow both physically and mentally in spurts through identifiable stages. Different children develop at different rates, but major developmental milestones pass in roughly the same order for all children.

Developmental considerations are important in selecting social studies content and teaching strategies. For example, a second-grade student is not likely to have the manual dexterity or spatial conceptualization needed to build an intricate toothpick model of a western frontier fort. Similarly, kindergarten and first-grade students are typically not able to appreciate or fully understand the duration of time involved in a decade. For such young children, the past is likely to be a mental construct without much depth, where yesterday seems to have happened just as long ago as last summer. Experience has also shown that prior to third grade it is very difficult for children to learn the relationship among cities, counties, and states. To children at this age, it is impossible to understand how they can be in a city, and also in a county and a state. This seems, to the child, like a logical fallacy: How can I be in three places at once? The dialogue in Figure 2-4 illustrates this idea. It shows the difficulty a child has in understanding that two cities can be in the same state. As you read the dialogue imagine the difficulties created by adding in the rather abstract idea of a county!

CHILD: (sensing that the car trip is taking longer than expected)

I thought we were going to Grandma's house in Tallahassee!

ADULT: (matter of factly)

We are. Tallahassee is in Florida.

CHILD: (detecting that within his experience when two things are in the same place you can see them both)

But you said we were already in Florida and I don't see her house!

ADULT: (responding logically as an adult)

That's because we are in Jacksonville right now.

CHILD: (incredulous that the adult now says they are in Jacksonville instead of Florida)

But I thought you said we were in Florida!

ADULT: (getting annoyed. . .)

We are in Florida! We're just not in Tallahassee yet!

CHILD: (not understanding how you can be in Jacksonville and Florida at the same time)

But you just said we were in Jacksonville!

ADULT: (unable to relate. . .)

We are. We're also in Florida.

CHILD: (wondering how come Jacksonville can be in Florida and you can see it but Tallahassee you can't)

But you said Tallahassee was in Florida!

ADULT: (tuned out. . .)

It is.

CHILD: (so if I can see houses and this is Florida, one of them must be Grandma's)

So where is Grandma's house?

• •

F I G U R E   2 - 4
Trip Dialogue

Experiential Readiness

Children with the same developmental level may have radically different life experiences. While development is, in part, a function of experience, here the term *experiential readiness* indicates the body of knowledge a student has gained from prior learning.

Experiential readiness prepares us to benefit from instruction by providing prerequisite knowledge and skills. Much of social studies learning is dependent on prior (and often missing!) knowledge and experience. For example, young students will not be able to follow a teacher's request to "Put your index finger in the upper right-hand corner of the map" unless they know which finger is the index finger, the difference between right and left, and the concept of corner.

Experiential readiness plays a role in the child's ability to grasp intended meanings and maintain interest in instruction. In general, the more you know, the easier it is to make sense of and stay interested in new material. Skilled elementary teachers know that they must develop missing and required background knowledge as a part of their social studies lessons.

Community Concerns

Communities across the United States exhibit great variety in wealth, religious affiliation, ethnicity, economy, size, and many other conditions. A topic that generates great interest among students in Peoria, Illinois, may prove senseless and boring to students in Brownsville, Texas. A topic that produces no community reaction in Orlando, Florida, may prove controversial in Bloomington, Indiana.

In general, it is important for the teacher of social studies to be sensitive to the unique characteristics of the community in which he or she teaches. These characteristics may provide opportunities for exciting social studies lessons. For example, a community that is experiencing a prolonged water shortage may be an excellent location for lessons focusing on water conservation and public policies controlling water use. The same lessons might flop if taught in a water-rich area such as the gulf coast of Florida, or the western part of Oregon. Elements of geography, history, and political science combine in determining how communities react to water shortage situations. Teachers who know their communities can add this vital information to their curriculum decision-making process.

District Guidelines

The most important factor controlling your selection and implementation of content will be the teaching directives provided by your school district. School districts vary in the degree to which they mandate or demand certain content and teaching methods. Some districts will prescribe a sequence of instruction that every teacher follows. Such districts may adopt a specific textbook or other material and require that it be taught. Other districts will provide a suggested curriculum and leave decisions about how and when to deliver the instruction up to the individual teacher.

It is your responsibility to make sure that you are following the letter and spirit of school-district policies. You should be aware, however, that considerable variation in practice is normally present in every school district. For example, you may get substantially different answers about instructional requirements depending on whether you ask your school's principal or the district's curriculum coordinator. Ultimately, you may have to answer, at least partially on your own, the what, when, and how of your social studies teaching.

Finally, just as it is your responsibility to carry out the district-mandated curriculum, it is also your responsibility to inform your school administration if you believe change is needed in district curriculum policies. Complaining about the supposedly "mandated" use of a textbook to colleagues but holding your tongue on this issue with curriculum supervisors or district administrators is being less than honest. It also fails to show the kind of intelligent leadership we need from teachers if we expect our schools to serve the needs of our democracy well.

Special Needs of Children

An essential factor to consider in selecting and implementing social studies lessons is the special needs of children. You may have a student in your class who is extremely shy. Another student may have a very negative attitude toward minorities. Yet another student may be coping with a learning disability.

The important point is that social studies is the ideal place to soften and bend the curriculum so that it may address some of the very real learning needs of the students you teach. We all need human understanding and, in the final analysis, that is what social studies is all about. The teaching techniques and ideas presented throughout this book demonstrate how social studies can help you achieve the kind of warm and accepting atmosphere that helps all children learn.

DISCUSSION QUESTIONS

1. Should special interest groups be ignored or silenced? Or do we have an obligation to listen to all of them and attempt to accommodate all of their wishes? Explain your position.

2. Which of the factors that influence the selection and implementation of curriculum are most important? Why do you say so? Give an example to support your position.

3. If you are teaching in a community that draws its livelihood mainly from a major distiller of alcohol or a large brewery, would it be okay to use this business as the basis for field trips or as a case study designed to help students understand the role of advertising and other aspects of economics? Explain your position.

CONCLUDING THOUGHTS

The roots of social studies have often been traced to the first formal schools established by European colonists. In fact, attempts to preserve culture and induct children into the prevailing society existed long before the Europeans came to North America. The many different Native-American nations handed down rich oral histories and well-developed social values to their children. Native-American cultures influenced the formation of our nation's government and economic life and remain an influence on contemporary culture in the United States today.

The history of social studies reflects the intellectual, social, and cultural turmoil that accompanied the development of our diverse nation. The ties that bind us will always be counterbalanced by events and viewpoints that create divisions. In many circumstances altruistic behavior may serve to benefit one's personal interest. But self-interest may also cause individuals to abandon or denounce the welfare of fellow humans.

Given recent cultural and technological trends, it seems likely that the future will bring more challenges and changes to social studies instruction. Disputes will continue over whose history should be taught and which nations should be studied. Little will remain unchanged or unchallenged. Let us hope that social studies continues to evolve; that it remains responsive to the needs of children, their local communities, our nation, and the world; and that it builds pride in our diversity as well as our unity.

REFERENCES AND SELECTED READINGS

Akenson, J. E. 1987. Historical factors in the development of elementary social studies: Focus on the expanding environments. *Theory and Research in Social Education* 5(3):155–171.

Atwood, V. A., and Finkelstein, J. M. 1987. Social studies in kindergartens: A status report. *Social Education* 51(7):526–532.

Bradley Commission on History in Schools. 1988. *Building a history curriculum: Guidelines for teaching history in schools.* Washington, D.C.: Educational Excellence Network.

Bruner, J. 1968. *The process of education.* New York: Bantam Books.

California State Department of Education. 1988. *History-social science framework for California public schools kindergarten through grade twelve.* Sacramento, CA: Bureau of Publication Sales.

Educational Development Corporation. 1972. *Man: A course of study.* Washington, D.C.: Curriculum Development Associates.

Epstein, T. L., and Evans, R. W. 1990. Reactions to charting a course: Social studies for the 21st century. *Social Education* 54(7):427–429.

Finkelstein, J., Nielsen, L. E., and Switzer, T. 1990. Primary elementary social studies instruction: A status report. Paper presented at the National Council for the Social Studies Convention, St. Louis, MO.

Finn, C. E., Jr., and Ravitch, D. 1988. No trivial pursuit. *Phi Delta Kappan* 69(8):559–564.

FitzGerald, F. 1980. *America revised: History schoolbooks in the twentieth century.* New York: Random House.

Hahn, C. L. 1985. The status of the social studies in the public schools of the United States: Another look. *Social Education* 49(3):220–223.

Hertzberg, H. 1981. *Social studies reform: 1880–1980.* Boulder, CO: Social Science Education Consortium.

Jenness, D. 1990. *Making sense of social studies.* New York: Macmillan.

Kohn, A. 1993. *Punished by rewards: The trouble with gold stars, incentive plans, A's, praise, and other bribes.* Boston: Houghton Mifflin.

Larkins, A. G., Hawkins, M. L., and Gilmore, A. 1987. Trivial and noninformative content of elementary social studies: A review of primary texts in four series. *Theory and Research in Social Education* 15(4):299–311.

LeRiche, L. W. 1987. The expanding environments sequence in elementary social studies: The origins. *Theory and Research in Social Education* 5(3):137–155.

Lybarger, M. B. 1991. The historiography of social studies: Retrospect, circumspect, and prospect. In *Handbook of research on social studies teaching and learning*, ed. J. P. Shaver, 3–15. New York: Macmillan.

Mehlinger, H. D. 1992. The national commission on social studies in the schools: An example of the politics of curriculum reform in the United States. *Social Education* 56(3):149–153.

Morrisette, I., Superka, D. P., and Hawke, S. 1980. Recommendations for improving social studies in the 1980s. *Social Education* 44:570–576, 653.

NCSS. 1989. *Charting a course: Social studies for the 21st century*. Washington, D.C.: National Commission on Social Studies in the Schools.

———— 1994. *Expectations of excellence: Curriculum standards for social studies*. Washington, D.C.: National Council for the Social Studies.

Ornstein, A. C., and Levine, D. U. 1989. *Foundations of education*. 4th ed. Boston: Houghton Mifflin.

Ravitch, D. 1984. The continuing crisis: Fashions in education. *American Scholar* 53(2):183–193.

Content in the Social Studies Curriculum

TYPES OF SOCIAL STUDIES CONTENT

As stated in Chapter 1, social studies draws its content principally from the social sciences and humanities. As a result, it is logical to think of social studies content being divided into such individual disciplines as history and geography. In the practice of teaching, however, it is also important to know the type or category of content being taught. Being aware of the type of content you are teaching can help you select appropriate teaching strategies, making learning more efficient and pleasant. The content of the social studies is often broken down into the categories of facts, concepts, main ideas and generalizations, skills, attitudes, and values.

FACTS: THEIR NATURE AND IMPORTANCE

Facts are discrete pieces of information known through direct experience or observation. It is a fact that today's date is _____ and that the weather is _____ outside. It is a fact that the time right now is about _____ here in _____. Of course, it's a different time if you go very far west or east of here!

Facts are also statements about items that are known to have existed or happened. It is a fact that President John F. Kennedy was assassinated. It is a fact that Ronald Reagan was the fortieth president of the United States and served two terms in office.

Facts are statements that are held to be correct at a certain time and place. Today, the capital of Indiana is Indianapolis; it used to be Corydon. The capital of Georgia is Atlanta; it used to be Milledgeville. Ronald Reagan was a one-term president until November 1984, when he was reelected to his second term in office.

Facts are statements that are tied to a specific place, culture, and/or time. An assortment of facts commonly known by citizens of the United States in the 1990s include such statements as: Tallahassee is the capital of Florida; U.S. astronauts Neil Armstrong and Buzz Aldrin walked on the moon on July 20, 1969; and George Bush and Bill Clinton were the forty-first and forty-second U.S. presidents.

Why Is Factual Learning Important?

Having certain facts is important to daily functioning. For example, if you live in a dorm, the fact that "breakfast is served between 6 and 8 A.M." is important to know. If you spend money, knowing a dime is equal to ten pennies is important. If you are responsible for monitoring your own or another's health, knowing that normal oral body temperature is 98.6 degrees Fahrenheit is important. Failure to know these facts can cause hunger, loss of material benefits, or even death.

Fact learning is also important because having certain facts is considered a cultural or social imperative. We expect the person on the street to know the name of the current president, the name and present location of the state capital, and lots of other cultural information such as the number of points scored in a football touchdown. Failure to know these facts causes embarrassment simply because people expect that we will have a command of such facts.

Fact learning is also important because controlling a body of factual information is an essential basis for claims to power and expertise in modern society. Consider for a moment the role factual learning plays in a medical or legal education. A patient wouldn't have very much confidence in a doctor who didn't know the names of the bones in the body or a lawyer who lacked knowledge of legal statutes and case law in his or her area of expertise. Simply put, factual learning is the basis of these and many other professions. Having a command of such factual knowledge is a good part of the expert's claim to authority. Jobs requiring very little factual knowledge are likely to be low-wage occupations.

A final reason for considering factual learning important is because factual knowledge forms the base for higher levels of intellectual functioning. Just as having a command of certain facts is basic to daily functioning, so too, is factual learning a prerequisite to higher-level intellectual functioning. Of course, some higher-level thought can occur without all of the facts, but time and time again, in natural sciences and other fields, we have seen our best thinkers' ideas invalidated by the discovery of a new fact!

The Role of Facts in Social Studies

Now that you have a firm grasp on the nature of facts, stop a moment and think about their role in social studies. History and geography, arguably the disciplines that dominate social studies, are full of factual information. Consider the potential number of names and dates to memorize from history. Or consider the number of places to locate on the globe and the long lists of exports and imports for each country. Acquiring such factual information is often taken to be evidence of sufficient learning in these subjects. Yet experts in these disciplines consistently maintain that such factual learning is only the beginning of learning in these areas. Facts are recalled best when connected to higher-order content. Thus, higher-level content (addressed in the remainder of this chapter) should also be mastered.

Some Ways to Teach Facts

Teachers have used many techniques to help students learn factual material. The technique selected may depend upon the nature of the factual material, the learner's ability, or the availability of instructional resources. Figure 3-1 lists common fact-teaching techniques and provides an example of each.

Remember that psychologists typically make a distinction between short- and long-term memory. Short-term memory lasts only briefly, perhaps only seconds in certain circumstances! It is limited in capacity, typically

Brute memory	Brute memory involves willfully remembering something without any particular strategy or tactic to aid your recall. Essentially, it's like saying, "I'm going to remember this."
	Example: "I'm going to remember that Frankfort *is the capital of Kentucky (not Louisville!)."*
Chaining	Chaining involves associating the fact to be remembered to some verbal, visual, or tactile experience.
	Example: The alphabet song is a verbal chain learned to teach the names of the letters. Recognition of the shapes of the letters is often accomplished by associating pictures of supposedly common objects (such as a cow for "C") with large-scale representations of the letter.
Chunking	This involves dividing facts to be learned into smaller subsets to aid memorization and recall.
	Example: Learning the states and capitals by dividing up the United States into discrete geographic regions is chunking.
Mnemonics	Mnemonics involves creating a sentence or word to represent the items to be recalled.
	Example: Every Good Boy Does Fine and "FACE" help students recall the names of the lines and spaces in music.
Part-whole relationships	Recalling one element stimulates the recall of the others.
	Example: The five Great Lakes include Lake Erie and . . .
Involving both brain hemispheres	Creating some affective associations may aid in learning.
	Example: Telling a joke or an anecdote about a particular event helps people remember the event.
Songs/Chants	Songs and chants combine elements of chaining and involvement of both brain hemispheres in learning.
	Example: The Fifty Nifty States song
Games	Games are another way to tap both brain hemispheres by making learning fun.
	Examples: People bingo, classroom concentration, and classroom baseball

FIGURE 3-1

Techniques for Teaching Facts

accommodating only seven disrelated elements (for example, a phone number like 542-4416, given in random order). The trick of fact teaching is thus to aid the learner in achieving long-term memory of the desired factual content. The fact-learning strategies briefly described in Figure 3-1 help in this process. Using the facts and recalling them over an extended period of time will also help in long-term retention.

A Fact-Teaching Model

Figure 3-2 provides an overview of a direct instruction model for teaching facts. The model may be used at all age levels and with all types of factual material. Read through the model and try to imagine yourself teaching the facts it uses as an example. Use an atlas or wall map to locate the major rivers and lakes in the United States.

Children are required to learn many facts as a part of their basic education as citizens. This will be easier if you follow the general procedures of the fact-teaching model and heed some time-tested advice.

STEP DESCRIPTION	SAMPLE DIALOGUE
1. Provide an overview of the facts to be learned. Identify the facts by name and show them to the learners.	*"Today we are going to begin learning the names and locations of the major rivers and lakes of the United States. Our map of the United States shows these bodies of water clearly." (Teacher points out the rivers and lakes on the wall map.)*
2. Give a rationale for learning the facts.	*"Knowing the location and names of these bodies of water will help you understand the geography of the United States. All citizens of the United States should know something of our nation's geography so they can be aware of what life is like for fellow citizens in other states."*
3. Select the method of instruction that is most appropriate for the number and type of fact and the level of the learner.	*"To help you learn the names of the major rivers and lakes I'm going to go over them with you as a group several times. Then we'll play a naming game in teams. After the game each of you will have an opportunity to copy the rivers and lakes on your own outline map. Tomorrow we'll play another little quiz game that uses the facts."*
4. Engage in mass practice sessions. (Mass practice involves intensive 15- to 30-minute sessions focused on learning the facts.)	*"Okay, we've got 20 minutes left before the dismissal bell. Let's all try to fill out a new outline map. Make sure you get the rivers and lakes in the right place and that you label them correctly."*
5. Distribute practice over time to allow for thorough learning.	*"It's Friday, so it's time to play our quiz game again. I'm going to form different teams today."*
6. Test, then review and test again.	*"Last week Joy and Tina got perfect scores on our lakes and rivers test. After we review, I'm going to see who else might get a perfect score."*
7. Use the facts as naturally required in lessons.	*"How many of you heard the news last night about the flooding in the Midwest? Let's look at the map and see what cities and towns were affected."*

FIGURE 3-2
A Fact-Teaching Model

Some Advice on Fact Teaching

Fact learning can be challenging and fun if you, the teacher, put effort into making it so. But regardless of how much effort you put into making fact learning fun, you'll find that some children have more trouble than others in mastering the material. The guidelines offered here can help you overcome the difficulties most new teachers experience when teaching for factual-learning outcomes.

Perhaps the most important and challenging step in fact teaching is to consciously link one or more important concepts, main ideas, generalizations, or skills to the facts you want students to learn. Doing this gives students a framework to tie their facts to and helps bare facts take on meaning and significance.

Once students have an understanding of the significance of the facts they are learning, the next task is to pick a fun way of helping them learn the facts. Making fact learning fun also helps students feel that it is easy.

Occasionally, teachers fail to help reluctant students make a serious commitment to their fact learning. Some questions you might want to ask a reluctant fact-learner are, "How long do you want to go on not knowing _____?" "Do you know what could happen if you don't learn these facts?" "Is there something I can do to make this easier for you?"

In undertaking fact learning it's important to reward effort as well as success. Too often children who struggle with fact learning fail to have their efforts recognized. A personal word of appreciation for good effort can go a long way toward motivating continued effort and eventual success. Children may enjoy keeping their own progess charts in fact learning. Exaggerations of success will be easily detected in follow-up assessments.

My last piece of advice is give up when it becomes apparent that the fact-learning task has overwhelmed or demoralized your students. Few facts are so important that their acquisition warrants ruining a school year or a child's self-concept. Freeing unsuccessful—as well as successful—students to move on to other, fresh learning tasks breathes new life into learning gone stale.

DISCUSSION QUESTIONS
◆ ◆ ◆ ◆ ◆

1. Are facts more important in social studies than in other areas of the curriculum such as science or language arts? Explain your opinion.

2. Since facts are fundamental building blocks thought essential by many educators to higher forms of learning, is it only fitting and proper that fact learning should dominate a student's basic learning in any content area? Give examples to support your view.

3. What is the difference between facts (as defined here) and truths? Is it appropriate and useful to think of truths as value judgments or generalizations that can be supported or called into question by facts?

CONCEPTS: THOUGHT AND COMMUNICATION ESSENTIALS

Concepts are ideas that can usually be expressed in a single word. A few examples are *man, woman, student, Indian, lake, peace, love, hate,* and *division of labor.* Another common way in which concepts are defined is to say that they are "categories of meaning" for which we can find many specific examples. Thus, every genetically "male" human is an example of the concept *man* (although admittedly, some are far worse examples than others!). The same statement may be made for *students, lovers,* or any other concept.

Concepts are important because they greatly facilitate thought and communication. Take, for example, the economics concept of *externality.* Unless you've had specific instruction on this concept you are unlikely to be able to think explicitly in terms of it when making economic decisions. Similarly, if you don't know the concept, I would be willing to bet that you haven't been using it in your conversations lately! Concepts are also important because they allow us to classify (for example, creek versus stream versus river) and free us to deal with abstractions (for example, you can think about relationships with others without actually having the person present).

All concepts are represented by labels or symbols, either verbal, written, or symbolic. A heart (♥) is often taken as a symbol for love. In fact, the group of letters l-o-v-e is also simply a symbol or label standing for the abstract category of meaning "love."

Concepts are defined by a set of essential characteristics or properties that specify the intellectual limits of the category of meaning and distinguish the concept from other concepts. Items that fail to have the essential characteristics are not considered examples of the concept.

Figure 3-3 invites you to discuss and define three widely known concepts from geography. Fill in definitions of the concepts using your own knowledge, and then answer the discussion questions that follow.

CONCEPT	DEFINITION
Urban	
Suburban	
Rural	

FIGURE 3-3

Three Concepts from Geography

DISCUSSION QUESTIONS

1. Where is your college or university located? Is it in a rural, suburban, or urban area? How would you support your judgment?

2. How do these three concepts facilitate thought and communication among business-people, city planners, politicians, and everyday citizens? What are some other concepts they frequently use?

3. Are concepts more, less, or equally important compared to facts? Support your answer with at least two examples.

How Concepts Get Taught

Random life experiences and the memorization of definitions are two of the most common ways in which concepts are learned. Both of these ways of learning concepts have their drawbacks, however. Learning concepts through life experience can take a long time and can produce incomplete and inaccurate understanding of the concept. Learning through the simple memorization of definitions produces limited learning. Imagine reading a definition of the concept *building* having never seen a building or been in one. Can a person who has never seen or entered a building honestly know the concept by reading: "something that is built; a structure; an edifice"? Clearly, the answer is, "No!"

To assure greater accuracy and depth of understanding, curriculum theorists and researchers have identified several efficient ways of helping students learn concepts. Some of the strategies they have identified are inductive and others are deductive. Some are more teacher-directed than others.

Taba's Concept Development Lesson Strategy   Hilda Taba developed an approach to teaching concepts based on the assumption that the teacher must aid the student in the process of developing conceptual understandings by providing firsthand experiences. Taba felt that firsthand experience was essential to real understanding of a concept (Fraenkel, 1992; Taba, 1967).

At the simplest level, Taba's concept development strategy may be seen as a three-step process involving listing, grouping, and labeling items. This is an inductive teaching strategy that is teacher-initiated and -moderated. Students have a high level of interaction with the material. The teacher functions as an aid or facilitator of the students' work. Figure 3-4 provides an overview of the Taba concept development lesson strategy using a series of photographs depicting contemporary farm life in the Midwest.

Many concepts can be taught using Taba's strategy, including *landscape*, *nature*, *city*, *suburb*, *farm*, *desert*, and others, where there is a large amount of observable, tangible phenomena that can logically be subsumed under this same "umbrella." In many cases these phenomena may be imagined to be arranged in an hierarchy or outline format with the key concept at the head.

The Taba concept development strategy is a well-tested and much-enjoyed approach to concept learning. Its basis in firsthand experience for students, its emphasis on student thinking, and its demand for the construction of meaning make it one of the most valuable approaches to teaching concepts for primary-age children.

TEACHER QUESTIONS	STUDENT RESPONSES	EXPLANATION
• *"What do you see or notice in this picture?"*	• *"I see a big barn."* • *"I see some cows."* • *"I see a tractor and a truck."* • *"I see some pigs and some chickens."*	This process continues for all of the different photographs. The teacher lists the items as the students mention them.
• *"Do any of these things go together?"* • *"If so, why?"* • *"What reason do you have for putting them together?"*	• *"Tractor and truck go together because they both have engines."* • *"Cows, pigs, and chickens go together because they are farm animals."* • *"The barn and the equipment shed both go together because they were made by people."*	This process continues until the students run out of logical groupings. The teacher visually identifies each group with colored chalk or a unique symbol.
• *"What would you call these groups that you have formed?"* • *"Is there a word that we can give to each group?"*	• *"The tractor and truck are both farm equipment."* • *"The cows, pigs, and chickens are farm animals."* • *"The barn and equipment shed are buildings."*	This goes on until all of the groups have been labeled.
• *"Could some of these things go in a different group?"* • *"Could some belong to two groups?"*	• *"Yes, tractors and trucks are made by people, so they could go together with the barn and shed."*	This continues until the students can find no new relationships. The teacher keeps track of new groupings with colored chalk or symbols.
• *"Can someone make a sentence or give me a word that describes how several or all of the groups go together?"*	• *"Some of our groups are things that come from nature, like the group that has trees and flowers, and the group that has wild animals like birds and squirrels."* • *"All these things are a part of farm life."*	The teacher keeps track of which groups go together. When the groups have been identified as fitting under a single label, this should become the name of the concept represented in the photographs.

FIGURE 3-4

Steps in the Taba Concept Development Lesson Strategy

Positive-and-Negative-Example Concept Development Strategy

A second strategy used to teach concepts is based on the presentation of positive and negative examples. Well researched and highly efficient, this direct instruction approach to concept learning is applicable to all ages. The basic steps in this strategy, as applied to the concept of *money*, are outlined in Figure 3-5.

Stop for a moment and think about the characteristics of this concept development strategy. Notice that this strategy, like Taba's, demands thinking and invites student participation. Note too that the positive-and-negative-

SUGGESTED STEPS	SAMPLE DIALOGUE
1. Identify the concept by name and state its major attributes while showing two or three clear positive and two or three clear negative examples of the concept.	*"This is money (holding up a $1 bill). Money is made by the government and takes the form of either metal coins or paper bills that can be used by anyone to make purchases. Money has a value that is printed or stamped on its face, and people have to accept it for payment. (This process gets repeated for at least two other clear positive examples.) This is not money (holding up gold ring). The government didn't make it. It has no preset value stamped on it, and people do not have to accept it in payment." (This process gets repeated for several other clear negative examples.)*
2. Have students define, as a group, the major attributes of the concept.	*"Okay, let's try to define what money is. Who can give me one characteristic of money? Who can give me another?"*
3. Present less clear and mixed positive and negative examples, having the students state the major attributes each time.	*"Okay, I'm holding up a blank check that I just tore from my checkbook. Is it money? What do you think? Andre, you've got your hand up. Are you thinking of one of the characteristics of money? (Andre nods yes.) Well what is the characteristic, and does my blank check have it? (Later . . .) And what do you think this is? Is this money (holding up a $500 saving bond)? Do you want to come and look at it more closely? Which criteria does it meet? Which (if any) criteria does it not meet?"*
4. Have students locate and share their own new instances of the concept.	*"Now I want each of you to identify one example of money and one example that is not money. I'll give you a few minutes to decide on the positive and negative examples you want to use."*

FIGURE 3-5

Positive-and-Negative Example Concept Development Lesson Strategy

example strategy may be used on almost any concept. Indeed, it is difficult to think of a concept that could not be taught using this strategy.[1]

Try to articulate reasons for the strategy you like best. Do you prefer the questioning approach of Taba or the telling approach of this strategy? Do you like the efficiency and controlled nature of the positive-and-negative-example approach, or are you more attracted to the open-ended questions (and less predictable answers!) of the Taba approach? Finally, try to imagine yourself

---

[1]Intangible concepts that are difficult to teach include *love, patriotism, prejudice, culture, friendship, peace,* and many others. Such concepts are not easily represented by tangible, observable phenomena and they often do not have a readily apparent hierarchical structure.

preparing to teach a concept lesson based on your favorite strategy. Can you think of everything you need to do before you begin teaching? Can you imagine what you'll say and what the children will most likely respond?

Concept Augmentation   Once students have a basic understanding of a concept, expand or augment their learning by presenting new and more complex instances. Many children, for example, have a woefully narrow conception of Native Americans. To them, all Native Americans may be "Indians" with teepees and Pinto horses. Television may have left the impression that all Native Americans came from a single culture and that they never advanced into modern time. Native Americans may be seen as simple savages, rather than as contemporary fellow citizens and worthy human beings whose history and present-day life add depth and diversity to our national identity.

Methods for augmenting concepts are as diverse as the teacher's imagination. They include field trips, resource speakers, trade books, movies, simulations, cultural fairs, and many other strategies. Expanding and refining our store of social studies concepts should be both pleasant and instructive. It is through such learning that we develop future citizens with the promise of becoming humane and competent leaders.

DISCUSSION QUESTIONS

1. A friend and colleague of mine once said that if he could change one thing about elementary schoolteachers he would focus more of their lessons on key concepts than on facts. If this happened, how would it change the nature of a typical child's school experience? How would it change your teaching tasks? How would it change testing practices?

2. Are all nouns concepts? Are verbs concepts too? How about conjunctions and prepositions? Is there any word that isn't a concept? Support your response with examples.

3. The high frequency of technical concepts is part of what makes social studies challenging to learn. Should teachers attempt to teach all new concepts to students by one of the two methods described in this chapter, or can they speed things up by quickly defining some of the less important concepts and simply assuming students know the others?

MAIN IDEAS AND GENERALIZATIONS: CONCLUSIONS OF THOUGHT

Main ideas and *generalizations* are types of social studies content that combine or make use of facts and concepts to form descriptive or predictive statements about people's behavior. For example, the descriptive generalization, "Most elementary education students are female," is based in facts revealed through surveys of elementary education students. (You may want to test this generalization with your own class and others that have preceded you through the program, to determine if it holds true for your institution.) Given knowledge of the gender status of present and past elementary education students, we could make a predictive generalization or hypothesis stating that if, in general, things remain the same, we would expect that future classes of elementary education students will also be mostly female.

Within elementary social studies textbook series, district curriculum guides, and other curriculum materials, there is seldom any distinction made between generalizations and main ideas. There are, however, some qualitative distinctions that exist between these two similar types of content that should be explicitly noted. Becoming sensitive to these distinctions will help you determine an appropriate teaching approach for any specific main idea statement or generalization.

Generalizations

Social scientists produce generalizations about people's behavior based on research they have conducted. Such generalizations are open to inspection and refutation by other social scientists investigating the same phenomena. Generalizations, when supported by numerous studies and accepted by informed critics, are often used to support theories, the highest level of content developed by social science.[2]

A *social science generalization* is a statement that expresses a relationship between two or more social science concepts. Social science generalizations are formed as a result of research involving direct observation, document analysis, surveys, and other methods of gaining information about people's behavior. Generalizations often take the form of descriptive statements that allow people to understand, explain, and predict human behavior. Generalizations are usually expressed in the form of complete sentences. They are supposed to have universal application within the frame of reference to which they apply. This means that the validity of the generalization must not be easily or frequently contradicted.

Generalizations may be taught by showing students examples that fit or exemplify the generalization statement. This direct instruction approach is efficient, but it amounts to little more than a lecture and it treats students as passive receptors of preexisting knowledge about human behavior. Figure 3-6 presents an alternative, inductive strategy for teaching generalizations to young children. In the example, the teacher wants students to see the relationship between increasing the number, weight, size, and speed of cars and trucks and the construction needed to accommodate these changes. He presents the students with a collection of photos that show the history of the North American auto industry and asks the students to notice how the scenes change as time progresses.

---

[2]Theories of social behavior are typically not taught in the elementary social studies curriculum so they are not addressed here.

SUGGESTED STEPS	SAMPLE DIALOGUE
1. The teacher selects and presents data for the students to examine.	*"Look at this collection of photographs that I brought in. The photos show scenes of car and truck traffic ranging from the early 1900s up to the present."*
2. The students are asked to examine/organize/ analyze the data and to look for evidence of similarities or trends in the data. They may be told specific things to look for or they may be asked to examine the data in an unstructured manner if it is likely that they will find the generalization sought.	*"Pass the photographs around and examine them closely. See if you can tell which photos are the oldest and look for the changes that take place over time."*
3. Students are asked to make supportable statements that hold true for the entire set of data examined. These are generalizations.	*"Terrance, you and Tonya seem to be ready to make a statement about what you've seen. Let's hear it."* Terrance: *There are fewer cars and trucks in the older pictures.* Tonya: *Yes, and the roads are smaller.*
4. The teacher and other students examine the data to see if the statements are supported.	*"Terrance has noticed that there are fewer cars and trucks in the older pictures and Tonya has noticed that the roads are smaller. Let's check to see if that's true. . . . Now that we agree that the photographic evidence supports the statements made by Terrance and Tonya, let's see if we can make a sentence that expresses the relationship between the increasing number of cars and trucks and the increasing size of roads. I'll start you out"* (teacher moves to the chalkboard).

FIGURE 3-6

An Inductive Strategy for Teaching Generalizations

Of course, there are many other items that students might notice in the photographs. For example, as time passes, the cars progress from being small, light, low-powered, and slow to being larger, heavier, high-powered, and fast. There is a greater diversity of models and colors available. Trucks have gotten bigger and more powerful. They too have experienced design diversification. Finally, the roads have had to change to accommodate these improved vehicles. Curves have had to be banked in order to facilitate higher-speed travel. Crash barriers have been erected to reduce deaths, and a whole system of standardized signs and signals have been installed across the nation to regulate traffic flow. If the students can discover these and other generalizations through their analysis of the photographs, then they've certainly learned a good bit of content relevant to the development of our nation.

Main Ideas

Textbooks and other curriculum materials often place generalizations together with other statements under the heading "Main Ideas." While generalizations are certainly among the "main ideas" to be gained from the material, a close inspection often reveals that most of the statements listed do not have the descriptive or explanatory power of a true social science generalization. Main idea statements may be simple definitions such as, "A truck farm is a place where vegetables are grown" or "A market is a mechanism for exchanging goods and services." Other main ideas may be simple statements of facts such as "Christopher Columbus arrived in the New World in 1492" or "Chicago is (at present) the largest city in the Midwest."

While main ideas are worthy of being taught, they do not warrant the same attention that should be devoted to true social science generalizations. Indeed it is difficult to imagine a social scientist arriving at statements like the previous ones as a result of research. For this reason, main ideas will not be the topic of inductive lessons like those used to teach generalizations. More often, main ideas are assumed to be gained from independent reading, teacher lectures, or class recitations.

The ten statements that follow may be classified as either generalizations or main ideas. Read the statements and decide whether you think they are main ideas or generalizations.

EXERCISE 3-1   Distinguishing Main Ideas from Generalizations

1. People in communities set up rules to solve problems and help everyone get along.
2. The nineteenth amendment to the U.S. Constitution guaranteed women the right to vote.
3. Over three hundred years ago, people from England, Spain, France, and Holland started colonies in the United States.
4. Improvements in communication and transportation are essential to industrial development.
5. Large cities tend to be located near navigable rivers, large lakes, seas, and oceans.
6. A pioneer is a person who does something or goes somewhere first.
7. Fibers from cotton are spun together to make thread.
8. If a community loses its major base of business or industry people will move away.
9. A generation is a group of people born at about the same time.
10. Martin Luther King, Jr. was an ordained minister who preached nonviolence and led many protests for African Americans' civil rights.

Answer Key 1. generalization 2. main idea 3. main idea 4. generalization 5. generalization 6. main idea 7. main idea 8. generalization 9. main idea 10. main idea

DISCUSSION QUESTIONS

1. Available research indicates that most elementary grade level children cannot identify the main ideas in their social studies textbooks through independent reading (Baumann, 1983). Assuming that this research conclusion holds true for your class, what kinds of activities or strategies does this imply you must do as a teacher if you want your students to benefit from reading their textbooks?

2. Are generalizations any more important than main ideas? If so, what evidence or reasoning do you cite as a basis for your position? If not, how would you defend yourself against the charge that you are belittling the work of social scientists?

3. Why do experts think that it is better to have children arrive at a generalization through an inductive process than to simply give children these products of academic work? How do you suppose they arrived at this position (that is, what evidence may have influenced their opinions)?

SKILLS: INTELLECTUAL PROCESSES FOR PRODUCTIVITY

The acquisition of intellectual skills is a critically important outcome of education. For our purposes, *skills* are defined as mental behaviors used to process or produce written, verbal, behavioral, visual, or tactile material or stimuli. It should be recognized that many intellectual skills are manifested through physical (psychomotor) behavior. In addition, it must be acknowledged that all skills are underlaid by or make use of various facts, concepts, and other forms of implied knowledge.

There are many lists of social studies skills and it is likely that your school district will include a list in its curriculum guide. The teacher's edition of most popular elementary social studies textbooks will also contain a list of skills supposedly infused throughout the instruction associated with the pages of the textbook.

While differences exist among the skills lists used by different states, school districts, and textbooks, they would be likely to include map skills (treated in Chapter 7), problem-solving and decision-making skills, questioning, hypothesizing, critical-thinking, and social participation skills.

Problem-Solving and Decision-Making Skills

The thinking operations typically identified in education include observing, describing, comparing, classifying, inferring, predicting, and hypothesizing. Thinking is also often divided into levels according to Bloom's taxonomy, which specifies knowledge, comprehension, application, analysis, synthesis, and evaluation as the six types of thinking people use (1956).

Direct instruction in thinking involves the use of these operations and levels of thought in the specific content being taught. Research has shown that expert thinkers in one area are not likely to be sophisticated thinkers in other disrelated areas (Penner and Voss, 1983). For this reason, it is important to teach problem solving and decision making within the content areas where these skills are desired.

Problem Solving   Problem solving may be thought of as a specialized type of thinking. Thinking, in general, implies such intelligent behaviors as recalling information, using concepts, and applying knowledge to accomplish some task. Problem solving implies the use of knowledge and intellectual skills in order to gain some specific end. Depending on the problem, the skills required could be observing, describing, comparing, classifying, inferring, predicting, and hypothesizing. Similarly, depending on the problem, you may spend more time recalling, comprehending, applying, analyzing, synthesizing, or evaluating.

Before going any further, it's important to define what is meant by the term *problem*. A problem is a task for which a person doesn't have an immediate ready-made answer or solution. *Problem solving* is finding the means to a distinctly conceived end or goal.

A true problem exists when three conditions are present: (1) an individual has a clearly defined goal whose attainment is desired; (2) blocking of the path to the goal occurs; and (3) deliberation takes place causing the individual to better define the problem, identify possible solutions, and test them for feasibility. Imagine you are driving to school and suddenly your car sputters and rolls to a stop. Your goal is to get to school and your normal pattern of behavior used to achieve that goal will not work since your car has just stopped running. At this point deliberation takes place and you begin processing a series of questions designed to make you familiar with the context of the problem. Questions such as, "Where am I? Is it safe to get out of the car? What does the gas gauge say? Could it be broken? Will the motor start again?" will be asked.

A four-step problem-solving model makes sense in social studies since it applies well to everyday life problems. The four-step model is presented in Figure 3-7.

Research has shown that quite a number of factors are related to high-level problem-solving ability. Among them are: relatively high I.Q.; high reading comprehension scores; high computation scores; high spatial aptitude scores;

---

1. Get to know the problem (which means understanding the setting, determining relevant facts, and perceiving implied relationships).

2. Choose what to do or select your plan of attack.

3. Carry out the plan.

4. Reflect on what happened.

• •

FIGURE 3-7
A Four-Step Problem-Solving Model

ability to note likenesses, differences, and analogies; ability to estimate; lower scores on text anxiety; and use of formal problem-solving strategies.

Commonly used formal problem-solving strategies are displayed in Figure 3-8. As you read the list think about which strategy you tend to use most. Also, consider whether certain strategies work better than others for particular types of problems.

---

1. Guess and check.
2. Look for a pattern.
3. Make a list of possible causes.
4. Make a visual model, table, or graph.
5. Act it out.
6. Eliminate possibilities.
7. Work backwards.
8. Restate and refine the problem.
9. Identify known and unknown information.
10. Identify a subproblem and solve it.
11. Solve a simpler, related problem.
12. Change your point of view and check for hidden assumptions.
13. Generalize to other similar situations or problems.

FIGURE 3-8
Commonly Used Problem-Solving Strategies

Decision Making   Decision making at its simplest is binary choice making. It may be as simple as deciding whether to wear a coat or not, determining whether to cross the street now or a moment later, or choosing to obey a teacher's request for silence. These situations make it clear that most of the decisions we make are not truly instances of problem solving.

As decision-making situations become more complex, however, they demand increasingly more thought and can indeed become true problem-solving experiences. Decisions that are important deserve careful consideration. A five-step decision-making model is often recommended for important decisions. The steps are shown in Figure 3-9.

Let's use the decision-making model in Figure 3-9 to practice making a common economic decision. Imagine that you have been invited to a formal dance and that you need a new dress or suit to make your best appearance. See if you can identify the criteria you would use in making your decision. Was cost a criterion? How about style? Compare your list with that of another student. Can the class come up with at least ten criteria?

1. Recognize the decision occasion.

2. List the various alternatives available.

3. Determine criteria for making the decision.

4. Use the criteria to evaluate and rate the various alternatives.

5. Make your choice.

FIGURE 3-9
A Five-Step Decision-Making Model

DISCUSSION QUESTIONS

1. Do you recall explicit problem-solving or decision-making instruction taking place in your own elementary education? If so, share your experience(s) with others in the class, describing how you felt about what you learned. If you did not experience any explicit problem-solving or decision-making instruction, how do you account for that reality? Do you suppose teachers felt it was unimportant? Do you suppose teachers felt it was too difficult to teach or that it wouldn't be tested (so why bother)?

2. Are good problem solvers and decision makers born that way or are these things that can be learned? Explain your position. Assume you are right. What are the implications of your position for classroom instruction? Assume you are wrong. Now what are the implications of your position for classroom instruction?

3. Think back carefully to the last time you had a significant problem to solve or a decision to make. How did you do? Were you successful? Are there things you would change now that you can look back on the situation? Could the help of a good advisor or well-developed instruction have made a difference in your performance? Explain your position.

Questioning, Hypothesizing, and Critical-Thinking Skills

Questioning, hypothesizing, and critical thinking are important elementary social studies skills. Typically, children arrive at their formal schooling experience full of questions and simplistic thinking about the social world. Encouraging the exploration of answers to their questions and the development of more accurate thinking about social phenomena is especially important to fostering interest in social studies. Let's examine how questioning, hypothesizing, and critical-thinking skills can be easily incorporated into K–6 social studies.

Questioning   Young children naturally ask some of life's most challenging questions: "Where is God?" "Why don't you make more money?" "If slavery was bad, why did people do it?" "Why did white settlers take the Indian's land?" and even "Why don't I have more friends?" Sadly, as children progress through the elementary grades, their precocious questioning behavior begins to diminish. An optimist might infer that this was because they had already received good answers to their most pressing questions, but it is more likely that children learn that such questions are considered inappropriate and that adults do not like to be asked questions that they cannot easily answer.

The broad and engaging content base of social studies naturally invites an endless succession of questions. In fact, the more you know, the more questions you have! In addition, the citizenship goal of social studies in a democratic nation demands that students be encouraged to ask questions of persons in authority.

Students may be encouraged to ask questions in a variety of ways. Here are a few:

- Share the questions you've posed and follow them with an invitation for students' questions: "Are there other things you would like to know?"
- When a student asks a question, make sure you really listen, and follow the question with a response that helps the student think about how to determine the answer.
- Begin new units of study by making a list of students' questions that they would like to have answered. Keep this list and return to it periodically to expand it and check off the questions that have been answered.
- Periodically, take some time at the end of class to allow students to ask questions concerning the content they are learning.
- Ask the students to pose questions that might be included in a unit test. Have the students assess the questions and determine which they feel are best.
- Place a question box in the room and have students deposit their questions that didn't get answered by the end of the class period. Review these questions and consider starting the next class with them.

As you begin to work with children on the development of their questioning skills, it is important to let them know that teachers and parents have a legitimate right to make certain decisions and may disapprove of children's questions regarding these areas of life. For example, many adults do not want to be questioned by their children about why the child has to go to bed, or must stop watching television, or take a bath. Failure to warn children of this potential may result in complaints from parents and other adults who are suffering under a barrage of unending questions.

Hypothesizing for Research   A *hypothesis* is a statement that expresses an inspectable relationship between two or more phenomena. Hypotheses usually take the form of "if x, then y" statements. A hypothesis related to economics might be: *If* demand for an item goes down, *then* the price will go down. Of course, the hypotheses of children will seldom be so formal. They are more likely to sound like guesses or conclusions. A child might say, "If our school had more computers we would learn more." Recognizing the implied "then" and helping the child inspect the reasoning behind the statement are important teaching behaviors. Hypothesizing can be encouraged by frequently asking "what if . . ." and "why . . ." questions. Figure 3-10 shows a series of informal hypotheses related to some of the social sciences and humanities. As you read

Economics	If the cost of candy doubled children would get less and then their dental health would improve.
Sociology	If neighborhood gangs had more recreational activities available they wouldn't get into so much trouble.
Geography	If our country didn't have any rivers there wouldn't be any floods.
Religion	If everyone was the same religion there wouldn't be any problem with school prayer.

FIGURE 3-10

Hypotheses Suitable for Research by Young Students

the hypotheses, identify how young students might conduct an investigation designed to prove or disprove their statements.

Children's research into social reality should be guided with patience and understanding. The logic children use to explain social phenomena may seem incredibly naive. Their hypothetical solutions to problems may reflect a real lack of knowledge and experience that good teaching may address in a positive atmosphere of shared inquiry and adventure. An important point to remember is that young students should never be laughed at or belittled because of their naive thinking—no matter how amusing it is to adults. Informative firsthand experiences and invitations to shared investigations are appropriate responses. Simply correcting a child's thinking is a tempting quick solution, but it is never as convincing as collaborative investigations and firsthand experiences. Chapter 14 on inquiry instruction addresses these ideas in detail.

Critical Thinking   Critical thinking involves making judgments about quality, correctness, goodness, or suitability. Critical thinking is essentially *evaluative* thinking. It calls on the learner to be critical.

Even the very young can be taught to exercise critical thinking and make independent judgments. Kindergarten children might be asked to judge the correctness of several statements you make about the weather. So on a sunny, hot, windless day, you might contend that it was cold, cloudy, and downright blustery—allowing the children to correct your silly and obviously incorrect perceptions. Clinging tenaciously to your story, you might maintain that just moments ago it was very cloudy and cold and that something just changed the weather. The children, of course, should detect that this too is a misperception and maintain their own judgments about the weather.

If critical thinking can be done with young children, then it is certainly possible to do it with older students. Drawing on students' growing skills in questioning and hypothesizing, lead students to challenge the conclusions offered in their textbooks, look for exceptions to rules, and continually ask, "Is that right? Do I really believe that?" By adopting this perspective, you turn learning from a process of passive absorption to one of active and selective knowledge filtration.

DISCUSSION QUESTIONS
◆ ◆ ◆ ◆ ◆

1. If questioning, hypothesizing, and critical thinking are so important, why weren't they offered more in your social studies classes?

2. Are skills "habits of the the mind" that once learned will never fade? If that is so, does it make sense to spend more time teaching skills than other forms of content?

3. Isn't it dangerous—or at least unwise—to teach children how to question and criticize? Shouldn't you cooperate with a parent who wanted you to eliminate this type of teaching in your classroom?

Social Participation Skills

Social participation skills involve such learned mental behaviors as active listening, conflict resolution, and persuasive speaking. Social participation skills are among the most important skills that an individual can have. They are used far more often than other skills we learn in school, and lacking social participation skills may prevent us from ever realizing our full individual potential.

Social participation skills affect the way we meet and communicate with other people. They influence our self-confidence in unfamiliar settings, and they often help determine the success we will have in life. To imagine the importance of good social participation skills, simply think what a mother might tell her son and daughter prior to letting them eat dinner with another family for the first time. Or imagine the importance of good social participation skills during a parent-teacher conference, a presentation at the Parents and Teachers Association meeting, or a call made to a local school board member concerning your views on mandatory drug testing of new teachers.

Despite the importance of good social participation skills, they are often learned only by chance, acquired through trial-and-error learning, haphazard reinforcement, and unconscious modeling. In school, the teacher has the ability to influence the learning of social skills through direct instruction, demonstrations, modeling, and role playing. Examples of social participation skills that can and should be taught include basic manners in greeting and introducing people, using the telephone directory and making calls for assistance, and writing an opinion letter to the editor of the local newspaper. When teaching such social skills it is important to allow the students to question why we have adopted these particular mannerisms. It is also appropriate to compare our cultural practices with those of other cultures. Providing school-based opportunities for children to understand and practice these culturally determined social participation skills should be a legitimate and valued part of the social studies program.

Figure 3-11 provides a summary of research- and experienced-based conclusions about skill teaching. Following these guidelines will help assure that your first skill-teaching sequence is productive and pleasant.

These proven skill-teaching guidelines work best when applied within a model skill-teaching sequence, such as the one described in Figure 3-12.

---

1. Skills have to be formally and explicitly taught.

    a. Mental processes must be discussed and described to the point where children can verbally tell their peers how to do the skill.

    b. Provide opportunities to think about and describe the skill as it is being performed.

2. Skills have to be taught and practiced several times to be learned.

    a. Opportunities for feedback and reteaching are required.

    b. Use frequent initial practice and then distributed practice.

3. Skill exercises must be directly related to the content of the course and the existing experiences of the students.

4. It is better to focus on thoroughly learning a few skills, taught one at a time, than to try to teach many skills simultaneously.

5. Skill-learning sessions should be short and pleasant, especially in the primary grades.

6. Students should be encouraged to judge their own success at the skill.

F I G U R E   3 - 1 1
Guidelines for Teaching Skills

---

1. Identify the skill by name and define or describe it.

2. Describe how the skill is used, why it is important, and/or how it will benefit the students.

3. Demonstrate the skill from its beginning to its end, making sure that your demonstration is a well-planned model of desirable practice.

4. Demonstrate the skill again, talking through the steps as you perform them.

5. Lead the class in performing the skill in a step-by-step, slow-motion fashion on simplified material. Monitor all work for accuracy.

6. Provide opportunities for shared and independent practice. Monitor for accuracy.

7. Ask students to describe the skill verbally to one another and to you.

8. Repeat steps 3 through 7 as required for students needing remedial help.

9. Test the performance of the skill.

10. Provide intensive and then distributed practice.

F I G U R E   3 - 1 2
The Skill-Teaching Sequence

ATTITUDES AND VALUES
· · · · ·

Attitudes and values are also important forms of social studies content. Because they are important and because teachers are often confused about their role in teaching attitudes and values, they are treated separately in Chapter 17.

CONCLUDING THOUGHTS
· · · · ·

As you begin to teach social studies to children in your own classroom, remember that the quality of your social studies content is critically important. Content refers to all of the facts, concepts, main ideas, generalizations, skills, attitudes, and values that are the focus of your instruction. Content can be powerful or trivial. It can be interesting or boring. Dressing up trivial and boring content with cute methods is a common practice in all subject areas, but it is a particularly negative practice in social studies, where there is so much important content to be offered. I urge you to offer powerful content to your students. It makes sense to direct your instructional efforts toward conveying powerful content, not to waste them on trivia or other learnings that are below the capacity of your students.

Make sure you do *your* homework and teach accurate, up-to-date content. Too often the content conveyed is ten to twenty-five years out of date. The only way to combat this problem is for you to take the initiative to be your own best student. That may mean going to the library once a week, calling a specialist at the local university, and subscribing to journals such as *Social Education, Social Studies and the Young Learner,* or *National Geographic.* It will most certainly mean reading a daily newspaper and a weekly newsmagazine, listening to the various news programs on television and radio, and being involved in your community. Grading students' papers is important and I know that you'll have plenty of that to do. But your homework must not stop there. You must consider it your professional business to be an active, enthusiastic learner who is intellectually alive. Exercising your inquisitiveness and building your store of knowledge are lifelong pleasures you can model for all students.

Finally, make sure you teach children something that is new and useful. Of course that's a tall order, but the content focus of lessons should be something that piques students' interest. In addition, students should be able to see that owning the content will be useful to them, not just in some remote, adult future, but also tomorrow, as they interact with their friends and families. So test your content periodically to see if it meets the twin demands of newness and usefulness to the students. If it doesn't, perhaps you're slipping into a mode of teaching and level of professional conduct that is less than you desire.

REFERENCES AND SELECTED READINGS
◆ ◆ ◆ ◆/◆

Angell, A. V. 1991. Democratic climates in elementary classrooms: A review of theory and research. *Theory and Research in Social Education.* 19(3):241–266.

Bakler, A., and Stoltman, J. P. 1988. *The nature of geographic literacy.* ERIC digest no. 35. Bloomington, IN: ERIC Clearinghouse for Social Science/Social Studies Education.

Baumann, J. F. 1983. Children's ability to comprehend main ideas in content textbooks. *Reading World* 22(4):322–331.

Bloom, B. S. 1965. *Taxonomy of educational objectives: Cognitive domain.* New York: David McKay.

Borich, G. D. 1992. *Effective teaching methods.* New York: Merrill.

Downey, M. T., and Levstik, L. S. 1991. Teaching and learning history. In *Handbook of research on social studies teaching and learning,* ed. J. P. Shaver, 400–410. New York: Macmillan.

Fraenkel, J. R. 1992. Hilda Taba's contributions to social studies education. *Social Education* 56(3):172–178.

Martorella, P. H. 1991. Knowledge and concept development in social studies. In *Handbook of research on social studies teaching and learning,* ed. J. P. Shaver, 370–384. New York: Macmillan.

NCSS. 1980. *The essentials of the social studies.* Washington, D.C.: National Council for the Social Studies.

Parker, W. C. 1991. Achieving thinking and decision-making objectives in social studies. In *Handbook of research on social studies teaching and learning,* ed. J. P. Shaver, 345–356. New York: Macmillan.

Penner, B. C., and Voss, J. F. 1983. *Problem solving skills in the social sciences: Methodological considerations.* ERIC document no. ED242612. Pittsburgh: University of Pennsylvania Learning Research and Development Center.

Petrini, G. C., and Fleming, D. B. 1990. A history of social studies skills. *Theory and Research in Social Education* 18(3):233–247.

Semelman, S., and Daniels, H. 1993. *Best practice: New standards for teaching and learning in America's schools.* Portsmouth, NH: Heinemann.

Taba, H. 1967. *Teacher's handbook for elementary social studies.* Palo Alto, CA: Addison-Wesley.

Wyner, N. B., and Farquhar, E. 1991. Cognitive, emotional, and social development: Early childhood social studies. In *Handbook of research on social studies teaching and learning,* ed. J. P. Shaver, 109–120. New York: Macmillan.

CHAPTER 4

Planning for
Social Studies

(A fourth-grade class early in the year . . .)

MS. DIX: Take out your pencils and a blank sheet of paper. We're going to draw maps of our state today.

BETH: Can I sharpen my pencil?

MS. DIX: Yes, Beth you may sharpen your pencil. *(Turning toward the chalkboard and pulling down two maps that have lain untouched since school opened one month ago . . .)*

MS. DIX: Let's see if one of these has a good image of our state.

DONNA: I don't have any paper!

MS. DIX: Borrow some from Linda. She's got a sheet she will lend you. Is everyone ready now?

BILL: Do we live in Illinois or Indiana?

IMAL: We live in Illinois! You should know that!

MS. DIX: Yes, we should all know that by now, and today we're going to draw a map of our state! Okay children, how should we start? Can everyone see the state of Illinois here on this world map? It's not very big, but it's right here under this blue area that's called Lake Michigan.

THEL: We used to live in Michigan when I was in kindergarten.

JOSH: You lived in a lake?

MS. DIX: No, Josh. Thel means she lived in the state of Michigan.

IMAL: Are we going to start our maps now?

MS. DIX: Okay, let's start. Draw a vertical line on your paper like this....

Fade . . . (Ms. Dix draws a dark vertical line on the chalkboard.)

WHAT MAKES SOCIAL STUDIES PLANNING SPECIAL?

The opening vignette presents the type of dialogue that might result from a hastily planned fourth-grade social studies lesson. The dialogue is fictional, but represents a composite of things that can go wrong in almost any inadequately planned social studies lesson. Let's take a moment and note some of the problems demonstrated.

First, it should be clear that some simple steps such as providing drawing paper and making sure that the students had sharpened pencils before starting the lesson would have improved the initial focus of the instruction. Proper planning would have also alerted Ms. Dix to the need for good state and regional maps and perhaps even put her in touch with specialized maps or creative ideas for accomplishing her desired objective.

In addition, Ms. Dix's lesson lacked a clear conception of the prior instruction and learning needed to help early fourth-grade children draw their first maps of Illinois. For example, the students would have benefited from some preliminary visualization activities designed to familiarize them with various physical features of the state. These activities could have included such things as making three-dimensional models of the state out of clay, cardboard, or other materials; games designed to help students become familiar with the locations of major cities, interstate highways, rivers, lakes, and agricultural regions; and activities based on print or audiovisual presentations about Illinois state geography. Offering such experiences prior to asking students to draw freehand maps provides the base of knowledge needed to carry out the assignment and make it a worthwhile activity.

Planning in social studies, of course, has similarities to planning in other areas of the elementary school curriculum. Lesson plans will have the same basic components: outcome-oriented objectives, a listing of needed materials, procedures for implementing activities, and planned evaluation strategies. Plans must also meet the requirements of your particular school district and offer experiences that fulfill the required formal curriculum. Finally, plans should take advantage of materials that will help you provide effective instruction for all of your students.

Planning for social studies also presents some unique challenges, including addressing the nonsequential scope and sequence of social studies, the critical importance of background experience, openings for differences of opinion that exist within the social studies curriculum, the limitations of social studies textbooks, and special techniques used in evaluating students' learning in this content area.

Nonsequential Scope and Sequence

Although topics in the expanding environments scope and sequence follow an assumed developmental progression, content from much of the traditional social studies scope and sequence could be taught earlier or later with equal ease. There is little reason to restrict first-grade children to studying families or third-grade children to studying communities. Similarly, there is no reason to believe that students should master basic geographic concepts prior to gaining their first knowledge from history.[1]

The lack of substantial research to support the expanding environments social studies scope and sequence is one reason that alternative content is often adopted. In fact, professional organizations have expended much effort in developing and promoting the adoption of detailed scope and sequence documents in history, geography, economics, and civics—four of the core content areas of social studies.[2] School districts and state departments of education also establish recommended scope and sequence documents for elementary social studies. Finally, textbook and other publishers attempt to market products that fit the recommendations of the various professional organizations, states, and school districts.

A nonsequential scope and sequence is significant to social studies planning. First, it means that you as the teacher may have considerable leeway in selecting topics. If you are free to depart from the state-mandated formal social studies curriculum, or better, if your social studies curriculum provides a substantial degree of freedom, then you can teach topics that better meet your students' unique needs, interests, and abilities.

Of course, setting sail into uncharted waters entails new obstacles and opportunities. One significant obstacle in tackling a new or little taught area of content is the potential lack of teaching resources. Another is lack of parental and professional approval. Questions may come up regarding whether third graders are ready, for example, to hear different opinions about efforts to save an endangered species such as the spotted owl.

A second implication of the nonsequential scope and sequence is the freedom it gives you to change the order of (or to entirely skip) specific chapters in the textbook.[3] Jumping ahead of your colleagues when you are teaching a sequential-textbook-based social studies curriculum may prevent conflicts over scarce teaching resources such as videos, games, simulations, and trade books. Your instruction may benefit by asking whether teaching different topics will serve your students better than simply following the topics covered in the textbook or official curriculum guide.[4] Making such decisions puts you and your students more directly in charge of the curriculum. This is

---

[1]The strongest exception to the statement that social studies has a nonsequential scope and sequence lies in the area of map and globe skills. In this specific area of geography, evidence suggests that there may be a developmentally appropriate scope and sequence.

[2]The recommendations and contents of these documents, developed by recognized experts and extensive national review processes, are included in Chapters 6, 7, 8, and 9.

[3]The topics of textbook units and chapters are seldom truly sequential. It is true, however, that reading levels increase from first to last chapters. U.S. history textbooks are the exception to the nonsequential rule, since they are often ordered chronologically.

[4]You must be aware of whether your district allows departure from its official curriculum guide. If it does not, ask for permission to teach an alternative topic as part of your district's ongoing efforts to develop new curriculum and promote professionalism among its teachers.

a justifiable position given the nonsequential nature of the social studies curriculum, the benefits gained by increasing students' ownership of the curriculum, and the political socialization demand for power sharing in our democracy.

DISCUSSION QUESTIONS

1. Does the lack of a research-supported, developmentally based scope and sequence inhibit or enhance prospects for effective K–6 social studies instruction? Argue both sides of this question.

2. What would be the results or consequences if math lacked a well-accepted scope and sequence? Would these same results or consequences apply to other areas of the curriculum? Explain your position.

3. Imagine you have just taught a unit to your first-grade class on an important social science concept (for example, prejudice or social class) that is not normally treated in your school's curriculum. How would you handle parental complaints that such teaching was detrimental and unnecessary, or peer disapproval based on the belief that this content was too sophisticated for first graders?

Importance of Background Experience

A student's background of experience is the single most important factor influencing his or her learning in social studies. Students who have traveled extensively, lived in different areas of the country, or read widely are often enthusiastic about social studies. When a student can say "Hey, I've been there!" or "I just finished reading a book about that!" teachers can motivate other students' interest by tapping into the informed student's background of experience.

Taking into account your students' experiences is essential to social studies instruction. Factors such as the school's geographic setting and the socioeconomic status of the students will affect your ability to teach about specific social studies topics. Students living in a rural midwestern setting may have difficulty relating to instruction about cities based on a case study of San Francisco. Similarly, students from the inner city of Miami may lack interest in a textbook unit on the Amish of Indiana. This does not mean that social studies instruction must always deal with the familiar. Instead, it alerts you to the importance of motivation and the need to provide missing background experiences as a part of your instruction.

Regardless of your instructional setting, it is important to remember that in most cases, you will have different backgrounds of experience among the students in your class. Many teachers take an inventory at the beginning of each school year in an effort to get to know parents' occupations, family travel experiences, and other information useful to their social studies instruction.

These differences work both for and against you. On the positive side, you can use individual student and family experiences to enrich your social studies instruction. On the negative side, natural variability in background experiences means that you will have to give extra help to some students while others move on to other topics or receive enrichment experiences in the same content area.

Because of its content, social studies planning often involves using community resources. You may need to locate someone in your community who has lived in or recently visited a place you are studying; you will have to become familiar with local historic places and local geographic features; and you may want to start your own collection of travel brochures, maps, and photographs to further illustrate the places studied in your curriculum. Using such resources can help provide missing background experiences.

Remember that experience and background knowledge play an enormous role in promoting students' understanding and enjoyment of social studies. Where background knowledge is lacking, students often view social studies as difficult and boring. In fact, you'll direct much of your effort at developing students' missing background of experience. Pumping life into something that would otherwise remain remote and unreal is critical to making social studies instruction powerful.

Recognizing Differences of Opinion

A final unique aspect of planning for social studies is the fact that differences of opinion exist within all social studies topics. Family life, the typical focus of first-grade social studies under the expanding environments scope and sequence, is the source of many differences of opinion. As an illustration of this fact, Figure 4-1 lists a few of the areas where different opinions exist surrounding family life.

Planning to include and manage differences of opinion is a key to effective social studies instruction at all grade levels. Pretending that all people hold the same opinion is unrealistic and fails to live up to the professional standards established by NCSS in its *Essentials* statement (see Chapter 2). Handled correctly, recognizing differences of opinion is one of the quickest and easiest ways to breathe life into social studies content. Handled incorrectly, it may detract from students' learning and raise parental and professional disapproval. Gaining the instructional good that can come from recognizing differences of opinion is so important that I have devoted a separate chapter (Chapter 20) to this area of social studies teaching.

EXERCISE 4.1

Take any grade-level theme from the expanding environments scope and sequence (see Chapter 2) and generate a chart similar to that shown in Figure 4-1. Repeat this exercise with a subtopic such as transportation, farming, medicine, sports, or pets.

SAMPLE TOPICS	POTENTIAL DIFFERENCES OF OPINION
Birth	Should parents tell their first-grade child where babies come from?
	Should parents help older siblings deal with feelings of jealousy when a new baby brother or sister arrives?
	What limits should apply to an older child's caretaker responsibilities for a new baby in his or her family?
Work	Should children be told if a parent loses his or her job?
	Should parents pay children for household chores?
	When, if ever, should a father's (or mother's) work take priority over family (or child-rearing) responsibilities?
Leisure	Should children have some say over a family's recreation and leisure activities?
	Is it appropriate for a father (or mother) to spend a night out with the boys (girls)?
	How much television should children be allowed to watch after finishing homework?
	Should parents restrict what children view on television, limiting them to educational shows?
Sleep	Should brothers and sisters sleep in separate rooms after the age of three? What if families can't afford this?
	Should a sixth grader be able to stay up until 10 P.M.?
	Should parents punish a child for wetting the bed?
	If a child insists on having bedroom lights left on each night, is that all right?
Eating	Is cold cereal with 2 percent milk a sufficient breakfast for young children?
	Should parents let children leave food on their plates?
	Should parents serve different food for their children if the children don't like what the adults are having?
	Should parents let children select their own breakfast cereals? What if they only choose junky sweet stuff?
	Would you serve a dessert to a child who would not or could not finish his or her meal?

FIGURE 4-1

Differences of Opinion Surrounding Family Life

UNIT TEACHING

. . . . .

The unit approach to teaching is used in all areas of the curriculum and at all grade levels. Textbook chapters are logically similar to units (although taken by themselves, they may be poor examples!). Social studies commonly uses the unit approach. Knowing why the unit approach makes sense, what makes a great unit, and how to develop one, are important to your success as a social studies teacher.

Why the Unit Approach Makes Sense

A *unit* is a thematically linked, coherent collection of lesson plans, designed to accomplish a limited set of instructional goals. Units have a beginning, middle, and end. The beginning of the unit arouses students' interest in the topic, provides an overview of unit activities and content, explains why learning this content is important, measures students' present level of background knowledge about the topic, and tries to provide a context for the unit by explaining relevance to other already learned topics or experiences. The middle of the unit develops the major concepts, main ideas, generalizations, skills, values, and attitudes through a sequenced set of activities that provide for a variety of learning styles and abilities. The end of the unit allows students to summarize and reflect on their efforts, share products of their learning, and evaluate their understandings.

The unit approach offers great variety and flexibility of many topic changes throughout the year. It also provides an opportunity for developing the depth of coverage needed to aid students' understanding. It helps students view subjects as coherent topics, making the year more manageable for teachers and students alike.

What Makes a Great Unit?

A great social studies unit teaches great content. Great content is intellectually powerful, up-to-date, and interesting to students. It includes more than just factual information; it incorporates social science and humanities concepts that are new to the students.

Great social studies units also make intelligent use of literature, drama, art, and music. Teachers integrate these subjects as a means of improving social studies learning. This means students aren't studying literature, drama, art, or music for their own sake as subjects during their use in social studies. The goals and objectives remain centered in social studies. Excellent social studies units make use of reading, writing, and mathematics in the same way; these subjects play the supporting role but aren't the focus of learning.[5]

Excellent social studies units also vary the pacing and variety of instruction offered. Students receive some choice of activities, and adaptations are offered for students with different learning styles and special needs. Excellent units provide for slower and faster students through such instructional devices as independent activities, group projects, learning centers, and contracts. Finally, excellent units make use of instructional aids such as bulletin boards, dioramas,

---

[5]Instruction that is truly integrated simultaneously accomplishes objectives from two or more subjects (Alleman and Brophy, 1991).

homework, periodic quizzes, and progress charts to keep the focus on the learning clear and present.

Steps in Developing a Unit

Developing a really good social studies unit takes lots of planning and time. An outstanding unit may take months to build simply because of the time needed to collect ideas, organize, and compose the various parts. Figure 4-2 lists the steps to follow in developing a unit.

---

1. Identify the topic. Narrow topics that allow greater depth of instruction are better than large topics that force superficial treatment. Ideas for topics may come from anywhere, but the best sources are the interests of students, the experiences of the teacher, and content related to the established curriculum.

2. Develop background. Use both the regular adult library and your curriculum resource center. Build content background, and search for student materials. Gather teaching ideas. Locate teacher-made units by searching an on-line or CD-ROM version of the Educational Resources Information Center (ERIC) database.

3. Develop a content outline. This outline clearly identifies what your unit teaches. The content outline may contain facts, concepts, main ideas, generalizations, skills, attitudes, and values.

4. Write the goals and objectives, remembering that objectives must describe how the students will demonstrate mastery of the content.

5. Describe the initiating, developmental, and closing activities for the unit. Be careful to properly sequence the instruction and make sure that it fully teaches the content you have specified for your social studies unit.

6. Plan the unit evaluation, taking care to make sure it fairly assesses each student's learning and covers all of the objectives.

◆ ◆

FIGURE 4-2
Steps in Developing a Unit

The Importance of Long-Range Planning

High-quality social studies instruction requires long-range planning. Planning for the long haul involves knowing what units you will be teaching months from now. Some teachers like to sketch out a yearly plan that shows the units they will be implementing each month throughout the entire school year. Doing long-range planning gives you time to identify community resource people, secure district- and school-owned curriculum materials such as videos and kits containing historical artifacts, and write to key contacts such as state travel bureaus or chambers of commerce. As you do long-range planning do not neglect to consult your district's curriculum guide, read the activity suggestions in the Teacher's Guide for your textbook, contact your social studies supervisor

The instructional goals of this unit are to:

- help students become familiar with the industrial, commercial, and agricultural regions of our state

- make students aware of the relative size and location of major cities in our state

- acquaint students with the climate of our state

- help students learn the locations and names of major rivers, rail lines, and highways

- build cartographic understandings and skills focusing on the use of symbols, color, map legends, scale, and grid coordinate systems

F I G U R E   4 - 3

Sample Goal Statements for a Fourth-Grade State Geography Unit

to ask for suggestions, and search ERIC for free instructional resources. Figure 4-3 displays some typical unit goal statements.

The unit goal statements shown in Figure 4-3 are general or broad statements of desired outcomes that may be attained only over a considerable period of work. Goal statements may bring to mind imagined student behaviors, but they are traditionally phrased as nonobservable statements of desired instructional outcomes. A final point: a single goal statement may give rise to many instructional objectives that contain discrete observable behaviors students perform as a result of content learned through one or more planned activities. Figure 4-4 on page 68 presents a diagram showing this relationship for one of the state geography goals.

SPECIAL CONSIDERATIONS IN SOCIAL STUDIES LESSON PLANS

Lesson plan formats and requirements vary from school district to school district. Many school districts require that teachers keep a plan book describing the sequence of daily subjects and breaks and specifying the topics and instructional materials covered each week. A plan book might show social studies being alternated with science on a unit-by-unit basis, with social studies (or science) instruction placed in one or more of the afternoon periods. If a third-grade class were studying mass transportation as a focus in an urban communities unit, the plan book might read as shown in Figure 4-5 on page 68.

Obviously, a teacher's plan book communicates only the briefest notion of intended instruction. The experienced teacher mentally plans the steps needed to make the intended instruction happen smoothly. For example, on Monday, prior to showing the video, the teacher might have the students raise their hands if they have ever ridden on a subway. Additional questions would help focus students' attention on the major ideas presented in the video. Such questions

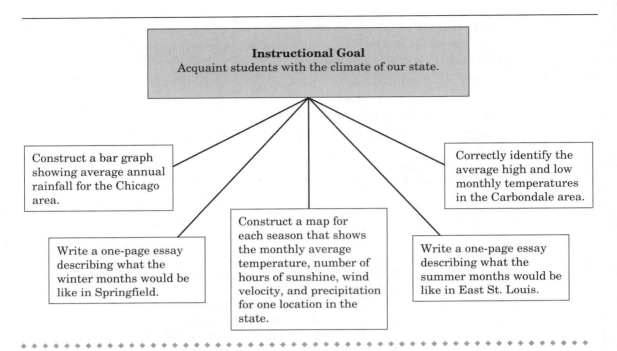

FIGURE 4-4

Geography Unit Climate Goal and Related Objectives

are a part of the instructional procedures used to gain maximum benefit from the video, but the plan-book sample does not show them.

Similarly obscured by the abridged nature of the plan-book content is (are) the instructional objective(s) of the video-viewing activity. Chances are good that valid instructional objectives are contained in the teacher's guide for the video, although these printed guides commonly disappear after a few uses. So exactly what were the students to learn as a result of viewing the subway video? Answering this leads to specifying the instructional objective for this day's

SUBJECTS	MONDAY	TUESDAY	WEDNESDAY	THURSDAY	FRIDAY
Social Studies	Introduce *subways* using video.	Read textbook pp. 46–48 (subways) and do Checkup questions.	Take a field trip on the Metro subway.	Begin a mural on the subways.	Finish the mural; write assessment stories.

FIGURE 4-5

Plan-book Sample

lesson. Figure 4-6 lists a few of the potential instructional objectives that might be stated for our imaginary video on subways. (You'll notice that specifying the objectives forces us to imagine the content that might be featured in the video.)

Of course, other objectives might have been imagined for the subway video. The point is that viewing the video should result in some gains of content knowledge related to this mode of transportation. Geography, history, economics, and government all play a role in helping the student understand the nature and function of subways. Knowledge we, as adults, take for granted is not obvious to younger members of our society, so part of your task as a teacher of social studies will be to reveal this knowledge and share your own understandings with children. The exercise that follows gives you a chance to practice stating objectives for other parts of the week-long subway transportation focus.

As a result of viewing the video on subways, the student will be able to:

1. name the city and year of the first subway to run in the United States

2. list the kinds of workers needed to build and maintain a subway system

3. write a short paragraph describing at least three problems common to subway systems and the ways in which the systems have attempted to overcome these problems

FIGURE 4-6
Objectives for the Subway Video

EXERCISE 4.2

Take each day's activities listed in the plan book and write the implied instructional procedures and objectives. Compare your work with that of a classmate.

For the purposes of teacher training, lesson plans, at a minimum, contain an instructional objective, procedures for teaching, materials required, and a statement of how the student's learning will be evaluated. Additional required components often include a lesson title, specified grade or ability level, and plans for enrichment, remediation, or extension. Different instructors typically request slightly different formats for lesson plans, so it is best to be certain that your lesson plans meet the expectations of your particular instructor.

Social studies lesson plans have the same components and follow the same formats as lesson plans for other subjects. Similarities in appearance and format, however, do not reflect the differences in lesson planning that apply to social studies instruction. Differences lie in the attention you must give to specialized vocabulary and concepts from the social sciences and humanities, the need for experiential background, the changing nature of social studies content, the fuzziness of right answers, and the challenge of higher-order thinking.

Specialized Vocabulary and Concepts

Specialized vocabulary and concepts often give students trouble learning social studies. Examples of vocabulary include people, place, and thing names (for example, Mussolini, Caribbean, NATO), and the specialized use of common words (for example, class, movement, occupation). The social sciences and humanities are also rich in highly specialized conceptual content such as: externalities (economics), megalopolis (urban planning), androgyny (anthropology), and agnostic (religion). Because knowledge of specialized vocabulary and concepts plays an important role in aiding students' learning, it is a good practice to acquaint students with prerequisite vocabulary and concepts prior to instruction. To meet this need you may do something as simple as informally defining vocabulary or introducing prerequisite concepts as a first step in the instructional sequence. Alternatively, you may teach an entire lesson on prerequisite concepts or require students to use their dictionaries or the textbook's glossary to look up specialized terms. Regardless of your approach, it is important to be sensitive to the presence of specialized vocabulary and concepts that students must understand if they are to benefit from social studies instruction.

Need for Experiential Background

The best-laid social studies plans will flop if students lack appropriate experiential background. Students who have grown up in a wealthy suburb near Chicago will have a different worldview and background of experience than children from Baker, Oregon, or Odessa, Texas. Knowing your students' backgrounds, interests, and abilities is essential to good lesson planning in social studies.

Variation in background of experience exists within communities too, due to family relocation and other factors. Even within the same community, students may have had very different social studies instruction in prior grades. In some cases, students may never have experienced social studies instruction in the primary grades. As a result, you cannot assume that certain knowledge and skills are in place when you receive your students at the first of the year. This is a significant contrast to reading, writing, and arithmetic, where prior instruction based on a highly similar scope and sequence may be assumed.[6]

Changing Nature of Content

A third area of difference in planning for social studies is the rapid change that takes place in the content of the social sciences and humanities. As a result of new scholarship, knowledge in the social sciences and humanities continues to advance at a rapid pace. New concepts and theories are born and old ones

---

[6]You are well advised to become familiar with students' abilities in these areas too, since it is amazing how much may be forgotten over a summer break!

discarded. Scholars redefine and enrich key concepts based on the most recent research. They collect and publish new factual data at an astonishing rate. Even history changes as better scholarship brings to light new documents and improved interpretations of past events.

Because of this continual change, it is important to check the facts, concepts, and generalizations offered in social studies materials. Teachers should alert children to the potential of outdated information in social studies materials. Students should consult current sources of information and be challenged to explain the cause(s) of noted differences.

Fuzziness of Right Answers

The fuzziness of right answers adds yet another dimension of difference to the task of planning for social studies. Remember that it is not unusual for social science experts to disagree on the answers to fundamental questions in their disciplines. Thus, for example, economists quarrel over the definition of full employment and dispute the appropriateness of the numbers used to provide an index of youth unemployment. Criminologists debate the causes of juvenile delinquency and social psychologists expound a new theoretical explanation of achievement failure among middle-class African-American males. A political scientist and a historian publish within the same year drastically different interpretations of the significance of Richard Nixon's presidency, often conflicting in their analysis of the same events and evidence.

Such developments are unsettling, especially to individuals who feel that it is their job to deliver well-defined, flawless knowledge to students. The tentative and ever-changing nature of social science knowledge requires teachers who are comfortable with a degree of uncertainty and who can admit that they don't know all of the answers. Teachers can help students understand this fuzzy-answer problem by gathering perspectives from a number of sources during their instruction. They can also help students see that different people are likely to see the same event or issue from different perspectives, thereby leading students to question the correctness and completeness of any single version of the truth.

Challenge of Higher-Order Thinking[7]

Earlier, I stated that social studies must go beyond factual information—that it must include higher-order content such as concepts and generalizations. Higher-order thinking requires students to do more than memorize facts and concept definitions. Higher-order thinking occurs when students do such things as form value judgments, state hypotheses, make inferences, and take

---

[7]Higher-order thinking is featured as an integral part of the chapters in Part III, and it is represented in the lesson plan examples contained in Part II and in the discussion questions offered throughout the book.

grounded positions on issues. For example, in learning about urban decay and renewal, challenge students to state hypotheses concerning the factors that led to decline and eventual renewal. They might investigate why immigrants continue to locate in urban centers despite crime, poverty, and poor-quality public schools. Encourage conversations between students and their parents on these (and many other) social studies questions.

USING THE TEXTBOOK

Textbooks play a central role in many social studies lessons, even in the lower elementary grades. Experts agree that textbooks have improved substantially in the last decade; however, all textbooks have instructional limitations that teachers must overcome.

Treating the Textbook Chapter as a Teacher-Modified Unit

Teachers often treat their social studies textbook as a collection of units that can be modified and expanded to better meet the needs of students. To understand how your young students are likely to react to reading the content of the textbook, try to gauge the instructional effectiveness of a textbook by looking through the chapters using a student's mindset. Carefully examine the photographs, charts, and maps. Determine whether students will feel the content is important. Ask yourself whether the material will interest your students and brainstorm ideas on how to present it in engaging ways that go beyond daily reading. After you have analyzed the student's textbook, consult the teacher's manual to see if it gives you useful ideas for teaching the material.

Strengths and Weaknesses of Textbooks

Textbooks are a valuable instructional tool—even in the primary grades. The student text offers a guide to what experts have judged to be age-appropriate for your class. The photographs contained in the book may serve as a valuable source of topic-focused, visual information if analyzed and used to foster thinking. The map content may be your best source of instructional material for developing these skills. And the teacher's edition may be especially helpful in suggesting activity ideas, determining appropriate instructional objectives, and identifying additional instructional resources. Textbooks provide each student with a social studies "document." When textbook reading is supplemented with other materials and teaching strategies, effective instruction is promoted.

Textbooks have their drawbacks, however. They are notorious for offering only limited or thin coverage of topics. They generally present only the positive side of the world, neglecting problems, conflicts, and prejudices children and

HOW TO USE A TEXTBOOK

- As a summary statement that can be read after other activities

- As a reference tool, read to find answers to individual questions

- As a stimulus for forming questions, clarifying concepts, or starting discussions

- As a source of visual information on a topic

HOW NOT TO USE A TEXTBOOK

- As a way to introduce a new topic of study

- As a whole-class reader, read by students out loud each day

- As a means of keeping students quiet and in their seats

- As the single authoritative source on a topic

FIGURE 4-7
How To Use a Textbook

their families face in their everyday lives. Textbooks are also limited in their ability to include all of the logically relevant and important subtopics associated with their major themes. They are unable to adapt to the interests and abilities of each student, and they provide little help in assessing students' higher-order thinking. Figure 4-7 summarizes some of the ways in which a textbook should and should not be used.

How to Use the Textbook Intelligently

Seldom, if ever, are all students within a classroom on the same reading level. Some students will read with better comprehension than others, some will read better out loud and some will read better silently. It's not uncommon to find more than a full-grade-level difference between the top and bottom readers in a classroom. Few, if any, teachers would expect all children to use the same basal reader. Yet it's not uncommon for teachers to disregard their knowledge about teaching reading when it comes time to use their social studies textbook. Too many teachers pass out the same social studies textbook to all students and expect them to use it in the same way. This violates effective reading instruction guidelines and it certainly sours social studies as a school subject for those students who have reading problems.

The goal of social studies is to acquire content knowledge and skills from the social sciences and humanities. Because of this, never pass out social studies textbooks just to have students practice applying reading skills. When students use their textbooks, tell them what facts, concepts, main ideas, or generalizations, they will gain by reading. Keeping the class quiet, killing time, and polishing reading skills are not legitimate objectives for social studies instruction![8]

---

[8]Note that there are certain reading skills—such as skimming for facts, detecting bias, or inferring the author's point of view—that should be practiced in social studies. The practice of these skills should come hand in hand with valuable social studies content learning, however, and never stand alone as an empty exercise in reading skills instruction.

Take the time to introduce students to parts and features of the book: the table of contents, glossary, subject index, and aids within the chapters such as highlighted words, subject headings, or other symbols and other types of codes. Help them learn to use the textbook to answer questions on their own. Keep older editions of the textbook and single copies of other publishers' textbooks available for reference. Use dictionaries, atlases, almanacs, and encyclopedias for double-checking facts and gaining additional information to augment the textbook.

Rather than reading out loud to cover the material in the textbook, ask students to paraphrase what a passage says in their own words. In grades 4 through 6, after students have read an assignment silently, randomly assign paragraphs to students around the room and ask them to tell the class what the paragraph says. This will help all students to follow along and read each paragraph for meaning. Ask upper-grade-level students to complete study guides or keep reflective journals.

You may recall from your own school experiences that social studies books are hard to read. Simple readability formulas don't reflect some of the persistent problems in reading social studies materials. The frequency of new concepts can be quite high. In addition, social studies books are full of specialized vocabulary that can cause trouble. Preparing students for their encounters with such stumbling blocks to comprehension can do much to enhance the learning gained from reading the textbook.

EXERCISE 4.3
. . . . .

Check out a social studies textbook written for grades 4, 5, or 6. Look through a chapter for examples of roadblocks to reading comprehension previously described. Share the examples you find and tell how you might overcome these problems through prereading activities.

Accommodating the Reading Levels of Children

There are many techniques for accommodating the different reading levels of students. All or some combination of the suggestions shown in Figure 4-8 will prove helpful in your teaching.

Building Social Studies Vocabulary

One of the outcomes of good social studies education should be an increased vocabulary of social science and humanities terms and concepts. Keep a written list of new social studies vocabulary words on a flip chart visible and easily accessible to all students. Because of the specialized meanings associated with many social studies terms and concepts, it is advisable to develop vocabulary in context. Use terms in sentences taken from the textbook and employed in classroom conversations. Students should use crossword puzzles,

1. Rewrite the passages of the textbook. The teacher, an aide, or an older student may rephrase passages using a lower-grade-level vocabulary and shorter sentences.

2. Record the passages and have the students who need help—or simply want to listen—gather and read along as they listen to the tape.

3. Have an older or more able student read the textbook to the students in need of help.

4. Use buddy reading, pairing more able with less able students so reading difficulties can be overcome with personal attention.

5. Locate audiovisual resources that treat the same topic and allow all students to use them.

6. Gain access to other textbooks or print materials on the same topic written at a lower grade level.

FIGURE 4-8

Ways to Accommodate Different Reading Levels

word-finds, the spelling/vocabulary baseball game, people bingo, classroom concentration, and other instructional devices to reinforce the learning of social science and humanities vocabulary.

Summary

It is likely that you will be given—and urged to use—a social studies textbook. Remember that textbooks are not designed to be autoinstructional resources. They are not intended to be used as whole-class readers or as sole-source social studies programs. Reducing social studies to a daily seatwork routine consisting of reading the textbook and answering the questions provided in a workbook or end-of-chapter summary is highly unprofessional. Experts rightly denounce such low-effort, low-gain teaching. Textbooks can be a valuable resource if used intelligently. You, the classroom teacher, are responsible for using your textbook in an intelligent and professional manner.

EVALUATION

Everything gets evaluated, either formally or informally, fairly or unfairly. For example, individuals informally evaluate and compare such geographic features as mountains, beaches, and forests. People may develop preferences for certain flora ("I just love to look at the dogwoods in spring bloom") or fauna ("There's nothing quite as cute as baby bunnies"). Of course, cultural phenomena are evaluated too. We form preferences for clothing ("I like that jacket, but I think it looks a little too big on me"); music ("People are unfair when they criticize rap music; some of it is really good"); literature (*I'll Fly Away* is the best children's book on homelessness); and food.

People—students, parents, teachers, professors, and others—are also evaluated whether or not they like it. We judge people for their physical appearance and for internal characteristics such as intelligence, humor, and personality. Most people find it difficult to meet someone, or even look at a stranger across a room, without forming impressions of one sort or another. The informal evaluation of people is reflected by such unexpressed thoughts as, "Boy is he handsome; I'd like to meet him!" or "What a slob; I hope I never look like that!" Assessments of intelligence and personality are often informal, but may be formally evaluated through established tests and assessment protocols. The fact is, we can't escape the judgments others make about us. At best, all we personally can do is hope that others' judgments about us are fair—and guard against making unfair judgments about others.

Teachers take on special responsibilities regarding the evaluation of their students. The act of teaching is supposed to cause individual gains in learning that take place as a result of the teacher's and student's efforts. Teaching a class without evaluating your students' learning progress would be like conducting an orchestra and never hearing the sound it makes. As teachers, we can't escape the responsibility of evaluating the learning of our students. The following sections develop a context for understanding the unique aspects of evaluation in social studies and offer specific suggestions for assessing the social studies learning of K–6 students.

Phases and Functions of Evaluation

Teachers must make defensible judgments about each child's readiness for instruction. This is called *diagnostic evaluation*. Once instruction is underway, teachers and students need to monitor the learning process and adjust it if needed. This is called *formative evaluation*. At the conclusion of instruction, *summative evaluation* strategies add additional evidence concerning how well each student met the learning objectives of the planned instruction and how well the teacher, the planned series of activities, and the curriculum resources met or exceeded their desired levels of performance.

Evaluation provides feedback to students, teachers, parents, and the public regarding student learning performance. Evaluation can improve a teacher's educational methods; determine a more appropriate placement for a particular student; inform decisions about promotion, retention, or the need for summer school; and give the public an indication of the performance of their community's schools.

Make every effort to ensure that evaluation in social studies is unbiased as to sex, race, culture, or other individual or group characteristics. In addition, because social studies has such a broad content base and a nonsequential structure, there is little reason to use an evaluation system designed to prevent the future progress of students who have not mastered the present material.

Such an approach may make sense in mathematics or even reading and language arts, but not in social studies.

Of course, all types of content learning can be evaluated. Fact and main idea learning are easily assessed. A student's conceptual knowledge can be assessed by determining whether he or she can separate examples from nonexamples. Students may show they understand a generalization by showing that it applies to many other cases. Skill learning is typically assessed by asking students to perform a task that involves applying the skill. The affective and participatory dimensions of social studies may also be assessed; however, these goal areas present special problems that must be carefully considered.

Despite the fact that social studies has established claims to certain attitude, value, and participation goals related to democratic citizenship preparation, teachers' assessments of effort, attitudes, personal values, or participation is difficult, and most likely inappropriate. This is partly because the data gained on such characteristics is often simply impressionistic, leaving the teacher open to indefensible judgments. It is also inappropriate because our civic creed demands that we allow individuals a right to hold unpopular opinions and that we protect their personal freedom—even if we disagree with their ideas and conduct—as long as it is not illegal. For these reasons, it is best to teach students to accurately self-assess their own attitudes, values, efforts, and civic participation.

Evaluation Process Includes Students

Evaluation is a process composed of a series of planned actions that take place over time. The evaluation process starts once teachers and students begin establishing goals and objectives for instruction. Teachers must share goal- and objective-setting power with students in the subject area of social studies. This does not mean turning over all power to the students, but soliciting thoughtful student input and allowing some student choice. You, the teacher, may still insist on having certain goals and objectives; others you may be willing to change or completely replace as a result of students' suggestions. After goals and objectives have been codetermined, you have answered the "what" question of instruction; you know what the desired results of your instructional efforts are supposed to be.

Once teachers and students have stated instructional goals and objectives, they may begin to think about ways of assessing whether the desired learning has occurred. They may make decisions to collect and grade homework assignments, to use chapter tests, and/or to grade students' reports to obtain information about how well students met the required objectives. Regardless of the data collected, the conscious application of criteria to it is essential to the formation of judgments about merit or worth. These, too, must be codetermined with the students in the area of social studies. Of course, good teachers will gather information from many sources to help ensure that students have several opportunities to demonstrate their knowledge.

No written policies prevent students' participation in evaluating their learning experiences; it is simply authoritarian attitudes and tradition that have locked students out of this important participation opportunity.

Grading and Evaluation

Evaluation is not synonymous with grading. The assignment of a grade to a student's test, paper, or overall subject performance at the end of a grading period, is an action taken as a result of evaluation. The evaluation process provides the data on which grading decisions are based. Ultimately, the accumulation of grades results in other decisions and actions being taken, such as designating a particular student as bright or another as average or another as slow.

A grade is a label representing someone's judgment. Any symbol system that communicates performance to the student is a grade. Thus, a happy face, a check mark, a star, or any other symbol that has evaluative meaning may be a grade. If the symbol system has a widely known meaning, such as As, Bs, and Cs, it may communicate performance to a broader audience.

Because social studies seeks to develop informed, caring, and active, future citizens it is important to use evaluative activities to foster self-judgments and to initiate discussions of how good a student's performance must be. Such an approach puts students in the decision equation and prepares them to take the role they must assume as citizens.

Types of Evaluative Information

Involving students in designing and implementing the evaluation strategies applied to their learning has direct implications for the typical assessment strategies used to judge learning gains. Typical evaluation strategies can also be adapted to allow for a degree of individuality in learning, the fuzziness of right answers, and higher-order thinking that goes beyond the recall of facts.

Teachers may gain greater student involvement and foster better self-assessment in the use of true-or-false, multiple-choice, matching, and fill-in-the-blank test items, by several strategies. For example, students may contribute test items that will be included if they meet acceptable standards. Another tactic is to allow students to answer a specific self-selected portion of the items (say 50 percent) on a test that has intentionally been made twice as long as normal. This strategy promotes choice and may also help discourage copying. Yet another strategy is to allow students to write an explanation of the reasoning they used to arrive at a particular answer to a multiple-choice, true-or-false, or matching test item.

In the realm of informal assessment techniques, students may help construct checklists that will be used to determine whether all the parts of an assignment have been completed. They may discuss and help determine the relative importance of criteria that will be applied to reports and construction projects.

Students should also be informed of steps to take if they are dissatisfied with the outcome of their teacher's evaluation. These steps might include such things as redoing an assignment or discussing the assignment in the presence of a parent or guardian.

For many decades, teachers have had students compile work folders that contained tests and samples of other items such as homework, end-of-chapter review question answers, and reports related to their social studies learning. When students are involved in determining what the contents of such work folders will be, when such folders include only examples of work that the students are most proud of, and when they are compiled for presentation as a prelude to employment, graduation, or some other goal such as a grade, these folders are commonly called *portfolios*. Portfolios originated in the world of performance art such as photography and acting. Today, educators have adapted the portfolio concept to their classrooms as a form of authentic assessment. When students are allowed to construct portfolios for grades, the criteria for assessment should be well known and coderived between the students and their teacher. Reducing portfolios to a single letter grade is a difficult (if not entirely misguided) task.[9]

Let's return now to the dialogue that opened this chapter and imagine the kinds of evaluative information that might be collected in order for a teacher to form a fair judgment of each student's learning. In her lesson, Ms. Dix was just about to have the students draw freehand maps of Illinois. Let's assume that Ms. Dix had indeed done many of the activities recommended in my analysis of her lesson. Let's also assume that she had wisely chosen to enlist the support and input of her students in planning, carrying out, and evaluating her geography-focused instruction on Illinois. (You might wish to look back at Figures 4-3 and 4-4 to reacquaint yourself with the focus of Ms. Dix's unit.) Here are some ways in which students could have their learning gains assessed:

1. A teacher- and student-made end-of-unit test could be given. The test might include true-or-false, multiple-choice, matching, fill-in-the-blank, and short-answer questions. The weight of the final test could be codetermined. Students could be encouraged to write explanations of their choices if they felt they had picked an incorrect answer.

2. If contracts are used, students might agree to keep a checklist of the assignments they completed and self-check components of the assignments prior to turning it over to Ms. Dix.

3. Students might be encouraged to videotape unit project presentations and include them in a portfolio containing maps they had made, reports on

---

[9]I say that it is misguided because it seems that one of the original inspirations for using portfolios was to get away from assigning a single letter grade to represent a student's progress or performance. Personally, I would stubbornly resist the task of grading portfolios, not only because it is difficult, but because it represents a violation of a major reason educators wanted to adopt them.

books they had read, field-trip diaries, and interviews they conducted. This portfolio might list all of the unit goals and identify which items helped to satisfy each goal.

4. Individual conferences could be held with each student where the teacher shared her own observations and impressions concerning the student's work and reviewed samples of completed and ongoing work. This conference might also be used to help the student set goals and identify additional resources for future work.

CONCLUDING THOUGHTS
· · · · ·

Providing instruction in social studies is a joy to many teachers. They love the human content and the power of the social sciences and humanities as lenses for personal enlightenment and social improvement. Such teachers enjoy planning new social studies units and slowly improving their existing units. They are continually shopping for new teaching ideas, better instructional materials, and additional community resources.

Teachers who offer highly involving social studies instruction realize that they also must take extra steps to ensure that their evaluation of students' learning is meaningful and fair. These teachers often view evaluation as an integral part of the teaching-learning process. They attempt to make evaluation a shared responsibility that promotes students' desire to learn and offers a means for detecting learning gains. They know that when their approach to evaluation is clear, when students have some say in designing the evaluation plan, when multiple methods and many chances are used to help students show what they know, students are likely to feel good about the fairness of the grades they receive.

DISCUSSION QUESTIONS
· · · · ·

1. If students participate in the planning and evaluation of social studies, aren't they likely to demand similar input in other curriculum areas? How would you explain such power sharing in one area and not in others?

2. Since background of experience is so important to success in social studies, is it fair to evaluate all students similarly even when you know that some come from disadvantaged backgrounds?

3. Imagine attempting to take effort into account in grading students' reports on famous Americans. Student A has great difficulty with what you think is an easy person. Student B easily completes a report on a person who you thought might be difficult. Should you reduce student B's grade because the report turned out to be easy? Should you reduce student A's grade for making an easy report difficult? On what hard data (for example, time spent, drops of sweat produced, number of complaints voiced) could you base your judgments of effort?

REFERENCES AND SELECTED READINGS

Alleman, J., and Brophy, J. 1991. A caveat. Curriculum integration isn't always a good idea. *Educational Leadership* 49(2):66.

Aoke, T. T. 1991. Layered understandings of orientations in social studies program evaluation. In *Handbook of research on social studies teaching and learning*, ed. J. P. Shaver, 98–105. New York: Macmillan.

Bauman, J. F. 1983. Children's ability to comprehend main ideas in content textbooks. *Reading World* 5:322–331.

Hoge, J. D. 1986. *Improving the use of elementary social studies textbooks.* ERIC digest no. 33. Bloomington, IN: ERIC Clearinghouse for Social Studies/Social Science Education.

Larkins, A. G., Hawkins, M. L., and Gilmore, A. 1987. Trivial and noninformative content of elementary social studies: A review of primary texts in four series. *Theory and Research in Social Education* 15(4):299–311.

McCutcheon, G. 1981. Elementary school teachers' planning for social studies and other subjects. *Theory and Research in Social Education* 9(1):45–66.

Woodward, A., Elliott, D. L., and Nagel, K. C. 1986. Beyond textbooks in elementary social studies. *Social Education* 1:50–53.

fostering Learner Involvement

WHICH TEACHER WOULD YOU WANT TO BE?

Two fifth-grade teachers are introducing their students to a new unit on life in colonial America. Each approaches this task in a different manner. Read the scenarios and decide which teacher you'd want to be more like.

SCENARIO ONE

Mr. Abbot tells his students that the next chapter in their social studies book is on colonial America.

> *"We found out in the first chapter that Native Americans were already here when the Europeans began to arrive. We learned that the first permanent settlement was established by the Spanish and that it was called St. Augustine. Now we're going to move forward in time to examine the expansion of the European colonies along the east coast of what is now the United States. You'll learn about Jamestown and Plymouth, two of the earliest settlements.*
>
> *Amy, will you please distribute the books? We'll read the first five pages silently and then review before the end of the period."*

SCENARIO TWO

Coming in from lunch, Ms. Baldwin's students found a note taped to their locked classroom door. It said simply: COME TO ROOM 5-C. Arriving at what they knew was a vacant classroom, Ms. Baldwin greeted them decked out in an old-fashioned, long dress; a shawl; "granny shoes"; and wire-rimmed glasses. She had pulled her long ash-blond hair back into a bun. Cooled by the fall air, nearly empty, and intentionally unlit, the vacant room seemed a bit spooky. Two rows of wooden benches stretched across the width of the room.

> *"Come in children and take a seat on one of the benches. Boys sit on the left side of the aisle and girls on the right. Your writing assignment is on the board. Use the writing slates and the chalk I've provided and begin copying."*

The writing assignment welcomed the students to a colonial-period classroom. It briefly explained the separation of boys and girls, the lack of pencils and paper, and the crude seating, lighting, and heating arrangements.

After a few minutes of working with the old-fashioned slates, Ms. Baldwin began answering the students' many questions. She encouraged questions about all aspects of colonial life and listed these on chart paper.

Returning to their room, the students found a collection of books on colonial America. They spent the last part of the day browsing through this treasure, adding questions to their list and sharing answers that they had already found.

INTRODUCTION
* * * * *

The opening scenarios paint a drastically different picture of social studies learning. I'd far rather be in Ms. Baldwin's class than Mr. Abbot's and I suspect you would too! Ms. Baldwin has put much effort into planning and securing resources. She's captured the students' attention with suspense and drama. She's involved students in setting the direction of their learning and she's provided a degree of freedom in their first exploration of learning resources. Many of the resources she's gathered can be shared with other teachers and reused year after year. Ms. Baldwin's unit is off to a great start. Let's examine a few of the teaching techniques she can use to keep her instruction going well.

In this chapter, you'll learn how to create a positive classroom environment for social studies, foster involvement through a variety of activities, use families and other community resources to support social studies, ask effective questions that foster higher-order thinking, and manage small-group instruction. You'll also learn how technology resources can benefit your social studies teaching.

I'm certain that you'll want to refer to this chapter many times during your planning for social studies. It's packed with useful ideas and strategies that can significantly improve your social studies instruction.

CLASSROOM ATMOSPHERE FOR SOCIAL STUDIES
* * * * *

The teacher forms, in large measure, the learning atmosphere of a classroom. His or her approach to instruction affects the classroom atmosphere in a dramatic way. An authoritarian teacher fits well in what is often termed a "back to basics" approach to instruction. The authoritarian teacher and the back-to-basics approach to instruction call up images of students sitting in straight rows, taking turns reading aloud, filling out worksheets, and keeping their hands to themselves. Students are excluded from the instructional decision-making process because the entire curriculum has already been determined by experts. Quite obviously, the atmosphere of an authoritarian, back-to-basics classroom fails to meet the requirements of high-quality social studies instruction.

The classroom atmosphere for high-quality social studies instruction must be open. An open classroom atmosphere implies that students will feel free to ask questions, make guesses, challenge the "authority" of their textbook's content, and interact with one another. Students view the teacher not as a dictator, dispensing predetermined bits of knowledge, but as a guide and leader who offers learning opportunities and consults with them. Figure 5-1 shows characteristics of an open classroom environment.

Note that all areas of the curriculum, including social studies, may be taught in a back-to-basics, authoritarian style. Similarly, students' learning in all areas of the curriculum would benefit, in certain respects, from an open classroom environment.

An open classroom environment is characterized by

- student input into planning, instruction, and evaluation decisions
- questions being asked and guesses being made without fear of ridicule
- flexible grouping and lots of academically focused social interaction
- a sense of security and protection from persecution and harassment
- positive attitudes toward learning the knowledge offered in school
- a variety of instructional materials and creative activities
- a constructivist view of knowledge.[1]

FIGURE 5-1
Characteristics of an Open Classroom Environment

Because of its citizenship goal and focus on the vast content base of social sciences and humanities, social studies lays the strongest claim of all subject areas to the necessity of an open classroom environment. Students must begin experiencing citizen involvement and critical thinking during social studies instruction in the early primary grades. Similarly, input into content selection makes sense given the opportunity for exploration of social studies' substantial subject matter base.

Sometimes teachers may feel that the school administration, colleagues, and even parents desire a back-to-basics approach to schooling. Principals may reinforce a skill approach to reading or math that teachers implement through a particular basal textbook series. If this is the case, you may find it highly beneficial to depart, during social studies, from the authoritarian tone that dominates most of your typical class day. Students are more likely to accept demands for correct answers, worksheets, and testing routines in math if you provide them with a more open approach in social studies. Students quickly accept the idea that social studies is a "doing" time, an opportunity to have their voices heard, a chance to work on creative projects, read more than just a single textbook, and ask questions that place them in the roles of detectives and social science researchers. They will also value having input into the planning and evaluation of their social studies learning.

FOSTERING INVOLVEMENT THROUGH ACTIVITIES

Because of its broad subject matter, teachers can easily use a variety of activities in social studies. Activities are selected based on the objectives to be achieved, the abilities of students, the availability of materials, educational

---

[1]The constructivist philosophy views knowledge as being constructed in the mind of the learner. It stresses the sense-making experiences and mental manipulations that students must engage in to gain meaning.

policies and philosophies, students' preferences, and several other factors. Offering a variety of learning activities reduces boredom and helps students learn key content.

The word *activity* refers to all manner of objectives-focused undertakings. Reading a book is an activity, and it can be an engaging—even exciting—activity. Filling out a worksheet is an activity, and even the lowly worksheet has occasionally risen to capture students' interest. Figure 5-2 displays the variety of activity types typically used in classrooms.

It makes sense to use all of these activities in social studies, but not in all other content areas. For example, field trips, debates, case studies, role plays, and mock trials make sense in social studies, but not in math and some other subjects in the K–6 curriculum. The existence of so many exciting ways to teach social studies makes the repetitive use of a textbook-lecture-worksheet approach unnecessary and unprofessional. Professional teachers skillfully use a variety of activities to heighten students' interest and achievement.

- Lectures
- Recitations and drills
- Skits or plays
- Mock trials
- Oral reports or speeches
- Collaborative writing
- Guest speakers
- Field trips
- Games
- Conducting surveys
- Traditional crafts and processes
- Map making
- Multimedia reports

- Discussions
- Debates
- Simulations
- Case studies
- Values education strategies
- Independent writing
- Panel discussions
- Role plays
- Independent reading
- Doing observational research
- Running a class government
- Treasure hunts and orienteering
- Constructing models and dioramas

FIGURE 5-2

Types of Classroom Activities

Construction and Processing Activities

Teachers can greatly enhance students' involvement and interest in social studies by construction and processing activities. *Construction activities* are opportunities for students to make models or replicas of items or places used in the past or present. *Processing activities* call for students to duplicate the steps people use to acquire the food, clothing, shelter, and other consumer goods. Figure 5-3 provides a listing of sample construction and processing activities.

Students can

- make a model of a city they are studying
- churn fresh cream into butter
- follow pioneer tanning instructions to create a buckskin coin pouch
- use clay to model land features near their school
- sew authentic costumes from other cultures or historical periods
- construct replicas of pioneer toys and dolls
- conduct a mock trial to learn about the juvenile justice process
- cook a Thanksgiving dinner on a wood stove, making everything from scratch
- create a replica of a real frontier fort out of twigs and split corrugated cardboard
- pan for gold or create a sluice box at a local creek
- recreate an authentic archaeological dig in a remote area of the school yard
- card and spin cotton and wool and then knit or weave it into fabric

FIGURE 5-3
Construction and Processing Activities

As much as is possible, allow students to experience making, doing, and constructing as it was originally practiced. There is a huge difference between making a Thanksgiving meal from scratch and popping a frozen turkey dinner into the microwave. Opportunities for learning abound when students use authentic methods. Don't overlook opportunities to involve resource persons in the community; they are often pleased to be invited to guide the students' work.[2] Finally, make sure that children have an opportunity to demonstrate their skills and present their projects to authentic audiences.

INVOLVING THE FAMILY AND COMMUNITY

Families should be involved in their children's education. Of all the school subjects, social studies offers the greatest variety of opportunities for family involvement. Seek parents' involvement on the basis of their occupations, leisure pursuits, travel, ethnic heritage, political affiliations, religion, linguistic ability, cultural knowledge, and civic roles. Parents or guardians need to play a significant role in helping students complete social studies projects. They should be proudly present when students demonstrate their social studies

---

[2]Since most children in the United States grow up in urban areas, I would highly recommend a fall field trip to the country. Attempt to locate a family farm close by and spend the day observing and participating in harvest activities. Your PTA/O may be able to help fund the trip—and compensate the farm family for its time. Arrange to see a cow milked, a chicken prepared for cooking, and a canning demonstration. And don't forget to teach some map skills on your trip!

learning. Offer them an opportunity to contribute to every social studies unit that their children have during the school year.

Your invitation to involvement and continuing efforts at establishing good school-home communication are keys to parent involvement. To start, survey your parent population during the first weeks of school to determine how to involve them in supporting your social studies instruction. One approach is to send a note home that lists the topics and major activities children will be experiencing during the first semester or quarter of the school year. Parents can return the note indicating any knowledge, tangible resources, or contacts they have that would support their child's social studies instruction.[3] Also, ask them to indicate whether they would like to be directly involved in any of the major activities, such as field trips, that their children will be experiencing in their social studies curriculum.

Parents are an important link to the community. Through their places of work, leisure activities, and civic and religious associations, parents and guardians have contacts that can increase the value of your social studies instruction. Larger cities have ethnic neighborhoods, diverse ethnic and religious associations, foreign consulates, international businesses, museums, cultural events, special interest groups, and state and federal government offices that can augment your social studies instruction. Use these resources wisely to significantly improve the quality of your social studies instruction. The first steps in contacting these resources must, of course, be yours. However, parent volunteers may be able to do some of the calling and "legwork" that is nearly impossible for you given your teaching schedule. Long-range planning is necessary if you wish to secure the support of parents and community resources.

EFFECTIVE QUESTIONING PROCEDURES

Developing skill in posing good questions is essential to elementary social studies instruction. For the purposes of classroom instruction it is probably most important to differentiate between convergent and divergent questions, thought and feeling questions, and questions that require inferences, as opposed to concrete, literal responses. Thinking of questions in terms of these three dimensions will help increase student participation in lessons and simultaneously raise the level of students' intellectual activity. Let's look at each question type and then analyze a few examples.

Convergent Versus Divergent Questions

A divergent question invites more than one "right" answer. An example of a divergent question is, "What do you suppose it was like being a soldier during the Civil War?" A convergent question, on the other hand, seeks a single, correct

---

[3]Note that it is far more likely that parents will have expertise or resources related to the social studies than to math, language arts, reading, or even science.

answer. An example of a convergent question is, "What was the name of the man who assassinated Abraham Lincoln?"

Divergent questions allow learners' thinking to spread out and take different avenues to arrive at a response. Divergent questions are important because they reduce the threat of giving a wrong answer. The diversity of students' answers may stimulate additional thinking. Remember that just because a question has more than one right answer does not guarantee that all answers will be correct. There are incorrect answers to divergent questions.

Take out a piece of scrap paper and number it from 1 to 10. Go ahead, do it. Now read the questions listed in Figure 5-4 and attempt to classify them as divergent or convergent. Put a "D" or "C" next to your numbers. Try to resist peeking at the key until you're done!

---

1. Who was the first president of the United States?

2. What is the name of a state that lies west of the Mississippi?

3. What are some differences between Republicans and Democrats?

4. In what year did the Civil War end?

5. What feelings might parents have when their child is very ill?

6. How might our nation be different if schoolchildren could vote?

7. What are some things that could happen when the main wage earner in a family can't find work and runs out of unemployment benefits?

8. In which decade was the Korean War fought?

9. Why hasn't a woman been elected president of the United States?

10. What eye colors do we have represented in our room?

Answer Key[4] **1.** convergent (1789–1797, George Washington) **2.** divergent (There are 24 right answers) **3.** divergent **4.** convergent (1865) **5.** divergent **6.** divergent **7.** divergent **8.** convergent (1950s) **9.** divergent **10.** convergent (Note that there will be classrooms with just one eye color.)

◆ ◆

FIGURE 5-4
Typical Social Studies Questions

Thought Versus Feeling Questions

Keeping emotions, attitudes, beliefs, and values out of social studies is one reason students occasionally feel the subject is too dry. Ignoring the affective dimensions of human existence creates a fragmented and incomplete view of

---

[4]It should be noted that divergent versus convergent may be viewed as a continuum, from questions having only one or very few right answers (convergent or more convergent), to questions having several or very many right answers (divergent or more divergent).

social studies. People act the way they do not just because of cold, logical considerations, but also because of their feelings. Good social studies instruction can help focus attention on the affective dimensions of life by asking questions that tap feelings. Such questions may directly ask students to respond to their own or others' feelings. Other questions more indirectly do so. Get out your slip of paper again and look back at the questions in Figure 5-4 and try to decide which ones tap into the affective dimension. Place an "F" next to each question that you think taps the feeling dimension of life. Now check the following key to see how you did.

Answer Key[5] 1. thought 2. thought 3. thought and/or feeling 4. thought 5. feeling 6. thought 7. thought and/or feeling 8. thought 9. thought and/or feeling 10. thought

Literal Versus Inference Questions

The answers to some questions are literally right before your eyes; such questions are called *literal comprehension questions*. A question that asked you to identify the three dimensions of questions being presented in this section of the textbook would be literal. All you would have to do is look and see (or recall) that they are divergent versus convergent, thought versus feeling, and literal versus inferential.

Questions that require the learner to go beyond the information presented are termed *inferential*. To answer such a question, the learner must make an inference based on available evidence. Every inference is based on multiple assumptions that may or may not be accurate. Inferences based on quantitative data are often called *projections*. But even data-based projections are based on assumptions. Take your paper again and look back at the list of questions in Figure 5-4. Try to determine which questions require making an inference and write an "I" by each. Check your answers against the following key.

Answer Key[6] 1. literal 2. literal 3. inferential 4. literal 5. inferential 6. inferential 7. inferential 8. literal 9. inferential 10. literal

---

[5]The difference between thoughts and feelings is blurred in many instances. Some individuals may have feelings strongly associated with referents that for most others are nonemotional. It's okay to disagree with my ratings!

[6]It is possible to ask questions that call for an inference that are also convergent. For example, you could be asked to look at the number of this page and infer what the next page number will be. This, of course, is a low-level inference, but it makes the point that there may be only one right answer to a question calling for an inference. Normally, questions that call for literal comprehension require that the respondent knows the answer. If the answer is unknown, then there should be no way that an inference process could allow the respondent to arrive at the right answer. For example, there is no way that a person could arrive, by an inference process, at the answer to question 2. Such information is either known or it is unknown.

More Information on Questioning

Research on questioning has shown that most questions asked in the classroom are low-level, recall-type questions. Questions that require students to show their understanding, to apply what they have learned, to analyze a new set of circumstances, or to synthesize and evaluate are absolutely mandatory if we want to foster higher-level thought in our classrooms. Do any of the questions shown in Figure 5-4 require higher-level thought? Write an "H" by those that you feel do and then compare your judgments with mine.

Answer Key The questions that require higher-level thought are 3, 5, 6, 7, and 9.

Imagine sitting in a class with a teacher whose major approach to instruction is to ask questions that come straight out of the textbook. Further imagine that this teacher asks questions that mainly call for students to supply a missing word in a sentence—the word often being a date, a name, or a definition. Such a teacher might ask questions like, "Who were the first Americans?" "What do we call the earth's largest bodies of water?" and "The signing date of our Declaration of Independence was . . .?" Ten minutes of such questions would seem like an eternity.

These are clearly poor questions. Perhaps the teacher who overuses such questions believes that social studies is a trivia contest. Or maybe he or she is just not well prepared to teach.

Just as it is possible to form poor questions, it is also possible to use ineffective questioning procedures. For example, asking questions in a set pattern is less effective than using a random sequence. Two examples of set patterns that are ineffective are (1) asking questions by going up and down the rows, and (2) asking questions by tables. If, for example, Terra, Tonya, Tammy, and Tina are in row 1 and they know that the teacher is directing questions to Albert, Abbie, Alice, and Amarrie in row 4, then they are likely to "tune out" the lesson until they realize that they are back in the spotlight. Some teachers tend to ask their first questions to students in the front of the room and gradually work their way back toward students sitting in the rear. Others ask questions more often to boys or to European-American students or exclusively to students' who raise their hands. Students who wish to participate are frustrated by such teaching failures and others use this weakness as an opportunity to daydream.

When a lesson calls for some well-planned systematic questioning, use a random sequence of question asking in order to keep the maximum percentage of students engaged in the lesson. When students can't predict whom you will call on next they are likely to stay engaged in the lesson. Further foster engagement by really listening to students' responses and following up with one or more probes. Students will start listening to each other's responses and be ready to refine, elaborate, or correct a response when you follow these suggested procedures.

Wait Time

These techniques are only part of the solution to good questioning. Research has shown that students learn more when you, as the teacher, enforce a 3- to 5-second wait time prior to selecting a respondent.[7] Students will quickly learn that you want thoughtful responses to your questions; they'll know not to attempt to answer until you either call a student's name or ask for volunteers to raise their hands. This approach gives *all* students time to think and develop responses. Really listening to students' answers and waiting again—at least 2 seconds—before you probe, ask for another student's response, or comment yourself, finishes the artful act of good teacher questioning.

You'll have to practice these techniques to become proficient. I'd recommend practicing with a small group of friends playing the role of students. Select a topic that you can really discuss, one where people will have different opinions. Perhaps your instructor will provide some class time for this activity.

SIMULATIONS AND INSTRUCTIONAL GAMES

A simulation is an exercise that models some selected aspect of reality as authentically as possible. When simulations have elements of competition, strategy, and chance, they are referred to as simulation games. A wide variety of simulations, simulation games, and instructional games are available for K–6 social studies instruction. A brief examination of instructional games, simulation games, and simulations will help give you an idea of the ways in which these aids to student involvement can improve your social studies instruction.

Games

You can turn virtually any content into a game format. Create board games that allow several players to follow a trail from start to finish based on their ability to answer content questions drawn from a student- or teacher-created deck. Adding chance cards, a spinner, or dice introduces an element of luck that compliments students' knowledge. Incorporate elements of skill and strategy through building in different levels of play or allowing students to make decisions that entail greater risk, while blocking an opponent's progress. Teacher's supply stores are a good source of ready-made games, many of which can be augmented or adapted to other purposes.

There are also quite a few varieties of whole-class games you may use to enhance your instruction. Once learned by the students, some of these games require very little set-up time and may be played for a very brief period of time, making them ideal content-focused "fillers" of that extra 5 or 10 minutes that occasionally arises even in the best-planned instruction. For example, you can

---

[7]Mary Budd Rowe (1974) did the original research on wait time. Virginia A. Atwood and William W. Wilen (1991) more recently reviewed the implications of wait-time research for social studies instruction.

divide the class into two teams and engage them in a variety of twenty-one questions where the focus is on some historic fact, geographic location, economic concept, or other social studies content that students have just learned. You announce, "I'm thinking of something we just learned about in our lesson today. Let's play twenty-one questions since we've got a few minutes left before lunch. I'll toss a coin to see which side goes first."

Knowledge baseball, classroom concentration, go to the head of the class, and people bingo are additional examples of whole-class games that may be used to motivate learning. You may have played some of these content-focused games in your own schooling experiences. Your instructor may have played one or more of these games as a part of this course.

Simulation Games

Perhaps the most well-known simulation game is Monopoly®. It blends elements of real-estate and urban-industrial development of the early twentieth-century United States in a board-game format. Basic economic concepts, such as *rent*, are embedded in the game, but not authentically portrayed or used as a focus for learning. The geography knowledge game Where in the World Is Carmen SanDiego?® is similar to Monopoly® in that it uses a rather artificial conception of detective work (the simulation aspect of the game) to involve students in learning place-name geography and a few geography concepts and skills. There are many other simulation games—some more game than simulation and others more simulation than game. The dividing line is often a judgment call.

If you use a simulation game in your classroom, remember that your business is to focus the fun on learning. As a result, you may need to do some preexperience teaching to focus students' attention on the valuable content that they might otherwise miss. You may also want to periodically debrief the experience, drawing associations with other real-life examples. In my opinion, it would be a mistake to allow children to play a simulation game such as Monopoly® without taking these recommended instructional steps. Even then, you might find a better approach to the content once you began to realize how much effort it was going to take to turn the Monopoly® experience into valuable learning.

Simulations

As noted, simulations attempt to model some selected aspect of reality as authentically as possible. Many teachers plan to use a simulation as a part of a broader unit they have developed for their students. In some cases it is possible to modify and augment the content of the simulation so that a major part of the content learning is accomplished or reviewed during its use. This approach helps justify the amount of time needed to fully implement a good simulation. Simulations are equal to other instructional techniques in fostering content learning and they are superior to many other approaches in developing positive student attitudes.

Simulations have been created for a wide variety of content. Interact is the largest producer of noncomputer-based simulations in social studies. Figure 5-5 lists some K–6 social studies simulations from their catalog.

TITLE	DESCRIPTION	GRADE/ABILITY/TIME
Apple Valley School	A simulation of pioneer life in a one-room schoolhouse	Grades 2–4 avg to above, 5–6 avg; 15–35 students; 10+ hours
Canada	Travel agencies plan family vacations in the Canadian provinces	Grades 5–8 avg to above; 20–35 students; 10–15 hours
War Lords of Japan	A simulation of the shogun history of feudal Japan	Grades 4–6 above; 7–8 avg to above; 20–36 students; 15–20 hours
Zoo	Members of a community work to save their local zoo	Grades 2–5 avg to above; 15–35 students; 15 hours
Museum	A simulation of the creation of a community museum	Grades 4–8 avg to above; 15–40 students; 15–25 hours
Discovery 3	A simulation of early American colonization	Grades 5–8 avg to above; 15–35 students; 15–23 hours
Agency	A simulation of competing advertising agencies	Grades 5–8; 10–35 students; 10–15 hours
Newscast	A simulation of a television news team's coverage of present or historic events	Grades 5–8 avg to above; 12–35 students; 7+ hours
Galaxy	A simulation of a space society on the brink of civil war	Grades 5–8 avg to above; 20–35 students; 13–22 hours
Explosion	A society struggles to solve its population problems	Grades 5–8 avg to above; 18–35 students; 10–25 hours
Mummy's Message	An archeological expedition explores a mysterious pyramid	Grades 4–8 avg to above; 12–35 students; 9+ hours
Dig 2	A simulation of the archeological reconstruction of a vanished civilization	Grades 4–8 avg to above; 15–35 students; 15–21 hours
World	A simulation of how nations develop and become involved in power struggles	Grades 5–8 avg to above; 20–35 students; 15–25 hours
Honor	A simulation of coming of age in Native America before the horse	Grades 4–8 avg to above; 15–35 students; 10–15 hours
Cigarettes on Trial	A simulation of a trial to ban the sale, manufacture, and use of cigarettes in America	Grades 5–8 avg to above; 10–35 students; 1–2 hours

FIGURE 5-5
K-6 Social Studies Simulations Available from Interact[8]

[8]Interact, P.O. Box 997-Y92, Lakeside, CA 92040, 1-(800)-359-0961.

Beyond regular simulations is the rapidly expanding collection of computer-based simulations. Oregon Trail® is perhaps the best-known computer simulation in social studies. Developed by the Minnesota Educational Computing Consortium (MECC), Oregon Trail® simulates the trek west that thousands of American families made in the late 1800s. MECC tried to make Oregon Trail® as realistic as possible. As with its other software, MECC provides excellent teacher-support materials to compliment this computer-based simulation. Tom Snyder Productions offers a variety of teacher-friendly simulations for Apple II, Macintosh, or IBM-compatible computers. More information is provided about computer-based simulations beginning on page 103.

DEVELOPING PRESENTATION AND PERSUASION SKILLS
◆ ◆ ◆ ◆ ◆

Within the areas of citizenship and civic life few talents have greater importance than presentation and persuasion skills. Of course, politicians need such skills, but opportunities for using them arise for all citizens. A simple discussion among friends can lead into an informal presentation with attempts at persuasion when different points of view exist. Presentation and persuasion skills take a written format when a citizen writes a complaint letter to a business or government agency. Community leadership opportunities arise within the church, the school, the workplace, and other groups.

Language arts shares responsibility with social studies for developing presentation and persuasion skills. In social studies, you should place the emphasis on developing a well-reasoned point of view rather than on such characteristics as word use, poise, enunciation, and eye contact. Accordingly, expose students to all sides of an issue and give them an opportunity to develop their own positions. Follow with small-group discussions so that students can practice presentation and persuasion skills in a nonthreatening context.

Have students practice presentation skills by giving reports on social studies projects to the whole class. Reports can take a variety of formats, ranging from straightforward presentations to those supplemented by posters, various forms of drama, or computer-generated graphics. Presentation skills are also developed as students write the results of inquiry projects and perform for groups such as the PTA/O.[9]

Presentations verge over into persuasion opportunities in a variety of situations. For example, students might investigate and then discuss different solutions to school problems in the lunchroom, hallways, or rest rooms. In this

---

[9]Educators have come to realize that when significant learning has taken place, students should be given an opportunity to demonstrate their accomplishment. Such culminating experiences as presentations not only give recognition to the students, but they also create a positive link with parents and the public, demonstrating valuable contributions that schools make to our society

situation, it is important to tie reasoning about the attempts to persuade others of the best possible solution to the results of the investigation.

Persuasion opportunities arise quite frequently in classroom life. For example, students might discuss and make decisions regarding fund-raising project ideas. Teachers could encourage students to responsibly voice a grievance with the principal. Students could write letters to the editor on local issues such as the school board's decision to delay the purchase of new textbooks.

Opportunities to responsibly practice presentation and persuasion skills should be frequently provided as a part of the social studies program. These are the skills that citizens need to function effectively in public forums such as town council, PTA/O, and school board meetings. These same skills are used in a variety of other situations such as in an issues-focused discussion on the bus ride to work, in advocating for your child in a parent-teacher conference, and when requesting a raise for work well done.

PROMOTING SMALL GROUP INSTRUCTION

Much of schooling takes place in whole-class activities and settings where it is essentially each child for himself or herself. This focus on individual competitiveness can become excessive, although, to an extent, individual competitive effort does determine our success in certain aspects of life. Increasingly, however, our success in life is influenced by how well some group of which we are a part functions. To drive this point home, imagine the frustration a disruptive and unruly class causes students who want to learn. Or think about how difficult it would be to live a peaceful life in a neighborhood plagued by gangs and violence. Or imagine attempting to grow into a healthy adult if you were trapped in a highly dysfunctional family. Perhaps you have experienced some of these situations, or have friends who have. Clearly, groups influence our ability to succeed. The better functioning our groups, the easier it is to achieve our individual goals.

It should come as no surprise to you by this point in the book that I believe that social studies should promote a healthy group atmosphere and positive social interaction among students. If students must work by themselves in math, language arts, and science, so be it. But social studies, because of its direct concern with the civic health of our society, should begin building genuine feelings of commitment to the group's welfare when schooling first begins. Developing positive citizenship attitudes is a goal of social studies instruction mainly achieved through social interaction, not through book learning.

Teachers must provide opportunities for social interaction as an integral part of social studies instruction to help students achieve the positive citizenship commitments our society desperately needs. Social interaction opportunities arise naturally as children pursue the content goals of social studies. For example, a first-grade lesson on the family might allow students to engage in dramatic play centered on the contributions that each family member makes to daily living in the family unit. In subsequent lessons, allow children to form multiple imaginary families that interact by planning a picnic or a neighborhood cleanup or offering assistance to one another in imaginary situations of need. Facilitate this type of dramatic play by providing props and allowing time for the interaction to develop, or even taking part, on occasion, in modeling new roles. Plan projects and activities designed for group work. For example, you might have several small groups in your class work on different parts of a large mural depicting city life, or a fourth-grade class might explore their school using five teams based on the five themes of geography.

Assessing group-work activities is based, in part, on the success of *everyone* in the group—and on the children's own assessments of their success. This causes each child to feel as though he or she is responsible to the other group members for producing a good result.

Getting children to work together productively takes some effort and know-how. Occasionally, teachers, even experienced teachers, throw up their hands and exclaim, "I just can't get this bunch to do group work. They're too disruptive!" Some teachers even apologetically confess that they "aren't any good at doing group work." The following material will help you prepare to begin small-group social studies instruction in your future elementary classroom.

Guidelines for Group Work

The first and most fundamental step in starting group work is making sure that you really have a task that is suitable for more than one person. A good group-work task is one that would naturally benefit from having many people work on it. To determine if a task is fertile ground for group work, ask yourself if more people would speed the work, if the work can be easily divided into separate or shared tasks, whether there are enough materials to support group work, or if more people will add to the quality of the product. If your answers to these questions are positive, then it is likely that you have identified a task that is compatible with group work. Here are some common group-work tasks for grades K through 6:

- Forming clean-up teams that help straighten up the room (kindergarten)
- Making a fingerpaint collage to show a social studies concept such as *mountain, farming,* or *seasons* (first grade)
- Doing team interviews of grandparents for a unit on the family (second grade)
- Taking part in a treasure hunt that exercises map skills (third grade)
- Building a paper maché or cardboard map of the state (fourth grade)
- Functioning as a team in taking a survey of other classrooms (fifth grade)
- Dividing up into groups to complete different parts of a report on a foreign country being studied (sixth grade)

All of these are examples of group work because the nature of the task makes it clear that the product (or process) will be better if two or more students put their heads together to do the work. Note, for example, that older children might perfectly well conduct an interview alone, but that with second-grade children, it is better to have a two- or three-student interview team to bolster confidence and ensure more thorough questioning.

Managing Small-Group Instruction

Managing groups requires planning and a degree of vigilance. You'll need a clear conception of what you want students to do and how you expect them to go about their work. The younger and more unaccustomed students are to group work, the more planning detail and vigilance are required. As you monitor the progress of your first group work, try to overlook minor problems, letting the students arrive at a solution. If they cannot, and if you get called over, make your expectations regarding group behavior clear. Don't allow misbehavior. Remove the student(s) who are causing problems. End the group work if necessary. Figure 5-6 expands on these basic recommendations.

---

1. Defer small-group work until you've firmly established your management of the class. This may take up to four or five weeks.

2. Begin group work gradually, with a carefully selected group of students who are well-behaved and capable of working independently.

3. Assign a task that is simple, well-defined, and one that really requires group participation for success.

4. Discuss group roles and responsibilities. Inform the group of your intention to monitor their progress and remind group members that working in such a setting is a privilege that you can remove. Tolerate no misbehavior and remove any student who misbehaves. Terminate the group-work project if the majority of the students are disruptive.

5. Have the rest of the class engaged in individual assignments while giving guidance to the small group.

6. Have resource materials readily available for the group.

7. Monitor group work and provide support and guidance as required. Encourage the independence of the group whenever possible.

8. Have the group report to the class, sharing their work product. Call attention to the good behavior of the group and use them as a model for others as you begin to expand group work to the whole class.

FIGURE 5-6

Guidelines for Small-Group Work

Committee Work

Committee work is a special kind of group work that all teachers should use. A *committee* is a *representative* body that functions to accomplish some aim, goal, or purpose *for everyone else*. The important point here is that in committee work, students get an opportunity to be responsible, not just to their teacher, but to their own classmates.

The best example of committee work that arises in the elementary school occurs when teachers form committees to organize a class party. Typical committees for a class party include entertainment, decorations, refreshments, invitations, and cleanup. In preparing for a class party, each child in the room should be working on a committee and feeling the responsibility of trying to plan and carry out something that is pleasing to his or her classmates. A smart social studies teacher will have students review the work of the different committees to provide feedback on their performance. If you undertake such a review, take care to ensure that individuals' feelings are not hurt by rudeness. One strategy to prevent hurt feelings is to ask each committee to construct a feedback form that other students anonymously complete. Other committees teachers might want to form are a book selection committee, committees that investigate classroom problems, and committees that help prepare for events such as open house.

Given a good start in their early elementary school years, students will be more likely to take part in volunteer committee work throughout their school experience and on into their lives as productive members of their communities.

Cooperative Learning

Cooperative learning is a form of small-group instruction teachers structure to enable the efforts of each student to contribute to the overall success of the group. In a cooperative-learning situation, one student's success enhances the success of his or her peers. Schools typically don't do enough cooperative learning. In part this is because educators typically conceptualize learning as an individual phenomenon, but it is also probably a holdover of the tutorial model of instruction.

The research on cooperative learning has been quite positive. It shows good academic gains and improved attitudes toward learning and fellow students. Cooperative learning also has been shown to have a positive impact on the performance of minority students. There are quite a few different approaches to cooperative learning. In the approach called Student-Teams-Achievement Divisions (STAD), students are divided into learning groups that compete for recognition and team scores determined by each student's improvement over previous instruction. The Teams-Games-Tournaments (TGT) approach has students play games designed to improve their learning with team improvement scores contributing to individual test scores. A third, and perhaps best known approach, is called Jigsaw or Jigsaw II. In the Jigsaw approach students each have a piece of the required information and teach each other so that they may score high on individual tests.

Regardless of the approach you use, or whether you make up your own, several elements are critical to the success of cooperative learning. First, students need to clearly understand the nature of the learning task and the method by which you want them to accomplish their goal. You should form the cooperative-learning groups, keeping in mind an even distribution of ability and a good mix of personalities and other characteristics such as race and sex. Monitor the functioning of your cooperative-learning groups, quickly resolving any impasses that might damage the outcome of their efforts. It's important for the groups to experience success in their first few cooperative-learning episodes. Students need to feel that the extra effort they put into their own learning benefited the group *and* raised their own individual performance. Finally, it's important to assign roles within cooperative-learning groups that students can actually fulfill. (A real problem will erupt if, for whatever reason, a student fails to fulfill his or her obligations to the group.)

I've already stressed the role that students should play in planning and evaluating their learning experiences. Cooperative learning is no exception to this rule. Allow students to share responsibility with you in determining who takes on what task within each cooperative group. Also, ask them to evaluate their own individual and group performance. They need to see that this evaluation, done well, influences the final grade or score given to their work.

Small-group work, committee work, and cooperative learning are important teaching techniques you must master as a part of your social studies instruction. Done right, they will contribute immensely to your classroom atmosphere and greatly improve students' learning while building the kind of caring future citizens our world needs.

INDIVIDUALIZING INSTRUCTION THROUGH LEARNING CENTERS

Learning centers are an excellent way to individualize all subjects in the K–6 curriculum. The characteristics of good learning centers are similar across subjects. They include clear instructions that allow students to work independently, a degree of student choice of activities, the provision of methods for self-checking work results, clear rules for center use, and high-interest, hands-on activities that make use of a variety of materials. While all centers should share these characteristics, social studies learning centers can go a step further to include elements of decision making and recognition of differences of opinion. For example, in a center on map skills, include a decision-making activity that challenges students to design their own islands and then decide the best locations for resorts, heavy industry, big port cities, power plants, military bases, universities, and farming activities. Introduce differences of opinion by having students debate the best locations for these elements of society. Taking things a step further, have students design campaigns to attempt to persuade nonaligned class members that their proposed locations were the best.

Regardless of the type of centers you set up in social studies, it is important that they appear as a visually inviting area of the classroom where two or more individuals can independently work on engaging activities. You will need to introduce students to the center and perhaps even train one or two center experts to help if difficulties arise. Learning centers can function as a supplement to ongoing social studies learning or they may become the sole source of social studies instruction when several are in operation at the same time. Replenishing center supplies, mending or replacing worn materials, and adding new activities and resources help guarantee that your centers stay attractive and useful. Upper-grade-level children can be made a more integral part of their center learning by being given some of these maintenance responsibilities.

USING COMPUTER TECHNOLOGY

In the early 1990s microcomputer technology reached a point where significant learning outcomes could be attained by a diverse body of users. Every dollar spent on hardware and software bought five times the power and better capabilities than anything imaginable just one or two years before. Schools had begun replacing their first hardware purchases with newer, more powerful machines priced at less than half what their first computers had cost. The 256K, paper-covered, 5¼-inch floppy became a 1.4 megabyte, plastic-encased, 3½-inch high-density disk. The 20-megabyte hard drive became a double-speed CD-ROM drive capable of reading libraries of shining disks, each capable of storing the equivalent of a complete encyclopedia set. The tiny flickering green screen transformed into a picture-sized, high-resolution color monitor. The 8-bit, 10-megahertz CPU became a 32-bit, 100-megahertz RISC CPU. DOS disappeared as the Macintosh® user-interface led to Windows 95® and other GUIs. Stand-alone programs started to add translators so they could read and write files from other company's products. Crude, low-powered integrated applications matured into highly capable, multi-purpose productivity tools. Computers were networked within buildings and linked across the nation and globe through high-speed modems. Black-and-white ink-ribbon impact printers hardly as capable as electric typewriters became color laser printers capable of producing photolike images. Cryptic menu-oriented, mostly text information services became user friendly icon- and window-based showcases of graphics, sound, and entertainment. The fifty-pound, steel-clad desktop machine was replaced by a mostly plastic notebook-sized laptop machine that had greater performance, simpler design, and made better use of the earth's precious resources. The classroom with a computer became the rule rather than the rare exception.

- **CD-ROM** Compact Disk-Read Only Memory (A large-capacity, long-term storage medium used to distribute software and large quantities of information)

- **CPU** Central Processing Unit (The "engine" that drives the computer—its "brain")

- **RISC-CPU** Reduced Instruction Set Chip (A CPU that uses a smaller number of instructions but cycles them more quickly to achieve greater performance)

- **DOS** Disc Operating System (DOS is an acronym that has come to stand for the command-line interface used on original IBM and compatible microcomputers. This interface was replaced by Windows® during the early 1990s.)

- **GUI** Graphical User Interface (A system of icons, pull-down menus, and windows that allow a user to operate his or her computer. GUI is pronounced gooie.)

FIGURE 5-7
Computer Acronyms

The progress made in computer technology is beginning to completely revolutionize teaching and learning. The impact on social studies instruction will eventually be immense as the walls of the classroom dissolve under the flow of information that is washing in tidal wave proportions toward all forms of users. Let's examine what present and near-future uses of this technology in K–6 social studies are possible.

Using Word Processors, Spreadsheets, Databases, and Presentation Software

Teachers can accomplish many of the social studies writing activities identified in Chapter 19 (pages 334–335) using a word processor. If you have a large-screen monitor or an LCD overhead display, use the word processor as a more flexible—and permanent—chalkboard or chart paper. Have the class view and critique a draft of a thank you letter prior to printing. Display two competing small group's versions of a letter to the editor and merge them into a final draft signed by the whole class. Beyond letters, students can use the word processor for social studies reports. Use the publishing and page-layout features of today's contemporary word processors to create professional-looking travel brochures for the places students are studying. Use a thesaurus, grammar, and spelling checker to help keep the focus on social studies ideas and off these aspects of language arts instruction.

Spreadsheets offer students an easy way to analyze the data they collect from social science surveys. Their integrated graphing capabilities provide instant bar, line, and pie graphs to help bring the numbers into visual perspective. Have students account for scrip collected and dispersed from banks, stores, and government offices in Mini- or Micro-Society (see Chapter 8). Student volunteers can help account for the real-dollar funds used for classroom field trips and other activities related to the social studies program.

Have students construct databases for a series of cities, states, or nations being studied. Categories might include population estimates broken down into age or ethnic groups, per-capita income, education information, climate data, government officeholders, state symbols, and other information. Students could prepare and keep current a database of all places and people (such as famous Americans) that their social studies curriculum mentions. As the database grows, the categories used to characterize each entry naturally increase. Research and enter missing information on earlier entries as an ongoing center activity. Students could begin to draw upon the database as an intellectual resource, noting similarities and trends. Share student-constructed databases with other classes in the school and around the world using free electronic bulletin boards and widely available telecommunication services.

Use presentation packages that facilitate the development of electronic slide shows as a replacement or augmentation to students' social studies reports. Students may also form their own electronic portfolios using presentation packages.

Getting On Line: The Information Highway

A computer with a modem, communications software, and access to a phone line can connect students with the world. Commercial on-line services such as Prodigy®, America Online®, and CompuServe® are beginning to provide an array of forums and other services that can help bring global and multicultural perspectives to social studies instruction. A teacher with an account on any of these services can arrange to have her students communicating with similar students in a variety of other cities around the nation and the world. Many states have set up free networks designed to facilitate communications among educators for sharing lesson plans, curriculum guides, samples of students' work, and e-mail. Access to Internet provides the capability of searching for information resources around the world on virtually any topic. Commercial and state-sponsored on-line networks often provide access to the teaching plans that accompany CNN Newsroom, a half-hour news production designed for grades 6 through 12 that can be downloaded or captured for use as a part of current affairs instruction.[10]

Commercial on-line services provide access, sometimes at extra expense, to rich database sources that can be used for student research and supplemental information on a variety of social studies issues and topics. For example, CompuServe® offers access to Knowledge Index®, a source of approximately one hundred databases covering many subjects. Included in the Knowledge Index® databases are a collection of U.S. newspapers that can be searched by

---

[10]CNN Newsroom is a noncommercial production of Turner Broadcasting. Schools can videotape this news program, aired each day at 4:30 A.M. EST. At present there is no charge for this service.

words that appear in the title and lead paragraph. This resource gives students (and their teacher) the capability of quickly locating articles that deal with virtually any aspect of society. The files on many of these newspapers go back for eight or more years and are seldom more than a few days behind the current issue. The complete text of any article can be captured and used later, either directly by students or after revisions by the teacher.

Using CD-ROM Databases and Other Commercial Software

Anyone who has spent even a few minutes with the increasingly popular multimedia encyclopedias knows that they are exploring a learning resource vastly improved over printed encyclopedias. Of course, the content of encyclopedias falls predominately within the spheres of the social sciences and humanities. Scientific articles make up much of the remainder of the material. The new multimedia encyclopedias offer full-motion video clips, thousands of color photographs, sound recordings of famous speeches, and easy searching capabilities that speed access to their many topically indexed articles. A subject like women's history is easily accessed and leads to multiple features on famous and ordinary American women. Students will see photographs and full-motion video clips. They'll be able to quickly gain the basic information needed to place these women in their historical context and compare their actions with contemporary events.

Multimedia encyclopedias are being augmented by specialized, topically focused multimedia products such as ABC Interactive® series with its focus on famous Americans, presidential elections, international relations, and social problems. Scholastic Software offers its Point of View® laser-disk series on state and national history. For example, *Struggles for Justice I* details the trials and triumphs of Native, Latino, and African Americans and *Struggles for Justice II* offers newsreel footage, still images, reenactments, and audio clips on women, labor, and immigrants.

Computer simulations such as Oregon Trail® offer learning opportunities that far outstrip anything previously available—with the exception of reality. Tom Snyder Productions' (TSP) *Decisions, Decisions* and *Choices, Choices* software offers whole-class or small-group simulations based on a variety of social issues and real-life problems. TSP's *Timeliner* and *Chronos* software offer specialized time-line databases teachers can modify and print out. Popular atlas software such as MECC's *USA GeoGraph II* and *Mac USA* combine modifiable, full-color, up-to-date maps and almanac-type data that can be explored, edited, and incorporated into handouts or students' reports.

Computer-based technology is bringing a rich stream of information into the classroom. It is expanding students' learning options and making higher-order thinking tasks a more fundamental part of everyday social studies instruction. The trends toward evermore powerful and easy-to-use computers and software will continue. Teachers and schools that ignore these resources imperil not only their own existence, but the future viability of our society.

REFERENCES AND SELECTED READINGS

Atwood, V. A., and Wilen, W. W. 1991. Wait time and effective social studies instruction: What can research in science education tell us? *Social Education* 55(3):179–181.

Bunting, E. 1991. *Fly away home.* New York: Clarion Books.

Chesler, M., and Fox, R. 1966. *Role playing methods in the classroom.* Chicago: Science Research Associates.

Eisenberg, H., and Eisenberg, L. 1984. *The handbook of skits and stunts.* Martinsville, IN: American Camping Association.

Ellis, K. 1993. *Teacher questioning behavior and student learning: What research says to teachers.* ERIC document no. ED359572. Bloomington, IN: ERIC Clearinghouse for Social Studies/Social Science Education.

Fisher, A. L. 1985. *Year-round programs for young players: One hundred plays, skits, poems, choral readings, spelldowns, recitations, and pantomines for celebrating holidays and special occasions.* Boston: Plays, Inc.

Hunt, T., and Renfro, N. 1982. *Puppetry in early childhood education.* Austin, TX: N. Renfro Studios.

Renfro, N. 1984. *Puppet shows made easy.* Austin, TX: N. Renfro Studios.

Rowe, M. B. 1974. Relation of wait-time and rewards to the development of language, logic, and fate control: Part II-rewards. *Journal of Research in Science Teaching* 11(4):291–308.

————. 1986. Wait-times: Slowing down may be a way of speeding up. *Journal of Teacher Education* 37(1):43–50.

Shaftel, F. R., and Shaftel, G. 1982. *Role playing in the curriculum.* 2d ed. New York: Prentice Hall, Inc.

Stahl, R. J., and VanSickle, R. L., eds. 1992. Cooperative learning in the social studies classroom: An inviation to social study. *NCSS Bulletin* No. 87. Washington, D.C.: National Council for the Social Studies.

Vockell, E. L., and Brown, W. 1992. *The computer in the social studies curriculum.* New York: Mitchell McGraw-Hill.

The Content Disciplines of Elementary Social Studies

INTRODUCTION

Part Two presents the intellectual foundation upon which social studies rests. Each chapter focuses on a particular social science, presenting a brief overview of the discipline's history and content, and then offering one or more statements about what portion of that content can be appropriately taught to K–6 children. Each chapter closes with two discipline-focused, sample lesson plans and other instructional resources.

As you begin reading Part Two, you'll find that these chapters are filled with content outlines of the social science disciplines and other types of curriculum content information. I do not expect you to recall the details in these rather long lists of content.[1] Personally, I would attach more importance to understanding the narrative sections that present, connect, and draw conclusions about these figures. I do hope, however, that you will recall the fact of the existence of these figures and have some awareness of the general type of information that each presents.

Part Two is a necessary component of any social studies curriculum and methods course because if you can't personally buy into the importance of teaching elementary grade level students the content that forms social studies, then you can't justify its inclusion in the school curriculum. So as you explore the chapters in Part Two, I hope you'll keep asking yourself if you support instruction for K–6 students that features this content.

---

[1]Individual instructors may, at their discretion, however, identify certain elements that they wish students to recall.

The content of these chapters may be used (1) to help you identify appropriate and important ideas for K–6 lesson plans and units, and (2) as an intellectual "yardstick" to measure the quality of published curriculum materials. You may want to retain this book as a reference to use in your teaching career for these same purposes.

One final word is in order. Please do not mistake my presentation of each separate discipline's content as an endorsement of a separate disciplines approach to elementary social studies. While some instruction in elementary school may indeed take this form, units that integrate two or more of the social sciences and/or humanities disciplines are desirable. You may want to practice planning a topically focused integrated unit that draws important content from a number of the different disciplines.

C H A P T E R   6

History: The Roots of Knowledge

A fourth-grade boy, dressed as an early California Spaniard, puts together a hand-crafted lamp while on a school field trip.

THE DISCIPLINE'S PERSPECTIVE

History is the most mature academic discipline included in social studies. The discipline of history traces its origin to ancient Greece where Herodotus produced, in about 430 B.C., his *Researches*. Written accounts of events go much farther back, of course, to the inscribed clay tablets from Ebla, Mesopotamia (Syria) dated circa 2350 B.C. However, these and other subsequent written accounts up to the time of Herodotus were largely produced as a matter of religious devotion, self-aggrandizement, or political propaganda. Because of his devotion to accuracy, Herodotus is often cited as the "Father of History" as an academic discipline that provides disinterested accounts of events. To develop a greater understanding of history, it is appropriate to further consider the nature, purposes, and content of this discipline.

The Nature of History

History is the study of the what and the why of past human events. Historians reconstruct and interpret chains of human actions through time to account for the development of human societies, groups, significant conditions, and events.

Seen as a process, history is what historians do—namely, construct accounts of the past based on firsthand analysis of all manner of evidence. Examples of this sort of work include interviewing survivors of wars, analyzing the diaries and personal letters of individuals, and using old courthouse records to trace marriages, deaths, land acquisitions, and trials.

Historians' study of the past brings them to a deep understanding of events. It allows them to see the past from the vantage point of the past. Professional historians specialize in particular periods or aspects of history so that they can engage in the type of in-depth study that will provide new insights into the past. Discovering the truth about the past and improving the accuracy of existing beliefs and accounts are the goals of academic history. These goals lead historians to be concerned with the validity of individual pieces of evidence (Is this document real or phony?), the accuracy of the information provided (Given that this document is real, is the content accurate, biased, or constructed for the purpose of deception?), and corroboration (Are there other sources that point in the same direction?).

Seen as a product, history is what historical research produces. Historians publish the results of their research in academic journals and give presentations at conferences for other historians. Occasionally, historians serve as authors, consultants, or reviewers in the production of biographies, textbooks, television documentaries, and fictionalized accounts of the past.

Figure 6-1 identifies three types of history. Each is analyzed in terms of its intended audiences, goals and purposes, and content qualities.

The chart in Figure 6-1 shows that typical school textbook histories, the ones we all read with varying degrees of interest, are only moderate in accuracy. This

TYPE OF HISTORY	INTENDED AUDIENCES	GOALS AND PURPOSES	CONTENT QUALITIES
Academic	Historians	The pursuit of truth about the past; to gain tenure and promotion; to stay employed	High accuracy Narrow scope Elaborate detail
Textbook	Students Teachers School officials Parents	To convey widely accepted views and information about the past; to make money for authors and book companies	Moderate accuracy Broad scope low detail
Popular	Consumers	Entertainment; to make money for authors and companies	Accuracy varies Medium scope Detail varies

FIGURE 6-1
Types of History

low level of accuracy is not due to intentional or unintentional omissions, but rather is a function of a single book not being able to provide the depth of coverage needed to give substantial detail. To grasp the seriousness of this problem, imagine, for a moment, that you are a historian who has written over a hundred papers and articles on the Industrial Revolution as it developed in the United States. You know virtually everything there is to know about this topic. Now imagine having to reduce your knowledge into two or three pages. Impossible? Yes! But worse, now imagine seeing what you have finally submitted to the editor come back to you as one page written at the fifth-grade level. If you can imagine this, then you'll understand why the typical survey-type history textbooks have only moderate accuracy and a very low level of detail. The amount of time covered by these books prohibits them from achieving the goals of accuracy and detail.

Concepts and Topics of History

Regardless of whether the history is academic, textbook, or popular, the same themes and ideas appear at the roots of the story. While the time period or events may change, history always addresses these themes and ideas. Figure 6-2 lists historical concepts and themes. Time periods for U.S. and world history are shown in the figure. Before you look at the conceptual outline, jot down on a sheet of paper ten history concepts and ten major periods or events from U.S. and/or world history. Now try to find the concepts you listed in sections I through IV of the outline. Give yourself an "A" if you find 9 or 10 of the concepts, a "B" for 8, a "C" for 7, a "D" for 6, and an "F" for 5 or less. Repeat this process for the major periods or events shown in section V of the outline.

I. Major Historical Concepts
  A. Chronological Order/Sequence of Events
    1. Cause and effect
      a. Antecedent conditions/Decision-making opportunities/Responsibility and need for action
      b. Alternatives/Consequences/Solutions
      c. Multiple causation
    2. Time periods
      a. Time perspective/Cultural perceptions
      b. Periodization
    3. Continuity and change
      a. Patterns of change
      b. Progress from change
      c. Rate of change
      d. Maintenance of traditions, institutions, etc.
  B. Commemoration
    1. Achievements
    2. Contributions
    3. Challenges
  C. Conflict and Compromise
    1. Independence and interdependence
  D. Cultural Heritage/Connections to the Past
    1. Traditions
    2. Collective memory
    3. Historical empathy
  E. Power
    1. Influence
    2. Leadership
    3. Authority
      a. Rules/Laws
II. Major Values Developed by History
  A. Historical Perspective
    1. Historical ethnocentrism
  B. Skepticism
  C. Empiricism
  D. Pluralism/Humanism
III. Major Historical Processes
  A. Synthesis
    1. Hypothetical thinking
    2. Document analysis

    3. Corroboration
IV. Core Content of History
  A. Prehistory
    1. Indigenous populations
  B. Exploration and Conquest
    1. Explorers
  C. Settlement/Migration/Immigration
    1. Settlement patterns
    2. Characteristic lifeways
  D. Conflicts and Alliances
    1. Internal conflicts and alliances
    2. International conflicts and alliances
    3. Conflict resolution
  E. Industry/Trade/Commerce
    1. Famous business leaders
    2. Famous labor leaders
  F. Agriculture
    1. Farming
    2. Forestry
    3. Ranching
  G. Government
    1. Development of government
    2. Legislation and policy
    3. Government programs and actions
    4. Operation of government
    5. Heads of state
    6. Other government officials
  H. Military Establishment
    1. Growth and development of services
    2. Generals and other officers
    3. Other soldiers
    4. Major wars and campaigns
    5. Descriptions of specific battles
    6. Milestones in military hardware and tactics
  I. Politics
    1. Development of political parties
    2. Political parties, platforms, and actions
    3. Political leaders
  J. Inventions and Applied Technology
    1. Transportation
    2. Communications media

(continued on next page)

FIGURE 6-2
Conceptual Outline of History[1]

[1]This outline is adapted from the Social Studies Content Descriptor Project, Educational Products Information Exchange Institute. Used by permission.

3. Famous inventors
K. Science
   1. Scientific discoveries and advances
   2. Famous scientists
L. Medicine
   1. Medical advances
   2. Disease
   3. Famous doctors
M. Religion
   1. Development of a religion
   2. Religious leaders
   3. Religious doctrines
   4. Religious controversies and conflicts
N. Education
   1. Development and practice of formal education
   2. Practice of informal education
   3. Famous educators
   4. Famous schools and universities
V. Chronological Outlines of History
A. United States History
   1. Early history (1500–1608)
   2. Colonial development (1608–1763)
   3. Revolutionary era/Founding period (1763–1789)
      a. Causes of the Revolutionary War
      b. The Revolutionary War
      c. Articles of Confederation
      d. Framing and ratification of the Constitution
   4. Early nation building (1787–1828)
      a. Establishment of constitutional government
      b. Early political party development
      c. Territorial expansion
      d. Sectionalism
      e. The Monroe Doctrine (1823)
      f. Development of the branches of of government (1800–1817)
   5. Jacksonian democracy (1828–1840)
   6. Social reform and utopian movements (1828—1848)
   7. Manifest Destiny (1836–1850)
   8. Slavery, sectionalism, and the Civil War (1848–1861)
   9. Civil War and Reconstruction (1861–1877)

   10. The winning of the West (1860–1890)
   11. The rise of industry (1870–1900)
   12. The Progressive Era (1900–1915)
   13. World War I (1914–1918)
   14. Post-World War I and the Roaring Twenties (1919–1930)
   15. The Great Depression and the New Deal (1929–1945)
   16. World War II (1941–1945)
   17. The Cold War and the 1950s (1941–1960)
   18. New Frontiers and the Great Society (1960–1968)
   19. Vietnam (1965–1973)
   20. Watergate and its aftermath (1973–1980)
   21. The Reagan administration (1980–1988)
   22. The Bush administration (1988–1992)
B. World History
   1. Emergence of humankind (2,500,000 B.C.–30,000 B.C.)
   2. Early human culture (30,000 B.C.–6000 B.C.)
   3. Early civilizations (6000 B.C.–300 B.C.)
      a. Nile Egypt
      b. Mesopotamia region
      c. Indus River Valley
      d. Yellow River (China)
   4. The Greeks (1500 B.C.–300 B.C.)
   5. The Romans (1500 B.C.–476 B.C.)
   6. Early Christianity (1 A.D.–476 A.D.)
   7. Later development in Non-European regions (1000 B.C.–1600 A.D.)
      a. India
      b. China
      c. Japan
      d. The Americas
   8. The Middle Ages (476–1500)
      a. The Holy Roman Empire
      b. The Dark Ages
      c. Feudalism
      d. The rise of Islam and spread of Arabic cultures
      e. The Crusades
      f. Mongolian hegemony in Eurasia

(continued on next page)

♦ ♦

FIGURE 6-2, continued
Conceptual Outline of History

g. Growth of the Church

h. The Byzantine Empire (330–1453)

9. The Renaissance (1350–1600)

10. The age of European exploration and discovery (1400–1600)

11. The Reformation (1500–1600)

12. Early nation building in Europe (800–1700)

   a. England

   b. France

   c. Russia

   d. Spain

13. The Age of Reason (1550–1775)

   a. Scientific Revolution (1550–1700)

   b. Age of Enlightenment (eighteenth century)

14. The Industrial Revolution (1750–1850)

15. The American Revolution (1763–1783)

16. The French Revolution (1789–1799)

17. The Napoleonic Era (1800–1815)

18. The Congress of Vienna and its aftermath (1815–1848)

19. Nineteenth-century nationalism in Europe (1860–1900)

20. Nineteenth-century industrial development in Europe (1850–1900)

21. Reform movements in England and Europe (1850–1900)

22. European imperialism (1870–1914)

23. World War I (1914–1918)

24. The Russian Revolution (1917–1938)

25. Treaty of Versailles and the League of Nations (1919–1938)

26. The rise of Fascism/Nazism (1920–1938)

27. The Great Depression (1920–1938)

28. World War II (1939–1945)

29. The Cold War (1945–1990)

30. Problems of Second and Third World Nations (1950–199?)

31. Problems with world environment (1960–199?)

32. Incipient global community (1960–????)

FIGURE 6-2, continued
Conceptual Outline of History

EXERCISE 6-1
◆ ◆ ◆ ◆ ◆

1. Now that you have read through the outline, look back at sections I through IV and identify in your mind a specific example of each concept based on the history you have learned. If you have difficulty, check out an elementary or secondary school U.S. history textbook and look for examples.

2. Select one of the time periods or topics in the U.S. history outline and then identify the concepts from sections I through IV that seem to match it best. Repeat this process for at least one additional time period from section V.

3. Select three of the time periods in the U.S. history outline and write down what you think fifth-grade students should learn about it. Check out a copy of a fifth-grade social studies textbook and compare what you have written with what is presented there.

4. Select three of the time periods in the world history outline and write down what you think sixth-grade students should learn about it. Check out a copy of a sixth-grade social studies textbook and compare what you have written with what is presented there.

Figure 6-3 provides another view of the content of history instruction based on an analysis of five elementary social studies textbook series (Hoge and Crump, 1988, 22–23). The generalizations stated were formed from the conceptual content and are representative of the main ideas taught to children by these series.

HISTORY CONCEPT CLUSTERS	EXAMPLES OF GENERALIZATIONS
Achievements **Contributions** **Challenges** **Commemoration**	**(K–3)** People are remembered for the special things they do. **(4–6)** When people or groups meet special challenges they are honored for their contributions.
Cause and effect **Alternatives** **Cconsequences** **Solutions**	**(K–3)** Actions have consequences. **(4–6)** The alternative solutions to any problem carry different consequences.
Change **Patterns** **Progress**	**(K–3)** People change as they learn and grow. **(4–6)** Patterns of living change over time with progress.
Chronological order **Sequence** **Time periods** **Connections to past, present, and future**	**(K–3)** People can recall the past and guess what will happen in the future. **(4–6)** We are connected to the past through a chronological sequence of events. **(4–6)** The past can be divided into time periods.
Conflict **Compromise**	**(K–3)** People and groups often settle conflicts through compromise. **(4–6)** When efforts to compromise fail, conflicts between people and groups occur.
Cultural heritage	**(K–3)** A person's ancestors are a part of his or her cultural heritage. **(4–6)** Each group of people or nation has a cultural heritage.
Freedoms **Rights** **Justice**	**(K–3)** All people want freedom, rights, and justice. **(4–6)** The struggle for freedom, human rights, and justice has occurred in every society.
Decision-making responsibility	**(K–3)** As we become more responsible we gain the right to make more decisions. **(4–6)** Leaders' decisions must take into account their responsibility to others.
Influence **Leadership** **Power**	**(K–3)** People who are leaders influence others' lives as they exercise power. **(4–6)** Leaders use varying powers to influence people and achieve their purposes.
Authority **Rules** **Institutions**	**(K–3)** Leaders use their authority to make and enforce rules. **(4–6)** People have always been guided by the authority established through their social, religious, and political institutions.

FIGURE 6-3
Concepts and Generalizations for K–6 History Instruction

The Purposes of History

If you asked people on the street,"Why bother to study history, what's the purpose?" they would likely say that the reason is to help us gain a sense of who we are and to prevent us from making the same mistakes over and over again.

In addition, I believe that young students should also learn something about the nature of history. For example, they should learn that even though historians work very hard to study the past and share their insights with us, the historical record is incomplete and never will be completed. Students should experience firsthand the methods that historians use. All history instruction must help make the past real to children and it must build insights into their own personal lives and contemporary events.

Prestigious panels of historians and educators as well as state departments of education have developed many different lists of desired outcomes for history instruction. Let's examine what may become the most influential list of history-learning outcomes ever devised and promoted—the National History Standards that grew out of *America 2000*.

WHAT K–6 STUDENTS SHOULD KNOW

In April 1991, President George Bush released *America 2000* and set in motion a drive to establish world-class standards for education in the United States. History was prominently named as one of the content areas where students would demonstrate competency in achieving national standards at grades 4, 8, and 12.[2] Funding established the National History Standards Project, administered by the National Center for History in the Schools at the University of California, Los Angeles. The standards development process was an immense task, spanning more than three years and involving many organizations and individuals with an interest in improving history instruction in the United States.

The efforts of the National History Standards Project resulted in a large document that defines the historical-thinking skills and historical content understandings desired for all students in grades K through 12. Figure 6-4 presents a selection of the thinking skills identified for grades K through 6.

In addition to describing strands of thinking skills to be developed in history instruction, the National History Standards Project specified the historical content understandings students should gain. Figure 6-5 offers an overview of the understandings desired for kindergarten through fourth grade.

For grades 5 through 12 the National History Standards Project identified ten eras of U.S. history and developed separate content understanding statements for each era. There is far too much material to include it all here, but the eras and the content understanding statements are shown in Figure 6-6.

---

[2]*America 2000: An Education Strategy. Sourcebook* (Washington, D.C.: U.S. Department of Education, 1991).

I. Chronological Thinking

- Distinguish between past, present, and future time.
- Identify in historical narratives the temporal structure of a historical narrative or story.
- Establish temporal order in constructing their [students'] own historical narratives.
- Measure and calculate calendar time.
- Interpret data in time lines.
- Create time lines.
- Explain change and continuity over time.

II. Historical Comprehension

- Reconstruct the literal meaning of a historical passage.
- Identify the central question(s) the historical narrative addresses.
- Read historical narratives imaginatively.
- Evidence historical perspectives.
- Draw upon data in historical maps.
- Draw upon visual and mathematical data presented in graphics.
- Draw upon visual data presented in photographs, paintings, cartoons, and architectural drawings.

III. Historical Analysis and Interpretation

- Formulate questions to focus their inquiry or analysis.
- Identify the author or source of the historical document or narrative.
- Compare and contrast differing sets of ideas, values, personalities, behaviors, and institutions.

- Analyze historical fiction.
- Distinguish between fact and fiction.
- Compare different stories about a historical figure, an era, or an event.
- Analyze illustrations in historical stories.
- Consider multiple perspectives.
- Explain causes in analyzing historical actions.
- Challenge arguments of historical inevitability.
- Hypothesize the influence of the past.

IV. Historical Research Capabilities

- Formulate historical questions.
- Obtain historical data.
- Interrogate historical data.
- Marshal needed knowledge of the time and place; and construct a story, an explanation, or a historical narrative.

V. Historical Issues—Analysis and Decision Making

- Identify issues and problems in the past.
- Compare the interests and values of the various people involved.
- Suggest alternative choices for addressing the problem.
- Evaluate alternative courses of action.
- Prepare a position or course of action on an issue.
- Evaluate the implementation of a decision.

FIGURE 6-4
National History Standards Project
Thinking Skills for Grades K through 4[3]

[3]From *National Standards for History for Grades K–4.* Copyright 1994 University of California, Los Angeles: National Center for History in the Schools. Pp. 16–17.

Topic I. Living and Working Together in Families and Communities, Now and Long Ago

Students should demonstrate an understanding of . . .

1A family life now and in the past

1B the different ways people of diverse racial, religious, and ethnic groups and national origins have transmitted their beliefs and values

2A the history of their local community

2B how communities of North America varied long ago

Topic II. The History of Students' Own State or Region

Students should demonstrate an understanding of . . .

3A the indigenous peoples who first lived in their state or region

3B the first European, African, and/or Asian-Pacific explorers and settlers who came to their state or region

3C the various other groups from regions throughout the world who came into the students' own state or region long ago or in the recent past

3D the interactions among all these groups throughout the history of their state

3E the ideas that were significant in the development of the state and that helped to forge its unique identity

Topic III. The History of the United States: Democratic Principles and Values and the People of Many Cultures Who Contributed to Its Cultural, Economic, and Political Heritage

Students should demonstrate an understanding of . . .

4A how the U.S. government was formed and of the nation's basic democratic principles set forth in the Declaration of Independence and the Constitution

4B ordinary people who have exemplified values and principles of American democracy

4C historic figures who have exemplified values and principles of American democracy

4D events that celebrate and exemplify fundamental values and principles of American democracy

4E national symbols through which American values and principles are expressed

5A the movements of large groups of people into their own and other states in the United States now and long ago

6A folklore and other cultural contributions from various regions of the United States and how they help to form a national heritage

Topic IV. History of Peoples of Many Cultures Around the World

Students should demonstrate an understanding of . . .

7A the cultures and historical developments of selected societies in such places as Africa, the Americas, Asia, and Europe

7B great world movements of people now and long ago

8A the development of technological innovations, the major scientists and inventors associated with them, and their social and economic effects

FIGURE 6-5
National History Standards Project
History Content Understandings for Grades K through 4[4]

[4]Taken from *National Standards for History for Grades K–4.* Copyright 1994 University of California, Los Angeles: National Center for History in the Schools. Pp. 32–64. (These statements, slightly modified from the originals, were followed by grade-level-specific examples.)

Era 1 Three Worlds Meet (Beginnings to 1620)

Students should demonstrate an understanding of . . .

- the characteristics of the societies in the Americas, Western Europe, and West Africa that increasingly interacted after 1450

- early European exploration and colonization, and the resulting cultural and ecological interactions

Era 2 Colonization and Settlement (1585–1763)

Students should demonstrate an understanding of . . .

- the early arrival of Europeans and Africans in the Americas and how these people interacted with Native Americans

- how political institutions and religious freedom emerged in the colonies

- how the values and institutions of European economic life took root in the colonies and how slavery reshaped both European and African life in the United States

Era 3 Revolution and the New Nation (1754–1820s)

Students should demonstrate an understanding of . . .

- the causes of the American Revolution, the ideas and interests involved in forging the revolutionary movement, and the reasons for the American victory

- how the American Revolution involved multiple movements among the new nation's many groups to reform American society

- the institutions and practices of government created during the Revolution and how they were revised between 1787 and 1815 to create the foundations of the modern American political system

Era 4 Expansion and Reform (1801–1861)

Students should demonstrate an understanding of . . .

- the U.S. territorial expansion between 1801 and 1861 and how it affected relations with external powers and Native Americans

- how the Industrial Revolution, the rapid expansion of slavery, and the westward movement changed the lives of Americans and led toward regional tensions

- the extension, restriction, and reorganization of political democracy after 1800

- the sources and character of reform movements in the antebellum period and what the reforms accomplished or failed to accomplish

Era 5 Civil War and Reconstruction (1850–1877)

Students should demonstrate an understanding of . . .

- the causes of the Civil War

- the course and character of the Civil War and its effects on the American people

- how various reconstruction plans succeeded or failed

Era 6 Development of the Industrial United States (1870–1900)

Students should demonstrate an understanding of . . .

- how the rise of big business, heavy industry, and mechanized farming transformed America

- massive immigration after 1870 and the new social patterns, conflicts, and ideas of national unity developed amid growing cultural diversity

- the rise of the American labor movement and how political issues reflected social and economic changes

- federal Indian policy and U.S. foreign policy that emerged after the Civil War

(continued on next page)

F I G U R E 6 - 6

National History Standards Project Eras and Content Understandings for U.S. History[5]

[5]From *National Standards for History for Grades K–4*. Copyright 1994 University of California, Los Angeles: National Center for History in the Schools. Pp. 35–37.

Era 7 The Emergence of Modern America (1890–1930)

Students should demonstrate an understanding of . . .

• how progressives and others addressed problems of industrial capitalism, urbanization, and political corruption

• the changing role of the United States in world affairs through World War I

• how the United States changed from the end of World War I to the eve of the Great Depression

Era 8 The Great Depression and World War II (1929–1945)

Students should demonstrate an understanding of . . .

• the causes of the Great Depression and how it affected American society

• how the New Deal addressed the Great Depression, transformed American federalism, and initiated the welfare state

• the origins and course of World War II, the character of the war at home and abroad, and its reshaping of the U.S. role in world affairs

Era 9 Postwar United States (1945–early 1970s)

Students should demonstrate an understanding of . . .

• the economic boom and social transformation of postwar America

• the postwar extension of the New Deal

• the Cold War and the Korean and Vietnam conflicts in domestic and international politics

• the struggle for racial and gender equality and civil liberties

Era 10 Contemporary United States (1968–present)

Students should demonstrate an understanding of . . .

• major developments in U.S. foreign and domestic policies during the Cold War era

• major social and economic developments in contemporary America

FIGURE 6-6, continued

National History Standards Project Eras and Content Understandings for U.S. History

Figure 6-6 provides only the bare skeleton of the full document developed by the National History Standards Project. While some of these content understandings may be developed in the fifth grade U.S. history course, it is clear that most must be developed in grades 7 through 12. I state this even though each statement shown in Figure 6-6 has an illustrative 5th- and 6th-grade-level example.

Because a chronological survey of the same U.S. history never reaches the degree of depth and detail desired, many states and districts have attempted to partition the content in various ways. Assigning the earliest portion of U.S. history to fifth grade, the middle part to eighth grade, and the most recent to senior high school is one approach that has been tried. Of course, this chronological partitioning has its drawbacks, among them, the limitations of young learners attempting to understand and appreciate the importance of early events in our nation's history and the limited recall of the learning that did take place in fifth grade when the same students' twelfth-grade contemporary U.S. history course makes references to forgotten events and barely grasped ideas studied seven years ago. Some teachers maintain that repetition of history content is necessary if the material is to be remembered.

A second scheme, used to gain greater depth, is to allow the elementary, middle, and high-school U.S. history courses to be surveys, but to focus each survey on somewhat different events to be developed in much greater detail. The Revolutionary War, for example, may be developed in much greater detail in the elementary school survey, the Civil War in the middle-school survey, and our more recent wars featured in the high-school survey. All surveys contain material on all wars, but teachers agree to treat specific wars in greater detail at their respective grade levels. A similar variation on this approach is to agree to focus the different surveys on slightly different aspects of our nation's development, with, for example, the elementary survey placing a much heavier emphasis on social history and intergroup relations, the middle-grades survey giving extra emphasis to the development of commerce and technology, and the upper-level survey focusing more on political, diplomatic, and military affairs.

Because the content domain of history is so large, and because there is no single scope and sequence pattern limiting the topics studied as a part of K–6 social studies, it is difficult, if not impossible, to list everything that students might legitimately encounter in their studies. For example, the Bradley Commission on History in Schools (1988) proposed three alternative curriculum patterns that emphasized the role of history. Figure 6-7 displays these patterns.

PATTERN A	PATTERN B	PATTERN C
K Children of other lands and times	K Learning and working now and long ago	K Children's adventures: Long ago and far away
1 Families now and long ago	1 A child's place in time and space	1 People who made America
2 Local history: Neighborhoods and communities	2 People who make a difference	2 Traditions, monuments, and celebrations
3 Urban history: How cities began and grew	3 Continuity and change: Local and national history	3 Inventors, innovators, and immigrants
4 State history and geography: Exploration to 1865	4 A changing state	4 Heroes, folk tales, and legends of the world
5 National history and geography: Exploration to 1865	5 U.S. history and geography: Making a new nation	5 Biographies and documents in American history
6 World history and geography: The growth of civilization	6 World history and geography: Ancient civilizations	6 Biographies and documents in world history

FIGURE 6-7
Bradley Commission Curriculum Patterns

An examination of the Bradley Commission's alternative scope and sequence arrangements shows that pattern A follows the familiar expanding environments topics, but adds an explicit historical focus. History is also the primary focus of patterns B and C. Of course, it is possible to blend elements of all three patterns and, for example, present folk tales and biographies in all grade levels of pattern A.

Another view of what children should know from the study of history associated with the expanding environments approach to social studies is provided in Figure 6-8.

Kindergarten

- Recognize ways that they and their classmates have changed over time.

- Give examples of the ideas that "everything comes from somewhere" and that "everything has a history."

- Order events experienced during the day in their proper sequence.

- Differentiate between a correct and an incorrect narrative account of an event they have witnessed.

First grade

- Recount events from their own and their family history using concrete props such as photographs to aid the telling of their story.

- Know the names of at least two prominent figures from U.S. history.

- Correctly describe the sequence of their life events for a series of days.

- Show the ability to identify cause-and-effect relationships within the family life environment (for example, the stove wouldn't work so they had a cold dinner).

Second grade

- Know basic information about the history of the school and the neighborhood.

- Correctly sequence a series of experienced events to form a history for an entire week of school.

- Know the names of at least five prominent men and women from U.S. or local history and simple facts about their lives.

- Recognize and offer reasons for changes that have occurred in their school and community over the years.

- Show the ability to locate and use historical information related to the school and the community.

Third grade

- Recall factual information about the history of their own (or a nearby) city.

- Correctly sequence a series of events experienced by their own or a nearby city to form a history for an entire month.

- Know the names of at least ten prominent men and women from local and U.S. history and simple facts about their lives.

(continued on next page)

F I G U R E   6 - 8

History Learning Outcomes for the Expanding Environments
Scope and Sequence[6]

---

[6]These selected outcome statements were adapted from Hoge and Crump, 1988.

- Recognize and offer reasons for changes that have occurred in their city over the years.
- Show the ability to locate and use historical information related to their own or a nearby city.

Fourth grade

- Know the names of at least ten prominent men and women from their own state's history and simple facts about their lives.
- Identify key events, places, and people shaping the history of the state or region.
- Explain similarities, differences, and changes relating to periods of time, groups of people, locations, and resources.
- Identify how major landforms, waterforms, and resources influenced settlement patterns, development, and lifestyles.
- Demonstrate a knowledge of history as a subject by writing histories delimited to specific topics.
- Organize historical data in simple time-line format.

Fifth grade

- Know the names of at least twenty prominent men and women from U.S. history and simple facts about their lives.

- Identify major events and people contributing to the development and growth of the United States.
- Recognize cultural characteristics, motivations, and contributions of populations making up the United States and its neighbors.
- Identify problems and conflicts experienced by different regions of the United States and evaluate solutions in terms of their consequences.
- Examine the authenticity of historical documents and arguments.

Sixth grade

- Know the names of at least twenty prominent men and women from world history and simple facts about their lives.
- Identify significant changes in ages past and assess their influence on present and future conditions.
- Acquire and organize information needed to support or refute a historical argument.
- Pose historical questions or hypotheses and conduct research to determine probable answers.

FIGURE 6-8, continued

History Learning Outcomes for the Expanding Environments Scope and Sequence

Limitations in Learning History

In thinking about what historical content to teach children in grades K through 6, it would be wrong to conclude that virtually all topics and methods are appropriate. Substantial research evidence shows that elementary grade level children have difficulty learning history by simply reading a textbook or listening to lectures. Young students have a limited sense of time and chronology. Their limited background of experience makes the conceptual content of history and the remote geographic settings hard to understand. Finally, young children are unable to think formally—in a Piagetian sense—about history. This means K–6 students will have trouble dealing with historical abstractions, propositions, and arguments.

Fortunately, much can be done to overcome young students' difficulties in learning history. Using the following techniques will make history instruction meaningful to young students.

Techniques for Helping Young Students Learn History

Connecting children with the past is not difficult. The most immediate connection children have with the past is through their own personal and family histories. Beyond these lie natural connections with the past that exist in the school and the community. The immediate and remote past exist everywhere. The teacher's job is to draw out connections and help children develop a positive attitude toward learning about the past. Hands-on teaching techniques and building conceptual bridges between the past and the present help accomplish these goals. Figure 6-9 lists a number of popular ways to help children experience history.

Artifacts

Bring in old books, clothing, maps, farm and kitchen implements, or any other physical relic of the past. Allow children to handle and ask questions about these objects.

Photographs/Videos

Collections of historical photographs are available from local museums and historical societies. Libraries often have photo-essays in their collections. Commercial publishers are a source of historical videos, slides, and large-scale photographs.

Enactments/Skits

Set up skits to bring famous events and people to life. Script the scenes and provide necessary props and costumes. Devise new situations for the historical figures and have the class determine how the skit should be played.

Field trips

Call your school district's social studies supervisor and ask for a list of local historical sites. The list should include the name of a contact person, hours of operation, and fees. Study information about the site in advance, being careful to integrate the field trip with ongoing instruction.

Resource persons and interviews

Ask a parent or grandparent to come in and help you bring a historical period, place, or event to life.

Let the students do most or all of the interview. Contact your local historical society and see if they can identify a resource person who specializes in some particular aspect or period of history.

Children's literature

Use the rich resource of children's literature to increase understanding of the past. Ask your media coordinator to select a group of trade books that can support your topic. Bring these to class and allow the students time to explore. Read portions of a student-selected historical fiction or biography aloud each day.

Conceptual bridge building

Consciously build conceptual bridges to the past. Compare soldiers and leaders of the past to those of today. Compare cooking techniques of the past with those of the present. Show how the childhood experiences of the past are similar to and different from those of the present. Ask the students to explain why things were different (or similar) in the past.

Focus on social history

Social history is the history of common people. Medicine, childhood, women's work, farming, and entertainment are all examples of topics addressed by social history. Focusing on social history makes it easy for a child to relate to the everyday life experiences of past generations.

FIGURE 6-9
Ways to Help Children Remember and Enjoy History Instruction

DISCUSSION QUESTIONS

1. Assume that K–6 students received outstanding history instruction as a regular part of their social studies. What might we reasonably expect would be the results of such instruction for our society if everyone experienced it? Would we all be reading more historical fiction? Would we have more historical monuments? Would we have greater respect for our elderly? Explain your answer.

2. Is history instruction more important than geography instruction? Is it more important than economics, or other social sciences and humanities? Take a stand and support your answer with at least two concrete examples.

3. Critics charge that schoolbook history is often a biased, sexist, racist, and status quo account of the past. If that is so, how can we correct it?

ALTERNATIVE HISTORY

Up to this point, the chapter has presented a picture of history as it is represented in many textbooks, curriculum guides, and official documents. Little has been said about controversies and conflicts that exist within the field of history and little has been said about alternative views of history. The three types of history detailed in Figure 6-1 may have alerted you to the fact that most of the history we consume in our schoolbooks represents a majority culture perspective on events of the past. In addition, these historical accounts are often centered on only the most important political, military, and economic events. The development of social history is an attempt to counterbalance the tendency to dwell on only the most important people, places, and events.

Social history is the term applied to historical accounts of common people and events. Histories of childbirth, children's games, medicine, transportation, aviation, and rock and roll are all examples of social history. Originally spurned by academic historians, forms of social history are gaining increasing acceptance on university campuses. Included within the domain of social history is oral history—the recounting of historical events by people who experienced it, either directly or indirectly. Since children are often interested in social history and capable of conducting oral history investigations, let's explore some of the kinds of topics that are possible and guidelines for doing oral history projects in the classroom.

Oral History

Oral history is the verbal "storytelling" of "old timers" about the people, places, and events they experienced. *Storytelling* and *old timers* are in quotes for a reason. Oral history is actually more than simple storytelling; it is the purposeful collection of information sought to illustrate important understandings about past events, places, and people. The "old timer" may, in fact, not be so old, but in any case must be a person who had firsthand experience with the phenomenon of interest.

The goals and purposes of oral history are many, but foremost is developing historical knowledge and processes. The gift of oral history is that it naturally motivates student interest as history becomes real before their eyes. A secondary, yet important goal, is developing students' affection for history. In addition, the practice or doing of oral history involves using communication skills such as interviewing, listening, and writing. Here are some guidelines to follow in conducting an oral history project.

1. *Determine a topic.*   The first consideration in selecting a topic should be student interest. A second consideration is whether the students will be able to secure an adequate number of narrators on the subject. A final consideration is whether the students will be able to locate a sufficient amount of written or visual source material on the chosen topic.

    Some potential topics are:

homes and furnishings	recreation	superstitions
food	sports	celebrations
cooking/preservation	farming methods and	local industries
music	machinery	important individuals
schools	transportation	important events
churches	medicine (home and	special periods (for
clothing (function and	formal)	example, depression
style)	architecture and art	era)

2. *Seek administrative approval.*   Since an oral history project involves a fair amount of time and effort, it is important to secure the support of your principal before you get into the project. Stress how the project will fit into the social studies curriculum and also support language arts and reading skills. The administrator should know that the project will involve the expenditure of money for cassette tapes, mailing expenses, and perhaps photographs. In addition, it is also advisable to seek the support of your social studies supervisor.

3. *Begin.*   Collect artifacts and documents that relate to the topic you and your students have chosen. Use both primary and secondary sources. Engage the students in forming questions they would like to have answered. List and group these questions on chart paper, keeping them for future reference.

4. *Identify individuals in the community who might be willing to provide information about the topic.*   Ask friends, parents, local officials, and so on for recommendations of names. Keep a list of recommendations and remember to ask those people who are contacted for additional names of people who might be able to provide more information. In general, the file of names you keep should include addresses, phone numbers, and topics on which the person can provide information.

5. *Select the individuals who will provide the oral histories.* Selection criteria should include not only the topic or question the person can address, but also the accuracy of his or her memory, the detail and reliability of his or her observations, the individual's self-confidence, whether he or she enjoys talking to children, and his or her general outlook (hopefully positive!) on life. Initial contact should be made by the teacher, who must be responsible for assessing these factors. A good parent volunteer might also make these calls and contacts, especially if he or she becomes committed to the project. It usually takes two or three calls to set up the time when the narrator will come to the school for the telling of his or her oral history. Initial contacts should inform the narrator of the age and interest areas of the children, assure the narrator that the contact with the children will be informal, and probe whether the narrator has a collection of artifacts, documents, or photos that might support his or her story. Depending on the potential future uses of the oral history, a legal release may need to be signed by the narrator.

6. *Train students for the interviews.* Students need to become familiar with asking questions that allow a person to give an elaborated response. Such questions often begin with the words *how, why, who,* and *what.* Students also need to be taught to ask follow-up questions and how to listen attentively.

7. *Conduct the interviews in the classroom.* Arrange the room for comfort and audience visibility. Post a sign on the door to prevent interruptions. Make sure the person who is providing information knows that it will be recorded and possibly transcribed so that others may enjoy his or her recollections. Ask the person to sign a release form indicating approval for educational uses.

8. *Debrief the interview experience.* Write a thank-you note to the narrator. Highlight new information that came to light as a result of the interview and identify any new questions or leads that need to be investigated.

9. *Label (and possibly transcribe) the tape.* Make sure that the label contains an abstract of the topics covered and information gained in the interview.

10. *Produce the oral history book or document that will represent the class' investigation efforts.* Display your project at parents' night. Contact the local media to see if they wish to report on the project.

CHANGE IN THE FAMILY[7]

Grade: First
Topic: How do families grow and change over time?
Overview: Just as individuals and places have histories, families have histories, too. This lesson helps the child gain a broader focus on how time has changed and will continue to change the character of his or her family.
Objectives: As a result of this lesson, students will:

- recall the origin of their present family unit
- identify the changes that have occurred in their family since its origin
- describe probable ways in which their family will change within the next few years

Suggested Time: Three to five class sessions
Materials/Resources Needed: (A note home to parents about the lesson)

Suggestions for Teaching the Lesson

Opening the Lesson: Ask the students to name some things that grow or change as they become older (plants, people). Tell the students that just as these things grow and change over time, families do, too. Tell the class that you are going to show them how families grow and change over time by sharing the story of your own family's history.

Developing the Lesson: Share the history of your family, beginning with an event such as the meeting or marriage of your parents. If possible, show a photograph of where your family lived and point out its location on a map. Show changes in your family represented by new children (including yourself), moves to new homes, or other developments. Explain that the photographs and events you have chosen show part of the history of your family.

Ask the children if they know anything about how their own families began. Tell them that in the next few lessons they are going to learn about their own family's histories. Explain that all families grow and change over time and see if the students can name some of the ways in which change occurs. (For example, new children arrive, parents

divorce and remarry, a move occurs, older children leave for college or work, and so on) Once these are listed on the board, have the students help you form questions such as the following on the board:

Has our family ever lived anywhere else?

What were things like before I was born?

What were things like before any of us were born?

Are there other big changes our family has had?

Help the students "tailor make" their list of questions to suit their own family situation. Send the papers home with a note that explains the project and urges parents to help their child understand their family history. Urge parents to use photographs or other means of making the history of the child's immediate family more understandable and real. Encourage parents to help the children write short answers to the questions they have brought home and illustrate these with pictures if possible.

When most of the students have gained the historical information about their family, meet with groups of four to five students to share their stories. Stress that everybody and every family has a history, and that although there are certain similarities among many of them, that each is unique and valuable in its own way. Conclude that our history helps us know more about who we are and why we act and think and live like we do.

Closing the Lesson: Praise the class for finding out about their family histories. Point out that as time goes on their families will continue to change and new history will be written.

Conclude the lesson by discussing with the children what they think things will be like in six months, one year, two years, four years, and eight years. Encourage the students to talk with their parents about the future of their family and the changes that are anticipated. As individual students gain information about their family's future, share this with the class to encourage others to do likewise.

---

[7]Adapted from Hoge and Crump, 1988.

Evaluating the Lesson

Key questions for the students:

- What are some things that you know about your family history?

- What things have changed in your family since you were born?
- What changes are likely to happen in your family in the future?

CITY ORAL HISTORY[8]

Grade: Third

Topic: What do people remember about a big event in your city's past?

Overview: Most cities experience a number of significant events over a period of years. Large fires, floods, tornadoes, the loss or acquisition of a major league athletic team, the closing of a key industry, or the renovation of the downtown are history that we all experience. This lesson plan provides suggestions for creating an oral history of such an event.

Objectives: As a result of this lesson, students will:

- identify and corroborate a set of facts related to a major historical event
- describe in detail the significance of the event to the city's economy or its people

Suggested Time: Three to five class sessions

Materials/Resources Needed: Old newspapers, oral history resource people; cassette recorder (optional); duplicating machine (for sending home the event history); refreshments (for oral history resource people)

Suggestions for Teaching the Lesson

Opening the Lesson: Begin by preselecting the event that you wish to have the students investigate. This decision should be based on a consideration of the students' interests, the availability of resource people, and sufficient newspaper coverage. Once you have determined which event to investigate, begin by raising the students' interest with questions such as: Has anyone heard about (the flood that happened eight years ago)? What do you know about it? What effect did it have on our city? Have you ever seen pictures of it?

Tell the students that events such as this play a major role in the history of a city and that they are going to use the coming week to learn more about it.

Developing the Lesson: Read one or two carefully selected newspaper articles about the event. Show any photographs of the event and allow students' reactions to the information and visuals. Write any questions they may have on the board and encourage speculation regarding the answers.

On two successive days, bring in an oral history resource person who experienced the event. Let him or her tell the story of how they experienced or were involved in the event and encourage questions from the students. Use the articles, photos, and questions previously recorded on the board as vehicles for probing the resource person's knowledge of the past. Debrief the experience after he or she leaves and see if the students have any additional questions or insights based on their interview. Repeat this experience with the second oral history resource person.

Closing the Lesson: Have the students dictate, as a group, their own history of the event to take home to their parents. The history should include the who, what, when, where, why, and how of the event, a description of how they studied the event, and their statement of the significance of the event to their community. Encourage the students to have their parents read and discuss (with the child) their account of the historical event.

Evaluating the Lesson

Key questions for the students:

What do you know about (the major event) we studied?

Why was this an important event to our city?

---

[8]Adapted from Hoge and Crump, 1988.

Alternative Teaching Suggestions

If your students are strong readers, let them take home a photocopy of an old newspaper story written about the event. Have parents help the students read the article. Share and discuss what they learned on the next day.

If the event you choose turns out to have greater personal significance to the students (perhaps family members or relatives were involved) take the extra time to have these people come in and be oral history resources.

Visit the sight of the event. Take along a camera and photograph any commemorative plaques or other evidence that the event really happened.

Discuss how history and the present might be different if the event had not occurred.

◆ ◆

RESOURCES
◆ ◆ ◆ ◆ ◆

The resources for teaching history to children in grades K through 6 are substantial. Publishers offer a wide variety of children's books and audiovisual resources to support history learning. The ERIC system contains units of instruction and lesson plans on many aspects of history, including women's history.

Cobblestone is a history magazine for children, published ten times a year by Cobblestone Publishers, Inc., (7 School Street, Peterborough, NH 03458).

The National Center for History in the Schools (University of California, Los Angeles, Moore Hall 231, 405 Hilgard Avenue, Los Angeles, CA 90024-1521) conducts research on the teaching of history, publishes a newsletter, provides workshops and curriculum materials, and developed the National Standards for History Education.

The National Council for History Education, Inc. (26915 Westwood Road, Suite B-2, Westlake, OH 44145-4656) also promotes history instruction in the schools and produces a monthly newsletter. It also operates History-LINK, an Internet listserve for teachers of history.

The National Women's History Project (7738 Bell Road, Windsor, CA 95492-8518, 707-838-6000) publishes all kinds of women's history materials for kindergarten through twelfth grade. Included in their annual catalog is a broad range of multicultural women's history resources such as teaching posters, videos, activity and reference books, cassettes, computer software, plays, speeches, card games, biographies for young readers, and celebration supplies for women's history month.

The Social Studies School Service (P.O. Box 802, Culver City, CA 90232-0802, 1-800-421-4246) markets educational materials from a variety of publishers, much of it history based.

REFERENCES AND SELECTED READINGS

Bradley Commission on History in Schools. 1988. *Building a history curriculum.* Washington, D.C.: Educational Excellence Network.

California Department of Education. 1991. *Literature for history-social science kindergarten through grade eight.* Sacramento, CA: California Department of Education.

Cleaver, J. 1988. *Doing children's museums.* Charlotte, VT: Williamson Publishing.

Downey, M. T., and Levstik, L. S. 1992. Teaching and learning history. In *Handbook of research on social studies teaching and learning,* ed. J. P. Shaver, 400–410. New York: Macmillan.

Field, S. L., Burlbaw, L. M., and Davis, O. L., Jr. 1994. I think there's a storm in the desert: Children's narrative as historical understanding. *The Social Studies* 85(6):256–261.

Field, S. L., and Labbo, L. D. 1994. A pocketful of history. *Social Studies and the Young Learner* 7(2):4–7.

Hoge, John D. 1991. A survey investigation of students' historical time knowledge. *Journal of Social Studies Research.* 15:16–29.

Hoge, J. D., and Crump, C. 1988. *Teaching history in the elementary school.* Bloomington, IN: Social Studies Development Center, Indiana University.

Levstik, L. S., and Pappas, C. C. 1987. Exploring the development of historical understanding. *Journal of Research and Development in Education* 21:1–15.

_____. 1992. New directions for studying historical understanding. *Theory and Research in Social Education* 20:369-385.

National History Standards Project. 1994. *Progress report and draft standards, March 1994.* Los Angeles, CA: National Center for History in the Schools.

Reed, E. W. 1993. *Helping your child learn history.* Washington, D.C.: Office of Educational Research and Improvement, U.S. Department of Education.

Sewall, G. T. 1987. *American history textbooks: An assessment of quality.* New York: Educational Excellence Network.

Thornton, S. J., and Vukelich, R. 1988. Effects of children's understanding of time concepts on historical understanding. *Theory and Research in Social Education* 17(1):69–82.

Zaccaria, M. A. 1978. The development of historical thinking: Implications for the teaching of history. *The History Teacher* 11:323–340.

Geography: Making Sense of the Environment

The power and beauty of geography allow us to see, understand, and appreciate the web of relationships between people, places, and environments. At the everyday level, for example, a geographically informed person can appreciate the locational dynamics of street vendors and pedestrian traffic or fast-food outlets and automobile traffic; the routing strategies of school buses in urban areas and of backpackers in wilderness areas; the land-use strategies of farmers and real estate developers.

At a more extended spatial scale, the same person can appreciate the dynamic links between severe storms and property damage or between summer thunderstorms and flash floods; the use of irrigation systems to compensate for lack of precipitation or the connections between temperature inversions and urban air pollution episodes; the seasonal movement of migrant laborers in search of work and vacationers in search of sunshine and warmth.

At a global level, the geographically informed person can appreciate the connections between cyclical drought and human starvation in the Sahel or between the Chernobyl nuclear disaster and the long-term consequences to human health and economic activities throughout eastern and northwestern Europe; the restructuring of human migration and trade patterns as the European Union becomes increasingly integrated or as the Pacific rim nations develop a commonality of economic and political interests; and the uncertainties associated with the possible effects of global warming on human society or the destruction of tropical rain forests on global climate.

(Bednarz et al., 1994, 29)

THE DISCIPLINE'S PERSPECTIVE

Geography is the study of places on earth, how the people in those places use the land and water, and how they interact with one another and other areas or places. Geographers study the spatial distribution of phenomena, patterns of interaction, and use of resources by people in a certain place and time.

There are two main branches of geography: physical and cultural. Physical geographers study soils, climates, vegetation, and landforms. Cultural geographers study the relationship between people and earth, focusing on how human societies and culture influence the use of earth's resources. Cultural geography also stresses the importance of cultural perceptions of resources as determiners of land and resource use.

Geographic educators have collected substantial evidence showing that Americans are geographically illiterate. Surveys show that both students and adults lack knowledge of where cities, countries, and natural features are located within the United States and around the world (Bein, 1990; NAEP, 1990; Grosvenor, 1989). Yet geographic literacy entails more than being able to identify places. It also includes being able to explain why things are located where they are using the five fundamental themes of geography and other geographic concepts. A geographically literate person must also be skillful in the use of maps, charts, and globes (Backler and Stoltman, 1986).

The Five Fundamental Themes of Geography

Figure 7-1 describes the five fundamental themes of geography and provides sample questions, based on Washington, D.C., to illustrate each. The five fundamental themes are used to organize geographic-learning experiences and shape the development of curriculum materials. The themes are further explained in Figure 7-2, a conceptual outline of geography's content.

Concepts and Generalizations

Figure 7-2 displays an overview of the conceptual content of geography. Before you look at the outline, take a moment and jot down on a piece of paper ten concepts from geography (excluding the five themes shown in Figure 7-1). Now score yourself by locating your concepts in the content outline: expert geographer = 9 or 10; geographer = 8; junior geographer = 7; on your way to geographic literacy = 6; and below 6 = improvement needed.

EXERCISE 7-1

1. After you have read through the outline, look back at the physical geography section and list the terms that you have never heard of or know very little about. Look these terms up in a dictionary or, better, check out a high school or college geography textbook and read more about them.

THEMES	EXPLANATION	SAMPLE QUESTIONS
Location	The location of a feature on the earth's surface may be described in two ways. Absolute location gives the location in terms of a grid coordinate system such as latitude and longitude. Relative location describes the position of a place relative to other places.	"What is the latitude and longitude of Washington, D.C.?" "How much time does it take by car to get from Atlanta to Washington, D.C.?" "Is Washington, D.C. north or south of New York?"
Place	All places have unique natural and cultural characteristics. Natural characteristics include landforms and waterforms, climates, soils, vegetation, and animal life. Places are also given unique characteristics in the "built environment" by the people who live there.	"What waterforms are near Washington, D.C. and how do they affect its climate?" "Why are there so many museums in Washington, D.C.?" "Why does Washington, D.C. have so many different kinds of restaurants?"
Relationships within places	People modify and adapt to their environment based on cultural values, technological capabilities, economic conditions, and political ideology. Geography focuses on understanding such human-environment interactions within a given place.	"Why are economically depressed areas so close to the Capitol building in Washington, D.C.?" "Why isn't Washington, D.C.'s riverfront developed with more public parks and entertainment?"
Movement	The transportation of people, products, information, and ideas from one place to another defines regional and global interdependence. The geographical analysis of movement patterns can influence the planning decisions of individuals, businesses, and governments.	"How many people ride the Metro subway each day in their commute to work?" "What products arrive by railroad in the Washington, D.C. area? Where do they come from?" "Should Washington, D.C. further expand its Metro subway system?"
Regions	How political, economic, cultural, natural, or other types of regions form and change is of interest to geographers. Geographers use the concept of regions to examine, define, describe, and explain human activities.	"What economic regions exist within Washington, D.C.?" "Does the highly charged political atmosphere of the Washington, D.C. area end at the Capitol Beltway?"

FIGURE 7-1

The Five Fundamental Themes of Geography

2. Find a globe and locate the features shown in Section III.A.7. of the outline.

3. The five themes of geography are featured in Section I of the outline. Select one or two subpoints under each theme and write a question about Washington, D.C. that could be added to Figure 7-1.

4. Select a geographic process and use it as a key word for a computerized search of news articles featuring that process. Photocopy several of the articles and share them with the class.

I. Major Themes in Human Geography
  A. Location: Position on the Earth's Surface
    1. Absolute location
    2. Relative location
  B. Place: Physical and Human Characteristics
    1. Physical characteristics
      a. Natural resources
        (1) Mineral resources
        (2) Flora/Fauna resources
        (3) Energy resources
    2. Human characteristics
      a. Settlement patterns
      b. Architecture
      c. Economic activities
      d. Recreational activities
      e. Transportation and communication
         networks
      f. Demography
        (1) Birth/Death/Growth rates
        (2) Race/Ethnicity
        (3) Age distribution
        (4) Family structure
        (5) Infant mortality
  C. Relationships within Places: Humans and
     Environments
    1. Types of land use
      a. Agriculture
      b. Mining
      c. Logging
      d. Public/Private recreation
      e. Industrial/Commercial development
      f. Housing
      g. Other forms of land use
    2. Adaptations to natural settings
    3. Spatial distribution
      a. Population density
    4. Areal association
  D. Movement: Humans Interacting on the Earth
    1. Spatial interactions
      a. Migration
      b. Immigration

      c. Trade/Commerce
      d. Other forms of mobility
      e. Spread of ideas
  E. Regions: How They Form and Change
    1. Terminology and concepts
      a. Boundary
      b. Area
      c. Density/Diffusion
      d. Homogeneity/Heterogeneity
      e. Pattern
    2. Physical regions (see Physical
       geography)
    3. Political regions
    4. Economic regions
    5. Cultural/Social/Religious regions
II. Major Themes in Physical Geography
  A. Climate
    1. Major types
      a. Humid tropical
      b. Subtropical
      c. Dry arid/Semiarid
      d. Midlatitude (Continental)
      e. Polar
      f. Highland
    2. Weather phenomena
      a. Hurricanes
      b. Frontal systems
      c. Jet stream
      d. Thunderstorms
      e. Tornadoes
      f. Tsunamis
      g. Typhoons
    3. Weather components
      a. Temperature
      b. Wind
      c. Precipitation
        (1) Rain
        (2) Snow
        (3) Sleet/Hail
      d. Clouds/Cloud types
        (1) Fog/Mist

(continued on next page)

FIGURE 7-2
Conceptual Content of Geography[1]

[1]This outline is adapted from the Social Studies Content Descriptor Project, Educational Products Information Exchange Institute. Used by permission.

B. Landforms
 1. Continents
 2. Mountains/Mountain features/Major mountain chains
 3. Hills
 4. Plateaus
 5. Plains
 6. Coastal environments
  a. Deltas
  b. Beaches
 7. Dunes
C. Water forms
 1. Oceans/Seas
  a. Gulfs
  b. Bays
 2. Rivers
 3. Lakes
D. Soil
 1. Mineral resources
E. Flora/Fauna
F. Solar System
 1. Earth
 2. Sun
 3. Moon
 4. Other planets
G. Geologic forces
 1. Continental drift/Plate techtonics
 2. Volcanoes
 3. Earthquakes
H. Ecology/Conservation
 1. Ecosystems
  a. Forest
  b. Grassland
  c. Polar
  d. Desert
  e. Mountain
III. Geographic skills/Methods/Tools
A. Instruction about Maps and Globes
 1. Symbols/Legends/Keys
 2. Distortion/Projection
 3. Scale/Distance
 4. Cardinal/Ordinal directions
 5. Latitude/Longitude
 6. Rotation/Declination/Axis

 7. Earth/Map features
  a. Equator
  b. Tropic of Cancer/Capricorn
  c. North Pole
  d. South Pole
  e. Arctic Circle
  f. Antarctic Circle
  g. Prime meridian/Greenwich
  h. Time zones
B. Analysis or Use of Maps or Globes
 1. Special-purpose maps
 2. Physical maps
 3. Political maps
 4. Weather maps
C. Mapping Phenomena
D. Cartography (Making Maps)
IV. Geographic Processes
A. Immigration/Migration
B. Growth of Cities
 1. Urbanization
  a. Neighborhood/Ghetto formation
 2. Suburbanization
 3. Urban renewal
 4. Industrialization
C. Colonization/Settlement
D. Deforestation
E. Pollution
 1. Air
 2. Water
 3. Soil
F. Desertification
G. Weathering/Erosion
H. Domestication (Animals and Plants)
V. Commonly Used Geographic Study Divisions
A. Hemispheres
 1. Western
 2. Eastern
 3. Southern
 4. Northern
B. Continents
 1. Europe
 2. North America
 3. South America
 4. Africa

(continued on next page)

FIGURE 7-2, continued
Conceptual Content of Geography

5. Asia
6. Australia
7. Antarctica
C. Regions
  1. Middle East
  2. Far East

3. Latin America
4. Pacific Rim
5. Southeast Asia
6. Caribbean
7. South Pacific
8. Central America

FIGURE 7-2, continued
Conceptual Content of Geography

WHAT K-6 STUDENTS SHOULD KNOW

Children are natural explorers of their environment. They love to play with water, form sand into mountains, and make rivers in mud. They enjoy driving toy trucks up big hills, poking sticks into the ground to make a fence, and arranging tiny plastic figures about the landscapes they have created. Children are also keen observers of their environment. They wonder why leaves fall from trees, they enjoy watching plants grow in spring, and they love learning about the weather. All of this play and interest in the natural environment is fundamental content in the study of geography.

In part because of children's natural interest in the environment, geography instruction must begin in the primary grades. By the time they start kindergarten, most children are ready to expand their casual and natural study of geography. For example, they are ready to represent symbolically their daily experience of the weather by creating a weather chart showing the sun, clouds, rain, wind, and snow. By the time they enter the first grade, they are ready to show the high and low temperatures for the day with a giant bulletin board thermometer, and by the second grade, they can take pleasure in helping to chart the amount of daily rainfall for an entire month.

Geography instruction includes learning about time and space. Virtually all children are eager to mark the progress of the days until their next birthday or holiday. Learning how to use a calendar opens avenues for thinking about the seasons and the passage of time. Preschool and early primary grade level children are still mystified by the relationship between time and distance. They are just beginning to be able to tell their way back and forth between frequently traveled and nearby places. Such children need experiences designed to help them learn time and distance concepts such as *hour, minute, half hour, far, near, mile,* and *kilometer.* Through these experiences the beginnings of geographic learning take root in early elementary education.

The National Geography Standards

The National Geography Standards (Bednarz et al., 1994) were developed in response to geography being named one of the five core subjects in the *America 2000* education initiative. The purpose of national standards for geography "is to bring all students up to internationally competitive levels to meet the demands of a new age and a different world" (p. 9). The standards establish clear benchmarks for geography learning at grades 4, 8, and 12 and they will help ensure that all students have access to a challenging geography curriculum. Figure 7-3 displays the eighteen National Geography standards.

The geographically informed person knows and understands . . .

1. how to use maps and other geographic representations, tools, and technologies to acquire, process, and report information from a spatial perspective

2. how to use mental maps to organize information on people, places, and environments in a spatial context

3. how to analyze the spatial organization of people, places, and environments on earth's surface

4. the physical and human characteristics of places

5. that people create regions to interpret earth's complexity

6. how culture and experience influence people's perception of places and regions

7. the physical processes that shape the patterns of earth's surface

8. the characteristics and spatial distribution of ecosystems on earth's surface

9. the characteristics, distribution, and migration of human populations on earth's surface

10. the characteristics, distribution, and complexity of earth's cultural mosaics

11. patterns and networks of economic interdependence on earth's surface

12. the processes, patterns, and functions of human settlement

13. how the forces of cooperation and conflict among people influence the division and control of earth's surface

14. how human actions modify the physical environment

15. how physical systems affect human systems

16. the changes that occur in the meaning, use, distribution, and importance of resources

17. how to apply geography to interpret the past

18. how to apply geography to interpret the present and plan for the future

FIGURE 7-3
National Geography Standards[2]

These eighteen standards are further explained by a summary of learning behaviors that students in grades 4, 8, and 12 must demonstrate if they are performing at an acceptable level. For example, by the end of the fourth grade, students should be able to:

- use the five themes (location, place, human-environment interaction, movement, and regions) in geography as an organizational and integrated framework

---

[2]The National Geography Standards offer, for each standard, a rationale and detailed examples for grades 4, 8, and 12.

- possess solid command of basic geographic vocabulary and concepts
- use maps and globes to locate places and for gathering data for making basic location decisions (for example, where to situate a new video game arcade in the local area)
- apply the skills of place location using latitude and longitude as well as alpha/numeric grid systems
- present an environmental or cultural issue from more than a single perspective
- possess a global sense with a basic awareness of economic and political interdependence
- make simple comparisons showing the similarities and differences between places
- demonstrate how people have adapted to and been changed by their physical environment
- access basic geographic information from a variety of sources
- develop alternative solutions to geographic issues
- participate effectively in collaborative learning situations

The National Geographic Standards also specify five geographic skill areas. Figure 7-4 on page 138 lists these skills and representative abilities to be demonstrated by the end of fourth grade.

Geography Learning Experiences in the K–6 Expanding Environments Scope and Sequence

Figure 7-5 shows a proposed scope and sequence for K–6 geography instruction. The scope and sequence conforms to the topics typically treated in the expanding environments approach to social studies and uses the five themes of geography as its basis.

DISCUSSION QUESTIONS

1. Should children know the names and locations of the states? If yes, by what age? If no, why not?
2. If children were really taught the content specified in Figure 7-2, how would our nation be different? Would citizens "think geographically" about development issues in their communities? Would citizens of the United States be less self-centered in their view of the world?
3. How would you rate your own geographic education, especially that provided in elementary school? How do you account for the fact that it was as good or as bad as you have rated it?

MAP AND GLOBE SKILLS

Map-reading skills are more important today than ever before. One reason is because people are more mobile than ever before. Another reason is because maps are more complex than they used to be due to the steadily increasing

Ask geographic questions	"Where is it located?" "Why is it there?" "What is significant about its location?" "How is its location related to the locations of other people, places, and environments?" Distinguish between geographic and nongeographic questions.
Acquire geographic information	Locate, gather, and process information from a variety of primary and secondary sources including maps. Make and record observations about the physical and human characteristics of places.
Present geographic information	Prepare maps to display geographic information. Construct graphs, tables, and diagrams to display geographic information.
Analyze geographic information	Use maps to observe and interpret geographic relationships. Use tables and graphs to observe and interpret geographic trends and relationships. Use texts, photographs, and documents to observe and interpret geographic trends and relationships. Use simple mathematics to analyze geographic data.
Answer geographic questions	Present geographic information in the form of both oral and written reports accompanied by maps and graphics. Use methods of geographic inquiry to acquire geographic information, draw conclusions, and make generalizations. Apply generalizations to solve problems and make reasoned decisions.

FIGURE 7-4
Geographic Skills Demonstrated by Grade 4[3]

GRADE LEVELS AND GEOGRAPHIC FOCUSES	**GEOGRAPHIC CONCEPTS AND SUGGESTED LEARNING EXPERIENCES**
Kindergarten Self in space	1. Knows and uses terms related to location, direction, and distance (for example, up/down, left/right, near/far) 2. Recognizes a globe as a model of the earth 3. Recognizes and uses terms that express relative size and shape (for example, big/little, large/small, round/square) 4. Identifies school and local community by name 5. Recognizes and uses models and symbols to represent real things 6. Makes simple observations and describes the weather, the seasons, the school, the neighborhood

(continued on next page)

FIGURE 7-5
Geography Learning Experiences in the K–6 Expanding Environments Scope and Sequence[4]

[3]Bednarz et al., 47. Used by permission of National Geographic Society. (Skills to be demonstrated by grades 5 and 6 were not developed by the project, which focused only on standards to be attained by grades 4, 8, and 12.)
[4]Adapted from *Guidelines for Geographic Education*, 11–17.

GRADE LEVELS AND GEOGRAPHIC FOCUSES	GEOGRAPHIC CONCEPTS AND SUGGESTED LEARNING EXPERIENCES

First grade
Homes and schools
in different places

1. Knows the location of home in relation to school and the neighborhood
2. Knows the floor plan of the school and the layout of the campus
3. Uses simple classroom maps to locate objects
4. Identifies state and nation by name
5. Identifies seasons of the year
6. Describes characteristics of seasons and discusses their impact on people
7. Follows and gives verbal directions (for example, here/there, left/right)
8. Distinguishes between land and water symbols on globes and maps
9. Relates locations on a map/globe to location on earth
10. Describes similarities and differences among people in their own community
11. Describes similarities and differences between people in their own community and those in other places
12. Observes, describes, and builds simple models and maps of the local environment

Second grade
Neighborhoods—
small places in larger
communities

1. Makes and uses simple maps of the school and home neighborhood
2. Interprets map symbols using a legend
3. Knows and uses cardinal directions
4. Locates the home community, state, and nation on maps and globes
5. Identifies local landforms and waterforms
6. Identifies the types of transportation and communication used within the community
7. Describes effects of seasonal change on the local environment
8. Differentiates between maps and globes
9. Locates other neighborhoods studied on maps
10. Explains how neighborhoods depend on other neighborhoods to satisfy their wants and needs
11. Traces routes within and between neighborhoods using a variety of maps and models
12. Compares pictures and maps of the same area

Third grade
Community—sharing
space with others

1. Uses distance, direction, scale, and symbols in map reading
2. Helps prepare a community profile that includes features of the natural and built environment
3. Compares the home community with other communities
4. Compares rural and urban environments
5. Analyzes alternative uses of the environment in terms of positive and negative consequences
6. Describes how people depend on each other in communities including a focus on children, adults, and the elderly

(continued on next page)

FIGURE 7-5, continued
Geography Learning Experiences in the K–6 Expanding Environments Scope and Sequence

GRADE LEVELS AND GEOGRAPHIC FOCUSES	GEOGRAPHIC CONCEPTS AND SUGGESTED LEARNING EXPERIENCES
Third grade (continued)	7. Describes interaction in the community in terms of transportation and communication
	8. Describes how the community interacts with other communities and areas
	9. Determines the characteristics of a region and explains why the local community can be considered a region
Fourth grade The state, nation, and world	1. Interprets pictures, graphs, charts, and tables
	2. Works with distance, direction, scale, and map symbolization
	3. Relates similarities and differences between maps and globes
	4. Uses special-purpose thematic maps and maps of different scales
	5. Recognizes the common characteristics of map grid systems and map projections
	6. Discusses how regions are defined and how the regional concept is used
	7. Compares and contrasts regions on a state, national, or world basis
	8. Locates and describes major geographical features and regions
	9. Compares and contrasts major geographical regions in terms of their peoples, cultures, and environments
	10. Notes how regions change through time
	11. Demonstrates how people interact within and among states, nations, and the world
	12. Describes how people have adapted to and modified their environments in keeping with their values and understands how personal choices and behavior are related to life conditions of people in other places
	13. Examines the impact of technological advances on the built and natural environment
	14. Discusses how personal behavior could be changed to help solve a particular environmental problem
	15. Discusses how people of the world are linked by transportation and communication and how they help fulfill each other's needs and are dependent on each other
	16. Recognizes the relationships between human activities and characteristics of their locations (for example, work, recreation, shopping, education, religion)
Fifth grade United States, Canada, and Mexico	1. Recognizes distance, direction, scale, map symbols, and the relationship of maps and globes
	2. Works with latitude and longitude
	3. Uses maps, charts, graphs, and tables to display data
	4. Discusses location in terms of where and why
	5. Maps the correspondence between resources and industry
	6. Compares physical and cultural areas and regions within the United States

(continued on next page)

FIGURE 7-5, continued

Geography Learning Experiences in the K–6 Expanding Environments Scope and Sequence

**GRADE LEVELS AND
GEOGRAPHIC FOCUSES**

Fifth grade (continued)

**GEOGRAPHIC CONCEPTS AND
SUGGESTED LEARNING EXPERIENCES**

7. Maps physical and cultural regions in North America; explains how these regions are determined
8. Identifies, locates, and describes well-known economic areas in the United States, Canada, and Mexico
9. Compares the quality of life in various regions
10. Outlines regions within the United States, Canada, and Mexico on the basis of the location, movement, and concentration of different cultural groups
11. Compares and contrasts life in Anglo-America with life in Mexico and understands the interrelationships between these nations
12. Describes the positive and negative consequences of having other nations to the north and south of the United States
13. Describes the environmental deterioration in the United States, Canada, and Mexico related to growth and economic activity
14. Discerns ways in which personal choices and public decisions influence environmental quality
15. Identifies local, regional, national, and international problems that have geographic dimensions
16. Describes the territorial growth of the United States, Mexico, and Canada

Sixth grade
Latin America, Europe,
Middle East, Asia,
Africa, and Russia

1. Improves understanding of absolute location, relative location, and the importance of location
2. Uses maps, globes, charts, and graphs
3. Readily uses latitude, longitude, map symbols, time zones, and basic earth-sun relations
4. Gains insights about the interaction of climate, landforms, natural vegetation, and other interactions in physical regions
5. Uses cultural regions to study change in regions through time
6. Examines human-land adaptations in difficult environments
7. Perceives and analyzes migration patterns including rural to urban and between regions of different levels of development
8. Maps trade routes, particularly those connecting developed and developing nations
9. Divides several large regions into smaller regions based on race, language, nationality, religion, or some other cultural characteristic
10. Identifies important global problems with geographic dimensions and offers suggestions for improvement (for example, deforestation, desertification, pollution, and overfishing)
11. Plots distributions of population and key resources on regional maps
12. Examines relationships between personal and national choices and their consequences for people in other world regions
13. Explains problems with geographic tools and processes; suggests possible solutions

FIGURE 7-5, continued
Geography Learning Experiences in the K–6 Expanding Environments Scope and Sequence

number of buildings, roads, subdivisions, and cities. A final reason is that modern technology has supplied us with the ability to make maps more easily, and to make a great variety of special-purpose maps that communicate such things as rainfall, vegetation, temperature, and population density.

Because maps are so important, it is crucial that elementary social studies teachers internalize a few basic understandings about maps and follow some experience- and research-documented practices in teaching map skills to their students.

Basic Understandings about Maps and Globes

It is important to convey to children that maps are drawings that try to accurately show selected features of a place. Maps are a symbol system developed for the purpose of conveying spatial information about real places. It is important for children to understand that maps are never perfect and they never show all of the features that could possibly be included. Put another way, maps are selective abstractions of reality intended to convey specific information about the spatial distribution of phenomena.

Children's first mapping experiences should be done with familiar objects and locations such as their classroom or bedrooms. These maps should be quite simple, showing, in semipictorial form, only selected aspects of the chosen place. Initial errors in perspective (the "bird's-eye" or overhead view), distortion of scale, and minor errors in the location of objects should be expected. Building a three-dimensional model of a room in a shoe box, or using Lego® blocks to model a room, is an excellent way to intuitively introduce the ideas of scale, proportion, and relative location. Comparing different maps of the same area is another good way to introduce these concepts.

Once maps have been introduced, integrate their use into the daily routines of schooling. For example, use the classroom globe to locate a country mentioned by a child during current events or sharing period. Similarly, use a wall map of the United States to locate cities and states visited on children's family vacations. Opportunities for using maps will also arise during field trips, and during reading and language arts activities centered on specific places.

Periodically during their elementary school experience, give children the opportunity to make three-dimensional relief maps of places such as their school yard, neighborhood, suburb, city, county, state, and nation. These maps may be made of modeling clay, a flour-and-salt mixture, cardboard scraps, cereal boxes, paper maché, or any other available materials. Making maps is the best avenue to raise such questions as: How big should our map be? What features should be shown and how will they be made? Where is (*object X*) located in relation to (*object Y*) and how big should it be?

There are many types of globes available for classroom use. Major globe manufacturers make simplified physical/political globes for use in the primary grades. Such globes use large print and omit much of the detail included in upper-grade-level globes. Globes sold for school use often come with suggested teaching procedures. Children should learn that the globe is a model of the earth and that because it is round like the earth, it can show the surface of the earth without the distortion present in different world map projections. Globes are useful for demonstrating time zones, latitude and longitude, earth-sun relationships, and the great circle routes traveled by aircraft and watercraft.

K–6 teachers will also want to make use of computer-based atlases such as MacGlobe®, MacUSA®, PCGlobe®, and PCUSA®. These products provide easy access to simplified maps that may be displayed with or without cities, physical features, and natural resources. These maps may also be cut and pasted into students' reports or handouts developed by the teacher.

Introducing Map and Globe Skills in Grades K through 6

Figure 7-6 shows a sequence of sample learning activities for introducing map and globe skills in grades K through 6. The sequence is based on experience and available research evidence concerning what is instructionally appropriate for students at different grade levels. The sequence assumes that skills learned in earlier grades are retained and practiced in later grades, so this information is not repeated again in the figure. Due to differences among students, it may be necessary to adapt the skills shown at any grade level to meet the needs of your particular group.

Kindergarten

1. Describes the relative location of other persons or objects to himself or herself

2. Describes the relative location of objects shown in pictures ("The cat is on the chair next to the table.")

3. Maps facial features using paper plates, crayons, paint, and yarn

4. Maps the relative location of body parts by tracing around the body

5. Responds to instructions such as: point up/down; take two steps toward/away from me

6. Describes the natural and built environment between home and school, using terms like *hilly, flat,* a *river, trees, streets, stores, apartments,* and *houses*

7. Compares the natural and built environments in pictures of different places

8. Models landforms, waterforms, and features of the built environment in a sandbox

9. Describes the sizes and geometric shapes of objects and places

10. Recognizes a globe as a model of the earth and identifies land and water areas

(continued on next page)

◆ ◆

FIGURE 7-6
Introducing Map and Globe Skills in Grades K through 6[5]

[5]Adapted from *K–6 Geography: Themes, Key Ideas and Learning Opportunities* (Macomb, IL: National Council for Geographic Education, 1987), 7–44.

First grade

1. Draws a map of the classroom and talks about its features

2. Describes the location of the home in relation to the school

3. Names the home city or town and points to it on a simplified state map and/or globe

4. Names and points out the directions north, south, east, and west in the classroom

5. Points out continents and oceans on a globe and a world map and land and water in the local area

6. Compares the ways natural features appear in a picture, on a model, and on a map

7. Recognizes symbols as a means of communication

8. Creates a bird's-eye view map of familiar areas and objects

9. Recognizes that a map uses an overhead perspective, symbols to represent real things, and a key to explain symbols

10. Uses a map of the local area to estimate and classify distances between places (for example, near/far, nearer/farther, nearest/farthest)

11. Uses a map to trace routes students follow to and from school

12. Uses a map to identify regions in the local community (for example, shopping, residential, and industrial)

Second grade

1. Uses a map to identify the relative locations of places in and near the neighborhood

2. Builds models and draws maps to represent the location of places in the neighborhood

3. Uses cardinal directions to describe the location of places on maps and to orient oneself

4. Identifies by name continents and oceans on a globe and world map

5. Compares the appearance of landforms and waterforms on a picture, globe, and map

6. Discusses and helps make a class collection of the types of maps used to gain geographic/spatial information

7. Uses a map to draw a boundary around a neighborhood as students choose to define its limits

8. Compares older and newer maps and pictures to identify changes in the neighborhood over time

9. Uses maps to propose and evaluate routes for field trips or individual students' trips

Third grade

1. Uses a map and a globe to point out the location of the community, state, country, and continent relative to other places

2. Uses cardinal and intermediate directions to describe the relative location of places

3. Draws a map that shows the location of several landmarks in the community relative to the school

4. Locates places on a map using a number/letter grid reference system

5. Uses maps of the school, neighborhood, and community to design several different kinds of grid reference systems and test their ease of use and accuracy

6. Uses a map of the community to help decide where to locate a new shopping center

7. Draws a map of the community that shows natural characteristics

8. Interprets a diagram that shows the earth's rotation on its axis to explain the causes of day and night

9. Draws a series of maps to show how the natural and built environments of the community have changed over time

10. Visits a small community and draws a map of it

(continued on next page)

FIGURE 7-6, continued
Introducing Map and Globe Skills in Grades K through 6

Third grade (continued)

11. Locates on country and world maps, natural areas such as forests, deserts, and mountains

12. Locates and maps places where agriculture, manufacturing, and recreation are activities on which the community depends

13. Draws established political boundaries on a map of the community

Fourth grade

1. Describes the relative location of places on local, state, national, and world maps

2. Points out the North and South Poles, the Equator, the Tropics of Cancer and Capricorn, and the Arctic and Antarctic Circles on world maps and globes

3. Uses maps and globes to identify the four hemispheres

4. Uses latitude and longitude to identify the location of places on maps and globes

5. Locates, on maps, major cities, mountain ranges, river systems, and geographic regions such as deserts

6. Analyzes maps to locate patterns of movement involving people, ideas, and products

7. Analyzes maps to determine the relationships among climate, natural vegetation, and natural resources

8. Selects, from maps drawn to different scales, the one most useful to describe the characteristics of a place

9. Uses symbols to represent places in state, national, and world maps

10. Locates and draws boundaries around areas that can be classified as regions

Fifth grade

1. Maps the major land and water features of North America

2. Designs symbols as references for map interpretation, placing them in a legend, and using them on a map

3. Uses maps and globes with scales expressed in metric and customary units

4. Constructs maps to show areas involved in environmental problems such as floods and droughts

5. Computes distances between countries and/or five major cities of North America and your community

6. Compares maps of North America that show landforms, climate, and natural vegetation regions to maps that show where people live

7. Examines a variety of thematic maps to determine the criteria used to draw regional boundaries

8. Demonstrates that by altering criteria, the boundaries change (for example, the "Sun Belt," oil, and corn-producing areas)

Sixth grade

1. Identifies on maps and globes the relative locations of physical and cultural features in South America, Eurasia, and Africa

2. Finds the latitudinal and longitudinal extent of South America, Eurasia, and Africa

3. Compares the locations of selected cities in South America, Eurasia, and Africa in terms of geographic factors such as bodies of water, natural resources, and energy

4. Compares the climate, landforms, waterforms, natural vegetation, and ecosystems within and between South America, Eurasia, and Africa

5. Analyzes maps of South America, Eurasia, and Africa to determine human characteristics such as race, language, nationality, and religion

FIGURE 7-6, continued
Introducing Map and Globe Skills in Grades K through 6

CONCLUDING THOUGHTS

Children need systematic instruction with appropriate curriculum resources if they are to develop the content understandings needed for basic geographic literacy and future geography instruction. Carefully designed lessons on map and globe skills are essential components of schooling too.

There is no lack of definition concerning what should be learned in geography and when this learning should be accomplished. There is no lack of grade-level-appropriate learning materials. Providing the kinds of experiences described in this chapter will help ensure that our nation is prepared for the demands of a global society with geographically literate citizens.

LANDMARKS NEAR YOUR SCHOOL

Grade: Second

Topic: Mapping landmarks on the route to school

Overview: Many children are unaware of the landmarks they pass on the way to school. This lesson uses music to motivate discussion of landmarks passed on the way to school. Students locate the landmarks on a map of the school's attendance boundary.

Objectives: As a result of this lesson, students will:

- define the term *landmark*
- identify landmarks that they pass on their way to school
- map the landmarks on a map of the school's attendance boundary

Suggested Time: Three to five class sessions

Materials/Resources Needed: Videorecording or photographs of landmarks from the area around the school, large-scale map of the attendance zone for the school, recording of "Wheels on the Bus" (optional)

Suggestions for Teaching the Lesson

Opening the Lesson: Begin this lesson by singing the "Wheels on the Bus" song, but tell the students that you are going to add some new lines to the song such as: "The bus goes by the grocery store." Ask the students to name some other places that the bus goes past and when you've gotten five or six items, start the song, including the new lines.

When the song is over, tell the students that this lesson is about landmarks that the students pass on their way to school.

Developing the Lesson: See if the students can define what the word *landmark* means. (A landmark is a notable natural or built feature of the environment, something that stands out and grabs our attention due to its unique characteristics.)

Survey the students to see if they can identify any landmarks that they pass on the way to school. List their contributions asking students to tell why they think the place they have named is a landmark. Now show pictures of the landmarks that you have photographed or videotaped.

Show the large-scale map of the school attendance zone and ask the students if they can correctly locate any of the landmarks on the map. Provide necessary help and generate discussion about locations using street names and making reference to where the students live.

If the map is large enough, tape the photographs to it. (If you have used a videorecording, let the children color pictures on small pieces of paper to tape to the map.) If your school-zone map is too small, tape the pictures around the map and run strings to pins that mark the locations of the landmarks.

Closing the Lesson: Allow the students to locate their own homes on the map. Point out any patterns or groupings that appear. Review the landmarks that are passed by having each child create a written list to turn in. (You may need to write the names of the landmarks so that they can be copied or, alternatively, allow inventive spelling.)

Evaluating the Lesson

Key questions for the students:

What is a landmark?

What are some of the landmarks that you see on your way to school?

Where are they located (show me on the map)?

Alternative Teaching Suggestions

Take a walking tour of the landmarks, photographing them once again with the children in front.

Invite parents to come in and see the map of landmarks made by the students. Ask parents to go on a walking tour of the landmarks with their children.

MAPPING CULTURAL AND ETHNIC REGIONS

Grade: Fifth

Topic: Creating a cultural and ethnic region map of the United States

Overview: Students in the fifth grade may be unaware of the ethnic and cultural diversity that exists in the United States. In this activity students use an outline map of the United States and data concerning each state's ethnic composition to create a map of cultural and ethnic regions.

Objectives: As a result of this lesson, students will:

- determine and draw ethnic and cultural boundaries on an outline map of the United States
- make decisions about criteria to be used in determining ethnic and cultural boundaries
- create a map legend that explains the symbol and coloring system used to depict cultural and ethnic regions

Suggested Time: Three to five class sessions

Materials/Resources Needed: Almanac, PC-USA (optional), outline maps of the United States, colored chalk for shading areas on the map (overhead transparencies and markers may be used if preferred)

Suggestions for Teaching the Lesson

Opening the Lesson: Begin this lesson by asking the students to identify their own ethnic heritages. List the groups and then show the following data based on the 1990 U.S. census.

European American	81.0%	202.0 million
African American	10.0%	25.0 million
Hispanic American	6.0%	15.0 million
Asian American	2.5%	6.3 million
Native American	0.5%	1.3 million

Point out that these groups of people are not equally distributed across the United States. Tell the students that, for example, the African-American population was distributed with 11.3 percent in the Northeast, 10 percent in the Midwest, 18.8 percent in the South, and 5.6 percent in the West. Point out these regions on the outline map of the United States and shade them with colored chalk, showing the greater concentration in the South.

Ask the students if they know where the Hispanic-American, Asian-American, and Native-American populations are concentrated? Allow guesses, but challenge the students to tell how they could verify their guesses. (A current almanac would be a good place to start. Popular demographic software such as PC-USA or MacUSA will also have this kind of information.)

Developing the Lesson: Divide the class into four research groups, one each for African Americans, Hispanic Americans, Asian Americans, and Native Americans. Tell the groups that their task is to identify the percentage of the minority population for each of the fifty states. Once they have their data, they must decide how to show it on the outline map of the United States.

Closing the Lesson: Have the groups present their data, describing those regions that have the greatest concentrations of their minority. If overhead transparencies have been used, the maps can be superimposed over one another, presenting a diversity mosaic for the nation.

Evaluating the Lesson

Key questions for the students:

Why do some areas have larger concentrations of different racial and ethnic groups?

How did the maps you helped make show this information?

Alternative Teaching Suggestions

Divide the class into more groups to represent European-American ethnic groups and map these in addition to the minority groups.

Discuss how the presence of a particular minority group or ethnicity affects the culture of an area. For example, how are New Orleans and Louisiana affected by the Cajun culture that inhabits this region?

RESOURCES

The Geography Education Program, of the National Geographic Society, supports state-based Geographic Alliance organizations, provides summer institutes for classroom teachers, supports the development of curriculum materials, and promotes public awareness through Geography Awareness Week and its *Update* newsletter. For information write: Geography Education Program, National Geography Society, Washington, D.C. 20036.

Geography for Life: National Geography Standards 1994 is the official statement of K–12 curriculum standards for the United States, produced by the Geography Education Standards Project, developed on behalf of the American Geographical Society, the Association of American Geographers, the National Council for Geographic Education, and the National Geographic Society.

Guidelines for Geographic Education: Elementary and Secondary Schools, available from NCGE, explains the five themes of geography and how they should be used at each grade level in school.

Helping Your Child Learn Geography, prepared by Carol Sue Fromboluti, OERI, U.S. Department of Education, is available from the Consumer Information Center, Pueblo, CO 81009.

The Journal of Geography is published six times a year by the National Council for Geographic Education. It features a broad assortment of articles designed to improve the teaching of geography.

K–6 Geography: Themes, Key Ideas and Learning Opportunities, available from NCGE, describes learning activities that teach important geographic concepts, knowledge, skills, and attitudes.

Map and Globe Skills: K–8 Teaching Guide, by Barbara J. Winston, offers a discussion of general considerations in effective instruction, followed by a grade-level outline of a K–8 map and globe skills program.

National Council for Geographic Education [NCGE] (Leonard 16A, Indiana University of Pennsylvania, Indiana, PA 15705) distributes *Guidelines for Geographic Education: Elementary and Secondary Schools, Map and Globe Skills: K–8 Teaching Guide*, and *K–6 Geography: Themes, Key Ideas and Learning Opportunities*.

National Geographic Kids Network provides a series of curriculum units that use the power of telecommunications to help students conduct geographic investigations using computer-generated maps and charts. For information contact: National Geographic Educational Services, Washington, D.C. 20036, or phone 1-800-368-2728.

Update is published by the National Geographic Society (17th and M Streets NW, Washington, D.C. 20036) to provide teachers with educational materials and to publicize the education efforts of the National Geographic Society.

REFERENCES AND SELECTED READINGS

Allen, R. F., and Hoge, J. D. 1990. Literature study for geographic literacy grades 3 to 6. *Social Studies and the Young Learner* 2(4):3–6.

Backler, A., and Stoltman, J. 1986. The nature of geographic literacy. ERIC digest no. 35. Bloomington, IN: ERIC Clearinghouse for Social Studies/Social Science Education.

Bednarz, S. W., Bettis, N. C., Boehm, R. G., de Souza, A. R., Downs, R. M., Marran, J. F., Morrill, R. W., and Salter, C. L. 1994. *Geography for life*. Washington, D.C.: National Geographic Research and Exploration.

Bein, F. L. 1990. Baseline geography competency test: Administered in Indiana universities. *Journal of Geography* 89(6):260–265.

Cohen, H. G. 1986. First lesson in map use: The primary grader. *The Social Studies* 77(3):162–164.

Grosvenor, G. M. 1989. Superpowers not so super in geography. *National Geographic* 12:816–821.

Guidelines for geographic education: Elementary and secondary schools. 1984. Macomb, IL: National Council for Geographic Education.

Lockledge, A. 1991. Elementary place geography: Beyond memorization. *Journal of Geography* 90(1):33–36.

Melahn, D. 1989. Putting it in perspective: Geography activities for primary children. *Journal of Geography* 88(4):137–139.

Murphey, C. E. 1991. Using the five themes of geography to explore a school site. *Journal of Geography* 90(1):38–40.

National Assessment of Educational Progress. 1988. Geography assessment. Princeton, NJ: Educational Testing Services.

National Assessment of Educational Progress. 1990. *The geography learning of high school seniors*. Princeton, NJ: Educational Testing Services.

Stoltman, J. P. 1992. Research on geography teaching. In *Handbook of research on social studies teaching and learning*, ed. J. P. Shaver, 437–447. New York: Macmillan.

_____. 1992. *Teaching map and globe skills K–6: A teacher's handbook*. Skokie, IL: Rand McNally and Company.

Stoltman, J., and Libbee, M. 1988. Geography in the social studies scope and sequence. In *Strengthening Geography in the Social Studies*, ed. J. S. Natoli, 42–58. Bulletin no. 81, National Council for the Social Studies.

Sunal, C. S. 1987. Mapping for the young child. *The Social Studies* (July/August):178–182.

CHAPTER 8

Economics: Explaining Money and More

I really wanted the baby, at least that's what I thought when I first found out that I was pregnant. You know, your period is late and then you get worried. A home test showed it, so I was pretty sure it was for real. I didn't see a doctor for three months and didn't tell my Mom until after my first [doctor's] visit. The doctor said that the baby was healthy and that I was lucky that I didn't smoke or drink or do drugs. I had just turned fifteen and she said that I had to tell my Mom before the next visit.

My home situation isn't too good. I've got two younger brothers and my Mom works as a teller at the Bank of Boston. My father lives in Memphis and he sends money but it's not very much.

I waited as long as I could to tell my Mom because I knew it would hurt her. She wanted me to go on to college and all. I knew that she was going to be angry, but there was nothing I could do. I had started to show pretty bad several weeks after the doctor's visit and I think my Mom could tell something was wrong.

When we talked that night I wasn't surprised that Mom was more upset about what the baby would do to my life than the fact that I had been sexually active. When I told her I wasn't sure who the father was, that really upset her. She said she didn't know how she could feed one more mouth. I wanted to tell her I would go to work, but that didn't make sense with the baby needing me all of the time.

It was then that I began to realize what a jam I was in and how it was going to hurt my entire family and change the rest of my life.

INTRODUCTION

The opening scenario should activate feelings and thoughts about a number of issues, many of which have economic consequences for individuals and our society. Consider the following facts:

- Unmarried U.S. teenagers between fifteen and nineteen gave birth to 203,000 children in 1992.[1]
- We, as a nation, are number one in teenage pregnancy among the world's most advanced industrialized nations.
- We have, per capita, twice as many teenage pregnancies as the United Kingdom, three times as many as Sweden, and six times as many as the Netherlands.
- About half of our teenage pregnancies result in birth, one-third in abortion, and the remainder in miscarriage.
- Each year about 10,000 U.S. girls, fourteen and under, give birth.
- Families begun by teenage mothers cost the U.S. government about $21 billion in 1989.[2]

We'll come back to the opening scenario at the end of the chapter, but keep it in mind as we explore the discipline of economics. Much of what we'll learn here applies to everyday living—even an unexpected pregnancy.

THE DISCIPLINE'S PERSPECTIVE

Economics is the study of how goods and services are produced and distributed. Economists examine how individuals, families, businesses, and governments decide how to use their limited resources to meet everyday needs. They also investigate how to make systems of production and distribution work better.

As a field of study, economics had its beginnings in the tumultuous eighteenth century. The agricultural and later industrial revolutions, the colonization of North and South America, the declaration of the United States' independence, and the French Revolution reflect the world-changing influences that economic forces were exerting on the lives of people and nations. In 1776 Adam Smith published *An Inquiry into the Nature and Causes of the Wealth of Nations*, the first comprehensive analysis of the way economic forces shape society. Smith's central thesis, which lives on today as a guiding principle of free enterprise, was that people should be free to pursue their own economic self-interest with minimal government interference.

Economics is rich in conceptual content and this conceptual content forms the basis for an economic way of thinking. The development of these concepts

---

[1]*The Universal Almanac*, 1992, 294. (Figures were supplied by the U.S Census Bureau.)
[2]Shapiro, 1992, 14–15.

and the economic decision-making skills are the main outcomes of economics instruction with K–6 children.

Concepts and Generalizations

Like it or not, you deal with economics every day of your life, from conception to death. To illustrate this assertion, let's take a moment and focus on a single aspect of life: the personal and societal costs of the birth of a child. This single, significant event in the life of a person has broad economic consequences for both the individual and society. Let's consider the individual view first, imagining the economic costs (monetary expenses, nonmonetary productive resources spent, and the opportunities forgone) associated with the birth of a child. We will consider the monetary costs first.

Prior to the birth of a child there are monetary expenses for prenatal care. The office visits require physician's fees and the costs of any special tests and necessary vitamins or mineral supplements. Of course, trips to the doctor's office require money for gasoline and parking fees, or bus fare. As the mother's size increases, there is the cost of maternity clothes and/or alterations to existing clothes. At the birth of the child there are doctor's bills, hospital charges, and lab fees. If there are complications in the childbirth, costs go up dramatically. Of course, there are new expenses associated with daily living—a crib for the baby, diapers, ointments, powders, and specialized foods.

Parents also expend nonmonetary resources at the birth of a child. They may devote some area of the house or apartment, perhaps a whole room, to the new family member. Information about infant care and child rearing will have to be gained, so it is not uncommon for prospective parents to spend time, energy, and intellectual resources preparing for the new baby.

In addition to the monetary and nonmonetary expenses, a woman having a new baby has opportunity costs associated with the event. Opportunity costs are the value of what has to be given up to have the chosen alternative. A woman may lose some employment opportunity as result of having a baby. This loss could be small, such as a missed sale opportunity, or large, such as an extended loss of employment. Opportunity costs may extend beyond employment, however. The new mother may miss an opportunity for a vacation or some other activity that she can no longer afford or consider.

From the societal point of view, there are quite a few monetary expenses associated with the birth of a baby. Among these are government record keeping, regulation of health and insurance industries, public hospitals, childbirth services for mothers without health insurance or the ability to pay for proper medical care, government-funded health research, and educational outreach programs. Beyond this, each child added to the population base will need a seat in a public or private school classroom for thirteen years of formal education. Each child will be an added burden on the existing infrastructure of government-funded highways, sewage systems, the power supply, and law enforcement. The list could go on and on.

There are also nonmonetary expenses and opportunity costs for society. Governments have a limited number of resources with which to meet the needs of the community. Officials could allocate existing space in government offices and public hospitals to other uses. Planning and coordination efforts drain intellectual resources away from other areas. Society's opportunity cost associated with a woman's decision to have a new baby is the temporary or permanent loss of that woman for other purposes. If she, for example, had great artistic talent and chose to devote thirty years to child rearing, delaying, or never undertaking her work as an artist, then society loses the aesthetic benefits it would have otherwise gained.[3]

Figure 8-1 provides one view of the major concepts and ideas of economics. Before you look at the outline, take a moment and write down ten concepts from economics that you expect to appear in the outline. Give yourself one point for each that you find. Grade yourself: expert economist = 9 or 10; economist = 8; junior economist = 7; on your way to economic literacy = 6; and below 6 = improvement needed.

EXERCISE 8-1

1. After you have read through the outline, take a life event such as the birth of a child and go back through the outline, identifying the ways in which each of the concepts applies (if at all) to that event. For example, how does the economic idea of specialization apply to the birth of a child? Are there specialized doctors, services, goods, and markets associated with the baby industry? If the entire world followed Japan's recent trend of dramatically reduced fertility, what occupations or services would likely experience a recession? After you have finished an analysis of a life event such as birth, select another life event (such as death, graduation from college, marriage, or retirement) and repeat the exercise.

2. Make a short list of economics concepts that you know little or nothing about. Look up the terms in a dictionary, an encyclopedia, and a high-school or college economics textbook. Share your learning with the class.

3. Select a single term in the content outline and conduct a key-word search of recent newspaper articles. For example, conduct a search with the key word *taxes*. Report the results of your search to the class, sharing some of the article titles and, if possible, contents. If you have trouble finding articles with the key words you selected, attempt to explain why you obtained such poor results. (Is the concept unimportant? Is it too difficult for the common public to understand? Are reporters and editors more interested in covering crime and sports?)

---

[3]I want to note that it is possible—and in my opinion desirable—to put men and women on an equal footing in regard to career and family choices. The career *or* family choice is not applied to men and it should not be applied to women, although in contemporary society it often is. It is possible, of course, that the woman's service and success at child rearing will result in far greater good than what might have come from pursuing an art career without the child-rearing experience. Children, well raised, are of immense value to society.

I. Major Concepts and Ideas
  A. Scarcity
    1. Unlimited wants
    2. Needs
    3. Limited resources
    4. Resource allocation
  B. Opportunity Costs/Trade-Offs
  C. Productivity
    1. Specialization
    2. Division of labor
    3. Competition
    4. Interdependence
  D. Types of Economic Systems
    1. Traditional economy
      a. Bartering
      b. Mercantilism
    2. Command economy
    3. Free market economy
    4. Mixed economy
  E. Supply and Demand
    1. Price
    2. Advertising
    3. Entrepreneurship
    4. Other factors affecting supply and demand
  F. Economic/Financial Institutions
    1. Federal Reserve System
      a. Monetary policy
      b. Gold reserves
      c. Money
    2. Stock markets
    3. Commodity markets
    4. Banks and thrifts
      a. Checking accounts
      b. Saving accounts
      c. Credit/Loans
        1. Credit cards
        2. Home loans
        3. Auto loans
      d. State and federal regulation
  G. Factors of Production
    1. Natural resources
    2. Human resources
    3. Capital resources
  H. Markets and Competition
    1. Competitive
    2. Oligopoly
    3. Pure monopoly
    4. Marketing process
      a. Retailers
      b. Wholesalers
      c. Cooperatives
  I. Goods and Services
    1. Goods
    2. Services
    3. Economic utility of goods and services
    4. Economic value of goods and services
  J. Government in the Economy
    1. Regulatory agencies
    2. Wage and price controls
    3. Price supports
    4. Sources of revenue
      a. Local taxes
        1. Property
        2. Sales
      b. State taxes
        1. Income
        2. Sales
      c. Federal taxes
        1. Income
        2. Social security
        3. Gasoline and other consumption taxes
    5. Government spending
      a. Federal budget
        1. Defense
        2. Social programs
        3. Deficit
    6. Labor relations
      a. Minimum wage
      b. Child labor laws
      c. Safety regulations
      d. Collective bargaining
      e. Fair employment standards

(continued on next page)

◆ ◆

FIGURE 8-1
Conceptual Content of Economics[4]

---

[4]This outline is adapted from the Social Studies Content Descriptor Project, Educational Products Information Exchange Institute. Used by permission.

7. International trade
   a. Protective tariffs
   b. Quotas
   c. Trade coalitions
   d. Balance of trade
8. Public utilities
9. Public services
K. Economic Problems
   1. Unemployment
   2. Poverty
   3. Recession
   4. Depression
   5. Inflation
L. National Economic Goals
   1. Price and wage stability
   2. Full employment
   3. Market freedom
   4. Growth
M. Income
   1. Wages and salaries
   2. Dividends and interest
N. Gross Domestic Product
O. Business Organizations
   1. Sole proprietorship
   2. Partnership
   3. Corporations
P. Business Cycles
Q. Labor Unions
   1. Labor Laws/Bargaining process

   2. Labor/Management conflicts
   3. Nonunion companies and
      workers
R. Energy and the Economy
   1. Domestic and imported oil
   2. Coal
   3. Nuclear
   4. Solar and other
   5. Energy conservation
S. Developing Nations
T. Consumer Economics
   1. Budgeting
   2. Consumer agencies and services
   3. Saving and investing
U. Economic Change
II. Methods and Procedures
   A. Economic Decision Making
   B. Cost-Benefit Analysis
   C. Statistical Concepts
      1. Mean/Median/Mode
      2. Standard deviation/Variance
III. History of Economic Thought
   A. Adam Smith
   B. John Locke
   C. Karl Marx
   D. John Maynard Keynes
   E. Milton Friedman

FIGURE 8-1, continued
Conceptual Content of Economics

WHAT K-6 STUDENTS SHOULD KNOW

The National Council on Economic Education (NCEE) promotes the economic education of precollege students. The NCEE has developed a multipart *Master Curriculum Guide in Economics* that provides a plain-language explanation of economic concepts for K–12 teachers, sample lesson plans at each grade level, and a scope and sequence for teaching economics.

Economic Learning Experiences in the K-6 Scope and Sequence

Figure 8-2 shows the NCEE recommended scope and sequence of major economics concepts for grades K through 7.

While Figure 8-2 shows the major concepts teachers should introduce and reinforce at grade levels K through 7, it does not help teachers determine

CONCEPTS	GRADE LEVELS			
	K–1	2–3	4–5	6–7
Scarcity	N	R/N*	R/N	R/N
Opportunity cost and trade-offs		N	R/N	R/N
Productivity		N	R/N	R/N
Economic systems			N	R/N
Economic institutions and incentives			N	R/N
Exchange money and interdependence	N	R/N	R/N	R/N
Markets and prices	N	R/N	R/N	R/N
Supply and demand			N	R/N
Competition and market structure		N	R/N	R/N
Income distribution				N
Role of government		N	R/N	R/N
Gross national product				N
Unemployment			N	R/N
Absolute and comparative advantage and barriers to trade			N	R/N
Exchange rates and the balance of payments				N

*N = New content introduced   R = Content reinforced/reviewed

FIGURE 8-2
Economics Scope and Sequence for Grades K through 7[5]

exactly what they should teach about each concept. For example, what should you teach about the role of government in grades 2 through 3? Or, what should children learn about unemployment in grades 4 through 5? Answers to these questions are supplied by the NCEE curriculum materials featured at the end of this chapter.

Main Ideas and Generalizations for Economic Education

Figure 8-3 displays main ideas and generalizations from economics to teach K–7 children. As you read Figure 8-3, look back to the chart shown in Figure 8-2 to confirm the grade-level placement and conceptual base of the recommended main ideas and generalizations.

---
[5]Taken from *Economics: What and When*, 1988.

GRADE LEVELS AND CONCEPTS	MAIN IDEAS AND GENERALIZATIONS
K–1 **Scarcity**	Scarcity is the condition of not being able to have all of the goods and services that you want.
Exchange, money and interdependence	Trading goods and services with people for other goods and services or for money is called exchange.
Markets and prices	A price is the amount of money that people pay when they buy a good or service.
2–3 **Scarcity**	Scarcity requires people to make choices about using goods and services to satisfy wants.
Opportunity cost and trade-offs	Opportunity cost is the highest valued alternative that must be forgone because another option is chosen.
Productivity	Economic specialization occurs when people produce a narrower range of goods and services than they consume.
Exchange, money and interdependence	People exchange goods and services voluntarily because they expect to be better off after the exchange.
Markets and prices	A market exists whenever buyers and sellers exchange goods and services.
Competition and market structure	A market is a setting where buyers and sellers establish prices for identical or very similar products.
The role of government	Government provides some goods and services.
4–5 **Scarcity**	Like individuals, governments and societies experience scarcity because their productive resources are limited and their wants are virtually unlimited.
Opportunity costs and trade-offs	Whatever resources are used to produce a particular good or service, the opportunity cost is not being able to produce the next most valued alternative.
Productivity	A society can increase the level of output in its economy through specialization.
Economic systems	The U.S. economy is organized around a system of private markets in which prices for goods and services are determined.
Economic institutions and incentives	Profit is the difference between revenues and the costs entailed in producing or selling a good or service; it is a return for risk taking.

(continued on next page)

FIGURE 8-3

Main Ideas and Generalizations for Economic Education Grades K through 7[6]

[6]This is an abbreviated listing taken from *Economics: What and When,* 1988.

GRADE LEVELS AND CONCEPTS	MAIN IDEAS AND GENERALIZATIONS
4–5 (continued) Exchange, money and interdependence	Money is any generally accepted medium of exchange. Money has generally replaced barter as a more efficient system for exchange. The basic money supply is usually measured as the total value of coins, currency, and checkable deposits held by the public. Banks play a key role in providing currency and other forms of money to consumers, and serve as intermediaries between savers and borrowers.
Markets and prices	The market clearing or equilibrium price is the one price level at which quantity supplied equals quantity demanded.
Supply and demand	If the price of a product increases, quantity demanded will decrease and quantity supplied will increase. If the price of a product decreases, quantity demanded will increase and quantity supplied will decrease.
Competition and market structure	The level of competition in a market is largely determined by the number of buyers and sellers in the market.
The role of government	The government pays for the goods and services it produces through taxing and borrowing.
Unemployment	Unemployed people are those who are willing and able to work at current wage rates, but do not have jobs. People who are unemployed usually have less income to buy goods and services than those who have jobs. Governments provide income to some unemployed workers until they can find jobs.
Absolute and comparative advantage and barriers to trade	The quantity and quality of productive resources available in different nations vary widely.
6–7 Scarcity	Scarcity of resources necessitates making choices at both the personal and societal levels.
Opportunity costs and trade-offs	All decisions involve opportunity costs; weighing these costs and the benefits associated with alternative choices constitutes effective economic decision making.
Productivity	Productivity refers to a ratio of output (goods and services) produced per unit of input (productive resources) over some time period. Specialization and division of labor usually increase labor productivity. Productivity can be increased by providing labor with additional capital goods.

(continued on next page)

FIGURE 8-3, continued

Main Ideas and Generalizations for Economic Education Grades K through 7

GRADE LEVELS AND CONCEPTS	MAIN IDEAS AND GENERALIZATIONS
6–7 (continued) **Economic institutions and incentives**	In a market economy, the pursuit of economic self-interest is a basic motivation that leads people and businesses to provide goods and services that other people want.
Markets and prices	Relative prices refer to the price of one good or service compared to the prices of other goods and services, and are the basic measure of the relative scarcity of a product when prices are set by market forces (supply and demand). Relative prices provide the key signals used by consumers and producers to answer the three basic economic questions: What to produce? How to produce it? Who will consume it?
Supply and demand	Forces of supply and demand determine prices, which are measures of the relative scarcity of different products. Demand is the schedule of how much consumers are willing and able to buy at all possible prices in a given period of time. Supply is the schedule of how much producers are willing and able to sell at all possible prices in a given period of time. The level of competition among producers or buyers affects supply and demand forces and prices for different products.
Competition and market structure	An industry is made up of all the producers of identical or very similar products in a market area. Active competition among sellers results in lower prices and profit levels. A monopoly exists when only one producer sells a product that has no close substitutes.
The role of government	In a market economy, the government defines and enforces property rights and provides standard units of weights, measures, and money. Operating a government requires shifting scarce resources from the private to the public sector.
Unemployment	The labor force is composed of people age 16 and over who are either employed or actively seeking work. The unemployment rate rises during a recession.
Absolute and comparative advantage and barriers to trade	International trade is the exchange of goods and services between people and institutions in different nations. Exports are goods and services produced in one nation but sold to buyers in another nation. Imports are goods or services bought from sellers in another nation. International trade promotes greater specialization, and specialization increases total world output.

◆ ◆

FIGURE 8-3, continued

Main Ideas and Generalizations for Economic Education Grades K through 7

Economists use factual information, economic concepts, and generalizations to analyze economic issues, to answer economic questions, and make economic decisions. This sounds like—and is—high-level intellectual functioning. However, even children are capable of making economic decisions by applying economic concepts in a simple, five-step decision-making process. Figure 8-4 demonstrates how this might happen based on a nine-year-old child's opportunity to purchase candy with his allowance.

What economic concepts were used in the child's purchase of the chocolate candy? (Well, he wasn't thinking about the balance of payments or the concept of a pure monopoly, but he probably was thinking about concepts such as *price*, *wants*, *limited resources*, *money*, *sales tax*, and *opportunity cost*.) Did the child think about and use the concepts correctly? (For the most part he did pretty well for a nine year old.) Were there any flaws in the child's economic thinking? (It was not clear that he applied all of his criteria to each piece of candy.) Do you suppose the purchase satisfied the child? (My experience raising children would support the judgment that children are often well satisfied with their first candy purchases—at least as long as they have not bought something that's lip-puckering green-apple sour or tongue-splitting hot

STEPS	SAMPLE QUESTIONS
1. Recognize the nature of the decision occasion.	*"Wow, I've got a whole dollar to spend now that I'm getting an allowance. I'm going to buy some candy at the Minute Market!"*
2. Identify available alternatives.	*"Hum . . . Looks like my choice is between a ChocoBlok, a CocoCube, and a Fudge DeeLite! Which should I choose?"*
3. Identify criteria for making the decision.	*"I want something chocolate, but I don't like coconut or almonds. The cost has to be under a dollar after sales tax, and I want the greatest quantity I can get for my money."*
4. Evaluate alternatives using criteria.	*"ChocoBlok says it's imported, super high-quality chocolate. But it's not very large. That rules it out. However the CocoCube is huge! Let's see. The ingredients label says it's . . . Yuk! filled with almonds! Let's see, the Fudge DeeLite price is seventy-five cents. Hmm, with tax that will still be under a dollar."*
5. Make decision.	*"Guess that means I'm buying the Fudge DeeLite."*

◆ ◆

FIGURE 8-4

Steps in Making an Economic Decision

like a cinnamon jawbreaker!) If you had been there to advise the child, what else might you have had him think about in making the decision? Would you have included criteria like making sure that the product had an unexpired freshness date or that the wrapper was intact? Do you suppose it would be a good or bad sign if the Fudge DeeLite was the last piece left in a large box? Experience—and often unspoken criteria—clearly plays a role in making purchases of all types.

Children will learn to apply the economic decision-making process if you teach it as a skill (see Chapter 3 for a skill-teaching model) and consciously apply it in many real-life situations. Occasions for using the model arise naturally throughout the year. The gift giving that often occurs during the winter break provides an opportunity to have children bring in advertisements from catalogs and newspapers to do catalog shopping and comparison pricing in the classroom. Encourage students to follow the decision-making model for each gift they would like to buy. What common and special criteria should they apply to gifts they might select for mothers, fathers, sisters, and brothers? What criteria would they want to apply in developing their own gift wish list?

The teacher and students may also apply the decision-making model to a fund-raising project. The first application of the model will be in deciding what service or product to sell. Students should consider their production resources; determine needed space; and identify required raw materials, machines, knowledge, and skills. Once the product or service is ready to sell, the next occasion to use the model will be in deciding how to use their profit. Students may first have to make a decision among dissimilar alternatives such as giving the money to charity, purchasing a new piece of playground equipment, or buying new books for the media center. Once decided, children could reapply the model to determine which charity, what kind of equipment, or what book titles and reading levels to purchase. The fund-raising activities of elementary-age children are excellent opportunities for teaching them the economic decision-making process and concepts such as *price, labor, profit, capital, supply*, and *demand*. Learning by doing, a basic principle of early childhood education, clearly applies to economic education.

MICRO-SOCIETY AND MINI-SOCIETY

Mini-Society[7] and Micro-Society[8] are instructional systems that simulate the operation of private enterprise and government within a school or individual classroom. In developing their own society, students learn fundamental economics and citizenship content as they apply basic skills to their everyday living problems. Both Mini-Society and Micro-Society promote learning by doing and invoke real life, logical consequences for students' actions.

---

[7]Kourilsky, 1983.
[8]Richmond, 1973.

As a first-year teacher in an inner-city fifth-grade classroom, George Richmond had to gain control. Over a period of three months he tried many tactics, but achieved only momentary success. Finally, he introduced a token currency that he used as pay for schoolwork. Students used their earnings to purchase refreshments and school supplies Richmond brought in at the end of the month. Wisely, Richmond decided to expand his token economy and develop a genuine Micro-Society. He expanded the society by allowing students to take on jobs within the classroom, purchase property, open businesses, and establish their own government.

Today schools around the country use Richmond's Micro-Society approach to help teachers establish a classroom climate that focuses on learning useful content and skills. Micro-Society often runs in more than one classroom and may become a schoolwide activity that occupies one or two periods each day. Social studies conferences around the nation offer workshops designed to introduce teachers to the basics of Micro-Society and school districts may offer in-service training for their own teachers. Richmond's book, *The Micro-Society School,* offers a full description of this particular approach to the development of a school micro-community.

Mini-Society, like Micro-Society, engages students in constructing their own classroom community. Dr. Marilyn Kourilsky's Mini-Society differs from Richmond's Micro-Society in the degree to which her approach is systematically organized, supported by student materials, and, perhaps most importantly, in how students are enlisted into the creation of their classroom community. Instead of introducing a token economy first, as Richmond did, Kourilsky recommends beginning by first introducing a problem of a scarcity of a desired resource. Students then propose different solutions to the distribution of this scarce resource and follow their plan. After a few days of operation, the teacher calls the students back together to discuss how their proposed solution is working. She asks if the students are still frustrated in their ability to gain access to the scarce resource—usually some art materials, a popular learning center, or other learning resources. (They usually are.) If the students don't come up with it on their own, she suggests allowing them to pay for access to the resource. (Economists call this a market mechanism for allocating scarce resources.)

The students are then encouraged to make a short list of things they could be paid for—keeping their desks clean, handing in homework, or coming to school on time. The teacher then holds a contest to create a classroom currency and begins introducing money into the children's economy. Soon the children develop businesses, apply for jobs, establish a bank, and begin the operation of government. Figure 8-5 offers a summary of the steps needed to begin a Mini-Society.

Because of the amount of work involved in creating a Mini-Society, it needs to run for at least ten weeks. Teachers often implement their Mini-Society units right after lunch in the time slot allotted to social studies. A Mini-Society can run for an entire school year if it is allowed to evolve and maintains students'

1. Create or emphasize a scarcity situation in your classroom or school.

2. Organize a whole-class interaction/discussion group that will meet regularly to analyze and debrief Mini-Society experiences.

3. Ask the students to propose solutions to the situation and act on one.

4. Introduce the idea of a market-based solution to scarcity situations.

5. Ask the students to identify school-related work for which they could be paid so that they will have money with which to purchase scarce resources. Set the compensation for school-related work to between five and ten units of scrip for each week. Quality of work counts.

6. Develop a school or classroom scrip to be used for all Mini-Society transactions. Consider different designs. Have different denominations such as 1s, 2s, 5s, 10s, 20s, and 50s.

7. Have the students identify private enterprise businesses to own (for example, a bank, a newspaper, a baseball or football card trading store, and a flower shop) or government jobs that they would like to have (for example, mayor, chief of police, and prosecutor). Students must apply for employment. Businesses must purchase space and pay any permit fees.

8. Begin the operation of your Mini-Society. Model reality as closely as possible, but do not allow inappropriate businesses (for example, fireworks vendors, or "adult" bookstores). Address problems as they come up, using the entire class to make decisions and set policy. Apply the three Rs to Mini-Society-related tasks. Have fun!

◆◆◆

FIGURE 8-5
Steps to Start a Mini-Society[9]

interest. Teachers have involved students at all grade levels in Mini-Society activities, although it is more common to find them in the fourth, fifth, and sixth grades than the primary grade levels.

Several problems are typical in the development of a Mini-Society. One of the biggest is establishing a value for the classroom or school scrip. Questions will arise as to how much a unit of the school's money is worth. Of course, the value of the school's scrip can be allowed to fluctuate, much as real currencies do, but the value must be reported periodically so that students can judge the fairness of prices and wages.

Another problem concerning a Mini- or Micro-Society is getting together the financial backing to launch the entire operation. Kourilsky suggests that parents allow their children to work for a small sum of money—real money—to be used to make the first purchases of items that will be sold in the students' businesses. Parents may also make direct donations of money or salable items. Some Mini- and Micro-Societies have been successful in soliciting donations (either money or salable items) from local businesses. Of course, students may raise money to implement their Mini- or Micro-Society by manufacturing items

---

[9]These steps are adapted from Kourilsky, 1983.

PRIVATE ENTERPRISE	GOVERNMENT
Message delivery/Post office	Mayor
Advertising agency	City Manager
Toy store	Sheriff/Deputy
Newspaper	Chief of police
Health food shop	Detective
Beverage shop	Prosecutor
Card shop	Jailer/Warden
Tutorial service	Police officer
Flower shop	Fire marshall
Fragrance boutique	Code inspector
Comics exchange	City clerk
Sports card exchange	Sanitation director
Hair and nails salon	Sanitation worker
Lottery game	Welfare director
Office/School supply store	Employment office worker
Conflict resolution and arbitration service	Tax collector

FIGURE 8-6

Sample Occupations in a Mini- or Micro-Society

for sale or selling services. Figure 8-6 presents a list of private enterprise and government jobs that can be developed in a Mini- or Micro-Society.

CONCLUDING THOUGHTS

I hope you feel like you've gained some new content understandings, goals, and methods for teaching economics to children in grades K through 6. To me, it's nice to know that there are some exciting ways to teach practical and empowering economics concepts and skills. Our society needs more rational thinkers; more doers; better businesses; and more highly motivated, competent government workers. (Did you realize that you're going to be a government worker as a public schoolteacher?)

I promised that we would return to the opening scenario at the end of the chapter once we had a little more economics under our belts. My goal in using the scenario—and the other data about pregnancy and childbirth—was to involve you in the content of economics in a highly engaging and perhaps personal way. I was hoping that you could relate to what our young, unnamed teenage girl was going through and the lifelong consequences of any alternative course of action that she might take.

It's clear that economics is playing a big role in the young woman's life. For the vast majority of U.S. citizens, educational attainment and employment opportunity are related. Events that make it more difficult to get an education make it more difficult to make a good living. An individual who is in a poor position to benefit himself or herself is also in a poor position to benefit his or her society. So it makes sense to help everyone achieve his or her highest potential. Here are some tough discussion questions that you can bring up in class.

DISCUSSION QUESTIONS

1. Would it be wise to use our tax dollars to provide free day care for the young woman's child while she finished high school? What data would you need in order to take a stand on this question? Would you want longitudinal data concerning earnings for groups of young women who did and did not receive this service? Would you want to know how well their children grew up—whether they became productive members of society?

2. Imagine that you have been presented with convincing evidence that a tax-supported abortion (before the end of the first trimester) saved our society $10,000 over allowing our teenage mother to carry and birth the baby. An additional $5,000 would be saved on tax-supported day care. Would this information influence how you might feel about a first-trimester abortion as a voluntary alternative for our imaginary young woman? If yes, why? If no, why not?

3. Does society have an obligation to help its citizens such as our young teenage mother? If we fail to provide services such as tax-supported day care, special opportunities to complete high school, or tax-supported abortion, are we endangering our overall quality of life? Take a stand and explain the basis of your position.

COSTS OF A CLEANER SCHOOL

Grade: Third or fourth

Topic: Superclean schools and playgrounds require increased labor and capital resources.

Overview: Virtually everyone prefers a clean, neat, litter-free environment. The question economics poses is what quantity of resources, both labor and capital, should be devoted to this goal when other competing desires also demand resources. This lesson uses a school cleanup cost estimate to demonstrate the fundamental idea that all activity entails costs that must be compared and balanced with other desired goals and activities.

Objectives: As a result of this lesson, students will:

- identify cleaning and repair problems that exist in the school
- estimate the cost of cleaning and repairing the school (include cost of resources used, time, wages, and so on)
- define and give examples of the economic terms: cost, labor, capital, wage, opportunity cost
- practice decision-making, valuing, and discussion skills
- assess their own involvement in maintaining a better-kept school

Suggested Time: Three to five class sessions

Materials/Resources Needed: Interviews with the principal and custodian; clipboards for surveys (optional); visit from an economist and/or home economist (optional); visit from a commercial cleaning company (optional); visit from a commercial landscaping company (optional); posting paper (optional)

Suggestions for Teaching the Lesson

Opening the Lesson: Start this lesson by asking the students if they have noticed any areas of the school that need to be cleaned up. Accept appropriate answers, listing them on the chalkboard or posting paper. Ask the students if they know (1) how these areas get dirty, (2) who cleans them, and (3) how often this happens?

Have the students close their eyes and get very quiet. Tell them you want them to think of a very beautiful school environment. (They might imagine fresh paint in beautiful colors; sparkling clean windows; a variety of indoor plants, fountains, mirrors, fresh landscaping, and so on.) They should see the walls, the windows, the floors, the lawn areas, the playground, and entrances to the building. Once they see these things in their minds' eyes, ask them to imagine quietly walking with you through their superclean building taking in the sights, smells, and sounds. (Use language with lots of imagery, such as "We're walking very quietly down the hallway. The floor is gleamingly clean. It's so shiny you can see reflections of walls and lights in it" Continue on for a few minutes, ending your imaginary tour back at your own classroom.)

Have the students open their eyes and briefly share how they felt about their imaginary walk. Tell them that in this lesson they are going to help do a survey of the school's condition and determine the cost of improving it.

Developing the Lesson: Divide the class into survey teams of three or four to scour the school for signs of dirt and damage. Form teams for walls, floors, doorways, ceilings, bathrooms, lawns and shrubs, and the playground. Have each team write down their findings and report back to the room.

As a class, tour the school now, letting each group read its report as you pass through the building and grounds.

Upon returning to your classroom, involve the students in compiling a master list of the most important items to clean up and repair. Ask them to reason concerning the items that are most important and those that are least important. See if the students can identify what the cleaning or repair costs might be for each item. Include estimates of time (wages) involved as well as materials such as cleaning supplies.

Invite the principal in to react to the list and confirm or revise the cost estimates. Have the school custodian come in and explain the cleaning schedule for the school. Have him identify the areas that take the most time and share his perception of the list compiled by the class. See if the custodian thinks that better, newer, or additional equipment would help make the cleaning faster. Point out that economists call these *capital expenditures. Capital* refers to money or equipment used to provide a service or make a product. Ask the custodian if he or she feels there is enough time to correct the problems the class has noted without jeopardizing the completion of other custodial duties. Point out that economists call money earned for performing a job *wages*. Wages for labor are a part of the cost of producing a service or good.

Closing the Lesson: Review what the class has found out. Take suggestions for correcting the problems noted in the surveys. See if the children want to be a part of the solution by volunteering time or bringing in cleaning materials. If there are volunteers, ask them what they must give up in terms of other goals if they participate in the cleanup. Point out that time spent cleaning cannot also be spent learning; money spent on cleaning supplies cannot also be spent on candy. These are both examples of what economists call opportunity costs, the alternative forgone due to the choices made.

Evaluating the Lesson

Key questions for the students:

What cleaning and repair problems exist in our school and what are the costs of correcting them?

How do the economic concepts and terms we learned (cost, labor, capital, wage, opportunity cost) help to explain why the school looks like it does?

How do the principal and custodian view the cleaning and repair problems we noted?

What role should schoolchildren play in maintaining or correcting such cleaning and repair problems?

Alternative Teaching Suggestions

Invite commercial cleaning and landscaping firms in to give the class a cost estimate for correcting the problems they found in the surveys. Raise the money to pay for the service. Write an article for the school or local newspaper about the project.

Compare your school with another in a nearby location. Have a school board member react to the findings.

Discuss: What is the optimal level of cleanliness for the school (according to students)? What is the point at which the elimination of more dirt becomes too costly?

ECONOMICS OF SEXISM AND SMARTS

Grade: Sixth
Topic: Sexual status (gender) and schooling (educational attainment) are related to income.
Overview: Economists are great number collectors and sometimes the numbers they collect tell us much about our society. In this lesson students will graphically see the data that proves that EDUCATION PAYS. Students are also introduced to data that show our society's economic discrimination against women.
Objectives: As a result of this lesson, students will:

- examine and graph data showing the income benefits of continued education
- examine and graph data showing income-based sex discrimination
- offer and analyze guesses regarding potential explanations for the noted income differences

- practice decision-making, valuing, and discussion skills

Suggested Time: Three to five class sessions
Materials/Resources Needed: Colored chalk for composite graphs of men and women's incomes

Suggestions for Teaching the Lesson

Opening the Lesson: Introduce this lesson by asking the students if they have ever heard the statement "education pays." See if individuals in the class can explain what the statement means (the more education you have the more you will likely earn once you start working). Tell the students that in this lesson they will see and graph data that prove this statement. In addition, students will also be introduced to evidence of wage and salary discrimination against women in our society.

Developing the Lesson: Show the the following data on the chalkboard:

1989 Median Annual Income for Year-Round Workers, Age 25 and Over
(Categorized by Educational Attainment)

	Men
Elementary school	
8 years or less	$17,204
High school	
1 to 3 years	$20,623
4 years	$25,859
College	
1 to 3 years	$30,406
4 years	$36,845

(These data were taken from the 1991 *Universal Almanac*.)

Explain that a median income is like an average income, in that it tries to give us a picture of what the average person earns with a certain level of education. (The median is actually the midpoint in the distribution of salaries, the point at which 50 percent of the incomes are above and 50 percent below.)

Ask the students to perform some simple math. Have them calculate the added benefit of finishing high school as opposed to dropping out in the freshman, sophomore, or junior years ($5,236). Explain that the high-school graduate gets this much more money EVERY YEAR. Have them calculate how much extra income this would mean over a ten-, twenty-, thirty-, or fourty-year period (10 = $52,360; 20 = $104,720; 30 = 157,080; 40 = $209,440). Perform similar calculations for the benefits of obtaining a college education.

See if the students can explain why people with more education make higher salaries. (Answers will vary, but should include the fact that people with more education are often given more responsibility; direct the work of others; make important decisions that affect the welfare of the entire company and all of its employees; and society simply attaches a higher value to the work that requires a greater amount of education.)

Now add the data for women to the chalkboard.

	Women
Elementary school:	
8 years or less	$11,712
High school	
1 to 3 years	$13,222
4 years	$16,865
College	
1 to 3 years	$20,764
4 years	$25,908

Explain that studies consistently show that for similar jobs, levels of experience, levels of education, and levels of responsibility, women in the United States earn between 60 percent and 80 percent of what men make. (In fact, the 1994 *Universal Almanac* reported that the median weekly earnings for U.S. women working full time in 1990 were $348. This compares to $485 for men, representing a 30 percent difference.) Tell the students that this is called *wage and salary discrimination.* Point out that both business and government employers can be sued for wage and salary discrimination.

See if the students can explain why men make higher salaries than women. Probe their reasons to see if they feel that any of them are justified.

Closing the Lesson: Divide the class into two or three groups of boys and two or three groups of girls. Ask the groups to make either a line or bar graph of the data for their gender. Have them share their work and select the best characteristics from each graph to make a large line and bar graph on the chalkboard (use colored chalk) showing the data for both men and women in each graph.

Conclude the lesson by asking the students whether they would like to see the gender-based differences eliminated and what an individual might do to help bring about greater salary equity.

Evaluating the Lesson

Key questions for the student:

What is the relationship between educational attainment and annual income?

Do women in the United States earn the same wages and salaries as men?

How can we explain the differences in salaries between men and women and among the different levels of education?

Alternative Teaching Suggestions

Use a current almanac to find more recent data on wage and salary differentials. Interview an economist concerning the information you have found. Write an article for the school or local newspaper about the project.

Conduct a survey of parents regarding the wage and salary differentials. Try to determine if they are aware of the differences that exist and whether they approve of them.

RESOURCES

The resources for teaching economics to children in grades K through 6 are substantial. Publishers produce a wide variety of children's books and audiovisual resources to support economics learning. Manufacturers often produce consumer-education-oriented materials that are made available free or at a reduced cost. The ERIC system contains units of instruction and lesson plans on many economics topics.

The National Council on Economic Education (432 Park Avenue South, New York, NY 10016, 1-800-338-1192) produces a wide range of economic education materials and maintains a network of affiliated state councils. A sample of some of the NCEE curriculum materials follows.

Basic Economics Test is a two-form, nationally normed test of economics knowledge based on the NCEE master curriculum guide.

Children in the Marketplace provides eight complete lessons for children in grades 3 through 4 that teach such topics as scarcity and choice, production, prices and the market, consumer decision making and investment. 96 pages.

Choices and Changes is a series of innovative lessons and fun-filled activities designed to demonstrate the link between education and future employment in society. Includes a teacher resource manual, black line masters, and student journals.

The Community Publishing Company is a grades 3-through-4 instructional unit designed to teach basic economic concepts. Students conduct community research, publish, and sell their report.

Econ and Me is a set of five 15-minute video lessons for seven- to ten-year-old children. The segments focus on scarcity, opportunity costs, consumption, production, and interdependence. The accompanying instructional manual contains resources for extending the video lessons.

Economic Education Experiences of Enterprising Teachers, produced annually, provides descriptions of award-winning, teacher-made economic education units, grades K through 12.

Economics: What and When Scope and Sequence Guidelines, K–12 offers help in selecting and sequencing the economics content of the *Master Curriculum Guide*. Available from NCEE.

Economics for Kids provides worksheets and activity ideas for teaching economics concepts, grades K through 7. Published three times a year.

Economics for Kids: Ideas for Teaching in the Elementary Grades is a practical guide to information pertaining to what, when, and how to teach economics to young children. It provides fifteen instructional activities, a brief bibliography, and suggestions for using community resources. 64 pages.

The Economics of Food and Fiber provides a variety of activities teaching the economics of the food and fiber system for grades K through 6. Grades K through 3, 44 lessons, 382 pages. Grades 4 through 6, 78 lessons, 425 pages.

Elementary Economist, published three times a year, offers lessons for grades K through 7 on specific themes. Each issue contains a plain-language, adult-level summary of the theme to help teachers fully understand the topic.

Kindereconomy + is a one-semester set of real-world experiences that integrates math, language, and performing arts. The program reinforces learning experiences through games, learning centers, worksheets, and market surveys.

Learning Economics Through Children's Stories is a bibliography of fiction and nonfiction for children in grades K through 6. 128 pages.

Strategies for Teaching Economics Intermediate Level (Grades 4–6) is a collection of lesson plans designed to teach concepts and generalizations from economics. Includes black line masters and complete teaching procedures.

Strategies for Teaching Economics Primary Level (Grades 1–3) is a collection of lesson plans designed to teach concepts and generalizations from economics. Includes black line masters and complete teaching procedures.

Trade-Offs is an audiovisual series designed to present core ideas in economics to children age 9 to 13. The series consists of fifteen 20-minute videos that develop economic concepts and reasoning. This series is aired regularly over many public and school-district broadcast facilities.

REFERENCES AND SELECTED READINGS

Banaszak, R. A. 1987. *The nature of economic literacy.* ERIC digest no. 41. Bloomington, IN: ERIC Clearinghouse for Social Studies/Social Science Education.

Economics: What and When. 1988. New York: National Council on Economic Education.

Korithoski, T., and Saunders, N. 1994. Mathematics and the federal debt. *Social Studies* 85(1):36–38.

Kourilsky, M. L. 1983. *Mini-society. Experiencing real-world economics in the elementary school classroom.* Menlo Park, CA: Addison-Wesley

Richmond, G. H. 1973. *The micro-society school. A real world in miniature.* New York: Harper & Row.

Robinson, M. A., Morton, H. C., and Calderwood, J. D. 1980. *An introduction to economic reasoning.* Garden City, NY: Anchor Books.

Rohlf, W. D., Jr. 1992. *An introduction to economic reasoning.* New York: Addison-Wesley.

Saunders, P., Bach, G. L., Calderwood, J. D., and Hansen, W. L. 1984. *Master curriculum guide in economics. A framework for teaching the basic concepts.* New York: National Council on Economic Education.

Shapiro, A. L. 1992. *We are number one!* New York: Vintage Books.

Shug, M. C., and Walstad, W. B. 1992. Teaching and learning economics. In *Handbook of research on social studies teaching and learning,* ed. J. P. Shaver, 411–419. New York: Macmillan.

CHAPTER 9

Political Science:
Government, Law, and Politics

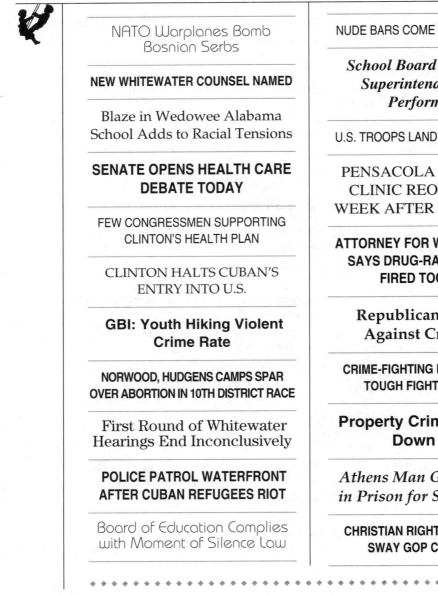

NATO Warplanes Bomb
Bosnian Serbs

NEW WHITEWATER COUNSEL NAMED

Blaze in Wedowee Alabama
School Adds to Racial Tensions

**SENATE OPENS HEALTH CARE
DEBATE TODAY**

FEW CONGRESSMEN SUPPORTING
CLINTON'S HEALTH PLAN

CLINTON HALTS CUBAN'S
ENTRY INTO U.S.

**GBI: Youth Hiking Violent
Crime Rate**

NORWOOD, HUDGENS CAMPS SPAR
OVER ABORTION IN 10TH DISTRICT RACE

First Round of Whitewater
Hearings End Inconclusively

**POLICE PATROL WATERFRONT
AFTER CUBAN REFUGEES RIOT**

Board of Education Complies
with Moment of Silence Law

NUDE BARS COME OUT OF CLOSET

***School Board to Evaluate
Superintendent's Job
Performance***

U.S. TROOPS LAND ON HAITIAN SOIL

PENSACOLA ABORTION
CLINIC REOPENS ONE
WEEK AFTER SHOOTINGS

**ATTORNEY FOR WINDER WIDOW
SAYS DRUG-RAID OFFICERS
FIRED TOO SOON**

**Republicans Line up
Against Crime Bill**

CRIME-FIGHTING BILL MOVES TO
TOUGH FIGHT IN SENATE

**Property Crime in Athens
Down 10%**

***Athens Man Gets 30 Years
in Prison for Selling Crack***

**CHRISTIAN RIGHT REBOUNDS TO
SWAY GOP CAMPAIGNS**

INTRODUCTION

The headlines featured on the opening page hint at the roles government, politics, and law play in our everyday lives. Indeed, it's hard to pick up a newspaper without bumping into such headlines. Sadly, many people skip to the sports page, the funnies, or society and advice columns. Worse still, articles on government, politics, and law may raise feelings of anger and frustration among citizens who do stop to read these stories. Sometimes these feelings come from a deep understanding of the issues and direct constructive involvement. But more often, they are assumed by individuals who haven't voted, aren't even registered, don't understand the issues or the processes, and are uninvolved in serving their home community. For the good of our nation, we need to turn this situation around and promote a more accurate and positive view of government, law, and politics.

As you may recall from Chapter 1, the fields of government, law, and politics are at the very core of the central citizenship purpose of social studies. After all, in the United States, it's *our* government, it's *our* laws, and like it or not, it's *our* politics! The roles we each play as a private person, as an employer or employee, and as a member of the public—a citizen of this great nation—are directly affected by government, law, and politics. The mission of social studies is to prepare children for their necessary involvement in government, law, and politics.

In this chapter, you'll gain an overview of the important and diverse content government, law, and politics hold for elementary social studies instruction. You'll become acquainted with what K–6 students should gain from this important portion of their social studies program. You'll see two examples of exemplary plans designed to teach portions of this important content. Finally, you'll gain an overview of the resources available to support your instruction.

THE DISCIPLINE'S PERSPECTIVE

The discipline of political science, perhaps because of its original academic and philosophical focus on the origins of government and law, is often thought of as the parent or foundation area for government, law, and politics.

As you might guess, political science traces its academic origins back to the period of Plato's *Republic*, though it would be correct to say that much earlier works, such as various books of the Old Testament, considered how a nation might be justly ruled.

Today, with a more empirical, data-based focus, political scientists study all activities of and influences on government from a national or international perspective. Topics of study include foreign policy; international law; national, state, and local governments; political institutions; political philosophy; government policies; party politics; public opinion; propaganda; and the influence of legislation on society.

You may be thinking, "Fine, but what does that have to do with young children?" Everything. Many of these very same topics are concerns, on a much smaller scale, in the everyday lives of children. For example, young children are naturally interested in the exercise of power and authority. They often test their own, attempting to determine who has control over what resources, what rules are to be strictly followed and what ones can be safely bent or altogether ignored. They want to know who is in charge and quickly determine whose authority must be obeyed under any given situation.

Within the family children generally know who bosses what—though they often have faulty explanations for the reasons behind rules caretakers enforce. Children hold misconceptions of the roles and powers of police, social workers, teachers, and many other types of government workers. In addition, they often fail to understand why they must get a vaccination before starting school, always use the crosswalk, attend one elementary school instead of another, and start school on a particular date; who determines the textbooks and other curriculum materials they use; and how standards for promotion are set.

Concepts and Generalizations

The conceptual content of political science, government, and law is substantial. To gain a quick overview of this content, examine the outline presented in Figure 9-1. But before you look over this outline, take out a scrap piece of paper and fold it into three columns. Label the columns "Government," "Law," and "Politics." In each column write five concepts that come immediately to mind. Now, as you examine the outline, circle or check each item that you find.

EXERCISE 9 - 1
◆ ◆ ◆ ◆ ◆

1. Now that you have read through the outline, look back at the Basic Concepts (I.A.) and Political Values (I.B.) sections and list the terms that you have never heard of or know very little about. Look them up in a dictionary or, better, check out a high-school or college textbook on government and read more about them.

2. Select one idea in Section II.B. that you have feelings about and write a one-page statement of your point of view. Turn this in to your instructor, inviting him or her to comment and open a written dialogue on this topic.

3. Many items are missing from the outline. Here are a few terms that got left out. Try to find where they would belong had they been included: impeachment, martial law, probation, bankruptcy, right to bear arms, government immunity, speaker of the house, Internal Revenue Service, nonmilitary foreign aid, Central Intelligence Agency.

4. Look up your local government in the phone directory. Based on the entries displayed there, expand the municipal government outline. What does this experience tell you about the other components of the outline?

I. Political Science
  A. Basic Concepts
    1. Natural rights
    2. Citizenship
      a. By birth
      b. Naturalization
      c. Rights and responsibilities
    3. Political power
    4. Government authority
    5. Government functions
      a. Establish order
      b. Provide services
  B. Political Values
    1. Rule of law
    2. Justice
      a. Equality under law
    3. Freedom
      a. Freedom of conscience
      b. Political freedom
      c. Freedom of speech
      d. Economic freedom
        1. Right to hold property
      e. Freedom of assembly or
         movement
    4. Right to security or life
    5. Separation of church and state
    6. Altruism/Public good/Patriotism
    7. Social equality (no nobility)
    8. Personal privacy
    9. Civilian control of military
II. Politics
  A. Political Participation
    1. Voting behavior
    2. Elections
    3. The role of media
  B. Political Ideas and Ideals
    1. Nationalism
    2. Federalism
    3. Majority rule
    4. Minority rights
    5. Proportional representation
    6. Political ideology
      a. Conservative
      b. Liberal

      c. Radical
    7. Political parties
      a. Democratic
      b. Republican
      c. Libertarian
    8. Public opinion
    9. Public disclosure
    10. Political rally
    11. Political platform
    12. Political patronage
    13. Party line vote
    14. Politician
    15. Political rank and file
    16. Political patronage
    17. Pork-barrel politics
    18. Pressure groups
    19. Propaganda and disinformation
    20. Bureaucracy
      a. Red tape
      b. Merit employment system
  C. Electoral Process
    1. Nomination
    2. Primary election
    3. Voting rights
III. Foundations of U.S. Government
  A. American Government Heritage
    1. Mayflower Compact
    2. The Colonial Period
    3. Declaration of Independence
    4. Colonial governments
  B. Principles of American Government
    1. Limited government
    2. Popular sovereignty
    3. Representative government
    4. Separation of powers
    5. Federalism
    6. Constitutional authority
  C. The U.S. Constitution
    1. Principles of the Constitution
      a. Federalism
      b. Separation of powers
    2. The constitutional convention
      a. Bill of Rights
  D. Freedom of Speech, Press, Religion

(continued on next page)

◆ ◆

F I G U R E   9 - 1
Conceptual Content of Political Science

IV. Federal Government Today
  A. Judicial Branch
    1. Supreme Court
    2. Court of Appeals
    3. District courts
  B. Legislative Branch
    1. Senate
    2. House of Representatives
    3. The legislative process
  C. Executive Branch
    1. The presidency
      a. Executive powers
        1. Military commander
        2. Legislative veto
        3. International treaties
    2. The vice-presidency
    3. The foreign service
    4. Foreign policy
    5. Fiscal policy
    6. International commerce
    7. The cabinet
    8. The federal bureaucracy
      a. Department of Agriculture
      b. Department of Commerce
      c. Department of Defense
      d. Department of Education
      e. Department of Energy
      f. Department of Health and Human
         Services
      g. Department of Housing and Urban
         Development
      h. Department of Interior
      i. Department of Justice
      j. Department of Labor
      k. Department of State
      l. Department of Transportation
      m. Department of the Treasury
      n. Department of Veterans
         Affairs
  D. Government Finances
    1. Revenues
      a. Income tax
      b. Social security receipts
      c. Borrowing

    2. Expenses
      a. Direct benefit payments
      b. National defense
      c. Interest on the national debt
      d. Grants to states and localities
  E. Government Oversight
    1. Regulation of commerce
      a. International trade agreements
      b. Domestic monopolies
    2. Reapportionment
      a. Redistricting
    3. Immigration and travel
      a. Passports and visas
V. National Governments
  A. Types of Governments
    1. Representative democracy
    2. Monarchy
    3. Dictatorship
    4. Communism/Centralized economy
  B. Functions
    1. Regulation of state governments
    2. Resolve conflicts between states
    3. International relations
      a. Diplomacy
      b. Trade policy
      c. Political terrorism
    4. National defense
      a. Intelligence services
      b. Military services
        1. Aggression deterrence
        2. Protection of commerce
      c. War
        1. Unlimited war
        2. Limited-objective war
        3. Cold war
        4. Police actions
        5. Blockades and embargoes
        6. Covert actions
VI. State Government
  A. State Constitution
  B. State Legislature
  C. State Courts
  D. Executive
    1. Governor

(continued on next page)

◆ ◆

FIGURE 9-1, continued
Conceptual Content of Political Science

2. Lieutenant Governor
E. State Services
   1. Education
   2. Business regulation
   3. Public assistance
   4. State militia
VII. County Government
   A. Courts
   B. Sheriff's Department
   C. Road Department
   D. Health Department
   E. Fire Protection
VIII. Municipal Government
   A. Mayor and City Manager
   B. City Council
   C. Municipal Services
      1. Sewers
      2. Water
      3. Roads
      4. Law enforcement
   D. Municipal Revenue
      1. Sales tax
      2. Licenses and fees
IX. Law
   A. Law Concepts
      1. Civil rights
      2. Due process
      3. The adversary system
   B. Components
      1. Courts
         a. Judges
         b. Sheriffs
      2. Lawyers
      3. Police
      4. Corrections
   C. Legal Rights
      1. Trial by jury
      2. Speedy and public trial
      3. Cross-examine witnesses
      4. Self-incrimination
      5. Legal representation
   D. Civil Law
      1. Consumer law
         a. Sales and service contracts

b. Warranties
c. Credit law
d. Deceptive sales practices
2. Housing law
   a. Fair housing practices
   b. Lease law
   c. Purchasing law
   d. Rent subsidy
3. Family law
   a. Marriage
   b. Child abuse and neglect
   c. Spouse abuse
   d. Divorce
      1. Child custody
      2. Alimony
   e. Death
4. Copyright law
5. Labor law
6. Organized labor
E. Criminal Justice Process
   1. Search and seizure
   2. Arrest
   3. Preliminary hearing
   4. Probable cause
   5. Parole
   6. Pardon
F. Criminal Law
   1. Crimes against property
      a. Arson
      b. Robbery
      c. Vandalism
      d. Larceny
      e. Extortion
      f. Burglary
      g. Forgery
      h. Embezzlement
      i. Receiving stolen property
      j. Car theft
   2. Crimes against persons
      a. Murder
      b. Rape
      c. Battery
      d. Assault
      e. Drug offenses

(continued on next page)

FIGURE 9-1, continued
Conceptual Content of Political Science

f. Sex offenses
G. Juvenile Justice
H. International Law
X. Legal and Political Issues
   A. School Desegregation
   B. Civil Rights Movement

C. Women's Movement
D. Affirmative Action
E. Rights of People with Disabilities
F. Abortion Rights
G. Gun Control
H. Immigration

FIGURE 9-1, continued
Conceptual Content of Political Science

WHAT K–6 STUDENTS SHOULD KNOW

Up until 1994 there were no national pronouncements concerning what elementary grade level children should learn in civics and government. However, the Center for Civic Education, as a part of the *America 2000* education initiative, developed National Standards for Civics and Government covering grades K through 12. Figure 9-2 displays the major organizing strands and content standards statements of the K–4 Civics and Government standards. Each content standard is phrased as a question in the standards document and followed by a rationale and achievement examples.

The amount of content contained in the National Standards for Civics and Government makes it impossible to offer more than a sample of how students are expected to demonstrate this important learning. Figure 9-3 shows the achievement examples for selected organizing questions. As you examine the contents of Figure 9-3 be aware that I have only selected one question for each strand. My hope is that by providing one example per strand you will be convinced that young children can achieve these standards and perhaps be motivated to investigate the other standards that are not represented.

The contents of Figures 9-2 and 9-3 should make it clear that much of what we hope children achieve in their civics and government learning is related to learning about the law. The next section develops in greater detail this important area of the social studies curriculum.

LAW-RELATED EDUCATION

Law-related education (LRE) began in the late 1960s as a part of a trend toward making social studies more relevant to the everyday needs of future citizens. The need for LRE was based on young people's observed lack of knowledge about the law and the increasing importance of law in our society.

Prior to the introduction of LRE, the main source of information students received about law came from high-school government classes where they learned how a bill becomes a law, studied the U.S. Constitution, and memorized the Bill of Rights. Many social studies teachers felt that preparation for citizenship needed to include more practical information about law and the legal

ORGANIZING STRANDS	CONTENT STANDARDS QUESTIONS
I. What is government and what should it do?	A. What is government? B. Where do people in government get the authority to make, apply, and enforce rules and laws and manage disputes about them? C. Why is government necessary? D. What are some of the most important things governments do? E. What are the purposes of rules and laws? F. How can you evaluate rules and laws? G. What are the differences between limited and unlimited governments? H. Why is it important to limit the power of government?
II. What are the basic values and principles of American democracy?	A. What are the most important values and principles of American democracy? B. What are some important beliefs Americans have about themselves and their governments? C. Why is it important for Americans to share certain values, principles, and beliefs? D. Why do disagreements about values and principles arise? E. What are the benefits of diversity in the United States? F. How should conflicts about diversity be prevented or managed? G. How can people work together to promote the values and principles of American democracy?
III. How does the government established by the Constitution embody the purposes, values, and principles of American democracy?	A. What is the U.S. Constitution and why is it important? B. What does the national government do and how does it protect individual rights and promote the common good? C. What are the major responsibilities of state government? D. What are the major responsibilities of local government? E. Who represents you in the legislative and executive branches of your local, state, and national governments?
IV. What is the relationship of the United States to other nations and to world affairs?	A. How is the world divided into nations? B. How do nations interact with one another?
V. What are the roles of the citizen in the American democracy?	A. What does it mean to be a citizen of the United Sates? B. How does a person become a citizen? C. What are some important rights in the United States? D. What are some important responsibilities of Americans? E. What dispositions or traits of character are important to the preservation and improvement of American democracy? F. How can Americans participate in their government? G. What is the importance of political leadership and public service? H. How should Americans select political leaders?

FIGURE 9-2

Content Standards in Civics and Government[1]

[1]From *National Standards for Civics and Government.* Copyright 1994 Center for Civic Education. Used with permission.

STRANDS	ACHIEVEMENT STATEMENTS
I.C. Why is government necessary?	To achieve this standard students should be able to: • explain the probable consequences of the absence of government and of rules and laws: (1) the strong may take advantage of the weak and act in their own selfish interests; (2) people may become disorderly or violent and threaten others' lives, liberty, and property; (3) people would feel insecure, unable to plan for the future, or to predict how others would behave • explain how government makes it possible for people working together to accomplish goals they could not achieve alone: (1) make laws to protect their lives, liberty, and property; (2) employ police, teachers, firefighters, and judges to carry out laws that protect their lives, liberty, property, and promote the common good • explain that the basic purposes of government in the United States are to protect the rights of individuals and to promote the common good
II.B. What are some important beliefs Americans have about themselves and their governments?	To achieve this standard students should be able to describe how the following beliefs operate in their own and classmates' lives: • importance of the individual's rights to vote, own property, enjoy liberty, and have freedom of religious and political views • importance of their school, community, state, and nation • importance of equality of opportunity and equal protection of the law • importance of respect for the law • importance of education • importance of work • importance of volunteerism
III.C. What are the major responsibilities of state government?	To achieve this standard, students should be able to: • distinguish between the national and state governments • describe the major responsibilities of each branch of their state government • describe important services their state government provides • describe how state government officials are chosen • explain how people participate in their state government (being informed and taking part in discussions of state issues; voting; volunteering their services; holding public office; serving on governing committees and commissions) • explain why it is important that people participate in their state government • explain how state government services are paid for

FIGURE 9-3

A Sample of Achievement Statements Contained in the National Standards for Civics and Government[2]

[2]From *National Standards for Civics and Government*. Copyright 1994 Center for Civic Education. Used with permission.

IV.B. How do nations interact with one another?	To achieve this standard, students should be able to: • explain how nations interact through trade, diplomacy, cultural contacts, treaties or agreements, military force • explain why it is important that nations try to resolve problems peacefully (promoting trade to improve people's standard of living, promoting peace to save human lives, protecting the environment, exchanging medical and scientific knowledge, exchanging students and teachers) • explain the basic purposes of the United Nations
V.D What are some important responsibilities of Americans?	To achieve this standard, students should be able to: • explain the importance to themselves, their family, school, community, state, and nation of individuals fulfilling such personal responsibilities as (1) taking care of themselves, (2) accepting responsibility for the consequences of their actions, (3) taking advantage of the opportunities to be educated, (4) supporting their families • explain the importance to themselves, their family, school, community, state, and nation, of individuals fulfilling such civic responsibilities as (1) obeying the law; (2) respecting the rights of others; (3) being informed and attentive to the needs of their community; (4) paying attention to how well their elected leaders are doing their jobs; (5) communicating with their representatives in their school, local, state, and national governments; (6) voting; (7) paying taxes; (8) volunteering to help less fortunate people in their communities; (9) serving on juries; and (10) serving in the armed forces

FIGURE 9-3, continued

A Sample of Achievement Statements Contained in the National Standards for Civics and Government

system that would help students stay out of trouble, sustain their own and others' rights, and help enforce the laws of their community, state, and nation.

A prominent group of organizations (their names, addresses, and services are detailed in the Resources section at the end of the chapter) have promoted LRE through the development of curriculum materials and training opportunities for teachers. Largely as a result of the work of these organizations and small seed grants from the federal government, each state now has its own law-related education network. These state-level organizations can put you in contact with resource speakers, locally produced curriculum materials, and programs of the national organizations.

The Law-Related Education Act of 1978 defined LRE as: "education to equip non-lawyers with knowledge and skills pertaining to the law, the legal process and the legal system, and the fundamental principles and values on which these are based." Educators have infused law-related education into the social studies curriculum throughout the country. Effective LRE is characterized by (1) active participation in the learning process, (2) a focus on critical thinking,

(3) the use of outside resource persons from the law community, and (4) considerable administrator and community support.

When most citizens think of law, they think of it as hard to understand and very difficult, if not impossible, to change. Many people see law as the image of authority and view police as "cops" whose sole purpose is to watch for crimes and harass people. Law-related education seeks to promote a much more accurate and healthy view of law. Law-related education attempts to accomplish the following learning outcomes shown in Figure 9-4.

Social studies lessons centered on the law should (1) provide students with an understanding of the principles, concepts, and values that underlie and guide the administration of justice in our democratic society; (2) promote positive

Students moved away from:	*Students moved toward:*
perceiving law as restrictive, punitive, immutable, and beyond the control and understanding of people affected	perceiving law as promotive, facilitative, comprehensible, and alterable
perceiving people as powerless before the law and other socio-civic institutions	perceiving people as having the potential to control and contribute to the social order
perceiving issues of right and wrong as incomprehensible to ordinary people	perceiving right and wrong as issues all citizens can and should address
perceiving social issues as unproblematic	perceiving the dilemmas inherent in social issues
being impulsive decision makers and problem solvers who make unreflective commitments	being reflective decision makers and problem solvers who make grounded commitments
being inarticulate about commitments made or positions taken	being able to give reasoned explanations about commitments made and positions taken
being unable to manage conflict in other than a coercive or destructive manner	being socially responsible conflict managers
being uncritically defiant of authority	being critically responsive to legitimate authority
being uncritically responsive to authority	being responsibly opposed to illegitimate authority
being illiterate about legal issues and the legal system	being knowledgeable about law, the legal system, and related issues
being egocentric, self-centered, and indifferent to others	being empathetic, socially responsible, and considerate of others
being morally immature in responding to ethical problems	being able to make mature judgments in dealing with ethical and moral problems

FIGURE 9-4
Law-Related Education Learning Outcomes[3]

---

[3]This chart was originally published by C. C. Anderson, 1980, 383–386.

attitudes toward the protection and exercise of our fundamental liberties and toward the thoughtful fulfillment of citizenship responsibilities; (3) encourage the useful application of basic skills and higher-order thinking skills such as critical thinking, decision making, and problem solving on law-related content; and (4) develop a willingness and ability to resolve conflicts by peaceful means. Lessons should center on concepts and topics such as those shown in Figure 9-5.

I. Laws Concerning Property Rights and Responsibilities
  A. Auto Theft
  B. Illegal Duplication of Print and Electronic Media
  C. Firearms
  D. Fireworks
  E. Trespassing
  F. Vandalism
  G. Breaking and Entering
  H. Receiving Stolen Property
  I. Forgery
  J. Shoplifting
II. Laws Concerning Crimes Against Persons
  A. Phone Harassment
  B. Assault
  C. Battery
  D. Sexual Abuse
  E. Rape
III. Laws Defining Just Procedures
  A. Due Process (Fair Ways to Find Things Out)
  B. Fair Ways to Set Things Straight
  C. Fair Ways to Distribute Benefits and Burdens
IV. Laws Defining Institutional and Familial Rights and Responsibilities
  A. Parents' Legal Rights and Responsibilities
    1. Education, discipline, medical care
    2. Child abuse and neglect
    3. Divorce and child custody
  B. Students' Rights and Responsibilities
    1. Attendance, truancy, tardiness
    2. Sexual, racial, or ethnic discrimination
    3. Search and seizure

    4. Proper deportment, attire, and language
    5. Religious beliefs (holiday celebrations, absences, pledge of allegiance)
    6. Lying or cheating
  C. Children's Legal Rights and Responsibilities
    1. Obedience (house rules, religion, friends in the home)
    2. Employment, allowance, and personal property
V. Laws to Promote Personal Safety and Public Welfare
  A. Gambling
  B. Underage Driving
  C. Laws Pertaining to the Sale and Use of Alcohol and Tobacco
  D. Public Obscenity
  E. The Illegal Possession of Controlled Substances
  F. Child Labor Laws
  G. Traffic/Pedestrian Laws
  H. The Juvenile Justice Process
    1. Key facts and concepts
    2. Juvenile diversion (alternatives to incarceration)
VI. Lessons on Key Legal Concepts and Values
  A. Authority
  B. Due Process
  C. Freedom
  D. Justice
  E. Privacy
  F. Property
  G. Responsibility

FIGURE 9-5
LRE Concepts and Topics for Grades K through 6[4]

[4]Adapted from the Georgia Law-Related Education Curriculum Supplements Project, Department of Social Science Education, University of Georgia, Athens, GA 30602.

Lessons designed to teach young children about the legal content shown in Figure 9-5 have been developed by a number of national projects. Sample lesson plans at the end of the chapter also illustrate how these concepts can be taught in the elementary grades.

DISCUSSION QUESTIONS
. . . . .

1. Did you ever experience lessons in your elementary school on any of this content? If you did not, why do you suppose that was the case?

2. Is it dangerous to teach children about the legal rights and responsibilities of teachers and families? Take a position and be ready to defend it in a class discussion.

3. If all U.S. citizens suddenly became highly literate in politics, law, and government (and politically active, too) how might our nation be different? How might such a development affect the activities of lobbyists and political action committees?

CLASSROOM CONSTITUTION OR WE THE PEOPLE[5]

Grade Level: 2–3
Author: Eloise Glorieux
Time Required: Two class periods
Concepts/Vocabulary: Responsibility, rules, constitution, government, preamble

Main Ideas

a. Rules are important for an orderly and functioning society.

b. A constitution, like that of the United States, provides criteria and a plan for making rules.

Objectives: As a result of this lesson, students will:

- describe what the Constitution of the United States is
- identify three parts of a constitution
- make rules that conform to a constitutional purpose

Instructional Strategies

Brainstorming possible classroom rules

Discussing rules for a classroom constitution

Voting on classroom constitution rules

Reenacting signing of the Constitution

Teacher Background

The Constitution of the United States of America is the basis for all government in our country. The Constitution establishes a framework for making and changing laws in our nation, for carrying out laws, and for interpreting them if disputed.

This lesson involves students in making their own classroom constitution. In so doing, students gain a greater understanding of the content and purpose of our state and federal constitutions.

Materials/Resources Needed: Two or three large pieces of manila tagboard or posterboard, markers, quill pen (large feather with quill, or pointed stick or pen with real or paper feather attached), ink or berry juice

Procedures

Period One

1. At the beginning of the school year, teachers generally review and/or establish school/classroom rules. Talk to students about what a rule is. Depending on the level of your children, you might have them look up the word in a dictionary. According to *MacMillan's Very First Dictionary* (1983), a rule is defined as: "something that tells you what you can do and what you cannot do."

    Let students give examples of rules ("You should always use crosswalks." "You have to stop at a red light.") List some of the rules on a chalkboard. Then let students suggest reasons for the rules. Help them see that there are common reasons for rules such as safety, order, and the protection of property.

2. Talk about how, when our country was very young, a group of citizens decided it needed a plan for rules for all the people in the country. These men wanted rules to help protect people's property, to keep people safe, and to make things orderly. They wanted rules that would protect the freedoms they felt were important. They wanted rules that would be fair. They wanted to establish general ways in which people could maintain control over government and even change the rules that govern them.

    To accomplish these goals, these early representatives wrote a constitution for the United States. (Write the word *Constitution* on the board.) The Constitution had several parts. The first part was a preamble (write on board) which gave the reasons for making the Constitution. The next part, the body of the Constitution, set forth a plan for making rules or laws and carrying them out. The Constitution concludes with a list of signees.

3. Explain that classrooms also need rules, and so that the class can make rules, it will first establish a constitution. Like the U.S. Constitution, it will have a preamble that gives the reasons (rationale) for the rules.

---

[5]This lesson plan was taken from the Georgia Law-Related Education Curriculum Supplements (GELRECS). This curriculum product is in the public domain and is available from ERIC as a microfiche document.

While the students are watching, write the preamble (the following version) on a piece of tagboard. Read it as you go and explain it:

We the students of Room _____, in order to form a more perfect classroom, establish fairness, ensure class happiness, keep us safe, increase class harmony, and guarantee our learning, do make this constitution.

4. Now tell students that their constitution will also have a plan for making rules to promote the ideals of the preamble. Both the U.S. and state constitutions have such a plan. Establish some guidelines for the students' rule making. Explain that you are calling the parts of the plan "articles," just as is done in the U.S. and state constitutions.

Article I. Rules for the students of Room _____ will be made by the students in the following manner. Rules will be suggested by students. Any rule must meet the guidelines that follow:

All of the students present must vote on each rule. To become a rule, _____ (all, a majority, two-thirds) of the students present must agree to it. Changes to rules must be made in the same manner.

Article II.

(a) Rules must meet the purpose of the constitution's preamble.

(b) Rules should only be made for important and necessary things.

(c) Rules should be stated so everyone clearly understands them.

(d) Rules should not be so broad that they become impossible to follow (for example, NO NOISE).

(e) Rules should apply to everyone in the class.

(f) Rules should be enforceable.

Copy the articles onto tagboard like the preamble.

5. Discuss Article II to be sure that everyone understands the guidelines. For each guideline, ask students for (or give) examples that would and would not work. Review the guidelines.

Point out that since the rules will be a permanent part of the classroom constitution, the students must be certain that they are satisfied with them.

6. Tell the students that they will use the constitution to make rules for the classroom tomorrow.

Period Two

Prior to class, write out the classroom constitution on a sheet of paper that students can sign.

1. Show the students the handwritten version of their constitution. Review it. Point out that the first part is the preamble and that it gives the purposes for the constitution. Name the purposes. Point out that the second part has the plan for making rules. Read this part with students. Then, point out that you have added a third part, a conclusion, to the constitution to make it just like the U.S. Constitution. The conclusion reads:

Done in Room _____ of_____ School, by the consent of the students present, on the _____ day of _____, in the Year of Our Lord, _____.

In witness, thereof, we have written our names.

2. Explain how the people who first established the Constitution of the United States of America signed the document. Talk about how they used a quill pen and ink.

Have each student use the quill pen to sign the constitution. Mount the signed constitution to display in the classroom.

3. Now it is time to use the constitution to make rules for the class. Ask students to suggest rules. (Some of the rules discussed yesterday may be applicable.) Be sure each rule fits the guidelines. After rules are listed, have students vote on each one. Use criteria in the constitution to see if each rule will pass. Make a copy of the approved rules to display in the room. Tell students that we will *all* live by these rules. If we find these rules are not acceptable, then as a class, we can amend, or change them.

4. As follow-up, reproduce copies of both the signed constitution and the rules. Invite students to soak their individual constitutions in a solution of brown paint and water to "age" them. These copies can be taken home and shared with parents.

Evaluation

- Give the following questions as a small test, or interview students to determine if they can answer them. (Or train two or three students to do the interviews for you and show them how to record answers.)
- a. What are the three parts of your classroom constitution? What is the purpose of each part?
  b. What is one purpose of your classroom constitution?
  c. What is one classroom rule made according to your constitution?
- Write the following on the chalkboard:
  The United States Constitution . . .
  a. is a plan for making rules for running the whole world
  b. tells what the people and the government can and cannot do
  c. tells other nations what they can and cannot do
  d. is a plan for making rules for running our country

  Ask the students to write their names on a sheet of paper. Read the statements and ask them to write the letters of the ones that are true. (Correct answers are b and d.)

Enrichment

- Let students decide what consequences should result if their rules are broken. Discuss what the consequences are for people who break laws in our country. It might help if you list some of these (going to jail, fines, community service, taking away of certain rights). Be sure that all consequences are fair. Talk to the students about the need to make sure that the consequence fits the rule.
- Ask the students to establish rewards for people who do follow the rules. Talk about how people who obey the rules and laws in our country also receive rewards. Help students establish rewards for the whole class if everyone follows the rules.
- Explain that the U.S. Constitution was amended (changed) to provide for rights for its citizens. Hold a classroom constitutional convention to devise a Bill of Rights for the class (or to otherwise amend the original document).
- Have students look up the names of some of the people who signed the Constitution. They can write down important biographical data on them. Suggested people might include: Alexander Hamilton; Benjamin Franklin; James Madison, Jr.; George Washington; William Few; and Abraham Baldwin.

DON'T TALK TO ME LIKE THAT![6]

Grade Level: 4–5
Authors: Sharon Fletcher and Kathleen Judge
Time Required: Three class periods
Concepts/Vocabulary: First Amendment, mental harassment, dignity, neglect, cruelty, exploitation, discrimination (racial/religious/gender/age), fighting words, slander, libel

Main Ideas

a. The freedom of expression guaranteed by the Bills of Rights of the U.S. Constitution is not absolute; there are restrictions on what teachers and students may say and do.

b. The United Nations' "Declaration of the Rights of a Child" sets standards for the humane and ethical treatment of children.

c. The National Education Association's "Code of Ethics of the Education Profession" provides standards for judging teacher conduct.

d. One person's rights end where another's begin.

Objectives: As a result of this lesson, students will:

- describe the rights to and limits on free speech
- develop a classroom document describing rights and responsibilities of class members

Instructional Strategies

Analyzing a verbal harassment scenario

Discussing free speech rights and limitations

Listing rights and responsibilities in two documents

---

[6]This lesson plan was taken from the Georgia Law-Related Education Curriculum Supplements (GELRECS). This curriculum product is in the public domain and is available from ERIC as a microfiche document.

Group writing of classroom declaration of rights

Teacher Background

Teachers are certainly experienced observers of the verbal abuse students hurl at one another. Most teachers instinctively try to establish a level of civility that is essential for learning. This lesson informs students that there are standards that both guide and limit our freedom of expression. More importantly, this lesson helps students see that these guidelines and limitations apply not only to them, but to all actors in the school setting.

Following are some of the vocabulary words used in this lesson. These definitions are provided for your convenience.

cruelty inhumane; an action that results in pain or distress to others

dignity worth; merit; worthiness; honor; reputation; self-respect

discrimination (racial/religious/gender/age) showing of difference or favoritism of treatment; to set apart; to show partiality (in favor of) or prejudice (against).

exploitation making use of others; utilizing or making unethical use of others for one's own advantage or profit; to turn something selfishly or unfairly to one's own advantage.

fighting words expressions likely to cause a breach of the peace; words that incite violence.

libel the intentional deed of writing, printing, or broadcasting of false information damaging to someone (A true statement is not libel.)

mental harassment to trouble, worry, or torment with repeated questions; irritate; create anxieties

neglect ignore; disregard; not to care for or attend to; be careless; overlook; despise; condemn; be negligent; slight

slander a spoken expression about a person that is false and damages his/her reputation (A true statement is not slander.)

Bill of Rights

Freedom of expression includes oral, written, and symbolic speech. An example of symbolic speech is the wearing of armbands to protest a war. The right to freedom of expression is broad in our society, but it is not unlimited. Speech not protected by the First Amendment includes:

- speech that presents a clear and present danger to others (The classic example of prohibited speech is shouting "fire" [when there is none] in a crowded theater.)
- speech that substantially disrupts or interferes with a governmental activity
- defamation (that is, slander or libel) This is speech that is not true and injures others. (However, public figures have less protection than private individuals.)
- fighting words (words that can incite a breach of the peace)
- obscenity and pornography
- speech inherent in crimes such as perjury and fraud

These limitations apply to both adults and children at all times and places. While attending school, students may have additional limitations placed on their freedom of expression rights. (For example, the content of a student newspaper may be censored by an appropriate school authority, and students may be prohibited from disrupting the educational process with verbal outbursts or symbolic behaviors.)

In general, courts have upheld suits based on sexual, religious, or racial harassment in the workplace. Verbal harassment in the school, regardless of its basis, opens the way for lawsuits that allege "emotional distress" caused by another's speech or actions.

Materials/Resources Needed: Posterboard, flip-chart paper, transparency, markers, pens

Handouts

1. Constitutional Rights to Free Speech

2. The Rights of the Child (United Nations)

3. Code of Ethics (National Education Association)

Procedure

Period One

1. Begin the lesson by reading the following scenario:

Katrina lived in a small house with her mother, two brothers, and two sisters. Because her mother supported the whole family by working in a restaurant, they had to be very careful with money. Katrina did not have many nice or stylish clothes. However, for her birthday, Katrina's mother bought her a bottle of bright red nail polish that Katrina had admired. Katrina and her oldest sister stayed up late that night doing their nails.

Mr. Wood, Katrina's fifth-grade teacher, was very strict and felt that fifth graders should not wear makeup or earrings. Katrina had never been in serious trouble or sent to the principal's office. As Katrina was walking into class to put her books on her desk, Mr. Wood noticed Katrina's bright red fingernails.

After the bell rang and the class was seated, Mr. Wood yelled, "Katrina! Come up to the front of the room!" He ordered her to stand in front of the class and told her to hold her hands out straight in front of her. Then he said, "Katrina, if you were meant to have red fingernails, you would have been born with them! This is disgraceful! Do not ever come into this classroom with your nails painted again!" Katrina hung her head and put her hands in her pockets as she walked sullenly back to her seat.

2. Lead a discussion of the scenario. Ask:

 a. How did Katrina feel after the teacher yelled at her? How would you have felt?

 b. Did Katrina have a right to paint her nails?

 c. Did the teacher have a right to criticize Katrina?

 d. How else could Mr. Wood have handled this situation?

 e. Did you ever feel like Katrina felt? (Try to elicit from students some of the vocabulary words presented in the Teacher Background.)

3. Ask the students to think about the scenario and discussion and tell you words that describe how a person feels when he or she has been hurt by someone else. List the words on the chalkboard, being sure students can define or understand them. (Encourage use of the words in the Teacher Background.)

Discuss: Should speech be limited? Should we be able to say whatever we wish? (Stress that the right to free speech has to be weighed against the possible harm it can bring to others; free speech is not limitless.)

Period Two

1. Distribute Handout 1, Constitutional Rights to Free Speech. Discuss what these rights mean, clarifying (a) that these rights are not absolute,

which means that the courts have allowed the government to put certain limits on freedom of expression, and (b) that these rights do not mean you can say whatever you want to say.

Ask students to guess what restrictions the courts place on free speech. Record their ideas on the chalkboard. Discuss and correct their responses, using the Teacher Background.

Point out that rights also carry responsibilities. Brainstorm with students the responsibilities the right to free speech carries (for example, the responsibility to not endanger others, the responsibility to have your facts straight, and the responsibility not to restrict unfairly the free speech of others). Record and discuss these responses.

2. Introduce the documents on Handouts 2 and 3, helping the students with any unfamiliar words and ideas. Help the class identify the rights and responsibilities presented in these handouts.

3. Clarify that while the Bill of Rights and the allowable restrictions are laws, the documents on handouts 2 and 3 are not. Ask: What is the difference? What are laws (a body of rules governing the affairs of people within a society; law consists of all rights, duties, and obligations that can be enforced by a society's government)? Be sure students understand why the "Rights of the Child" and "Code of Ethics" are not laws.

Period Three

1. Divide the class into six small groups. Tell the groups that they are going to create documents reflecting the specific free speech rights and responsibilities of members of the class toward each other, of members of the class toward the teacher, and of the teacher toward each member of the class. (Although the groups should work independently, each topic will be covered by two groups.) The documents, discussed at length during Period Two, can serve as models.

2. Have the matching groups meet to combine their results. Ask them to copy their document on the chalkboard, a piece of newsprint, or on a transparency.

3. Present the three lists of free speech rights and responsibilities one at a time, allowing for comments, corrections, and discussion. After a consensus is reached on a declaration of rights of expression in the classroom, a final combined document should be posted in the room and copied by everyone.

Evaluation

- Use the classroom declarations produced by the students during Period Three.
- Ask each student to write a paragraph about the following statement: "My rights to free speech end where others' rights begin."

Enrichment

- Have students list antonyms for words identified in Period One.
- Research famous individuals who were victims of harassment.

H A N D O U T 1 **Constitutional Right to Free Speech**
The First Amendment to the U.S. Constitution

Congress shall make no law respecting an establishment of religion, or prohibiting the free exercise thereof, or abridging the freedom of speech, or of the press; or the right of the people peaceably to assemble, and to petition the government for a redress of grievances.

H A N D O U T 2 **The Rights of the Child***

Although the specific rights of the child are not spelled out in the Constitution of the United States, the United Nations General Assembly, on November 20, 1959, adopted a document called "The Rights of the Child."

a. The document affirms the dignity and worth of the human person without distinction of any kind, such as race, sex, language, religion, political or other opinion, national or social origin, property, birth, or other status.

b. The document affirms that the child, by reason of his physical and mental immaturity, needs special safeguards and care including appropriate legal protection.

c. The document affirms that the child should be raised in conditions of freedom and dignity; be protected against all forms of neglect, cruelty, and exploitation; be protected from practices that may foster any forms of discrimination; be brought up in the spirit of understanding, love, tolerance; and be given an education which promotes the development of his/her moral and social responsibilities.

---

*Excerpted from the United Nations Declaration of the Rights of the Child.

HANDOUT 3   **Code of Ethics***

The Code of Ethics of the Education Profession indicates the aspirations of all educators and provides standards by which to judge their conduct. It was adopted by the National Education Association Representative Assembly, July 1975.

The following are selected, relevant points made in Principle 1, Commitment to the Student:

a. The educator strives to help each student achieve his/her potential as a worthy and effective member of society.

b. The educator shall not intentionally expose the student to disparagement or embarrassment (debasement).

c. The educator shall not on the basis of race, color, creed, sex, national origin, marital status, political or religious beliefs, family, social or cultural background, or sexual orientation unfairly:

1. exclude any student from participation in any program;

2. deny benefits to any student; or

3. grant any advantage to any student.

RESOURCES

The resources for teaching citizenship, and LRE in particular, to children in grades K through 6 are substantial. The ERIC system contains units of instruction and lesson plans on many government, law, and political topics.

American Bar Association (ABA) Special Committee on Youth Education for Citizenship, 541 N. Fairbanks Court, Chicago, IL 60611-3314. Publications include *Update on Law-Related Education*, free newsletters, pamphlets, and brochures.

Center for Civic Education (CCE) 5146 Douglas Fir Road, Calabasas, CA 91302-1467, (818) 591-9321. Publications include Law in a Free Society audiovisual kits on concepts of authority, justice, privacy, responsibility, property, freedom, participation, and diversity; soft-covered elementary, middle-, and high-school textbooks (*We The People*) with teacher's guides on the U.S. Constitution, and the *Drugs in the Schools* program.

Center for Research and Development in Law-Related Education (CRADLE) Wake Forest University School of Law, Box 7206 Reynolds Station, Winston-Salem, NC 27109, 1-800-437-1054. Publishes sets of teacher-written lesson plans such as *Teaching Our Tomorrows* and *Constitutional Sampler*. Publishes a newsletter, collections of lessons on special topics such as the 1992 elections, and operates a free LRE-network (phone 919-759-4709 using 1200/2400,8,1,N) with a conference area, bulletin board, and lesson plans to download.

---

*Excerpted from the National Education Association Code of Ethics for the Education Profession.

Constitutional Rights Foundation (CRF) Chicago office: 407 South Dearborn, Suite 1700, Chicago, IL 60605, 312-663-9057. Los Angeles office: 601 S. Kingsley Drive, Los Angeles, CA 90005. Publications include middle-school *Living Law* texts; minitexts with LRE lessons for integrating into history, geography, and government classes; *Bill of Rights* newsletter; simulations; and mock trials.

National Institute for Citizen Education in the Law (NICEL) 25 E Street, N.W., Suite 400, Washington, D.C. 20001, 202-662-9620. Publications include *Street Law; Teens, Crime, and Communities*; free newsletter; mock trials; and case studies.

Phi Alpha Delta Phi Alpha Delta Public Service Center, Suite 325E, 7315 Wisconsin Avenue, Bethesda, MD 20184, 301-961-8985. Materials focus on use of community resource persons (especially lawyers) in secondary school settings.

REFERENCES AND SELECTED READINGS

Anderson, C. C. 1980. Promoting responsible citizenship through elementary law-related education. *Social Education* 44(5):383–386.

Angell, A. V. 1991. Democratic climates in elementary classrooms: A review of theory and research. *Theory and Research in Social Education* 19(3):241–266.

Berman, S. 1990. Education for social responsibility. *Educational Leadership* 11:75–80.

Boyer, E. L. 1990. Civic education for responsible citizens. *Educational Leadership* 11:4–7.

Bragaw, D. H. 1989. In training to be a citizen: The elementary student and the public interest. *Social Science Record* 26(2):27–29.

Center for Civic Education. 1994. *National standards for civics and government.* Draft for Review and Comment, August, 19, 1994. Calabasas, CA.

Gallagher, A. F. 1989. Access to justice: K–6 strategies. *Update on Law-Related Education* 13(1):5–17.

Giroux, H. A. 1991. Beyond the ethics of flag waving: Schooling and citizenship for critical democracy. *The Clearing House* 64(May/June):305–308.

Greenawald, D. 1987. Making wrongs right. *Update on Law-Related Education* 11(2):11.

Gross, R. E., and Dynneson, T. L., eds. 1991. *Social science perspectives on citizenship education.* New York: Teacher's College Press.

Haas, M. 1988. Teaching about the president and the presidential election. *Social Studies and the Young Learner* 1(1):1–4.

Hickey, M. G. 1990. ". . . and justice for all." Teaching kids about the law. *The Social Studies* 81(2):77–79.

_____. 1990. Mock trials for children. *Social Education* 54(1):43–44.

Holmes, E. E. 1991. Democracy in elementary school classes. *Social Education* 3:176–178.

Kennedy, E. M. 1991. Educational service and education for citizenship. *Phi Delta Kappan* 6:771–773.

Larson, S. B. 1991. *Teaching citizenship through children's literature.* ERIC document no. ED286771. Bloomington, IN: ERIC Clearinghouse for Social Science/Social Studies Education.

Lewis, B. A. 1990. Cleanup crusade: Citizenship in action. *Social Education* 54(4):238–240.

The making of a citizen. 1988. *Instructor* 5:50–51.

McKinney-Browning, M. C. 1987. Law-related education: Programs, process, and promise. *The International Journal of Social Education* 2(2):7–14.

Nielsen, L. E., and Finkelstein, J. M. 1988. Citizenship education: Looking at government. *Social Studies and the Young Learner* 1(1):10–13.

Parker, W. C., McDaniel, J. E., and Valencia, S. W. 1991. Helping students think about public issues: Instruction versus prompting. *Social Education* 1:41–44,67.

Passe, J. 1988. Citizenship education: Its role in improving classroom behavior. *Social Studies and the Young Learner* 1(1):19–21.

Pereira, C., Dolenga, J., and Rolzinski, C. A. 1990. Teaching citizenship through community service. *Social Studies and the Young Learner* (Nov/Dec):1–4.

Quigley, C. N., and Bahmueller, C. F. 1991. *CIVITAS: A framework for civic education.* Calabasas, CA: Center for Civic Education.

Psychology and Social Psychology: Understanding Ourselves

"Ray's playground behavior troubles his classmates. He runs from one play group to another, interrupting and causing trouble. When children see him coming they turn their backs, expecting that he will barge in and do something disruptive. It's clear that something is wrong, but I haven't yet decided what to do."

"Sabrina's always so low-key. She's a sweet little girl, dressed up in ruffles and lace everyday. Judged by her appearance, you'd think she was on her way to Sunday school! I suppose that living with her Grandmother may be one of the reasons she comes to school looking like that. I'd like to help Sabrina develop more friends and come out a little bit more."

"Matt fits the trickster and roughhouse boy stereotype. If there's trouble, you can bet that Matt's part of it. He's always got a smart comment to make during social studies. I dread it when he raises his hand or calls out an answer. I wish I could get him motivated in the right direction. He could be a real leader instead of a troublemaker."

"I've never seen a student work harder than Jacob. He spent most of the first quarter learning about castles and built a really neat model with the help of his father. His report was word processed and included some excellent graphics that he drew himself. Here, take a look at it. I wish I could get all of my students to work as hard."

INTRODUCTION

The opening quotations hint at the complexity and challenge teachers face as they practice their chosen profession. What advice, if any, should you give to Ray's classmates? Should you worry about Sabrina? Is there any hope for a boy like Matt? Is Jacob really happy? Clearly, your answers depend, in large part, on a mountain of unsupplied contextual information. Another big factor in your answers is your understanding of psychology and social psychology.

While the opening quotations demonstrate the need for an understanding of human behavior on the part of teachers, every person can benefit from similar knowledge in his or her daily life. Even young children can make good use of knowledge from psychology and social psychology. This knowledge is included in the school curriculum as a part of social studies.

Psychology and social psychology play an important, but often hidden, role in social studies. Concepts and generalizations from these two disciplines apply directly to many of the topics typically included in the K–6 social studies curriculum. Much of the content from history and geography, for example, involves fundamental understandings of human nature derived from psychology and social psychology. Though these disciplines do not play a major role in the formal social studies curriculum, there is little doubt that further instruction on topics of psychology and social psychology would benefit young learners.

THE DISCIPLINE'S PERSPECTIVE

Psychology is the systematic study of mental activity in humans and other animals. Because psychologists attempt to explain why living things act the way they do, psychology is often termed a *behavioral science.* Psychologists recognize the influence of genetic inheritance, but focus more on learning and experience as influences on behavior. The discipline has always sought scientific explanations of human behavior, though psychologists developed many theories and basic concepts in laboratory settings experimenting on lower forms of animal life.

Psychology emerged as an independent field of study in Germany in the late 1800s. Its original focus was on understanding perception and sensation. By the 1880s psychology was being taught at a few U.S. colleges by such people as William James—recognized now as the father of American psychology—and G. Stanley Hall, who founded the American Psychological Association and was one of the first psychologists to specialize in child study. Other notable American psychologists include John Dewey, John B. Watson, Edward Thorndike, B. F. Skinner, Kurt Lewin, David Wechsler, and Carl Rogers.

The closely related field of social psychology is the study of how an individual's feelings, thoughts, and behaviors are influenced by others. Social psychologists investigate a large area of phenomena such as nonverbal communication, prejudice, aggression, conformity, group dynamics, child-rearing practices, leadership styles, socialization, interpersonal attraction, prosocial behavior, attitudes, and social inhibitions. Social psychologists study these phenomena within the framework of a theory such as attribution theory, modeling theory, consistency theory, autonomy theory, ego-defensive theory, or reinforcement theory.

Because of their focus on understanding individual and social learning during child development, teachers owe a great debt to psychology and social psychology. Many of our professional explanations of children's behavior employ concepts and theories from psychology and social psychology. For example, our explanations of learning, maturation, motivation, and emotion all stem from psychology and social psychology. Helping children gain these same intellectual footholds on personal and social reality is a worthy goal of social studies. (Sample lessons are presented at the end of this chapter. Chapters 14 and 15 also provide examples of how children gain learning footholds on important content from social psychology.)

Let's further examine psychology and social psychology by taking a brief look at their content. Figure 10-1 displays a conceptual outline of these disciplines. As you read the outline jot down the concepts that you believe should be taught to elementary school children. Share your list in the coming class.

I. Major Concepts/Ideas
  A. Biological Basis of Behavior
    1. The brain
    2. The nervous system
    3. Sensation
      a. Visual
      b. Auditory
      c. Taste
      d. Smell
      e. Skin
      f. Perception
      g. States of consciousness
        1. Fantasy/Day dreams
        2. Meditation
    4. Sleep
      a. Dreams
      b. Nightmares
  B. Learning
    1. Continuity of learning
    2. Classical conditioning

    3. Operant conditioning
      a. Behavior modification
    4. Social learning/Socialization
      a. Social perception
  C. Memory/Information Processing
    1. Short- and long-term memory
    2. Cognitive structures and schemata
    3. Explanations of forgetting
  D. Motivation
    1. Biological needs
    2. Social needs
    3. Psychological needs
  E. Cognition
    1. Cognitive development
    2. Types of thinking
      a. Associational
      b. Analogical and metaphorical
      c. Critical/Evaluative
      d. Creative
      e. Problem solving

(continued on next page)

FIGURE 10-1
Conceptual Outline of Psychology and Social Psychology[1]

---

[1]This outline is adapted from the Social Studies Content Descriptor Project, Educational Products Information Exchange Institute. Used by permission.

F. Language Learning
  1. Early language acquisition
  2. Language learning problems
G. Intelligence
  1. Concepts and definitions
  2. Measurement practices
  3. Hereditary influences
  4. Environmental influences
H. Psychology and Development
  1. Prenatal development
  2. Birth
  3. Infancy
  4. Childhood
  5. Adolescence
  6. Adulthood
  7. Later years
I. Theories of Personality
  1. Psychoanalytic theories of personality
  2. Humanistic theories of personality
J. Emotions
  1. Fear
  2. Hate
  3. Love/Attraction/Affection
  4. Joy/Pleasure
K. Psychological Disorders
  1. Mental retardation
  2. Depression
  3. Schizophrenia
  4. Sexual deviance
L. Personal Growth and Development
  1. Self-concept and self-esteem
  2. Interpersonal communications
    a. Active listening
    b. Nonverbal communications
    c. Conflict resolution
M. Topics of Social Psychology
  1. Attachment
  2. Aggression/Violence
  3. Conformity
  4. Altruism
  5. Prejudice
    a. Racial prejudice
    b. Sexism
    c. Ageism
    d. Religious prejudice
  6. Sex roles

  7. Attitude formation and change
  8. Values/Moral development
  9. Deception
    a. Lying
    b. Propaganda
II. Psychological Theories
  A. Psychoanalytic Theories
    1. Autonomy theory
    2. Ego-defensive theory
  B. Behaviorism Theories
    1. Reinforcement theory
    2. Modeling theory
      a. Role models
  C. Cognitive Theories
    1. Attribution theory
    2. Consistency theory
  D. Cognitive Development
  E. Existential Theories
  F. Biological Theories
  G. Humanistic Theories
III. Fields of Study
  A. Adolescent Psychology
  B. Child Psychology
    1. Play
  C. Developmental Psychology
  D. Clinical Psychology
  E. Educational Psychology
  F. Industrial Psychology
  G. Personality Psychology
  H. Social Psychology
  I. Cognitive Psychology
    1. Concept formation
  J. Group Dynamics
    1. Group morale
    2. Leadership styles
IV. Methods/Procedures
  A. Scientific Method
  B. Research Tools/Techniques
    1. Case study research
    2. Observational research
    3. Survey research
    4. Clinical research
    5. Experimental research
    6. Research terminology
    7. Statistical analysis

FIGURE 10-1, continued
Conceptual Outline of Psychology and Social Psychology

EXERCISE 10-1

◆ ◆ ◆ ◆ ◆

1. After you have examined the outline and made a list of topics that you feel are appropriate for young children, go back and see if you can determine some basis or criterion for your selections. Did you exclude topics that dealt with theories because you thought children incapable of understanding such high-level content? Did you select emotions as one of the areas that you felt were appropriate? (If so, why?) Did you include lying but not propaganda? Would you teach children about simple reinforcement theory but exclude knowledge from the Freudian-based psychoanalytic theories? Explain your answers. What do your choices say (if anything) about your perceptions of children and schooling?

2. Select one of the entries in the outline and do a computer search in *Psychological Abstracts* using the term in union with the term *children*. For example, search for "modeling theory" and "children." Locate, read, and bring to class one or more of the most interesting articles. Try to imagine incorporating the knowledge in the article into instruction that you could provide to young children. Imagine you selected the entry "Fear" (I.J.1.) and located an article about the abatement of fear in children. Discuss how to incorporate some of this content into social studies instruction for children.

3. Select a primary-grade-level social studies textbook and examine it for psychological and social psychological content. Keep the outline handy as you page through the book. If psychological or social psychological content isn't being taught, then what else is, and is it as important? Justify your response.

4. Using a college-level psychology or social psychology textbook, look up one or more of the following outline entries: attribution theory; modeling theory; prejudice; sexism; nonverbal communication; conflict resolution; depression; or love. Take notes on what you find. Write a position statement at the end of your notes that describes what you would be willing to teach young children about this topic. Turn this in to your instructor.

WHAT K-6 STUDENTS SHOULD KNOW

◆ ◆ ◆ ◆ ◆

There is no organized effort to promote teaching based on the content of psychology and social psychology within elementary social studies.[2] As a result, I offer you my own opinion of what teachers might include in their social studies curriculum. Figure 10-2 displays these judgments. As you examine the material, please remember to take a critical stance—these are just my suggestions! Note, too, that the sample main ideas and generalizations are totally of my making. Others could just as easily have been stated.

Social psychology and psychology are also responsible for much of what we know about the learning of higher-order skills such as decision making and critical thinking. Social psychology, in particular, is the source of much con-

---

[2]Jenness, 1990, 249–254.

CONCEPT OR TOPIC	SAMPLE MAIN IDEAS AND GENERALIZATIONS[3]
Perception	• People see, remember, and interpret things differently. • Checking your perceptions with someone else is a good way to verify your judgments and interpretations.
Fantasy/Daydreams	• Virtually everyone has fantasies and daydreams. • Fantasies and daydreams can cause you personal trouble if they occupy too strong a place in your life.
Sleep, dreams, nightmares	• Children need at least 8 hours of sleep to grow and learn well. • There are many positive things that people can do to help make sure that they get a restful night of sleep. • Remembering and sharing dreams with friends and family can be fun. • People who have frequent nightmares should seek counseling or psychological help.
Behavior modification	• Ignoring an unwanted behavior can often reduce its frequency. • Rewarding a behavior tends to increase its frequency.
Social learning/ Socialization	• Learning certain accepted ways of acting can help smooth relationships with others. • Different groups of people have different accepted ways of acting.
Social perception	• Many of the views we hold are gained from or influenced by others. • Perceptions derived from society regarding what is right or wrong or good or bad may have little to do with the inherent goodness or badness of the behavior. (For example, people consider burping at the dinner table rude in some countries and polite in others.)
Long-term memory	• Storing content learned in school in long-term memory usually takes effort. • There are techniques that can help you with the task of committing material to long-term memory.
Cognitive structures and schemata	• Trying to figure out how new knowledge fits into what you already know is important. • Drawing a knowledge web may help a person note relationships between old and new knowledge.
Biological needs	• Every living thing has biological needs for food, water, rest, and exercise.
Social needs	• Most people have need for social acceptance and recognition.

(continued on next page)

FIGURE 10-2

Sample K–6 Content from Psychology and Social Psychology

---

[3]These generalizations and main ideas may seem incredibly simplistic, provoking a reaction like "Doesn't everybody already know this!" Sadly, the answer is, no! Many children are being raised in situations where this knowledge is not being conveyed. Remember that part of the task of being a good social studies teacher is learning how and when to reveal the taken-for-granted adult understandings we possess.

CONCEPT OR TOPIC	SAMPLE MAIN IDEAS AND GENERALIZATIONS
Cognitive development	• Some kinds of learning may be difficult for young people because their mind has not grown to a stage where it can easily handle the new content. • Cognitive development can be halted or delayed by a number of factors, one of which is environmental deprivation. • Cognitive development continues through life and is enhanced by learning effort.
Intelligence	• There are many different kinds or facets of intelligence. • Intelligence is partly due to heredity and partly due to environmental influences. • Since we cannot influence heredity, it makes sense to do as much with the environment as practicable.
Later years	• Old people have special needs. • Sometimes friendship with a young person can help older people feel better.
Fear	• Fear is a normal emotion and can be a healthy reaction to dangerous circumstances. • Children should not have to live in fear of physical harm or psychological abuse. • Unfounded fears (phobias) are not normal and should be treated.
Hate	• Hatred is a strong emotion—usually accompanied by unfounded beliefs—that may cause people to take actions that hurt others. • Disapproval and dislike are milder emotions that people do not often use to justify behavior that hurts others.
Love/Attraction/ Affection	• All people want to be loved. • There are different kinds of love. • Mutual expressions of affection—that society considers age-appropriate—are good.
Joy/Pleasure	• Life brings people many forms of joy and pleasure. • Both work and leisure can be sources of pleasure.
Self-concept and self esteem	• A positive self-concept is important to your success and fulfillment in life. • People can influence your self-concept by how they act toward you. • A person who feels bad about himself or herself needs help.
Nonverbal communications	• A person's posture, facial expressions, and gestures can convey much about his or her present state of mind and physical well-being. • Sending nonverbal signals that are consistent with your verbal utterances adds strength to your message.
Conflict resolution	• Conflicts are a natural part of life. • Well-established methods for resolving conflicts really work and make violence unnecessary. • Anyone can learn how to resolve conflicts peacefully.

(continued on next page)

FIGURE 10-2, continued
Sample K–6 Content from Psychology and Social Psychology

CONCEPT OR TOPIC	SAMPLE MAIN IDEAS AND GENERALIZATIONS
Attachment	• Attachments to childhood toys, blankets, or other objects is natural and harmless in most cases. • Attachments to significant others—usually parents, grandparents, guardians, or other family members—are essential to good mental health.
Aggression/Violence	• Aggression and violence are largely learned behaviors. • Aggression and violence thwart the achievement of other personal and social goals. • Aggression and violence in the classroom are unacceptable.
Conformity	• It is common to want to be like other people and to have the things they have. • Conforming to some expectations for behavior is important. • Taken to extremes, conformity may have negative consequences for individuals and social groups.
Altruism	• Taking actions that benefit others produces a kind of personal satisfaction that cannot be attained by other means.
Prejudice, racism, sexism, ageism, religious prejudice	• It is wrong to harbor or express ill-founded thoughts that are damaging to others. • Refusing other people's rights, calling them names, or attacking them in any way is not acceptable.
Sex roles	• Most societies have differentiated domestic tasks and occupations based on gender status. • Rigid conceptions of gender-appropriate roles unfairly limit life's possibilities for both women and men. • Some individuals feel that rigid sex roles should be maintained; others want complete freedom from sex-role restrictions.
Values/Moral development	• People must develop morally as well as physically and cognitively. • Values are learned in the home, school, peer group, and church. • Certain values, such as honesty, are held by virtually all Americans.
Lying	• People lie for a variety of reasons—two of which are to stay out of trouble and to protect the feelings of others. • Lying can cause unforeseen trouble that a person may later very much regret.
Propaganda	• Learning the persuasion techniques used to promote products, ideas, and people can help us be better judges of the truth.
Role models	• Parents are often positive role models. • Having a good role model can help children develop into healthy adults.
Play	• Play is normal and healthy activity during childhood. • Adults may discourage some forms of play for a variety of reasons. • Learning how to play is an important childhood development task.

FIGURE 10-2, continued
Sample K–6 Content from Psychology and Social Psychology

temporary learning on the nature of beliefs, attitudes, and values. The topic of values education is so important to social studies that I have devoted Chapter 17 to it.

METHODS FOR TEACHING PSYCHOLOGY AND SOCIAL PSYCHOLOGY

Teachers can best convey psychology and social psychology content understandings to children through discussion of children's literature, role playing, and various forms of action research. Let's briefly examine how you can use these methods to accomplish important social studies content learning in each of these disciplines.

Children's Literature

Children's literature, especially the growing body of fiction that addresses interpersonal issues, offers a high-interest doorway to the content of psychology and social psychology. A book such as Howe's *The Hospital Book* (1994) can help children deal with, for example, the feelings of fear that can develop when a parent is admitted to a hospital. The book could be read individually by the affected child, but it would be better to read it aloud to the entire class over a period of several days. Take care to allow the children time to react to the content of the story. For example, have your students describe the emotions and thoughts of the actors, drawing inferences based on their own experiences. ("How did Marna feel when her mother got sick?") Ask the children whether anything similar has ever happened to them, allowing one or two volunteers to share their personal stories. ("Have any of your parents ever gotten sick?") Make sure that the children are understanding the key psychological and social psychological terms used. ("Sonya said that she felt real *upset* and nervous when her mom had to go and stay at the hospital. She had bad dreams and kept waking up. What does it mean when we say we feel upset? What are the kinds of things that can happen that are upsetting?")

Beyond giving students time to react to and process the content of children's literature focused on psychological and social psychological content, help children explore alternative ways to resolve problems that are presented. Have children examine the way the story resolves its main conflict, then help them consider other ways of resolving the main conflict and examine their likely consequences.

Using children's literature to accomplish the goals and objectives of social studies is an intelligent use of instructional time. You can still enjoy the story and follow it up with language arts activities during that period of the day. Your efforts to build an appreciation of literature are not hindered by social studies-focused discussions or follow-up activities, such as informal surveys, designed to anchor the book in children's everyday realities. Guides to children's literature, such as *A to Zoo* and *Children's Books in Print,* can help you identify topically focused stories to augment your social studies instruction.

Role Playing

Role playing is one of the most powerful techniques for learning social psychological content. The power of role playing comes from its active nature. Actors' involvement quickly taps into emotions, providing insights that cannot normally be gained through detached study or discussion. You can easily structure role plays to provide insight into such social psychological content as lying, cheating, stealing, rejection, sexism, racism, religious prejudice, conformity, cliques, bullying, defiance of legitimate authority, family problems, school problems, and interpersonal problems. Chapter 19 contains in-depth information on using role playing in social studies instruction.

Action Research

When students attempt to find answers to practical questions, issues, or problems within their own environment they are engaged in action research. *Action research* and *inquiry instruction* are terms that stand for much the same thing: taking steps to find things out when a question, issue, or problem arises. Chapter 14 is devoted to an explanation of inquiry instruction. It provides examples of students investigating cheating and rule-breaking behaviors in their own schools. In addition, it offers an overview of several action research methods such as surveys and observational studies.

Applying action research techniques to the content of psychology and social psychology allows students to move beyond their traditional role as passive consumers of information. It places students more in the role of scientific investigators attempting to discover and verify the ideas they have about the nature and causes of human behavior.

GO AWAY! WE DON'T WANT TO PLAY WITH YOU!

Grade: Second

Topic: What does it feel like to be left out?

Overview: Sooner or later children find themselves in situations where they are left out of a specific play group that they desire to be in. Learning to empathize with others who are left out can reduce playmate rejection behaviors. In addition, giving students strategies to help deal with rejection may lessen the hurtful effects of playmate rejection.

Objectives: As a result of this lesson, students will:

- identify emotions children typically feel when they are left out of a play group
- describe ways to resolve situations where someone is about to be left out
- select a constructive alternative course of action for a situation where someone is left out

Suggested Time: Two or three class periods

Instructional Strategies

Guided imagery

Role playing

Decision making

Art interpretation

Children's literature (in the follow-up)

Materials/Resources Needed: Crayons, paint, markers, art paper, *Lila on the Landing* by Sue Alexander

Suggestions for Teaching the Lesson

Opening the Lesson: Begin this lesson by asking students to sit up close to you on the floor with their arms and legs folded. Have them relax and close their eyes, freeing their minds of everything. Allow 5 to 10 seconds for the group to become quiet.

Once the students are quiet, ask them to imagine going to a new school where they don't know anyone. "Imagine you are all by yourself. Each day, when recess comes and after lunch, too, you try to get into the games other children are playing, but people just ignore you and won't let you play. When captains pick teams you stand with the group, but it always seems that the teams are full before anyone picks you. Even children playing

quiet games in small groups tell you to go away, saying that they don't want to you interfere."

Have the students open their eyes and describe how the situations made them feel. (Possible responses are sad, lonely, angry, hurt, depressed, and so on.)

Ask the students to raise their hands if they have ever had those feelings when they were left out and not allowed to be in someone's play group.

Allow two or three students who volunteer to tell about real situations that they experienced.

Tell the students that in this lesson they are going to learn more about how it feels to be left out. They will also learn how to deal with situations where someone is being left out.

Developing the Lesson: Introduce the following role-play scenarios:

Scenario 1:   Sam, Jane, and Daniel are playing catch with a Frisbee. They seem to be having a lot of fun. Megan comes up and asks to join in, "Can I play, too?"

Discuss some potential things that could happen in this setting and list them on the board. (Here are a few: Megan could be included; Megan could be excluded with some kind of excuse that was polite; Megan could be rudely excluded and, in turn, call the trio names as she was leaving; and Megan could try to jump into the game by stealing the Frisbee.)

Ask for volunteers to perform these different role plays. After each role play, analyze what happened and how it made the children feel. Allow the students to suggest new ways to handle the situation. Point out that it was probably easy to include Megan in this situation, but in some circumstances it might not be so easy.

Scenario 2:   Tonya and Anwar are using the teeter-totter. Opal comes up and asks to have a turn, "I never get a chance to use the teeter-totter."

Discuss some potential things that could happen in this setting. (Here are a few: Tonya and Anwar could say "Too bad, we got here first." Tonya and Anwar could ask Opal to wait a while or to go and try to find a friend who would ride with her.

Either Tonya or Anwar could get off for a while and let Opal ride.

Ask volunteers to play the parts of Opal, Anwar, and Tonya. After each potential resolution, analyze what happened and how it made the children feel.

Closing the Lesson: Distribute crayons, paints, markers, and art paper. Have the children fold the paper down the center and ask them to draw or paint a cartoon scene on the left showing a play scene where they have been excluded. On the right, have the children redo the scene showing how they could have been included. Have the students write cartoon bubbles to show what the characters are saying.

Allow the children to share their art interpretations. Display them on a bulletin board.

Evaluating the Lesson

Key questions for the students:

How might a child feel when he or she is left out?

What are some ways to resolve situations where someone is left out?

Follow-up Teaching Suggestions

Read and discuss *Lila on the Landing* by Sue Alexander.

CHILD ABUSE IS AGAINST THE LAW[4]

Grade Level: K–1
Author: Janice Habersham
Time Required: One class period
Concepts/Vocabulary: Abuse, protection from abuse, teacher's legal responsibility
Main Ideas
a. Children have the right not to be abused.
b. The law requires people who work with children to report suspected child abuse.

Objectives: As a result of this lesson, students will:

• be able to define child abuse
• be able to identify the child's right not to be abused
• be able to state who has legal responsibility to help a child suspected of being abused

Instructional Strategies

Listening to a short story of child abuse

Identifying evidence of child abuse in story

Discussing child-abuse law and teachers' legal responsibilities toward children

Teacher Background

In the law child abuse is defined as:

1. physical injury or death inflicted upon a child by a parent or caretaker thereof by other than accidental means;

2. neglect or exploitation of a child by a parent or caretaker thereof;

3. sexual assault of a child; or

4. sexual exploitation of a child (that is, conduct allowing, permitting, encouraging, or requiring a child to engage in prostitution or print or film/video child pornography).

Generally the following persons, if they have cause to believe that a child has been abused, must report such abuse: physicians, hospital or medical personnel, dentists, psychologists, podiatrists, registered or licensed nurses, professional counselors, social workers, family therapists, schoolteachers, administrators, counselors, child-counseling personnel, child-service personnel, and law enforcement personnel.

Check the law in your home state and identify any agencies that help protect children from child abuse.

A note of concern and caution: While figures vary some, research and experience suggest that there is a strong likelihood that at least one child in any classroom comes from an abusive home or may have experienced parents using abusive behaviors. You are cautioned to be alert to the feelings and needs of all the children in your classroom. It is also advised that you "nip in the bud" any comments that a child might make regarding his or her

---

[4]This lesson was adapted from the Georgia Law-Related Education Curriculum Supplements (GELRECS). GELRECS is in the public domain and available through ERIC.

own abuse. A child seeking to share such experiences needs to be heard, but not by the entire class. Tell the child that you want to hear what he or she has to say, but that it must wait until after the lesson. Later, after hearing what the child says, if you believe he or she has been or is being abused, your state's law may give you no alternative but to report this information to your principal. A child who comes forth with such comments needs to be given immediate access to a counselor or other professionals licensed to deal with child abuse.

Materials/Resources Needed: "The Little Match Girl" by Hans Christian Andersen, optional: filmstrip or videotape of "The Little Match Girl"

Procedure

1. Read "The Little Match Girl" to the group.

2. Discuss how the little girl in the story was treated. Her treatment is an example of child abuse.

   a. What evidence of child abuse was there in the story "The Little Match Girl"?

   b. How did the abuse affect the little girl's life?

   c. What might have happened if she could have been protected, by law, from child abuse?

   d. What might have happened if she had told her teacher? a neighbor?

3. Define child abuse for the students. (Abuse includes harsh physical treatment and emotional abuse, threats, and demeaning language or acts.)

   Read the following examples and ask related questions about what the child can do.

   a. Sometimes Ollie, age 12, misses school for a whole week. His pal, Matt, assumed that Ollie was sickly. One day Ollie tells Matt that when his mom gets mad at him, she locks Ollie in a closet for days. He shows Matt bruises on his hand from pounding on the door. He is always truthful. What should Matt do?

   b. Paula's mother constantly threatens to pour boiling water over her head if she doesn't obey. Her mother has never done this, but Paula is still afraid. What should Paula do?

4. Tell children that they have certain rights and that the law protects children from abuse. One of the rights of children is that they have the right not to be abused. Doctors, teachers, nurses, social workers, and day-care personnel are required to report suspected child abuse (see complete list in Teacher Background). Child abuse can be reported to the county Department of Family Children Services (DFACS).

5. Help the children distinguish between abuse and behaviors that are not likely to be seen as abusive. (Examples of behaviors not likely to be seen as abusive: mild spanking on the buttocks with hand, being sent to room for a limited time, having a privilege removed, or being yelled at)

6. Return to the discussion of "The Little Match Girl" and ask some of the same questions again. Note that the teacher is required by law to report a suspected case of child abuse. The neighbor is *not* required by law. Emphasize that a child who is being abused should ask for help.

Evaluation

- Class participation through discussion and response should allow the teacher to evaluate whether the objectives have been reached.

Enrichment

- Have children suggest possibilities for a new ending for "The Little Match Girl," in which she receives help.
- Have children draw pictures of people who will help an abused child.

THE LITTLE MATCH GIRL
by Hans Christian Andersen

It was bitterly cold; snow was falling and darkness was gathering, for it was the last evening of the year—New Year's Eve. In the cold and gloom a poor little girl walked, bareheaded and barefoot, through the streets. She was wearing slippers, it is true, when she left home, but what good were they? They used to be her mother's, so you can imagine how big they were. The little girl lost them as she ran across the street to escape from two carriages that were being driven terribly fast. One slipper could not be found, and a boy ran off with the other, saying that he could use it very nicely as a cradle some day when he had children of his own.

So the little girl walked about the streets on her naked feet, which were red and blue with the cold. In her old apron she carried a whole lot of matches, and she had a packet of them in her hand as well. Nobody had bought any from her, and no one had given her a single penny all day long. She crept along, hungry and shivering, the picture of misery, poor little thing! The snowflakes fell on her long golden hair which curled so prettily about her neck, but she did not think of her appearance now. Lights were shining in every window, and there was a glorious smell of roast goose in the street, for it was New Year's Eve, and she could not think of anything else.

She huddled down in a little heap in a corner formed by two houses, one of which projected further out into the street than the other, but though she tucked her little legs up under her she felt colder and colder. She did not dare to go home, for she had sold no matches nor earned a single penny. Her father would be sure to beat her, and besides, it was cold at home. They had nothing but the roof above them, and the wind whistled through that, even though the largest cracks were stuffed with straw and rags. Her little hands were almost dead with cold. Oh, how one little match would warm her! If only she dare pull just one from the packet, strike it on the wall and warm her fingers. She pulled one out —scr-r-ratch! How it spluttered and burnt! It was a warm bright flame like a little candle when she held her hand over it, but what a strange light! It seemed to the little girl as if she were sitting in front of a great iron stove with polished brass knobs and brass ornaments. The fire burnt so beautifully and gave out such a lovely warmth. Oh, how wonderful that was! The child had already stretched out her feet to warm them too, when out went the flame, the stove vanished, and there she sat with a bit of the burnt match in her hand.

She struck another. It burnt clearly, and where the light fell upon the wall, it became transparent like a curtain of gauze. She could see right into the room where a shining white cloth was spread on the table; it was covered with beautiful china, and in the center of it stood the roast goose, stuffed with prunes and apples, steaming deliciously. And what was even more wonderful was that the goose hopped down from the dish, waddled straight up to the poor child! Then out went the match, and nothing else could be seen but the thick cold wall.

She struck another, and suddenly she was sitting under the most beautiful Christmas tree; it was much larger and much lovelier than the one she had seen last year through the doors of the rich merchant's house. A thousand candles lit up the green branches, and gaily colored pictures, like those in the shop-windows, looked down upon her. The little girl reached forward with both hands—then, out went the match. The many candles on the Christmas tree rose higher and higher throughout the air, and she saw that they had now turned into bright stars. One of them fell, streaking the sky with light.

"Now someone is dying," said the little girl, for old Granny, the only one who had ever been good to her, but who was now dead, had said: "Whenever a star falls, a soul goes up to God."

She struck another match on the wall; once more there was light, and in the glow stood her old Granny, oh so bright and shining, and looking so gentle, kind, and loving. "Granny!" cried the little girl. "Oh, take me with you! I know you will disappear when the match is burnt out; you will vanish like the warm stove, the lovely roast goose, and the great glorious Christmas tree!" Then she quickly struck all the rest of the matches in the packet, for she did so want to keep Granny with her. The matches flared up with such a blaze that it was brighter than broad daylight, and her old

Granny had never seemed so beautiful nor so stately before. She took the little girl in her arms and flew with her high up, oh, so high, towards glory and joy! Now they knew neither cold nor hunger nor fear, for they were with God.

But in the cold dawn, in the corner formed by the two houses, sat the little girl with rosy cheeks and smiling lips—dead—frozen to death on the last evening of the Old Year. The dawn of the New Year rose on the huddled figure of the little girl, holding the matches, of which a packet had been burnt more than halfway down.

"She was evidently trying to warm herself," people said. But no one knew what beautiful visions she had seen, and in what a blaze of glory she had entered with her dear old Granny into the heavenly joy and gladness of a new year.

REFERENCES AND SELECTED READINGS

Bean, R. 1992. *Cooperation, social responsibility & other skills. Using the four conditions of self-esteem in elementary and middle schools.* Santa Cruz, CA: ETR Associates.

Derman-Sparks, L. 1989. *Anti-bias curriculum. Tools for empowering young children.* Washington, D.C.: National Association for the Education of Young Children.

Hipp, E. 1985. *Fighting invisible tigers: A student guide to life in "the jungle."* Minneapolis, MN: Free Spirit Publishing, Inc.

Howe, J. 1994. *The hospital book.* New York: Morrow Junior Books.

Jenness, D. 1990. *Making sense of social studies.* New York: Macmillan.

Kincher, J. 1990. *Psychology for kids. 40 fun tests that help you learn about yourself.* Minneapolis, MN: Free Spirit Publishing, Inc.

Schmitz, C., and Hipp, E. 1987. *A teacher's guide to fighting invisible tigers.* Minneapolis, MN: Free Spirit Publishing, Inc.

CHAPTER 11

Sociology: Exploring Contemporary Society

INTRODUCTION

The concepts and theories of sociology play a major role in aiding our understanding of groups within society. Along with social psychology and to a lesser
extent cultural anthropology, sociology provides the vocabulary we use to
describe virtually all areas of social life.

Sociology plays an important but hidden role in children's early socialization
into peer groups and school. In addition, sociological concepts are routinely
applied to the analysis of family life. Consider your own family relationships
for a moment. If you had brothers and sisters, how did your birth order
influence your relationships? Were you the bossy big sister or the little brat who
always wanted to be included in an older sibling's doings? How do you think
your position in the family influenced your upbringing—and even your choice
to become an early childhood educator?

Let's briefly examine the background and make up of this social science
discipline and attempt to gain some insight into how it contributes to elementary social studies.

THE DISCIPLINE'S PERSPECTIVE

Sociology is the study of the interaction processes and consequences of group
life. Sociologists seek to reveal and understand the patterns of human social
behavior that emerge in contemporary group living. As a result, sociology may
be thought of as the scientific analysis of groups functioning within society and,
on a much grander scale, the analysis of society itself. Sociologists focus on
such large- and small-scale social phenomena as education, marriage, social
mobility, crowd behavior, social status, subcultures, deviance, violence, and
family living.

The discipline of sociology is relatively new compared to history, geography,
anthropology, and the other social sciences and humanities that make up social
studies. Auguste Comte, a French philosopher, is credited with coining the term
sociology in 1838, asserting his belief that this new social science would
discover fundamental "laws" of human society similar to those being revealed
in physics, botany, and biology. It was not until the 1880s and 1890s that
sociology came to be recognized as an academic subject.

The United States dominated the field of sociology during the first half of
the twentieth century. This new academic discipline seemed ideally suited to
the study of many social programs and problems that accompanied our rapid
national development. As sociology grew, the sociological perspective spread
into the older social sciences and spawned the development of new fields such
as social psychology, criminology, demography, sociology of education, and
sociology of medicine. Despite this tremendous growth, attempts to build grand
theories of society resting on fundamental laws akin to those in the natural
sciences failed.

Figure 11-1 displays an abbreviated conceptual outline of sociology, restricted to eliminate excessive overlap with social psychology and cultural

I. Major Concepts/Ideas
A. Society
1. Social organization
a. Leadership
b. Social roles
1. Sex (gender role)
2. Family role
3. Citizen (public role)
4. Work role
c. Patterns of social interaction
2. Values
a. Personal
b. Religious
c. Social/Cultural
3. Attitudes
4. Beliefs
5. Social change
a. Types
1. Social
2. Cultural
3. Technological
b. Causes
1. War
2. Diffusion
3. Discovery/Invention
4. Social movements
5. New ideas
c. Theories of change
1. Social Darwinism
2. Functionalism
3. Conflict
6. Social control
a. Internal/External
b. Social status
1. Ascribed status
2. Achieved status
3. Occupational status
B. Groups
1. Ethnic
2. Racial
3. Occupation
C. Social Institutions/Agents of Socialization
1. Marriage

a. Interracial marriage
2. Education
a. Functions/Uses
1. Social
2. Economic
b. Phenomena/Practices
1. Tracking
2. Busing
3. Testing
3. Religion
a. Beliefs/Practices/Ceremonies
b. Religious fundamentalism
4. Mass media
a. Types
1. Newspapers/Magazines/Bulk mail
2. Televisions
3. Movies/Videos
4. Radio
5. Software/Computer networks
b. Use and impact
1. Information distribution
2. Entertainment
3. Advertising
c. Problems/Abuses
1. Censorship
2. Propaganda
5. Work
a. Labor unions
b. Professional associations
c. Work subcultures
6. Family
a. Functions
b. Problems
1. Divorce
2. Abuse
c. Rules/Governance
D. Social Phenomena
1. Substance abuse
2. Prejudice and discrimination
3. Crime
4. Poverty
5. Unemployment
6. Deviance

(continued on next page)

◆ ◆

FIGURE 11-1
Conceptual Outline of Sociology[1]

[1]This outline is adapted from the Social Studies Descriptor Project, Educational Products Information Exchange Institute. Used by permission.

7. Collective behavior
   a. Crowd behavior
   b. Social movements
   c. Fashions and crazes
8. Hunger
9. Social stratification
10. Social mobility
11. Segregation
12. Terrorism
13. Cultural lag
14. Ethnocentrism
15. Cultural pluralism/Diversity
16. Subcultures/Lifestyles
  E. Social Programs
   1. Poverty programs
    a. Welfare
    b. Aid to Families with Dependent Children

    c. Food Stamps
   2. Health programs
    a. Medicare and Medicaid
    b. Disease control
   3. Education programs
    a. Head Start
    b. School Lunch Program
   4. Population/Birth control
   5. Housing programs
II. Sociological Theories
  A. Social Learning Theory
  B. Modeling
  C. Labeling
  D. Social Darwinism/Evolution
  E. Theories of Deviance
  F. Role Theory
  G. Symbolic Interaction

FIGURE 11-1, continued
Conceptual Outline of Sociology

anthropology. Before you read the outline, however, I want you to jot down three reasons for why there are many more female than male elementary schoolteachers in contemporary U.S. society. Now as you examine the outline, see how many of your reasons can be tied to the sociological concepts it lists. Save your list and be ready to share it in class.

EXERCISE 11-1

1. Now that you have examined the outline, were you able to locate any of the reasons you cited for the predominance of women in teaching? Did any of your reasons have to do with our current cultural perception of women as being more nurturant than men? Did you feel that tradition played a big role in women's (and men's) occupational choices? Did you feel that women's selection of elementary schoolteaching as a career might have much to do with their perceptions of responsibilities that come with marriage and child rearing?

2. Look through the outline and identify one concept that you wish to know more about. Use your research skills to find out more about the concept. Report your findings in class.

3. Select a primary-grade-level social studies textbook and examine it for sociological content. Keep the outline handy as you page through the book. If sociological content isn't being taught, then what else is, and is it more important? Justify your response.

WHAT K–6 STUDENTS SHOULD KNOW

As with several other social sciences and the humanities, no official pronouncements guide what sociological content students might properly consider in grades K through 6. My own recommendation is shown in Figure 11-2. The figure presents potential concepts in the left column and sample activity ideas in the right column. As you examine the activity ideas see if you think you would feel comfortable dealing with this content in your own classroom and attempt to determine whether the activity is best suited to the primary or intermediate grades.

I hope you feel some of the activity ideas are attractive possibilities for social studies lessons. You can probably think of other ideas or different ways of implementing instruction on the same concepts that you would personally prefer.

CONCEPT	ACTIVITY IDEAS
Achieved status	• Hold brief ceremonies to commemorate their achievements • Interview parents regarding their own achievements in life. • Use children's literature to study people who accomplished great things as a result of hard work. • Study careers, noting the education and training required for successful practice.
Attitudes and values	• Do simple attitude surveys toward foods, sports, television shows, and so on. • Survey students' attitudes toward classroom and school policies. • Study parents' attitudes toward community problems and current events. • Take a widely held value such as honesty and attempt to develop criteria that could be used to determine when it might be appropriate to violate that value (for example, to be less than completely honest).
Citizen roles	• Write a classroom constitution and bill of rights. • Conduct an election to set up a classroom government. • Involve the students in settling conflicts, distributing work burdens, and allocating school resources.
Prejudice and discrimination	• Set up a skit or role play that depicts discrimination; reverse roles and ask students to help analyze why the discrimination was painful and wrong. • Read historical accounts of race and gender discrimination in the United States. • Interview parents about discrimination that they might have experienced.
Leisure	• Make a chart showing the favorite pastimes of the students. • Collect data on the favorite pastimes of students in other grade levels, then look for similarities and differences. • Set up a hobby and craft area in the classroom and share skills.

(continued on next page)

FIGURE 11-2

Selected Concepts and Activity Ideas for Sociology

Ethnicity
- Chart the ethnic heritage of students, going back two or three generations, then transfer this information to a world map.
- Invite parents or community members to come and present aspects of their ethnic heritage to the class.
- Following in-depth study, hold an ethnic festival day complete with foods, music, and costumes.

Etiquette
- Study "old fashioned" etiquette or etiquette associated with a particular cultural group; practice using these mannerisms.
- Establish special etiquette practices for your classroom.
- Role play situations to practice proper etiquette.

Family
- Make mobiles of the nuclear and extended families of each child in the class; start with the children on the top followed by living parents, aunts, uncles, and grandparents.
- Investigate family roles looking especially at who performs what work in the home; note if some chores are more often done by female children or mothers.

Fashions and crazes
- See if you can create a clothing, accessory, or phrase craze in your school.
- Investigate old clothing, hairstyles, and music fashions; have parents help locate photographs and bring in old clothing items.

Gender roles
- Make a list of fathers' and mothers' occupations; see if some are more often held by women than men or vice versa.
- Observe the playground to determine whether boys and girls do the same kinds of things. Keep a chart and discuss your findings.
- Make wish lists of future careers; see if they follow current gender stereotypes.

Leadership
- Allow different students to experience a leadership role in academic and other circumstances.
- Discuss the qualities of a good leader.
- Invite community leaders into the classroom to describe their jobs and tell about one specific episode where they had their leadership tested.

Name-calling
- Adopt a negative and a positive nickname for each student; use positive names in the morning and negative in the afternoon. Discuss the influence this had on students' feelings and the classroom atmosphere.
- Spend a day calling everyone in the room Ms. or Mr. using last names; discuss how this makes people feel.

Role model
- Identify older students in the school or neighborhood who can be looked up to as role models. Working in groups of two or three, create role-model reports that profile each student's hobbies, interests, and abilities; include photographs or video. Arrange for a classroom visit by the student and his or her parent(s).
- Invite adult role models into the classroom; ask them to focus on their early lives, paying particular attention to what influenced their success in life.

FIGURE 11-2, continued
Selected Concepts and Activity Ideas for Sociology

EXERCISE 11-2

1. Go to your curriculum materials center and check out a social studies textbook for any grade, K through 6. Page through the book looking for sociology content. In many cases you may have to look "between the lines and behind the topic" to find any sociology. Note your findings. Bring the book to class, along with your notes, and share what you've found.

2. Form small groups and develop an imaginary K–6 scope and sequence that stresses sociological content. Compare your work with other groups and attempt to reach consensus on unified curriculum. Mail your scope and sequence to a major textbook publisher along with a letter requesting better coverage of this content in future editions of their series.

DISCUSSION QUESTIONS

1. Now that you've begun to understand the important role that sociology could play in the social studies curriculum, how can you explain its general neglect? For example, do you attribute this neglect more to lack of knowledge about the discipline's content or more to people's fear of dealing with sociological concepts?

2. Why do you suppose sociologists haven't organized and attempted to promote early grade level study of content from their discipline in a fashion similar to historians?

3. First-grade social studies often focuses on different types of families, here and abroad. Students learn about different lifestyles and cultures and attempt to gain some perspective on their own family experiences. If you believe this study is beneficial, would you also support the study of other identifiable groups such as play groups, peer groups, and school gangs?

FAMILY RULES[2]

Grade Level: K–1
Author: Donna R. Bishop
Time Required: Two class periods
Concepts/Vocabulary: Rules, consequences, legal rights, legal responsibilities

Main Ideas

a. Families establish rules in order to promote safety, health, and order.

b. The law gives parents or guardians the right and responsibility to establish reasonable rules and to enforce them with reasonable punishments.

c. Good rules have a purpose, are clear, and can be followed.

Objectives: As a result of this lesson, students will:

- name examples of rules families have
- list the possible positive and negative consequences of following or failing to follow family rules
- identify children who are following family rules
- tell what makes good rules

Instructional Strategies

Data collecting on chart paper

Questioning rules followed at home

Decision making concerning what makes good rules

Discussing the consequences of following or not following rules

Teacher Background

Parents have considerable power over the lives of children under the age of eighteen who are not married or declared emancipated minors by a court. Parents can represent their children in court and they can require that the children live with them. They can expect children to obey reasonable rules and demands. Children do not, however, legally have to obey parents' rules or demands if they are illegal. Parents have the right to punish their children in a reasonable way, but children have the *right not to be abused*. State laws protect children from physical and/or emotional abuse. Parents also control the personal property of their children. Parents have a right, for example, to the earnings of a minor child, although many parents do not exercise that right.

It is the duty of each parent to provide for the maintenance, protection, supervision, and education of children until they reach the age of majority. Under the law, maintenance means food, clothing, housing, and medical care. The law also obligates parents to see that children go to school until they are sixteen. (Note that a "deprived child" is one who is without proper parental care or control, sustenance, education as required by law, or other care or control necessary for physical, mental, or emotional health or morals. If a court finds a child to be deprived, it can require certain behaviors of the parents.)

To provide supervision, parents make rules. It is the responsibility of the parent to establish rules for the well-being of the child, and it is the child's responsibility to follow these rules until he or she can make decisions on his or her own.

Materials/Resources Needed: Chart paper, headed as shown; magazines with pictures of children and families in a variety of settings; masking tape; marking pen; scissors

:(		:)

---

[2]This lesson plan was adapted from the Georgia Law-Related Education Curriculum Supplements (GELRECS). GELRECS is in the public domain and available through ERIC.

Procedure

Period One

1. Ask students to name things they "have to do" at home. List about ten of their responses on the middle section of the chart paper, making sure that the list contains a representative selection of typical family rules such as "Make my bed," "Be home by dark," and "Help wash the dishes."

2. Ask what happens if they *don't* do the things they have to do. List their responses on the chart paper in the left section under the "sad face." Probe to see if these bad things that happen make them feel bad, too.

3. Now ask what happens if students *do* what is asked of them or follow their parents' directions. Are they given special privileges, money, hugs, or smiles? List students' responses on the right section under the "happy face."

   Ask how they feel about their rewards for doing what they are supposed to do. Point out that sometimes we are not given anything for following rules, but that we may still feel good because we did what was right.

4. Redirect the students' attention to the middle column and ask what they call these things we all "have to do" at home? (They may be called home rules, rules, or family rules.)

   Write "FAMILY RULES" at the top of the middle section of the chart and point out that we have rules we follow at home just like our rules at school.

5. Point out that the happy and sad face sections are our *consequences*; they tell what happens if we do what is asked of us or if we fail to.

   Read the happy face column and tell students that this is what happens when we follow the rules. Then read the sad face column and tell them that this is what happens when we don't follow the rules.

6. Tell students that there are several ways of identifying a good rule.

   a. A good rule is clear. This means you can understand what the rule means. What if a rule said, "Never try to obfuscate the teacher's dictums"? Would that be a good rule? (No. Not unless, you know what it means.)

Have students look at the family rules on the chart. Check to see if they understand them. If not, make them clearer. (Be particularly careful of words or phrases that are vague or imprecise. For example, a rule could say, "Don't hit." But, don't hit what? a wall? a person? a ball? The rule needs to be clarified to say, "Don't hit people."

   b. A good rule can be followed. That means you can do what the rule says. What if a rule said, "All children must leave the room by flying out the windows"? Is it possible to do that? Is that a good rule? Have students look at the rules on the chart. Check to see that all of them can be followed. (Point out that some rules are harder to follow than others.)

   c. A good rule has a purpose. Ask: What if your class had a rule that said, "All children must wear paper rabbit ears to class every day." Is that a good rule? Would it be okay for an Easter party, but not every day? Is it silly? Does it have any sensible purpose?

Have students reexamine the family rules on the chart. For each one, write down its purpose—order, safety, health, and so on. Cross out any rules that do not seem to have a good purpose, but do not, at this point, try to generalize.

Period Two

1. Briefly review what was learned in the first period.

2. Distribute the magazines and ask the students to cut out pictures that show where a rule has been followed in a family. After about 5 minutes allow the students to come up one or two at a time and tape their pictures to the wall or chalkboard. Ask each child to explain the rule shown in his or her picture. With masking tape and marking pen clearly label each picture to show what rule is being followed.

   Now ask the students if they see two or more rules that have similar reasons that can go together. Have them explain their groupings (for example, rules to keep children safe at home, rules to keep the house clean and neat, and so on). Move the pictures so that they are in groupings.

   Summarize by stating that all families have rules to follow. Stress that rules help families get along, stay safe, and remain healthy. Explain that it is important to follow your family rules until you are old enough to make decisions for yourself. Until then your parents have a legal right to set up rules for you to follow, and you have a legal responsibility to follow those rules.

3. Tell the students that parents have a legal right to punish children (in a reasonable fashion) for not following the rules. (If necessary the teacher should go back over the negative consequences on the chart to give examples of reasonable punishment.)

Also, point out it is against the law for parents to make you do anything illegal. (Cite examples: steal, harm others, not tell the truth.)

Evaluation

- Have students divide a sheet of paper in half, and draw a picture of a family rule that is easy to follow on one side and a rule that is hard to follow on the other. Allow them to write about the drawings using inventive spelling.
- Ask students the following questions about their rules and pictures.
    a. What is the rule's purpose? Write the purposes on the board, and give them initials to aid students in labeling the drawings.

For example:

   S Safety

   O Order

   H Health

   b. Can these rules be followed if you try? Students should write "Y" or "N." Discuss any Ns.

   c. Are the rules clear? Discuss to check for understanding.

   d. What happens if you follow rules? What happens if you don't?

- Collect labeled drawings and use, along with observation, for evaluation.

Enrichment

- Have students suggest personal rules they would like to follow and write them on chart paper or the chalkboard. Examples of rules would be eating the right foods or completing assignments before lunch.
- Ask students to tell about any rules at home that are hard to follow, explaining why they are difficult. Encourage them to make a weekly progress report of the hardest rule to follow. These sheets could be taken home or left at school.

EXAMPLE OF PROGRESS REPORT

Name _____

My hardest rule to follow is _____

_____.

	Yes	Sometimes	No
Sunday			
Monday			
Tuesday			
Wednesday			
Thursday			
Friday			
Saturday			

DADDY'S WEEKEND DOINGS

Grade Level: Fifth

Content Focus: What fathers like to do on the weekend

Objectives: As a result of this lesson, students will:

- make statements that are limited generalizations concerning the weekend activities of their fathers
- help design a survey for data collection
- construct a graph that shows the results of their survey

Instructional Strategies

- Collecting information about what fathers like to do on the weekend
- Making graphs to show the results of the survey
- Discussing results and implications of the survey

Teacher Background

Husbands have significantly more leisure time than wives. In Western societies the family is the most important leisure group and adults spend a large proportion of their nonwork time with members of their families. Of primary interest is the influence of occupational status or prestige on choice of specific types of leisure activity. Leisure time includes both time spent alone and time spent with others in social and recreational activities, such as entertaining, exercising, watching television, and going out.

Recent studies have shown that leisure time is decreasing, not increasing as many experts had predicted. As a result, fathers may find themselves working on the weekend instead of spending time with the family. Tasks such as lawn maintenance and food shopping may intrude upon more relaxing leisure pursuits such as sports or entertainment.

Materials/Resources Needed: Paper, pencils, chart paper, markers or crayons, masking tape, construction paper, scissors, glue, computer, printer, and LCD projection panel

Procedure[3]

1. Start the lesson by asking what students do on the weekends. Do they have chores or do they mostly play? List all of the responses on the board. Have students look at the list. Ask if their fathers participate in the same activities on the weekends. (Mothers or guardians can be used as the focus for fatherless children.) Check those that are the same and add activities that have not been listed yet. Tell students the question they will investigate is, "What do fathers like to do on weekends?"

2. Using a computer and an LCD projection panel, work with the students to transfer and organize the information on the board into a paper survey instrument. The instrument might have different categories of typical leisure and weekend work activities such as sports, movies, dining out, lawn care, house cleaning, auto maintenance, and so on. (Note: If a computer or projection equipment is not available, consider working with a smaller subgroup of students.)

3. Divide the class into as many groups as there are classes to survey and arrange for an appropriate time for the group to visit the other classes to collect data. Make sure that the groups have enough copies of the survey for their assigned classes.

4. Involve students in compiling their data. (You may want to use the computer to aid this process, but it is also possible to simply list the categories on the chalkboard and post the numbers to it.)

5. Divide into the groups used to conduct the survey and distribute graphing materials. Ask each group to graph all of the data, or alternatively, ask different groups to graph different portions of the data. (For example, one group could do the sports data and another the work or chore data.)

6. Hang the different graphs in one area of the room and spend some time analyzing the results of the survey. Ask students to form generalizations about the weekend activities of their fathers.

Evaluation

- Were the students able to form generalizations about what fathers like to do on weekends?
- Did each student participate in constructing a graphic representation of the survey data?
- Did students actively assist in designing and implementing the survey?

---

[3]Before starting this lesson talk to other teachers to make sure it is all right to take surveys in their classes.

REFERENCES AND SELECTED READINGS

Atwood, V. A., et al. 1989. In the soup: An integrative unit. Part 1. *Social Studies and the Young Learner* 2(1):17–19.

Biskup, M. D., and Cozic, C. P., eds. 1992. *Youth violence.* San Diego, CA: Greenhaven Press, Inc.

Derman-Sparks, L. 1989. *Anti-bias curriculum. Tools for empowering young children.* Washington, D.C.: National Association for the Education of Young Children.

Field, S. D. 1992. An analysis of the disciplines in elementary school social studies textbooks, grades 1–4. *Georgia Social Science Journal* 23(1):33–40.

King, E. W., et al. 1994. *Educating young children in a diverse society.* Needham Heights, MA: Allyn and Bacon.

Rose, P. I., Glazer, P. M., and Glaser, M. P. 1990. *Sociology: Understanding society.* Needham Heights, MA: Prentice Hall, Inc.

Anthropology: Exploring Our Physical and Cultural Roots

The children carefully examined each object they pulled from the bag. A candy wrapper came out first. It was the wrapper for a chocolate Tootsie Pop®. Inside the wrapper was a piece of gum. "Ooo," said Charlotte, "this is sticky!" "Yuk!" exclaimed Tamara, "I can't stand this." Reginald placed the wrapper on the newsprint, marked a circle around it, and placed the number "1" in the circle next to the wrapper.

Angela began writing a description of the wrapper on her data collection chart. She wrote, "Chocolate Tootsie Pop wrapper with bubble gum stuck inside." Tamara remarked that whoever had eaten the Tootsie Pop® had probably also been chewing the gum. Charlotte agreed, adding that you couldn't eat a Tootsie Pop® and chew bubble gum at the same time. "You might swallow or choke on the gum," she reasoned.

Suddenly Angela bent over and picked up the wrapper again. "Did you notice this?" she asked, showing everyone in the group the red lipstick marks near the gum. "The gum came from a woman, or maybe a teenager, who was wearing lipstick! I'd better mention the lipstick marks in my description of the wrapper. It might be a clue to where our trash collection came from."

The next item out of the bag was a dried-out towelette with light smears of chocolate on it. Reginald took the towelette and placed it in a circle near the candy wrapper. He placed the number "2" in this circle. Angela began writing her description of the object. Suddenly Tamara interrupted, "I'll bet that's chocolate Tootsie Pop® on that towelette. See, it could have been an adult and a baby. Maybe it was a mother and her child!"

Bolstered by this thought, the children anxiously plunged into their analysis of the next object. . . .

INTRODUCTION
◆ ◆ ◆ ◆ ◆

The opening scenario attempts to capture some of the excitement fifth graders typically experience as they conduct a "trash dig." It's clear that the students are putting their writing and thinking skills to good use. More importantly, they are experiencing the thrill of doing anthropological fieldwork right in their classroom.

Let's briefly examine the discipline of anthropology, attempting to gain some insight into what content understandings this social science offers elementary social studies.

THE DISCIPLINE'S PERSPECTIVE
◆ ◆ ◆ ◆ ◆

The word *anthropology* literally means *study of human beings*. The field is often said to be divided into four major areas: physical anthropology, archaeology, anthropological linguistics, and ethnology. Anthropology is the study of cultural and biological human variation across time and space. Anthropologists are concerned with human origins, the development and diffusion of cultures, and variations in contemporary cultures. Anthropology is grounded in both the biological and social sciences. In addition, it draws on the humanities for its interpretations of cultural symbolism, art, and religion.

Anthropologists originally studied largely non-Western, primitive cultures by collecting artifacts, learning their customs, describing their social organization, and establishing their history. Up until World War II, anthropological studies were mainly of tribal societies in the South Pacific, Australia, Africa, and South America. Since the 1950s anthropologists have turned their attention toward smaller communities, life in urban settings, and studies of various groups within all modern societies.

Anthropology differs from sociology, social psychology, and political science in part because of the emphasis that anthropologists place on living among their informants, participating in life routines as they observe and record their field notes. This approach to research is called *ethnography* and has spawned sophisticated qualitative data analysis techniques used to organize and interpret voluminous quantities of anecdotal and descriptive notes.

Because anthropologists are involved in describing society and culture, they naturally use many of the same concepts, theories, and methods of the other social sciences. When appropriate, anthropologists may use surveys, questionnaires, and other research techniques to augment their field notes. However, anthropologists' continuing use of ethnographic research methods and their holistic concern with the comparative analysis of culture continue to differentiate their work from other fields.

Figure 12-1 displays a conceptual outline of anthropology. Before you read it, take a moment and write two short paragraphs. In the first, describe what you know about any ancient (prehistoric) culture. For example, you might name the culture and tell where they were located, when they lived, what their

I. Major Concepts/Ideas of Physical Anthropology
   A. The Fossil Record
      1. Strata
         a. Carbon dating
   B. Evolution
      1. Basic concepts
         a. Mutation
         b. Selective adaptation
         c. Gene pool
      2. Early primate evolution
      3. Evolution of Homo sapiens
         a. Material culture
         b. Stone caches/Tools
         c. Acclimatization
         d. Instincts
      4. Major stages of human evolution
         a. Paleolithic
         b. Mesolithic
         c. Neolithic
         d. Bronze Age
         e. Iron Age
   C. Human Variation
      1. Heredity influences
      2. Environmental influences
II. Major Concepts/Fields of Archaeology
   A. Archaeological Method and Evidence
      1. Archaeological site
      2. Archaeological debris
   B. Cultural Evolution
      1. Preagricultural
         a. Domestication
         b. Migration
      2. Postagricultural
III. Major Concepts/Fields of Cultural
   Anthropology
   A. Culture
      1. Ethnocentrism
      2. Enculturation/Socialization
      3. Acculturation/Change
      4. Cultural diversity
      5. Cultural adaptation
      6. Cultural relativism
      7. Universals
         a. Values
         b. Norms/Rules
            1. Folkways
            2. Mores
            3. Taboos
            4. Laws
            5. Customs
            6. Traditions
            7. Rituals
            8. Rites of passage
   B. Family and Marriage
      1. Family types
         a. Nuclear
         b. Extended
         c. Matrifocal
         d. Patrifocal
      2. Kinship
         a. Clan
      3. Marriage patterns
         a. Monogamy
         b. Polygamy
      4. Marriage practices
         a. Ceremony
         b. Dowry
         c. Endogamy
         d. Exogamy
   C. Economic Systems
      1. Pastoralism
      2. Slash and burn
      3. Nomadism
      4. Foraging
      5. Agrarian
      6. Industrial
      7. Postindustrial
   D. Religion
      1. Tribal religions
         a. Animism
         b. Priest/Priestess
         c. Shaman
      2. Religious symbolism
      3. Religious rituals
   E. Political Systems
IV. Anthropological Linguistics

FIGURE 12-1
Conceptual Outline of Anthropology[1]

---

[1]This outline is adapted from the Social Studies Content Descriptor Project, Educational Products Information Exchange Institute. Used by permission.

religion was like, or the types of tools they used. In the second, describe what you know about any contemporary non-Western culture. Now as you examine the outline, see if you can locate any of the concepts that appeared in your sentences. Save your sentences and be ready to share them in class.

EXERCISE 12-1

1. Now that you have examined the outline, look back at the paragraphs you wrote and see if you can add a sentence or two that expands or refines what you were saying. Did concepts in the outline activate this knowledge? Would you like to learn more anthropological information about the groups you targeted in your paragraphs?

2. Look back at the outline and identify one or two entries that you know little or nothing about. Look up the entry in a college dictionary, an encyclopedia, and a college-level introductory anthropology textbook. Write your findings on a single sheet of paper and be ready to explain your new knowledge to the rest of the class.

3. Select an upper-grade-level social studies textbook and examine it for anthropological content. Keep the outline handy as you page through the book. If anthropological content isn't being taught, then what else is, and is it more important? Justify your response.

WHAT K–6 STUDENTS SHOULD KNOW

No official pronouncements guide what anthropological content students might properly consider in grades K through 6. My own selections of potential concepts and related activities are shown in Figure 12-2. As you examine the activity ideas, see if you can visualize children at a particular grade level doing the recommended learning.

The activity ideas demonstrate that anthropology offers wonderful insights into culture that even very young children can appreciate. A key to this

---

CONCEPT

ACTIVITY IDEAS

Ceremonies

- Investigate the extent to which ceremonies play a role in school learning (Does the school observe a pledge of allegiance ceremony? Is there a flag ceremony each morning and afternoon? Are there ceremonies practiced in school clubs?)
- Videotape a common school ceremony as it happens at several different times or locations. Write a sequence chart noting common features. Make suggestions for improving the ceremony.
- Use students' suggestions to start one or more new ceremonies in your classroom. Discuss ways to elaborate or abbreviate the ceremony.

(continued on next page)

FIGURE 12-2

Selected Concepts and Activity Ideas for Anthropology

CONCEPT	ACTIVITY IDEAS
Cultural diffusion	• Examine instances of cultural diffusion present in the children's own lives (examples may come from borrowed linguistic terminology, music, clothing styles, and foods). Keep track of which cultures are most often represented and see if the children can offer reasons for this finding. • Use the Internet or some other means of international communication to solicit examples of how the culture of the United States influences life in other nations.
Cultural diversity	• Take simple, everyday events and determine how families from different cultures accomplish these tasks (some events to investigate are cooking, washing clothes, and celebrating birthdays). • Select a single food, such as an apple, egg, or rice, and investigate how different cultures prepare and use it. Hold a tasting party.
Cultural relativism	• Investigate what qualifies as "good table manners" in a variety of cultures; invite guests in to demonstrate appropriate and inappropriate behaviors. • Examine the ways in which children's families celebrate selected holidays. Seek adults' perceptions of their family traditions.
Family types	• Make mobiles of each child's family tree, going back two generations if possible; show only living family members. Analyze the mobiles for similarities and differences. • Investigate a culture (such as the Amish) that has extended family structure.
Folkways	• Select any daily living task associated with school (sharpening pencils, organizing homework papers, and so on) and share information about how different students accomplish this work. Examine how technology facilitates the work. • Observe how other classes go about their daily routines; keep notes and report your findings. Consider adopting any changes for the better.
Kinship	• Chart the kinship patterns of children in the class; note the number, gender, and age of relatives. • Read and discuss children's literature about kinship relations.
Norms	• Brainstorm and list the ideal norms of behavior in different school settings (for example, lunchroom, bathroom, playground, and classroom). Compare the lists and generate reasons why different behavior norms exist for these different locations. • Investigate school norms that parents experienced. Collect photographs from old yearbooks. Use parents as resource speakers.
Religion	• Learn about major world religions, focusing on religious customs, beliefs, and holy days. • Examine the creation stories of major world religions; compare them, looking for commonalities and differences. • Invite several parents from the same or similar religion to come in and describe how they celebrate a specific religious holy day; note differences and similarities.

(continued on next page)

FIGURE 12-2, continued
Selected Concepts and Activity Ideas for Anthropology

Traditions

- Interview parents regarding family traditions. Write and illustrate stories about your favorite family tradition.
- Select an occupation and examine it for traditions; ask a practitioner to explain the traditions' functions.

FIGURE 12-2, continued
Selected Concepts and Activity Ideas for Anthropology

appreciation is students' active involvement as participants in the culture-discovery process.

Anthropological content may be introduced through a growing body of children's literature focused on other cultures. As you explore these different cultures through literature, make sure you build conceptual bridges that allow comparisons with the children's own culture. Encourage children to form questions and find answers about these cultures. Suggested areas follow:

- Education—Is their school day like ours?
- Religion—Are there special religious holidays and customs?
- Family—What is the typical family like?
- Food—What are the most common breakfast, lunch, and dinner foods?
- Sports—Are there organized sports for children, like Little League baseball?
- Recreation—What do families do on the weekends?
- Television—Do they have children's programs?
- Childhood—What are the most popular games and toys?
- Clothing—What do children wear to school?
- Social problems—Do they have poor people?

Answering such questions may require extra research or contact with a knowledgeable cultural informant. Your efforts to explore other cultures through children's literature (and meaningful follow-up activities) will be richly rewarded with increased interest and cross-cultural understanding.

DISCUSSION QUESTIONS

1. Anthropology is the social science discipline most closely associated with the biological theory of evolution. Would you be opposed to introducing children to anthropological evidence of early hominids? Explain your position.

2. Is learning about cultural diversity different from the "multiculturalism" that has been attacked? What beliefs and views are associated (rightly or wrongly) with multiculturalism that may not be present in lessons about cultural diversity?

3. What taboos exist in our own society? What is the basis of, or reason behind, these taboos? What would likely happen to an individual if he or she broke these taboos? What would happen if everyone broke these taboos?

TRASH CAN ARCHAEOLOGY

Grade Level: 4–6

Overview: In this lesson students examine several different collections of trash and draw inferences concerning the activities of the people that created the trash and the location of those activities.

Time Required: One class period

Objectives: As a result of this lesson, students will:

- improve artifact observation skills
- form inferences regarding the use of objects and interrelationships among objects

Materials/Resources Needed: Plastic gloves for at least eight student "diggers," plastic garbage bags, trash from four different locations, clean newsprint and crayons or markers for displaying trash items and noting relationships, eight copies of the data inventory and analysis sheet (see attached handout)

Procedure

1. Tell students that today they are going to experience what it would be like to be real archaeologists. Explain that archaeologists examine artifacts from other, often vanished cultures in order to learn more about their lifestyles. Give an example of an archaeologist finding the abandoned campsite of a primitive culture in the Amazon River basin and unearthing fragments of woven baskets containing kernels of corn. Ask what conclusions might be drawn from this "find." (This group knew how to create woven baskets and may have eaten corn.)

2. Divide the class into four groups and distribute one bag of trash to each group. Ask the group to designate two diggers (who will extract the items from the trash bag), two data recorders (who will fill in the data inventory and analysis

form), and several data mappers (who will use crayons or markers to draw connections between and among items extracted from the trash bags).

3. Allow the groups to work independently for approximately 15 minutes, monitoring the quality of their artifact descriptions, inferences, and data maps. Encourage speculation about the nature of the people who created this trash. For example, were they all engaged in a single type of activity or does it appear that the trash they produced came from a variety of activities? Did the trash include food wrappers or wasted food? If so, what conclusions can be drawn about the people from these items? (Was it mostly sweets or mostly fast-food wrappers?)

4. Issue a 5-minute warning for task completion once the first group finishes its analysis.

5. Conclude the lesson by asking the groups to share their work. Allow students in other groups to ask questions and challenge conclusions.

Evaluation

- Did students improve their artifact observation skills?
- Were they able to form plausible inferences concerning the identity of the group that produced the trash?
- Were they able to form inferences concerning the use of objects?

Enrichment

- Visit a real dig site.
- Invite an archaeologist to come in and talk about his or her work.

TRASH-BAG DIG HANDOUT

Directions Name each item taken out of the trash bag. Then describe its condition. Follow the example given below.

ITEM Tootsie Pop candy wrapper

DESCRIPTION This wrapper had chewing gum stuck inside it. The wrapper came off a a chocolate Tootsie Pop. The wrapper was in very good shape and didn't show any signs of having been walked on or handled very much. There was a trace of red (lipstick?) on the inside of the wrapper near the gum.

ITEM _____

DESCRIPTION _____
_____
_____

ITEM _____

DESCRIPTION _____
_____
_____

ITEM _____

DESCRIPTION _____
_____
_____

ITEM _____

DESCRIPTION _____
_____
_____

ITEM _____

DESCRIPTION _____
_____
_____

ITEM _____

DESCRIPTION _____
_____
_____

ITEM _____

DESCRIPTION _____
_____
_____

ITEM _____

DESCRIPTION _____
_____
_____

FAMILY TRADITIONS

Grade Level: First

Overview: In this lesson children investigate and share their own family traditions.

Time Required: Two class periods

Objectives: As a result of this lesson, students will:

- define the word *tradition* using their own words
- give an account of a tradition that is a part of their own family heritage

Instructional Strategies

Teacher presentation/Demonstration

Role playing

Data collection and sharing

Art interpretation

Materials/Resources Needed: A note home about family traditions collection

Procedure

Period One

1. Write the words *family tradition* on the board and tell students about one or two of your own family traditions. (It would probably be best to share traditions that deal with common family events such as holiday cooking, holiday decorations, family sayings, and so on.)

2. Explain that a tradition is something done over and over again each year in much the same way. Ask the children if they are aware of any of their own family traditions. Have a few students share examples of traditions.

3. Show students the note. Tell them that you want them to take it home and help their parents decide which family tradition to write about.

4. Before distributing the notes, review what students are being asked to do by using a role play to act out a typical home scene. (You play the parent and ask for a child to volunteer. Have the child come home and show the parent the note and explain what the assignment is. Debrief the action. Repeat with another child if necessary.)

5. Distribute the notes.

Period Two

1. Ask the children to take out their notes. Have students raise their hands if they think they remember what tradition their parent(s) wrote about.

2. Invite these children up, one by one, to stand by you and "present" with your help what is on the paper. (You may have to read the note and then ask the child to add anything or react to the tradition.) Depending on how quickly this goes and the attention of the rest of the class, have more children come forward and share their family traditions. Extend the sharing portion of the activity to another day or two if required.

3. Ask the children to use crayons or markers to draw a picture of their family practicing its tradition. Post these completed pictures together on a bulletin board that will be displayed during the next open house.

Evaluation

- Meeting in small groups, ask students to define the word *tradition*.
- Ask each child to share one family tradition that he or she has learned about.

REFERENCES AND SELECTED READINGS

Barnes, B. R. 1991. Using children's literature in the early anthropology curriculum. *Social Education* 56(1):17–18.

Derman-Sparks, L. 1989. *Anti-bias curriculum. Tools for empowering young children.* Washington, D.C.: National Association for the Education of Young Children.

Ember, C. R., and Ember, M. 1990. *Anthropology.* 6th ed. Englewood Cliffs, NJ: Prentice Hall, Inc.

Harvey, K. D. 1993. Native Americans: The next 500 years. *Social Studies and the Young Learner* 5(3):1–3.

Hoge, J. D., and Allen, R. F. 1991. Teaching about our world community: Guidelines and resources. *Social Studies and the Young Learner* 3(1):19, 28–32.

Howard, M. C., and Dunaif-Hattis, J. 1992. *Anthropology: Understanding human adaptation.* New York: HarperCollins Publishers, Inc.

Williams, T. R. 1990. *Cultural anthropology.* Englewood Cliffs, NJ: Prentice Hall, Inc.

CHAPTER 13

The Humanities: Artistic Interpretations of Society

INTRODUCTION

Content from the social sciences forms the predominate substance of elementary social studies. As you may recall from the first two chapters, the social sciences are included in the K–6 curriculum as elementary social studies because they possess the power to give future citizens the understandings needed to function effectively in our democratic society. No other part of the curriculum shares the goal of developing social science content knowledge and skills.

Understandings about life, however, may also be gained from the humanities. To the extent that they may be employed as a means of providing understandings about life essential to effective citizenship in our democracy, religion, music, art, drama, and literature are also legitimate components of social studies curriculum. Of course, music, art, drama, and literature are included in the K–6 public school curriculum as subjects in their own right. Instruction in these four humanities is often devoted to the development of skills and appreciation, with little attention given to interpretations of what specific instances of these art forms say about the nature of our (or any other) society. When instruction in the humanities does address the social meaning and interpretation of music, art, drama, or literature, it is augmenting the role these subjects traditionally play in social studies.

Let's examine religion, art, music, drama, and literature in order to gain some understanding of what teachers might hope to include from these humanities in their K–6 social studies curriculum.

RELIGION IN THE SOCIAL STUDIES

Until quite recently, teachers typically avoided presentations and discussions about religion in their public school classrooms. Many falsely believed that the U.S. Supreme Court had outlawed any type of instruction about religion in public schools. Others who were knowledgeable of their right to teach about religion were still reluctant to mention religion due to fear of controversy and parents' disapproval.

Information about religion needs to be included as a part of the social studies curriculum because of the role religion has played in history—and continues to play in contemporary society. Put simply, explanations of why events happened as they did are often only partially correct if they ignore the influence of people's religious beliefs. In the United States and many other nations, religion is playing an increasing role in politics—especially as the political process is used to address morally charged social issues through the formation of government policies and laws. Children of all religious faiths, and those who are raised apart from any particular faith, need to be informed about the religious beliefs and practices of their fellow citizens if they are to fully understand both history and current events.

Recent thinking has altered many teachers' opinions about the need to offer children information on different world religions as a part of their basic education in social studies. To support this change, many authors and several organizations have provided guidelines for including religion in the social studies curriculum. These guidelines[1] suggest that study about religion should:

- strive for awareness and understanding of the diversity of religions, religious experiences, religious expressions, and the reasons for particular expressions of religious beliefs within a society or culture
- stress the influence of various religions on history, culture, the arts, and contemporary issues
- examine the religious dimension of human existence in its broader cultural context, including its relation to economic, political, and social institutions.
- be academic in nature, stressing student awareness and understanding, not acceptance or conformity
- emphasize the necessity and importance of tolerance, respect, and mutual understanding in a nation and world of religious diversity
- be descriptive, nonconfessional, and conducted in an environment free of advocacy

These guidelines represent only a start in understanding an appropriate role for religion in the public school social studies curriculum. Haynes and Kniker (1990) offer additional insights designed to help teachers avoid common pitfalls when teaching about religion. They remind us, for example, that what is taught about religion should be an integral part of ongoing social studies instruction. The information supplied about religion should be essential to understanding the events and peoples under consideration in the social studies curriculum. Haynes and Kniker advise that if a teacher is asked by children to reveal his or her own religious beliefs, he or she can either (1) state that his or her personal religious beliefs do not need to be interjected into the discussion, or (2) briefly describe his or her religious beliefs, adding that others honestly believe differently. Haynes and Kniker advise against role-playing religious ceremonies, noting that "such activities, no matter how well-intentioned, may violate the conscience of students and undermine the integrity of the faith involved" (306). Finally, teachers should work to avoid an atmosphere where students feel obligated to declare their personal religious affiliations, explain their faith, or defend their religious practices.

These guidelines for prudent pedagogy in the area of religion hint at, but do not clearly state, what is legally permissible concerning instruction about religion in public schools. Figure 13-1 presents a brief listing of legally acceptable practices.

I end this section on religion with my understanding of the current status of law on school prayer. You may already know that teachers or other individuals who are public school employees may not lead children in prayer of any type during the school day or while on school property. Children, however, are free to engage in silent voluntary prayer at any time of the school day, provided that such activities do not interfere with their ability to participate in regular school

---

[1]NCSS, 1990.

- It is not against the law to teach about religion in the public schools. Instruction about religion may be infused throughout the curriculum or provided in separate courses or special units.

- It is not against the law to study the major textual basis of any world religion when that printed material is presented objectively as a part of (1) a balanced secular religious education program, or (2) for the purpose of gaining literary or historical perspectives on regular school content.

- Public schools may teach about various religious and nonreligious perspectives on complex moral issues that confront society, provided that such instruction is presented without promoting or denigrating any particular perspective.

- States or local school boards may not mandate that the biblical story of creation be taught as an alternative or competing scientific theory to evolution.

- The biblical account of creation, and other religious explanations of creation, can be presented and discussed in a religious studies class or in situations where such accounts of creation are a legitimate focus of study.

- Holidays with significance to particular religions may be recognized and used as opportunities to teach about religion.

- Teachers may not use the study of religious holidays as opportunities to proselytize or display personal religious beliefs.

- Religious symbols are permissible only as temporary aids to objective instruction and may not be left in the classroom beyond the time of their use as a referent for instruction.

- Children may create artwork with religious symbols, but teachers may not encourage or discourage such products.

- Sacred music may be used as a part of academic study as long as it serves a sound educational purpose and is not used as a vehicle for promoting religious belief. Holiday programs should use predominately secular music, though it is permissible to include hymns or other sacred music.

FIGURE 13-1

What Federal and State Laws Permit in Regard to
Religious Instruction in Public Schools[2]

routines. In addition, courts have ruled that when schools provide access to facilities and special blocks of time to voluntary student-led groups, student groups formed for religious purposes must be accorded equal rights.[3]

---

[2]These statements were gleaned from articles noted in the references to this chapter and two brochures distributed by a broad coalition of religious organizations and the National Education Association, *Religion in the Public School Curriculum: Questions and Answers* and *Religious Holidays in the Public Schools: Questions and Answers*.

[3]Peach, 1986. This information should not be considered a substitute for professional legal advice.

MUSIC, ART, AND DRAMA
◆ ◆ ◆ ◆ ◆

Music, art, and drama offer diverse and unique views of human nature. The social studies shares responsibility with other areas of the curriculum for developing an appreciation of what these subjects convey about different societies and cultures.

Social studies makes selective use of these areas of the humanities to develop deeper understandings of what it means to be human. The emphasis is not on the development skills needed to produce music, art, or drama, but rather on consuming the perspectives and understandings these areas offer on living.

Lucy Fuchs (1993), in her book on humanities in the elementary school, suggests a number of ways in which teachers might assist children in developing an appreciation for these areas of content. Let's examine some of Fuchs' suggestions and see how they might be translated into meaningful instructional practices that could be a legitimate part of social studies instruction.

To incorporate art into your social studies classroom, Fuchs recommends periodically turning your classroom into an art gallery. To do this, you might work with your media center to display famous paintings that go with the historical subjects you are studying. Encourage students to make pictures similar to the art displayed. Based on their knowledge, they can imagine and draw other scenes of the period or location.

Encourage children to analyze famous paintings for evidence of what life was like in times past. Compare both masterpieces and student-created scenes with analogous contemporary artworks in order to gain a deeper understanding of past and present lifestyles. Have students note the social themes present in the artwork, and form generalizations regarding life in that time and place. Contact a contemporary artist and use his or her works as a springboard to discuss current social themes that reflect present-day society.

To develop music appreciation in the social studies classroom, have children listen to a variety of good music symbolic of each area, culture, or period studied. Accompany such listening with discussions of the human emotions, feelings, and thoughts developed by the music. Have students analyze music for social messages and images, looking up unusual words or phrases that typify the time, culture, and location. After hearing a number of selections appropriate to the topic, ask students to select a theme song symbolizing the content studied.

Involve elementary grade level children in making music as a part of their social studies instruction. For example, allow children to sing along to authentic folk songs as they engage in various construction projects. Ask them to create and sing new verses to the folk songs based on knowledge gained from their study. Bring authentic folk instruments or replicas to school and demonstrate them.

In the area of drama, involve children in performing plays and skits that match the content of social studies topics. Let students write original skits and plays to fit contemporary issues. Use puppet theater as a vehicle for dramatic expression for younger children as they gain knowledge about their families, schools, and communities. Have upper-grade-level students use reader's theater techniques.

Take advantage of local theater performances. For example, encourage children to attend the holiday performances of classic plays after studying the period and location in social studies.

LITERATURE IN THE SOCIAL STUDIES

Growth in the quantity and quality of children's literature has spurred increased interest in using this rich resource of socially focused content. Dianne Common (1986) notes that children's stories are a powerful way to increase students' interest in social studies. Dry factual knowledge, she points out, is made meaningful when students' imaginations are put to work on these "particulars" by the power of literature. Students learn how to feel about events as they identify with story characters and vicariously experience the story's plot. Stories work to increase students' involvement in content, she contends, because they (1) reduce reality to a manageable, individual scale; (2) help us know how to feel about events; (3) offer an ending that freezes the flow of events; and (4) give teachers and students a common frame of reference from which to share their further study.

The National Council for the Social Studies (NCSS) has published for many years, in the April/May issue of *Social Education,* its annual guide to notable children's trade books in the field of social studies. The selections in this annual bibliography are reviewed by a panel of teachers who recommend books for grade levels K through 8, based on their high literary quality, emphasis on human relationships, and representation of diverse groups. The reviews are arranged under broad categories, include a brief annotation, and ordering information. Figure 13-2 displays a few samples of entries in the 1992 list.

Tom McGowan (1987) points out that activities generated from children's fiction can build a variety of citizenship skills. For example, help children build map skills by locating real places depicted in stories, tracing the movement of characters, and making imaginary maps of the location where a story takes place. Incorporate problem-solving skills by having students work out alternative strategies for resolving dilemmas faced by characters. McGowan notes that teachers should select books that confront issues important to citizenship, avoid stereotyping, and have good literary value. If teachers will use children's literature as a springboard to high-quality, hands-on social studies activities, then valuable content[4] can be learned.

Supplementing your existing social studies textbook with high-quality children's literature makes good sense. There are, however, some potential

---

[4]Recall that the word *content* refers to all forms of social studies content: facts, concepts, main ideas, generalizations, skills, attitudes, and values.

ANTHROPOLOGY

Fiesta! Mexico's Great Celebrations.

Elizabeth Silverthorne. Illustrated by Jan Davey Ellis. Millbrook. 64 pp. ISBN 1-56294-055-4, $13.90. (I & A).

This book provides comprehensive coverage of all types of religious and patriotic fiestas in Mexico and includes examples and directions for making objects and foods associated with the various celebrations. This excellent sourcebook, suitable for student use, contains a calendar of Mexican fiestas and a further reading list. Glossary. Index. RCS.

Houses and Homes.

Ann Morris. Illustrated with photographs by Ken Heyman. Lothrop. 32 pp. ISBN 0-688-10168-2, $14.00. (P).

This excellent book, sure to stimulate classroom discussion, features the various types of houses and homes in the global community and the culturally diverse people who live in them. Index. KA.

Rising Voices: Writings of Young Native Americans.

Edited by Arlene B. Hirschfelder and Beverly R. Singer. Scribner's. 115 pp. ISBN 0-684-19207-1, $12.95. (I & A).

The young people in this book write of identity, family, community, ritual, history, and the harsh reality of their lives. It is a must-read for students interested in contemporary Native American experience. Index. RPK.

BIOGRAPHY

Dear Dr. Bell . . . Your Friend, Helen Keller.

Judith St. George. Illustrated with prints and photographs. Putnam. 128 pp. ISBN 0-399-22337-1, $15.95. (A).

The author successfully weaves together the lives of Alexander Graham Bell and Helen Keller in this excellent biography of their lives. The book is both informative and moving. Bibliography. Index. JAA.

I Am Somebody! A Biography of Jesse Jackson.

James Haskins. Enslow. 112 pp. ISBN 0-89490-240-7, $17.95. (A).

Readers will be touched by the passion exuding from the pages of this book, which describes Jackson's early years, his work with the civil rights movement, the founding of People United to Serve Humanity (PUSH), and the possibility of a presidential bid. Bibliography. Index. BMM.

CONTEMPORARY ISSUES

Single Parent Families.

Richard Worth. Illustrated with prints and photographs. Watts. 128 pp. ISBN 0-531-11131-8, $12.90. (A).

This excellent, easy-to-read, and respectful resource covers many aspects of single parenting, using quotations and composites of real-life situations. Bibliography. Index. JS.

Recycle! A Handbook for Kids.

Gail Gibbons. Illustrated by the author. Little, Brown. 32 pp. ISBN 0-316-30971-0, $14.45. (P, I, & A).

This book explains the processes involved in recycling paper, glass, aluminum, plastic, and polystyrene. It also details how readers can recycle. VW.

FOLKTALES

How the Stars Fell into the Sky: A Navajo Legend.

Jerrie Oughton. Illustrated by Lisa Desimini. Houghton. 32 pp. ISBN 0-395-58798-0, $14.95. (P & I).

(continued on next page)

FIGURE 13-2
Selected Entries from the 1992 NCSS Children's Trade Book List[5]

[5]©National Council for the Social Studies. Reprinted by permission. These are only samples. Categories vary from year to year and some books may fit in more than one category. Key to abbreviations: P = K,1,2, (primary); I = 3,4,5, (intermediate); A = 6,7,8, (advanced). The closing initials are the abstractors' initials.

This poignant Navajo folktale is about lawmaking, patience, and confusion. The story of First Woman and Coyote is elegant, inspirational, and filled with splendid illustrations. JRG.

First Snow, Magic Snow.

John Cech. Illustrated by Sharon McGinley-Nally. Four Winds. 32 pp. ISBN 0-02-717971-0, $14.95. (P).

A lovely rendition of the Russian tale "The Snow Goose." The author provides a fresh approach to this tale; the illustrator provides visual images that evoke Russia. The combination is a cultural feast. JAA.

GEOGRAPHY

The Great St. Lawrence Seaway.

Gail Gibbons. Illustrated by the author. Morrow. 40 pp. ISBN 0-688-06984-3, $15.00. (P & I).

A journey through the Saint Lawrence Seaway describes the history, transportation, and engineering of the locks and canals connecting the world's largest inland waterway. Colorful illustrations accompany the clear, readable text. VW.

Kanu of Kathmandu: A Journey in Nepal.

Barbara A. Margolies. Four Winds. 40 pp. ISBN 0-02-762282-7, $14.95. (P & I).

Using engaging and varied photographs, Kanu, a third-grade city boy, takes the reader on a tour of the surrounding countryside. Glossary. JS.

LIFE AND HISTORY

Children of the Dust Bowl: The True Story of the School at Weedpatch Camp.

Jerry Stanley. Crown. 96 pp. ISBN 0-517-58781-5, $15.00. (I & A).

John Steinbeck's *The Grapes of Wrath* comes to life in this true story of Oklahoma children who build their own school at Weedpatch Camp. The compelling text is complemented by dozens of quality archival photographs. Index. JRG.

Working Cotton.

Sherley Ann Williams. Illustrated by Carole Byard. Harcourt Brace Jovanovich. 32 pp. ISBN 0-15-299624-9, $14.95.

An African-American girl relates the daily events of her family working in the cotton fields of California. This book contains rich illustrations that depict the hardship and oppression of long days and hard labor. A 1993 Caldecott Honor Book. BMM.

The Big Lie: A True Story.

Isabella Leitner with Irving A. Leitner. Illustrated by Judy Pedersen. Scholastic. 80 pp. ISBN 0-590-45569-9, $13.95. (I).

In an elegant style, a Holocaust survivor tells the story of her family's persecution by Nazis in Hungary during World War II and their escape to the United States. JS.

REFERENCE

The Visual Dictionary of Military Uniforms.

Edited by Louise Tucker. Illustrated with photographs by James Stevenson, Geoff Dann, and Tim Ridley. Dorling Kindersley. 64 pp. ISBN 1-56458-010-5. $14.95. (I & A).

Military uniforms labeled in specialized terms with color photographs and drawings will capture the interest of readers of all ages. Ceremonial dress, headgear, medals, footgear, armor, and uniforms worn in war are all part of this comprehensive visual dictionary. Index. VW.

SOCIOLOGY

The Memory Box.

Mary Bahr. Illustrated by David Cunningham. Whitman. 32 pp. ISBN 0-8075-5052-3, $13.95. (P & I).

This thoughtful and moving picture book recounts the way one family handles the approaching specter of Alzheimer's disease. A memory box is organized by Gramps to contain mementos of cherished experiences for his grandson. RCS.

(continued on next page)

♦ ♦

FIGURE 13-2, continued
Selected Entries from the 1992 NCSS Children's Trade Book List

Back Home.

Gloria Jean Pinkney. Illustrated by Jerry Pinkney. Dial. 40 pp. ISBN 0-8037-1168-9, $15.00. (P & I).

An eight-year-old girl's North Carolina homecoming explores the tensions that exist between urban and rural cultures. Teased by her cousin about her citified ways, she wonders if they can ever be friends. JRG.

A Forever Family.

Story and pictures by Roslyn Banish with Jennifer Jordan-Wong. HarperCollins. 48 pp. ISBN 0-06-021673-5, $14.00. (P).

Jennifer Jordan-Wong tells her own story of being adopted. While answering many questions on the subject, this photo essay introduces Jennifer's multiracial adoptive family and her African-American foster family. Glossary. JAA.

SONGBOOKS AND FOLK SONGS

Gonna Sing My Head Off!
American Folk Songs for Children.

Collected and arranged by Kathleen Krull. Illustrated by Allen Garns. Knopf. 160 pp. ISBN 0-394-81991-8, $20.00. (P, I, & A).

This history in song is a collection of sixty-two American folk songs. The illustrations are works of art. Index. JAA.

FIGURE 13-2, continued

Selected Entries from the 1992 NCSS Children's Trade Book List

drawbacks associated with this practice. Figure 13-3 lists the benefits and drawbacks of adding children's literature to the social studies program.

The benefits of supplementing your social studies textbook with children's literature outweigh the drawbacks. At a minimum, you should urge children to read trade books topically related to social studies and encourage students' contributions of added content and perspectives produced by such reading. You may also wish to model, reading adult-level material related to your social studies topics. Such reading is not only pleasant, but will add to your own

BENEFITS	DRAWBACKS
• It offers a way to add depth to standard social studies topics. • It offers a way to add nonstandard topics. • It adds a story-line format that can aid students' understanding. • It accommodates individual reading abilities if students are allowed to read different trade books. • It adds an emotional dimension often missing in textbooks.	• Censorship problems may arise as students encounter greater depth of standard topic treatment or explore new, nonstandard topics. • Biased or fictionalized points of view may go unnoticed and unchallenged. • Time will be lost that could have been devoted to other social studies activities.

FIGURE 13-3

Benefits and Drawbacks of Adding Children's Literature

knowledge of the events, people, and places that are the focus of your social studies instruction.

On occasion educators have suggested that children's literature alone be used to carry the social studies program. Advocates of this approach note that textbooks (1) are often considered boring by students, (2) cost a substantial amount of money, (3) tend to become the de facto curriculum, and (4) introduce subtle (and sometimes not so subtle!) demands to "cover" or read the entire book from front to back during the span of the school year. Moving completely away from a textbook, however, places a substantial burden on the teacher to identify literature that fulfills the district, state, and national curriculum goals for social studies. Allowing students to read independently in different books— even on the same topic—will certainly create a problem of sharing information and developing follow-up activities that are suitable for each student (or the entire group). If each child were allowed to read a different book, it would be hard to imagine how a teacher could stay up with the amount of library work and monitoring required to address each of the areas of the social studies curriculum guide. Reading the same book to the entire class would be a laboriously slow approach to content and virtually guarantee limited learning if that is the only social studies instruction offered. Finally, using only children's literature may deprive students of information needed to perform well on standardized tests. For these reasons, using *only* children's literature to teach social studies would create more problems than it would solve.

HANUKKAH: A CELEBRATION OF FAITH

Grade Level: Third
Time Required: Two class periods
Concepts/Vocabulary: Religion, culture, symbols, tradition

Main Ideas

- Many Jewish people incorporate their faith into every aspect of their lives.
- The celebration of Hanukkah is an eight-day affair.
- The menorah is lit every Hanukkah in remembrance of the army of Jews who fought for their religious freedom and the jar of oil that burned so long.
- The menorah is a symbol for the Jewish faith.

Objectives: This lesson should help students become acquainted with the meaning of Hanukkah and the religious symbols and rituals that are a part of it.

Instructional Strategies

Art expression

Guest speaker

Children's literature

Materials/Resources Needed: Children's book on Hanukkah; poster showing drawing of menorah, dates of Hanukkah celebration, and brief history; sample food items such as matzo, bagels, and lox; paper plates, napkins, and serving utensils; guest speaker

Procedure

Period One

1. Tell students that today we are going to learn about the Jewish holiday called Hanukkah. The reason we are discussing this holiday is because many Americans are Jews, and we need to recognize the importance of all religious faiths in our country.

2. Tell students that at the end of the lesson they should be able to tell what Hanukkah stands for, and give examples of how the Jewish people celebrate this holiday.

3. Show students the poster and go over the information it contains, allowing students to ask questions. Draw parallels to the major religious celebrations of Christians or other religions.

4. Read the children's book on Hanukkah, stopping to reemphasize the major points contained on the poster.

Period Two

1. Introduce the guest speaker and allow him or her to share personal memories of the celebration of Hanukkah.

2. Work with the guest speaker to teach the children a Hanukkah song and traditional dance, encouraging all of the children to participate. Compare the song and dance with examples from other religions and cultures.

3. Take students to a tasting table and allow them to taste the matzo, lox, and bagels. Encourage children's questions and allow the guest speaker to describe how these foods and others are prepared during the Hanukkah celebration.

Evaluation

- Review the information students have gained about Hanukkah.
- Do they know the symbolism and the story behind the Hanukkah celebration?

REFERENCES AND SELECTED READINGS

Adler, D. A. 1981. *A picture book of Jewish holidays.* New York: Holiday House.

Aggarwal, M. 1985. *I am a Hindu.* New York: Franklin Watts.

_____. 1985. *I am a Jew.* New York: Franklin Watts.

_____. 1985. *I am a Muslim.* New York: Franklin Watts.

_____. 1985. *I am a Sikh.* New York: Franklin Watts.

Common, D. L. 1986. Students, stories, and the social studies. *The Social Studies.* (Nov/Dec):246–248.

Fuchs, L. 1993. *Humanities in the elementary school: A handbook for teachers.* Springfield, IL: Charles C. Thomas.

Greenberg, J. E., and Carey, H. H. 1985. *Jewish holidays.* New York: Franklin Watts.

Haynes, C. C. 1990. *Religion in American history: What to teach and how.* Alexandria, VA: Association for Supervision and Curriculum Development.

Haynes, C. C., and Kniker, C. R. 1990. Religion in the classroom: Meeting the challenges and avoiding the pitfalls. *Social Education* 54(5):305–306.

Hughes, E. 1994. *Making a world of difference: A multifaith resource book for primary teachers.* London: Cassell.

Lawton, C., and Goldman, I. 1985. *I am a Jew.* New York: Franklin Watts.

McGowan, T. 1987. Children's fiction as a source for social studies skill-building. ERIC digest no. 37 (ED285797). Bloomington, IN: ERIC Clearinghouse for Social Studies/Social Science Education.

National Council for the Social Studies. 1990. NCSS position statement and guidelines on including the study about religions in the social studies curriculum, originally adopted November 1984. *Social Education* 54(5):310.

_____. 1993. NCSS children's trade book list. *Social Education* 57(4):197–208.

Peach, L. 1986. Supreme Court docket. Does religion belong in the schools? *Social Education* 50(3):166–169.

Selwyn, D. 1993. *Arts and humanities in the social studies.* NCSS bulletin 90. Washington, D.C.: National Council for the Social Studies.

PART THREE

Special Topics
and Methods

INTRODUCTION

I've written this section so that you can easily gain an understanding of the special topics and methods that make social studies an exciting and essential component of every child's education for democratic citizenship. These chapters contain much of the "heart and soul" of social studies.

As you examine these chapters, please realize that the topics presented here are not meant to be implemented as separate, isolated subjects within a social studies program. Instead, these topics and methods are meant to be infused throughout the ongoing social studies program. You should engage students in inquiry and multicultural learning experiences beginning in kindergarten. Similarly, all children should experience current events, global, and values education on a regular basis. In addition, you should support your social studies instruction with the careful integration of children's literature, math, reading, and writing. Finally, good social studies should help children gain footholds on methods by which they may peacefully resolve differences of opinion.

By the time you've completed studying this section, I hope you'll feel like you can go forth and begin your professional practice as a classroom teacher who is fully capable of designing and implementing high-quality social studies. Give yourself time to experiment with the different methods and approaches you've learned. Most of all, enjoy the privilege of being involved in preparing children for their future roles as responsible citizens of our nation and the world.

Inquiry Instruction

THE NATURE OF INQUIRY INSTRUCTION

One simple way of describing *inquiry instruction* is to say that it is teaching that helps students examine a significant question, issue, or problem they have encountered and brought to the teacher's attention. In inquiry instruction, students become investigators searching for knowledge, aided by their guide and coinvestigator—the teacher. Inquiry instruction can also be teacher-initiated if the teacher is able to create a genuine sense of wonder (a burning desire to know) that motivates students' investigation.

Before we go on, stop and think about the image of inquiry instruction just presented. Can you recall ever having a class where you and your fellow students set the agenda for a time by defining a question, issue, or problem that *you* wanted to investigate? Or were you ever in a class where the teacher raised a question, issue, or problem and got you so interested that even though you didn't set the agenda, you felt exhilarated about your involvement and the quest for knowledge? Close your eyes for a moment and search your past. Can you recall even one such experience?

Sadly, most students confess that they can only recall one or two inquiry experiences in their entire educational careers. For some it happened in a fourth-, fifth-, or sixth-grade classroom. For others it didn't happen until high school or even college. Tragically, many students failed to experience even one day of school where they felt the exhilaration of inquiry learning.

To learn more about the nature of inquiry instruction, let's contrast it with direct instruction and then consider more fully its two forms: student-initiated and teacher-initiated inquiry.

Inquiry Contrasted with Direct Instruction

In the traditional direct instruction approach to teaching, the teacher is visibly in charge. It's easy to think of him or her standing by the chalkboard leading a whole-class lesson. We can imagine students raising their hands to answer questions or volunteering to read passages from their textbook. Perhaps the teacher distributes a worksheet or shows a video. Maybe students are actively engaged in what is being taught. Perhaps they are interested, even intellectually stimulated, by the instruction being offered. It is more likely, however, that students are being polite. They are exercising their best classroom manners— sitting up straight, keeping their eyes open, trying to focus, focus, focus. In short, they are acting out the traditional school learning plot.[1]

Knowledge, in the traditional direct instruction approach, is conceived of as something that has already been discovered. Someone else, usually an adult

---

[1]I don't want to sound too critical of traditional direct instruction, since I do a lot of it and believe that most teachers will continue to use it in one form or another for the majority of their time in the classroom. Done well, direct instruction is effective at promoting many kinds of learning. Something can be said, too, for teaching students to focus, absorb knowledge, and practice the social conventions associated with traditional schooling.

with an advanced academic degree, has already conducted the experiments, done the surveys, or performed the research necessary to find the answers. This knowledge, greatly simplified and compressed, is now packaged in the form of school curriculum—textbooks, worksheets, videos, and lectures. The teacher's job is to deliver this knowledge using the most appropriate and efficient instructional methods for her students. The students' task is to absorb the knowledge and demonstrate, usually on a test, what they have learned.

In inquiry instruction, teachers are less visibly in charge.[2] In fact, they may not be seen, at first glance, in the classroom. The teacher could be sitting with a small group of students helping them make a decision about what resources they want to consult next. He or she might be examining a draft version of a student-created chart that summarizes the results of recently collected survey data. The teacher might be out of the room (while an aide monitors the class) ordering student-requested audiovisual materials or making appointments with resource persons the students want to interview.

Knowledge in the inquiry approach is something students create—or at least assemble and interpret. Students gain answers through applying various research strategies. The answers gained, in turn, depend upon the type (and quality) of the methods used and the sources consulted. Both students and their teacher view knowledge as tentative and conditional. Experts and published sources may or may not have the precise answers desired. Students may have to collect, organize, and carefully weigh a large quantity of information before they can reach any conclusions. Even then, their conclusions must be tested against new cases and situations.

In summary, inquiry instruction casts students and teachers in different roles than traditional direct instruction. Knowledge, too, is viewed less as something to absorb and more as something that learners create and use to make sense of the world.

Student-Initiated and Teacher-Initiated Inquiry

Let's examine an instance of student-initiated inquiry as a means of expanding our knowledge of inquiry instruction. Students won't just walk in one day and say, "Teacher, we'd like to do some student-initiated inquiry!" What will happen, more likely, is that some event will take place that captures your students' attention and causes a groundswell of questions, complaints, hasty explanations, challenges, or other exclamations. Such outpourings of emotions are most often derived from a question, issue, or problem that can be student-investigated. Your task as teacher is to capture this teachable moment and direct your students' launch into inquiry learning.

The main drawback associated with student-initiated inquiry learning is the lack of teacher planning and preparation time. This results because you never

---

[2]This does not mean that they have given up their authority or control of the classroom, however. They still direct the learning and are clearly in charge.

know what will ignite the students' interest. It might be an incident on the playground, a news item concerning the community, or even something students have read in their textbook. When the urge to know hits, latching on to it requires a willingness to set aside the time needed to engage in the inquiry learning process. Since students determined the focus, you as the teacher, must be willing to embark into an area where your own knowledge may be limited. You must also be willing to put in extra time helping students identify and secure the resources needed to carry out their inquiry.

Teacher-initiated inquiry begins when the teacher, through advanced planning, constructs an inquiry experience that she offers to students. One of the real tricks of offering teacher-initiated inquiry instruction is igniting students' desire to know. This is usually done through a springboard specifically designed or adopted for this purpose. If the springboard is effective, then students will launch into this preplanned inquiry unit with the same gusto they would normally reserve for self-generated questions, issues, or problems.

Figure 14-1 presents a simplified model of inquiry instruction. A brief hypothetical example of a fourth-grade class' investigation into cheating follows as an illustration of each step.

Here is an example of an inquiry experience taking place in a fourth-grade class. In the paragraphs that follow, you'll see students encounter a cheating problem that raises questions in their minds. The teacher uses the situation to initiate an inquiry instruction experience. She follows the model presented in Figure 14-1. Each step in the inquiry process is labeled.

STEP 1: Encounter Question, Issue, or Problem
Students encounter a question, issue, or problem that ignites their curiosity. They speculate about answers and review relevant prior knowledge.

STEP 2: Clarify Meanings of Terms
Students carefully define key terms using dictionaries and other expert sources. They settle on agreed meanings that will be used to guide their research.

STEP 3: Formulate Researchable Hypotheses
The initial question, issue, or problem is recast into one or more "if . . . then" hypotheses. Using these hypotheses and precise meanings for key terms, students can now identify exactly the data needed to complete their research.

STEP 4: Collect Data
Students finalize data collection procedures and begin collecting their data.

STEP 5: Assemble and Analyze Data
Students organize, tally, code, chart, and/or statistically summarize their data.

STEP 6: Present Results and Generalize
Students report results and draw conclusions. They attempt to generalize to other similar situations and phenomena and note the limitations of their study.

◆ ◆

FIGURE 14-1
Simplified Inquiry Model

DISCUSSION QUESTIONS
◆ ◆ ◆ ◆ ◆

1. Why do you suppose inquiry teaching isn't offered more?

2. What are the advantages of teacher-initiated inquiry as opposed to student-initiated inquiry? What are the drawbacks?

3. Should teachers restrict inquiry instruction mainly to gifted students (as it often is)? Why or why not?

STEP 1 Students encounter a problem.

(Ms. Cogins' fourth-grade class went totally silent when they saw the serious look on her face and realized how she felt. She waved a handful of tests, just taken yesterday, up in the air.)

MS. COGINS: I've got convincing evidence here in my hand that several of you cheated on this social studies test.

You know, it really hurt my feelings to think that some of you cheated. I don't believe that your parents would be very proud if they found out either. My guess is that the students who cheated on this test have probably cheated on other things. Maybe sports, or maybe some other subject.

When you get your tests back tomorrow, you'll know if you are one of the people I caught cheating. You'll see a zero on the top of your test and you won't be allowed to make it up.

I don't want any complaints about not being fair, either. If you want to appeal the grade, you'll have to get your parent or guardian to come in and see the evidence I've got. If you want to see me privately and apologize for cheating, I'll let you retake the test this one time for a new grade. See me at recess, lunch, or right after school if you want to apologize for cheating and retake the test.

(Hands shoot up as students attempt to cope with the situation.)

DONNA: How many students cheated on the test?

MS. COGINS: I'm not telling. Several.

TINA: I don't understand why anyone would cheat. We had plenty of time to study and the test wasn't hard!

TROY: I bet it's the same students that cheat in football! I saw . . .

MS. COGINS: That's enough, Troy. I don't want any wild accusations.

LATRELL: I'll bet it's people who forgot to study. They get to school and remember it's a test, but it's too late. So they have to cheat to keep from getting punished at home.

(Talk goes on. The next 15 minutes are spent discussing cheating. Ms. Cogins determines that the students would like to investigate cheating as an inquiry project. A vote is taken and all of the students want to participate.)

STEP 2 Students define terms.

(The last part of the period is spent defining terms that are important to their inquiry. Here is a part of the dialogue.)

MS. COGINS: Before we can go on, we really need to get clear about what we mean by cheating. For example, is it cheating on your homework to get your big brother to help you answer math problems if you're not understanding and really just letting him tell you what to write?

LATRELL: That's just like having a friend do your homework for you. You don't learn anything and it makes it hard to do well on the test.

TROY: Right, it's not really your own brain work. You haven't learned anything.

MS. COGINS: Okay. Is it cheating if you look on someone's paper to see if you marked the same answers?

SONJA: Not if you don't change your answer, it's not!

MS. COGINS: Wouldn't you be tempted to change your answer if you saw it was different?

SONJA: No. I'd think the other student was probably wrong.

MS. COGINS: So looking on other people's papers during a test is okay?

CODY: No. It's not! You'd never know who was cheating and who wasn't. Some people could be getting answers by looking on other students' papers.

(The class goes on and reviews other issues such as: Is cheating in sports like cheating on a test? If a teacher fails to mark a question wrong when it is wrong, is it cheating if you don't tell her about the mistake? The students develop the following definition of cheating: Cheating is doing something you know is wrong, like breaking a rule, in order to pass a test or win a game.*)*

STEP 3 The students form hypotheses.

(The next day the class breaks into three groups, each with its own hypothesis. With the aid of the teacher, each group decides how to conduct its inquiry. Group 1 decides to investigate whether cheating in one subject is likely to spill over into other subjects. Their hypothesis is, If a student cheats in one subject then he or she will be likely to cheat in another. Group 2 wants to find out why students cheat. Their hypothesis states, Students who are punished for bad grades cheat more often than students who are not punished. Group 3 decides to find out how students view the risk and reward of cheating. Their hypothesis states, Cheaters seldom get caught and believe that cheating improves their grade or performance.

Ms. Cogins agrees to contact the school's guidance counselor and psychologist to see if they would consult with the groups to help them develop their questionnaires and survey procedures.)

STEP 4 Students collect data.

(Students meet with resource people. Questionnaires are finalized and distributed. Here is part of the dialogue that took place between the guidance counselor [Ms. Ayers] and group 3.)

MS. AYERS: What was the question you wanted to investigate?

TYLER: We told you, it's whether cheaters think they'll get caught and . . . I forget the second part.

SONJA: And whether they believe it benefits them.

MS. AYERS: Okay. How would we go about doing that?

WILLIAM: We could just go around and ask, couldn't we?

MS. AYERS: Sure. What would you say?

WILLIAM: Well, you could just walk up to people and say, "When you cheat do you think you'll get caught?"

LATRELL: That's not going to work 'cause not everyone cheats and students who do cheat may not want to answer.

FLOYD: I think our survey would have to be secret.

MS. AYERS: Yes, I agree. We have a word for that. It's called an "anonymous" survey. Anonymous literally means "without names."

LATRELL: So we know our survey will have to be anonymous.

(Ms. Ayers works with the group to determine who they want to survey. The students decide that they want to include only fourth, fifth, and sixth graders in their survey. To save paper and make sure that reading problems don't influence the results, the students decide to construct a booth out of two refrigerator boxes. Respondents will enter one box and speak through an opening to the surveyor. Small groups of students will be brought to the booth throughout the day. The students create a data-recording system to capture their answers.)

STEP 5 Students assemble and analyze data.

KAYLIE: Okay, our first question just asked if they had ever cheated on a test in school.

LATRELL: Almost half said yes. We could make a pie chart split down the middle to show that.

SONJA: How many students was that?

WILLIAM: One hundred and thirty-four.

TYLER: So how are we going to show that almost all of those students never got caught?

LATRELL: And that they all thought it helped them get a better grade?

(This discussion goes on as the students work through the process of determining how to present their data.)

STEP 6 Students present results and generalize.

(Each group makes a poster that summarizes what they discovered. The groups also create skits that illustrate some of the major ideas in their findings. Students make presentations to other classes. Some parents attend the presentations.)

PARENT: Ms. Cogins, I can see that your class has done a lot of work on this project and learned quite a bit about cheating. What disturbs me is that none of the groups found out that cheating was wrong and that it can have terrible consequences when discovered.

MS. COGINS: We talked about that in class at some length. The students understand that it is wrong and that there are consequences. Just ask those that I caught two weeks ago.

PARENT: Don't you think it's damaging to let the students see that so many of their peers get away with cheating and feel it improves the grades they receive?

MS. COGINS: I can't deny that the data are disheartening. Once we began the surveys, I started to wish that the data looked different. I was afraid that it might increase cheating. I discussed this with the students and they were intrigued. Later in the year we plan to do a follow-up study to see if there is any change.

PARENT: Well, I'd be interested in coming back for that!

MS. COGINS: I'll make sure to call you when we do the follow-up.

It should be clear from this example that inquiry instruction places school learning in a new light. Knowledge is made meaningful. Intellectual activity has a clear purpose. Students have to apply many skills they have acquired and engage in higher-order thinking as they progress through the steps of the inquiry process. Let's take a moment and formally consider the roles of the teacher and students as they engage in inquiry instruction.

The Role of the Teacher

The role of the inquiry teacher is different from that of a teacher using direct instruction. For example, instead of telling students what to think, the inquiry teacher poses questions to spur students' thinking, offers suggestions regarding methods and sources to consult, and provides materials that help students conduct their investigation. Ideally, the teacher gauges the students' ability levels and places a reasonable burden on them to identify sources, methods, materials, and logic related to their inquiry. In general, the teacher declines to answer students' questions. Instead he might say something like, "I'm not sure. What do you think?" or "How would you go about doing that?" or "Do you think your data will really show what you want to know?"

Students will soon learn that they have thinking powers too, just like the teacher. They can think independently and even evaluate the quality of their own ideas. The more skillful the teacher is in asking questions, the more quickly students will sense the power of their own knowledge and intellectual abilities.

Evaluation is, perhaps, the most difficult task for an inquiry teacher. Clearly, the product of inquiry is not the only item to be evaluated. True, the quality of the product reflects the quality of the work that went into it. However, students may have learned much more than what they formally reported. Keep track of evidence of work and learning at each step of the inquiry model. Have students keep folders that document their contribution to the inquiry project. Record anecdotal information and conference individually with students to gauge their understanding and assess their level of participation. Finally, assess whether students are learning inquiry processes and skills, additional and valuable outcomes of this approach to instruction.

The Role of the Students

Students assume a different role in inquiry instruction, too. They must be able to work independently and in small groups in order to be a part of inquiry instruction. Greater degrees of assistance and increased structuring are necessary for younger students. For example, the teacher needs to offer much more assistance in formulating questions for a questionnaire because younger students will need more help with spelling, word meaning, and answer-recording techniques. The teacher also needs to add more structure to small group and independent tasks. Parents' help is needed, especially for younger students, if the inquiry project moves much beyond the school's immediate surroundings.

The most significant impact of the inquiry approach to instruction is the influence it has on students' attitudes toward learning and their views of knowledge. Suddenly they are no longer sponges soaking up whatever substance the teacher provides. Instead they have become self-propelled harvesters of knowledge, directing their own courses through vast fields of knowledge. They choose what to take in and what to bypass. The teacher's assistance is required only when a new direction is taken or in the event of trouble.

THE BENEFITS OF INQUIRY INSTRUCTION

It is clear that there are substantial benefits to inquiry instruction. A major benefit to the teacher is removal of the constant motivation burden. Once students' curiosity is piqued, there is little need for motivational tactics. Students' attitudes toward learning improve as they begin to sense the connections between knowledge and real-life concerns. Students begin to view knowledge as something they use—even create—to answer important questions, solve problems, and investigate issues.

Inquiry instruction involves several aspects of higher-order thinking. For example, students make judgments about the goodness, the truthfulness, and the applicability of information. They are choosing among alternatives and weighing the consequences of taking one course of action over another. They are solving problems that arise naturally as a part of any serious investigation of social reality. Finally, the students are seriously engaged in *metacognition*, thinking about thinking. All of this occurs while students gain practice in applying basic reading, writing, and math skills.

Beyond attitudinal and cognitive benefits are the social skills that students develop during inquiry instruction. They learn to lead as well as follow as they participate in the inquiry process. They develop listening and discussion skills as groups determine individual assignments. Interviewing skills are often needed as students make contact with resource persons or subjects who are the target of their study. Persuasion and presentation skills may be learned as students negotiate the details of task assignments and present their final report.

GUIDELINES FOR CONDUCTING INQUIRY LESSONS

Teachers use forms of instruction that they can understand and easily implement. At this point, I feel certain that you have a solid grasp of the nature of inquiry instruction, but you may be concerned about implementing it in your future classroom. Student-initiated inquiry may be especially threatening because of your inability to prepare for the experience. You may also be concerned about turning the whole class loose on such an involved learning experience. These fears lead to some suggestions that may help you get started doing inquiry with K–6 students.

First, don't attempt to turn the entire school day (or the entire social studies program) into an inquiry approach. It's sufficient to use the inquiry approach for only part of the instructional program. You may discover that doing inquiry oriented units for half of your instructional time is plenty to satisfy the students and meet the higher-level learning goals set for your social studies curriculum.

Next, I think it's important for teachers to make their first excursions into inquiry learning experiences ones that they have preplanned. Using the teacher-initiated inquiry approach allows you plenty of time to select an appropriate QIP (question, issue, or problem), to locate or devise a springboard that captures student interest, and identify the resources students will most likely need. Getting comfortable with teacher- initiated inquiry will build the confidence needed to embark on the adventure of student-initiated inquiry.

Finally, I urge you to consider running inquiry learning as a "sideshow" to regular social studies instruction. You might want to identify several QIPs related to each topic being studied and see if any of them tickle the curiosity of a sufficient number of students to launch an inquiry group. At first, I'd only allow a few students to get involved in the inquiry learning experience at any one time. Consider exempting these students from their regular social studies lessons. When completed, have them present their work to the rest of the class.

Even though you start with a small group, give every student an opportunity to be involved in inquiry learning experiences during the course of the year.

OTHER FORMS OF INQUIRY

At this point you may have the impression that inquiry instruction means doing survey research. I need to correct that impression by giving some examples of inquiry learning experiences that are not survey based. As you read each example, check to make sure that it meets the most basic requirements of inquiry learning.

Experiments

The answers to some questions are most appropriately determined by conducting experiments. For example, it is easy to set up experiments that test people's honesty. Here is an inquiry experiment that I call "the dropped dollar."

> Sam wanted to determine whether students would more frequently return a dropped dollar found lying on the playground or near the principal's office. She hypothesized that more children would return the dollar found near the principal's office, though she wasn't really sure why.
>
> Sam planned to run the experiment all week during social studies class and recess. No one but her partner and the necessary school authorities knew about the experiment. She stationed herself in an inconspicuous spot and observed the behavior of the students who found the dollar. Students who turned the dollar in were promptly thanked and those who walked away with the dollar were promptly confronted by her partner who claimed to have just lost the dollar. During the course of the week Sam and her partner ran their experiment successfully twenty-three times outside the principal's office and twenty-five times on the playground.
>
> Sam's data showed that more students returned the dollar when it was discovered right outside the principal's office. She and her partner wrote up their experiment and included a table that described their results. The last section of their paper speculated on why there was such a difference in the dollar return rate for the playground and the principal's office.

Can you think of other experiments that might be conducted by K–6 students? Experiments manipulate the conditions or circumstances under which people perform. The investigator then attempts to explain the observed differences. Students can conduct experiments on many aspects of social behavior. As a part of the ethics of experiments, it is important to debrief participants and make sure that the experimental procedures do not cause people embarrassment or other psychological harm.

Library Research

Quite often a trip to the library is sufficient to answer our needs for information. While library research is difficult for young children, it becomes increasingly possible for students in the fourth, fifth, and sixth grades. Inquiry on questions related to any of the social sciences or humanities can be conducted in a library. CD-ROM multimedia encyclopedias offer an attractive starting point for student inquiries. Specialized trade books and biographies are valuable sources of information.

Lee and her friends became interested in learning more about refugees and immigration when they found out that a new group of Cambodian children was arriving in their community and would soon be enrolled in their school. There were seventeen children in all, ranging from the kindergarten to the sixth grade. Temporarily, these children would be living with families in the community until their parents could join them in the United States. Lee's family was hosting two children, one who would be in the fifth grade with Lee and one who was in the second grade.

Lee was asked several questions in class the day she announced the imminent arrival of her new friends. "Why couldn't their parents come too?" "Was this happening in other towns and schools?" "Would these children speak English?" and "Why were these children called refugees instead of immigrants?"

Lee's teacher felt uncomfortable answering all of these questions on the spot, so she agreed to let Lee and her two friends go to the media center to look for answers. She suggested that they start with the multimedia encyclopedia looking up the terms *refugees* and *immigration*. An almanac would give data about immigration too, so she suggested that they check that second. Recent editions of newspapers might have articles on this, perhaps even the special group of children coming to their own town. The school's new subscriptions to several computer-based news services could also be tapped with the help of the media specialist. These sources would yield information about recent events related to the Cambodian children's arrival in the United States.

Lee and her friends agreed to give the class a report on what they found out. It took almost a week of social studies classes and several conferences with the teacher, but in the end they found the answers they sought.

Interviews

Some forms of inquiry learning experiences lend themselves mainly to interviews. Students may be interested in careers, or a particular career. They may seek to have some aspect of history clarified by a knowledgeable resource person. Or they may be interested in some aspect of local government or politics.

The CEO of Winterville was more than happy to come and answer the students' questions about changes planned in the town's parks. She had been involved with the planning commission and citizen's oversight group from the beginning and knew the plans well. Here is part of the interview:

STUDENT 1: Ms. Kelp, we've been learning about recent changes in the recreation plan and I want to know why the bike paths were dropped. Most of us ride bikes and we thought it was a good part of the plan.

MS. KELP: The bike paths were dropped for financial reasons. It costs quite a bit to build bike trails. We just didn't have the money.

STUDENT 1: But the paper said you were going to spend $135,000 to build a second boat ramp that got added to the plan after the bike trails were dropped.

MS. KELP: The idea for a second boat ramp was very popular. We have a lot of families that go boating and the first ramp was getting crowded.

STUDENT 2: How much money was saved by dropping the bike trails?

MS. KELP: We had budgeted $200,000 for bike trails.

STUDENT 3: So is it true that the money saved from the bike trails was used to build the boat ramp?

(Fade)

Product Investigations

Product investigations are among the more popular starting points for inquiry learning experiences. Manufacturers make product claims that students of all ages can investigate. If the claim is scientific, such as "Detergent X cleans three times better than the leading brand," then the nature of the inquiry is essentially science-centered. But many manufacturers make claims that are social-science-based. Claims such as "Our product is preferred 2 to 1 over the Brand X" suggest the use of a social-science survey technique.

A new brand of powdered drink mix was being advertised on television as more fun than others. The manufacturer also claimed that kids preferred its taste over the "older" drink mixes. The commercials showed children having lots of fun drinking large glasses of the bright-colored drink mix.

The students in Mr. Foley's second-grade class believed the advertisement and wanted to have the new fun mix at their next party. Mr. Foley challenged them to tell the difference between the two. With the students' help he set up an experiment to see if they could tell the difference. Each student was blindfolded and given six small cups of similarly sweetened drink mix. Two of the cups were orange, two grape, and two were strawberry. Monitors kept track of preferences and charted the data at the end of the experiment. The students were surprised to find out that only one of the flavors from the new company was judged superior to the product of the more established manufacturer.

Foxfire Projects[3]

The community-centered, inquiry-oriented projects that form what is termed the *Foxfire approach* are often focused on social studies. Originated by Eliot Wigginton, Foxfire projects were conceived as an instructional device to give

---

[3]The Foxfire approach to instruction was developed and nurtured by Eliot Wigginton, a high-school English teacher. Today, the Foxfire foundation supports a nationwide network of teachers who have adopted Foxfire methods for their classrooms. The material offered in this section represents a synthesis of the Foxfire philosophy and what is commonly referred to as the *project approach.*

high-school students content that could be converted into articles for their high-school literary magazine. What began as an attempt to foster the authentic application of writing skills by a high-school teacher became a philosophy of instruction that culminated in an award-winning magazine and a series of ten books that have sold over eight million copies.[4]

Teachers who attend the Foxfire workshops offered around the country by the twelve regional networks[5] learn a set of instructional principles used to guide Foxfire projects. These principles include such ideas as:

- All work must flow from students' desires and concerns.
- The role of the teacher is that of collaborator and guide—not boss.
- Students' project work must have academic integrity and enable mastery of state and local curriculum mandates for knowledge and skills.
- Projects clearly connect the classroom with the real world of the surrounding community.
- The outcomes of projects must reach a wider audience that students seek to serve, engage, or impress.
- Students should be engaged in ongoing reflection as an essential part of the activity.

To help students select potential projects, a first step often recommended by Foxfire trainers is to engage them in thinking about the most powerful learning experiences they have had in the past. As the students begin to identify these episodes, the teacher helps them identify the characteristics of the experiences that made them engaging, fun, and worthwhile.[6] Students are then invited to suggest projects that will engage them in the authentic application of skills and knowledge from social studies (or other areas of the formal curriculum).

In elementary social studies students might suggest projects related to the various themes and subthemes of the expanding environments curriculum, the ten strands of the NCSS standards for social studies, or some specific area of the national standards in history, geography, civics, or economics. Regardless of the area, students should attempt to identify a project that meets the principles of the Foxfire approach. Figure 14-2 displays a few examples of Foxfire projects.

---

[4]The information here came from a variety of sources and experiences. Sales figures and other kinds of information were verified in May 1995.

[5]Contact the Foxfire network nearest you by calling 706-746-5318 or writing to Foxfire, P.O. Box 541, Mountain City, GA 30562.

[6]Students often say that learning experiences were fun because the experience took them outside the classroom, allowed them to work with new and different materials, engaged their imaginations, was challenging, resulted in a product they were proud of, gave them valuable information or skills, and made them feel like they had done something valued by others.

PROJECT AREA	GRADE	DESCRIPTION	PRODUCT
Families (An expanding environments scope and sequence topic)	First	Students are interested in telling and comparing their birth stories.	Each child writes and illustrates a birth storybook. The books are displayed at open house.
Cities (An expanding environments scope and sequence topic)	Third	Students want to improve the park system of their community, which they perceive as being inadequate.	After investigating the park system the students put together, with the help of their teacher, a written proposal for a new park. The proposal includes results from a brief survey and a three-dimensional clay and cardboard model of the proposed park.
Global Connections (An NCSS standards theme)	Fourth	The closing of a foreign-owned company where many parents worked raises students' interest in determining how many other local businesses are foreign owned.	Students work with the chamber of commerce to complete a survey of business ownership. The results are presented to the city council and put into a brochure about the commerce of their city.
Science, Technology, and Society (An NCSS standards theme)	Sixth	The development of a violent new video game spurs disagreements about the influence of video games on students' school learning, grades, and values. Students conduct several investigations of different aspects of the disagreement.	Students produce a flyer for parents naming recommended and not recommended video games. Students work on an article for the local paper that presents their Foxfire project.
History (A national standards subject area)	Second	Inspired by a recent grandparents' day, students decide they want to construct a school history. They interview retired teachers, parents, and others to help reconstruct their school's history.	A full-page feature newspaper article is developed by a local reporter working with the students. A school history booklet is produced.
Geography (A national standards subject area)	Fourth	Students become interested in how their state's climate and location are related. They begin an investigation that leads to an understanding of general principles. Using this information they form guesses about other states' climates.	An Internet project involving fourth-grade students from around the United States is developed. Climate data are collected and analyzed.

(continued on next page)

F I G U R E   1 4 - 2
Examples of Foxfire Projects

PROJECT AREA	GRADE	DESCRIPTION	PRODUCT
Civics (A national standards subject area)	Fifth	Safe-schools legislation sparks students' interest in conducting a safety audit of their own school.	Students produce a safety profile of their school and present it to the principal. Safety hazards are discussed in the PTA meeting.
Economics (A national standards subject area)	Kinder-garten	Students complain that a popular toy can no longer be found at the local toy stores. With the help of their teacher they call the toy store manager who reports that she simply can't get enough of the toy.	Students write, with the teacher's help, letters to the manufacturer asking for a larger supply of the toy.

FIGURE 14-2, continued
Examples of Foxfire Projects

The following sample inquiry unit took place in a small midwestern school. The unit takes the form of a third-grade teacher's report of her first-ever inquiry experience. The names of the school and teacher are fictitious, however.

Ms. Carrera's Inquiry Unit

Based on frequent reports of misbehavior in the hallways, lunchroom, and playground, Ms. Carrera's third-grade class decided to find out what school rules were not being followed at Clinton Primary.

On Monday morning, students delivered letters explaining their study and soliciting input regarding the rules teachers thought were most important (see Figure 14-3).

Monday afternoon the students tallied the responses from the teachers. Each rule was put on the board and tally marks for each additional response was put beside the rule. Figure 14-4 shows what the data looked like.

On Tuesday, the students began their observations. Tally sheets were distributed and the students divided into four groups of six. Each student was assigned a station for one half hour. They marked each occurrence of an infraction. The students started at 8:00 A.M. and observed until reading class began at 10:00 A.M. They resumed after lunch break at 1:00 P.M. and completed their assignment at 2:30 P.M. Figure 14-5 shows what the tally sheets looked like.

Wednesday and Thursday students began the task of compiling the data they had gathered. The timetable was copied on the board and the tally marks each student had compiled were posted to the proper cells. This information is shown in Figure 14-6.

On Friday, before presenting to the other classes, Ms. Carrera's class discussed why they had more students talking at some times more than others. They came to the conclusion that at the start of the day there were more students in the halls and

---

March 17, 1994

Dear Clinton Primary Teacher:

Our class is conducting an investigation of students' rule-breaking behavior outside the classroom. In order to do this study, we need to know what rules you expect your students to obey when they are not in your classroom.

Please list the three rules you expect your students to obey when they are not in your classroom, and return this note by noon today.

1. _____

2. _____

3. _____

Please do not inform your students that they will be observed. No individual, teacher, or class will be identified. We are marking only the number of times we observe a rule being broken. We will share our results on Friday.

Sincerely,

Students, Room 51

FIGURE 14-3
Ms. Carrera's Students' Inquiry Letter

1. Be quiet in the halls.	21
2. Walk in the halls.	19
3. Keep hands and feet to yourself.	11
4. Respect school property.	6
5. Respect other people.	4
6. Stay in line.	3
7. No loud talk in the lunch room.	2
8. Don't chew gum.	1
9. Play on the blacktop.	1
10. Don't play in the rest rooms.	1
11. Obey the teacher.	1
12. Don't brag.	1

◆ ◆

FIGURE 14-4
Replies from the Teachers

there were not many teachers present to monitor them.

Other observations were that there were more talkers going to recess than returning from recess. The students also decided that more of their classmates ran to leave school than at any other time of the day because they were worried about missing their buses.

Ms. Carrera's students could not decide on a reason for students not keeping their hands and feet to themselves. Most thought it was mostly the first and second graders doing the pushing and shoving, but they did not tally that type of information.

Ms. Carrera's class enjoyed their inquiry learning experience and wanted to participate in another. Made more aware of the amount of talking in their building, they seemed to be more orderly in the halls than before.

STUDENT: _____

PLACE: _____

TIME: _____

RULE	TALLY MARKS
Be quiet in the halls.	
Walk in the halls.	
Keep hands and feet to self.	

◆ ◆

FIGURE 14-5
Tally Sheet Example

Rule Breaking at Clinton Primary

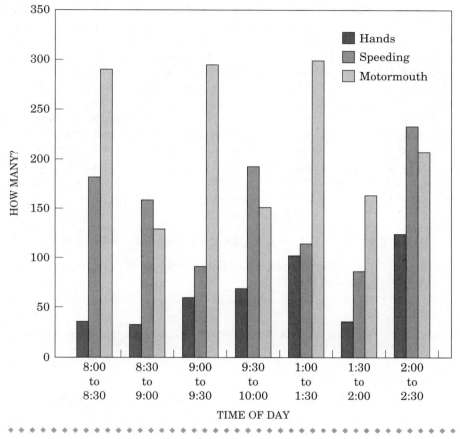

FIGURE 14-6
Results of Data Collection

CONCLUDING THOUGHTS

Inquiry instruction is a rewarding, but little-offered, learning alternative. It can be done with children at all grade levels and it takes many forms, from simple surveys to true experiments and extended library research.

Contrary to what some others have claimed, inquiry learning does not use teaching strategies or resources that differ from direct instruction. It does change the role of the teacher and the perspective of the student, and the way in which each looks at knowledge.

I urge you to try out inquiry learning in your own classroom. If you begin with a teacher-initiated inquiry unit, don't forget to put extra effort into planning your springboard experience. It must motivate the students to the degree that they actually want to learn the answers to the QIP you have so carefully framed. As the inquiry unit develops, try to remain flexible in your expectations and make the students' learning experiences fun.

REFERENCES AND SELECTED READINGS

Atwood, V. A. 1985. Bubble-good data: Product testing and other sources. *Social Education* 49(2):146–149.

Beyer, B. K. 1977. *Inquiry in the social studies classroom.* Columbus, OH: Charles E. Merrill.

Guyton, E. M. 1985. The school as a data source for young learners. *Social Education* 49(2):141–144.

Massialas, B. G., and Cox, C. B. 1966. *Inquiry in the social studies.* New York: McGraw-Hill.

Van Cleaf, D. W. 1984. Guiding student inquiry. *Social Studies* 75(3):109–111.

Wigginton, E. 1985. *Sometimes a shining moment: The Foxfire experience.* Garden City, NY: Anchor Press/Doubleday.

_____. ed. 1991. *Foxfire: 25 years.* New York: Anchor Books.

Multicultural Education

Board Demands Schools Teach "Superiority" of U.S. Culture

TAVARES, Fla. (AP) - The lesson today in Lake County schools: America is No. 1. But some teachers and parents say what's really being taught is bigotry.

With flag-waving gusto, the Lake County School board ordered its schools to teach youngsters that American culture is superior to any other. The policy was met with cheers in some corners, horror in others.

"The board's majority has made a mockery out of education in my county," said Ana Cowin, who has taken her son out of Leesburg High School in favor of a private school in Connecticut.

At a park near the county courthouse, Louis Williams said the board was acting in response to multiculturalism "being rammed down our throats."

"We need someone to look out for the Christian view, particularly in our school with our children," said Constance Older, a South Dakota teacher who retired to Leesburg.

The policy was adopted in a 3–2 vote May 10 [1994] after the school board in this fast-growing central Florida county of small towns and rolling hills recited the Pledge of Allegiance and listened to student musicians play "It's a Grand Old Flag."

It's the latest controversy since the board became dominated by members espousing conservative, traditional and Christian values.

The one-paragraph policy requires teachers to "instill in our students an appreciation of our American heritage and culture such as our republican form of government, capitalism, a free enterprise system, patriotism, strong family values, freedom of religion and other basic values that are superior to other foreign or historic cultures."

"I have never heard of an issue quite like this one," said Jay Butler, spokesman for the National School Boards Association, which represents 95,000 elected school board members. " 'Values' education . . . is something we hear about more and more with the rise of the religious right wing."

The 1,400-member Lake County teachers union sued the school board Tuesday to block the policy.

Associated Press news release 5/25/94. Used by permission.

INTRODUCTION

The article on the opening page touches on some of the feelings and issues surrounding multicultural education. I'm sure you can find some ideas in the article that you agree with, others that you feel are wrong, and still others that you may be unsure about. To help you prepare for this chapter, take a moment and reread the article, jotting down at least one statement or idea that you agree with, one you disagree with, and one about which you have mixed emotions. Keep these ideas in mind as you process the ideas in this chapter. We'll come back to the article near the end when we've learned more about multicultural education.

Multicultural education is a movement that seeks to adjust the K–12 school curriculum so that it includes the contributions and multiple perspectives of all groups that compose U.S. society.[1] Change away from a monocultural curriculum is needed to prepare all of America's children for their multicultural future, and to combat ignorance, racism, and ethnic hatred.

In this chapter you will learn about our multicultural heritage and future. You will gain deeper insight into the nature, goals, and methods of multicultural education. You'll also learn strategies for dealing with stereotyping; racism; parent disapproval; and your own lack of knowledge concerning ethnic, cultural, and racial minorities. The chapter concludes by stressing the importance of civic common ground and offering a selection of resources designed to help you become an accomplished multicultural-approach teacher.

OUR MULTICULTURAL HERITAGE AND FUTURE

Since the earliest times, North America has been multicultural. Distinct Native-American cultures existed across Canada, the United States, and Mexico. Many tribes maintained friendly relations, traded, and some intermarried with neighboring groups. A few had ongoing conflicts that ran deep into history. Adults' stories about the lifeways of other tribes were an interesting part of growing up, and doubtlessly our first approach to multicultural education.

The European colonizers that immigrated to North America came from different regions, spoke different languages, and worshipped in different ways. Conflict fueled by old-world attitudes and greed erupted as different groups sought to advance their own interests and repress others. Europeans from different regions founded separate communities. Settlements were also formed to serve people of a single religious affiliation. Pulling the colonies together to form a nation, and establishing a climate of religious tolerance was a substantial task for early European Americans. The Declaration of Independence and the establishment of our federal government were giant steps taken toward uniting our nation. The protections established by the U.S. Constitution and the Bill of

---

[1]Groups based on, but not necessarily limited to, race, ethnicity, social class, gender, sexual orientation, and religion are included in multicultural education.

Rights were not, however, extended to European-American women, Native Americans, or African Americans.

The struggle to accord all people equal rights, to establish and maintain a fair system of justice, to provide full access to economic opportunity, and to establish a climate of acceptance for diversity continues today. Multicultural education offers a means of peacefully working toward these societal goals. It is the primary means by which the youth of our nation learn to respect and support the cultural differences that make our vast nation an interesting and enjoyable place to live.

The need for multicultural education is stronger today than it was in the past. During the 1980s, approximately 33 percent of our population growth was from immigration.[2] This was a 10 percent increase over the rate of the 1970s and a 20 percent increase over the immigration rates that had existed since the 1940s. The countries of origin for immigration in the 1980s were, in order of magnitude, Mexico, the Philippines, China, South Korea, Vietnam, India, the Dominican Republic, Jamaica, the United Kingdom, Cuba, El Salvador, Canada, Haiti, and Iran. The 1990s have brought continued, and often increased, immigration from many of these same countries. By the year 2000, demographers estimate the United States will be only 72 percent European American, almost 13 percent African American, and 11 percent persons of Hispanic origin. Asian Americans and Native Americans will make up the remaining 4 percent. Compared with nineteen other major First World nations, the United States is the most ethnically diverse. Sadly, however, we are eleventh in tolerance of people with different ideas.[3]

Demographers estimate that one of every three people in the United States will be a person of color by the turn of the century. At present, students of color are the majority in twenty-five of the nation's largest school systems.[4] These present and future realities support the need for offering a strong program of multicultural education as a part of the total school curriculum. Social studies should serve as a focal point for this effort.

THE GOALS AND METHODS OF MULTICULTURAL EDUCATION

Imagine for a moment that you are a third-grade teacher and that a child from a different culture enrolls in your class one morning during the first month of school. Imagine further that no one else in your school is from the new child's culture. Close your eyes and try to picture the scene: you there as the teacher, receiving this new child.

What are your best wishes for this new class member as the year unfolds? Do you wish him or her great success? Are you looking forward to learning

---

[2]*The Universal Almanac*, 1994, 302.
[3]Shapiro, 1992, 107.
[4]National Council for the Social Studies, 1992.

more about the child's culture? What steps will you take to make the child's transition into your room, and this new American culture, a positive experience?

This imaginary scene takes place many times across the United States each year. Culturally different children face the task of making new friends and adapting to new ways of behaving. Teachers and their students welcome new, culturally different, classmates and gain lasting memories from this contact. Such contacts offer significant learning opportunities associated with the goals of multicultural education.

Authorities have specified many different goals for multicultural education. Let's examine the most commonly stated goals[5] and attempt to relate them to your imagined experience with the new third-grade student.

According to authorities, multicultural education should . . .

- help all children gain greater self-understanding by viewing themselves from the perspectives of other groups
- encourage children in the development of positive racial, cultural, and ethnic self-identities
- foster awareness of and respect for the diverse lifeways of different ethnic, racial, and cultural groups
- empower students with the knowledge, attitudes, and skills needed to function in other cultures and improve understanding among diverse ethnic, cultural, and racial groups
- encourage accurate interpretations of historical and contemporary events from diverse cultural, ethnic, and racial perspectives
- help students master essential reading, writing, and computational skills by accommodating learning styles, including culturally representative content, and showing diverse role models in all curriculum materials

Return for a moment to examine your imagined actions at the arrival of a new, culturally different student. How did your imagined actions fit with the goals of multicultural education? Did you imagine that your class was totally European American and that the new person was Jamaican American? Or was your imaginary class predominately African American and the new student Chinese American?

Regardless, did you see yourself greeting the child warmly and taking the time to properly introduce him or her to the class? Did you tour the student around the room and show him or her the locations of materials and classroom equipment? Was a desirable seat selected? Did you ask a volunteer to be the new student's aid during the coming days?

I hope you also felt it was appropriate to sit down with the new student and visit—just one-on-one—for a while. During this session you might have offered

---

[5]These goal statements were adapted from Banks, 1991; Ramsey, 1987; and the National Council for the Social Studies, 1992.

assistance and attempted to learn about the child's interests and background. Depending on language barriers and the relative novelty of the child's culture, you might have made plans to have your new student share some of this information with the entire class. As in many areas, doing the right thing depends on quite a number of factors. Most important are your sincerity, good will, sensitivity, and openness. Viewing the situation as an opportunity to enrich and expand your ongoing multicultural education curriculum is only natural. We'll learn more about what to do, and what not do, in the rest of the chapter.

One of the typical ways teachers introduce multicultural education into their curriculum is to feature a few selected representatives from each group, focusing on the contributions these individuals made. James Banks (1991) terms this the *contributions approach*, since it focuses on athletic and cultural heroes, ethnic holiday celebrations, and people of color who have made it in mainstream society. Teachers also include multicultural education by adding in special units that focus on a particular ethnic, cultural, or racial group. When teachers add themes, units, and concepts to the curriculum without changing its basic structure, this is termed the *additive approach*. Banks believes that both of these approaches leave much to be desired:

> Merely adding low-level facts about ethnic content to a curriculum that is already bulging with discrete and isolated facts about mainstream American heroes will result in overkill. Isolated facts about Crispus Attucks and the Boston Massacre do not stimulate the intellect any more than do isolated facts about George Washington or Abraham Lincoln. To integrate ethnic content meaningfully into the total school curriculum, we must undertake more substantial curriculum reform. (p. 12)

Banks makes it clear that he is *not* suggesting that we need to eliminate or disparage mainstream perspectives on U.S. society and culture. Instead, teachers should include mainstream perspectives along with many other ethnic and cultural perspectives. He terms this the *transformation approach* because it requires a transformation of the existing approach to the entire curriculum. He states, ". . . [the] Transformation Approach is not the addition of ethnic groups, heroes, and contributions, but the infusion of various perspectives, frames of reference, and content from different groups that will extend students' understandings of the nature, development, and complexity of the United States and the world" (24).

The highest-level approach to multicultural education, according to Banks, is the *social action approach*. It builds on the transformation approach, but requires, in addition, that students be a part of the curriculum decision-making process and that they take actions related to the concepts, issues, and problems they have studied.

Schools often blend all four approaches to multicultural education identified by Banks. Clearly, using only the first and second approaches leaves much to be desired. Encourage the use of multiple perspectives on all content and involve students in curriculum decision making and social action subsequent to their study.

RACISM AND SEXISM

It's important to note that prejudice reduction is a desired outcome of multicultural education. We all desire to be free of unwarranted adverse judgments and opinions. Harboring adverse feelings toward a whole category of people—despite mountains of evidence proving that a healthier view of reality would be better for everyone concerned—is a tragedy. Teachers play a special role in developing healthy attitudes and accurate knowledge in all areas of life. Prejudice by its very nature is a faulty view of reality and a personal fault we all have the power to correct and control. Let's examine how our mandate to control racism and sexism might take place in a real classroom.

Occasionally, teachers have a student who spouts off with comments that are inappropriate, incorrect, hurtful, and hateful. These comments often represent attitudes learned at home, so it is difficult, but not impossible, to directly confront the child that voices them.

Regardless of how innocuous—or how vile—the comment, it is appropriate for you to immediately silence the student. You can do this easily by simply stating that you don't allow any form of name-calling or sexist, ethnic, or racial joke-telling in your classroom. Depending on the age of the student and the level of disruption the comment caused, it may be appropriate to move toward the student, and get close enough to whisper that you would like to meet privately with him or her right after class. If your attempt to silence the student is successful, I'd recommend returning immediately to your lesson. Moralistic lectures that attempt to show students the errors of their comments seem to be ineffective and often invite additional inappropriate retorts. (Taking a week or more to conduct a real discussion or inquiry experience based on the comment and the feelings behind it can be quite beneficial, however.)

It is important to stress appropriate interpersonal behavior in all class activities. If your actions fail to silence sexist or racist comments from a student, then consider immediately sending the child to the office or placing the child in a quiet room. Maintaining the focus on content is important and protecting the dignity of all students is a fundamental duty of teaching.

Dealing with racial prejudice or sexism in the classroom is a concern of many teachers. Experience shows that few, if any, of us are free from prejudice. A recent issue of *Educational Leadership* revealed that sixth graders in a school on the outskirts of Washington, D.C., held the following racial stereotypes:

- Blacks are poor and stay poor because they're dumber than whites and Asians.
- Black people don't like to work hard.
- Black men make women pregnant and leave.
- Black boys expect to die young and unnaturally.
- White people are smart and have money.

- Asians are smart and have money.
- Asians don't like blacks or Hispanics.
- Hispanics are more like blacks than whites. They can't be white so they try to be black.
- Hispanics are poor and don't try hard because, like blacks, they know it doesn't matter.[6]

You might be thinking that these highly negative stereotypes were expressed by a bunch of budding white racists, but that is not so. In fact, the class expressing these attitudes was predominately African and Hispanic American. Only two children in the class were European American. The author of the article, their teacher, Mark Elrich, was shocked by what he learned from his students' views of contemporary society. His students firmly believed that African-American people were bad—not bad in the sense of "cool" or "tough," but bad in the sense of "evil" and "not good." These young African and Hispanic Americans held views toward their own racial and ethnic groups that can only be characterized as highly negative stereotypes.

Glen S. Pate (1981) published a summary of research on prejudice reduction that offered useful generalizations for classroom teachers. Figure 15-1 displays a summary of his findings. As you read the information, jot down memories and questions that come to mind and share these in the coming class.

Much of what can be said with regard to racial prejudice applies to gender prejudice. It is clear that different societies have different conceptions of what is appropriate social behavior for women and their daughters. It is also clear that these conceptions change over time, largely reflecting the actions that women have taken to improve their treatment in the legal system, workplace, church, and home.

Studies continue to show that women are the victims of employment discrimination and sexual harassment on the job. Despite recent gains, and the equalization of pay in some settings, women still earn, on average, only about $0.70 for every $1.00 a man earns.[7] The 1991 median income of women working full time was $21,245, compared with $30,332 for men. Women remain underrepresented in the leading professions and heavily concentrated in underpaid and less prestigious careers such as nursing, dental assistant, and elementary school teaching. Women in traditionally male occupations often hit a "glass ceiling" that prevents their rise to the top. Social attitudes and incipient sexism in education are doubtlessly responsible for women's traditionally lower SAT scores (for example, the average 1992 score for women was 875 compared with 923 for men) and lower college completion rates (19 percent for women and 24 percent for men).

---

[6]Elrich, 1994.
[7]Perry and Perry, 1991.

GENERALIZATION	KEY POINTS
1. Facts or information about another group are not sufficient to change attitudes.	• Facts *alone* won't reduce prejudice. • Knowledge is filtered by the receiver. • Perceptions of motives and situational variables are critical.
2. Class prejudice is confounded with racial prejudice and may be stronger.	• Social class prejudices are strong. • Due to past and ongoing economic, legal, and social discrimination, a disproportionately large number of minority group members remain in the lower strata of America's class structure.
3. An individual who has a high degree of self-acceptance will likely have a low degree of prejudice.	• Liking others is difficult if you don't like yourself. • Improving students' self-concepts will help reduce prejudice.
4. Students who work in interracial cooperative learning groups develop positive attitudes and cross-ethnic friendships.	• Use cooperative learning strategies. • Try to make sure interracial groups experience success. • Form interracial groups as a matter of frequent practice.
5. The cognitive, affective, and behavioral components of prejudice are not always, nor necessarily, interrelated.	• Do not assume that improved knowledge will result in improved attitudes and behaviors. • Set clear knowledge, attitude, and behavior goals for your prejudice-reduction efforts. • Behavioral changes may result in attitudinal changes; don't assume you have to change attitudes first.
6. Films and other media improve students' attitudes.	• Set clear objectives for media use. • Follow up media use with discussions and other activities.
7. Social contacts may reduce prejudice under certain circumstances.	• Help participants get to know one another as *individuals*. • Similar social status, age, and interests help produce positive contact. • Make sure leaders set a positive example. • Circumstances should favor cooperation—not competition. • Shared and attainable goals aid positive contact.

FIGURE 15-1
Research on Prejudice Reduction[8]

You can—and should—take positive actions to reduce sexism in society and school. Here is a short list of suggestions.

• Be aware of your own words and actions. (Are you using sexist language? Are your attitudes healthy? Are your actions fair to both girls and boys?)
• Identify sexist behavior in your colleagues and students. (You can do this in a tactful manner. Simply say something like, "I don't think it's fair to refer to all girls [women] as . . . " Then suggest more appropriate language or more correct thinking.)

---
[8]These generalizations and key points were adapted from Pate, 1981.

- Help your students identify negative stereotypes of girls and women. Point out examples that refute the stereotype. Question the meanings commonly given to such concepts as "strength," "beauty," and "success."
- Use mixed-gender groups and seating. Don't fall into teaching and management practices that separate boys and girls, like lining up boys and girls separately, or playing boys against the girls in competitions.
- Make sure that men and women resource presenters aren't always stereotyped. Arrange to have a female physician, a female hunter, or female business executive visit the class.
- Help your students imagine future careers uninhibited by traditional sex-role stereotypes. Support their drives for freedom and fair treatment in all areas of their lives.
- Don't tell gender-focused jokes, and if you are confronted with such behavior on the part of others, show your disapproval either by directly voicing your displeasure, or by breaking eye contact, refusing to smile or laugh, and silently walking away.

SOCIAL CLASS DIFFERENCES

One of the most potent determinants of an individual's overall lifestyle is social class. People in a particular social class share similar occupations, incomes, education, and life chances that set them apart from other social classes in the same society. Sociologists define *life chances* as an individual's opportunity to fulfill his or her potential.

Social class and social status are interrelated and usually similar; people of low social class typically have low social status. *Status* is the degree of social esteem that an individual or group enjoys in society. Some people with relatively high incomes may lack social status and, conversely, some people of high social status may lack high income. Peoples' learned desire for high status can influence virtually every aspect of life, from choice of clothing, to home, to those considered as potential mates. In the United States, status depends most heavily on one's occupation, which, in part, is achieved through individual effort.[9]

Sociologists refer to occupation and education as *achieved statuses*, recognizing the role the individual plays in climbing up the ladder of success. They term statuses about which individuals can do little, such as, disability, sex, race, or ethnicity, *ascribed statuses* because individuals cannot easily alter or hide these traits and they are not achieved through effort. As your experience might show, however, a person's ascribed status interacts with and limits—or facilitates—his or her achieved status.

---

[9]The phrase, "in part," is a key element of this sentence. For example, successful white males of upper-middle-class background often express the belief that they succeeded solely on their own effort. They may incorrectly discount—or completely disavow—the substantial "career boost" entailed by the cultural and social benefits of being an upper-middle-class white male.

A person of higher social class has more power in society. Power is the ability to carry out one's wishes in spite of resistance. It is the ability to get people to do what you want them to do. Personal power is the freedom of individuals to direct their own lives in a way that they choose. Social power is the ability to make decisions that affect groups, communities, or even a whole society.

A person's social class influences many aspects of life. Figure 15-2 shows the influences of social class for upper- and middle-class families versus lower-class families. As you examine the generalizations, remember that individual students may be exceptions to the rule. Also, focus on how these characteristics might influence your practice of teaching if you have a class that is predominately upper-, middle-, or lower-social class.

AREA	UPPER OR MIDDLE CLASS	LOWER CLASS
Child rearing	• stress independence; principles of right and wrong • punishment by withdrawal of love	• stress obedience to rules, staying out of trouble • punishment harsher and by physical means
Family	• more often two-parent families • many at higher income levels • couples socialize	• more often single-parent families • many below poverty level • women socialize with other women, men with men
Crime	• lower arrest and conviction rates • more forgery, tax evasion, fraud, and embezzlement • can afford better legal advice and defense	• higher arrest and conviction rates • more robbery, burglary, larceny, and auto theft • rely on public defender
Values	• have feelings of control over life • engage in long-range planning and able to defer gratification	• feel manipulated by forces beyond their control • pursue short-range goals, immediate gratification
Health care	• more likely to be covered by insurance • use private physician and private rapid-treatment centers • lower incidence of mental health problems; treatment by psychotherapy in private clinics for short periods of time	• less likely to be covered by insurance • use public health-care facilities, public hospital emergency room • higher incidence of mental health problems; treatment by electroshock, tranquilizing drugs in state institutions for longer periods of time
Religion	• more involved in church activities • membership likely in mainline Protestant groups	• less involved in church activities • membership likely in fundamentalists or revivalist groups

FIGURE 15-2
Consequences of Social Class[10]

[10]Adapted from Perry and Perry, 1991.

Of course, the information presented in Figure 15-2 presents a positive stereotype of upper- and middle-class American families and a negative stereotype of lower-class American families. These stereotypes may or may not be accurate for individuals. They are, nonetheless, found by research to be reasonably accurate for the majority of people.

Note that the mere existence of these consequences of social class membership does not reveal any reason or theory to explain why things are so. You would have to consult individual studies to gain the benefit of the researcher's explanation of the phenomenon he or she revealed. Recall that a good part of social studies instruction should aim toward helping students find answers to questions about why people act as they do, why they hold certain beliefs, and why society is like it is.

What impact does social class have on an individual's education? Does a person's social class tell us much about his or her experience and success in education? Figure 15-3 provides some data on this topic.

UPPER OR MIDDLE CLASS	LOWER CLASS
• more successful academically	• less successful academically
• values stress academic achievement	• values stress work and getting by
• better attendance	• more frequent cuts, absences, and tardies
• more often involved in soccer, swim team, and individual sports	• more often plays baseball and football
• more often involved in school government, honor society, newspaper, and academic and service clubs	• more often in FTA, FHA, FFA, and drill team[11]
• parents more likely to belong to PTA/O, help with homework, and talk about school and plans after high school	• parents less likely to express interest in school or give help with homework
• more likely to go to college	• more likely to stop education with high school

FIGURE 15-3
Consequences of Social Class for Education[12]

This information should alert you to the need to take specific actions in your classroom that help level the educational playing field.[13] Here are some suggestions.

---

[11]FTA, Future Teachers of America; FHA, Future Homemakers of America; FFA, Future Farmers of America.

[12]Compiled from statistical data published by the U.S. Department of Education, National Center for Education Statistics, 1992.

[13]Jonathon Kozol's 1991 book, *Savage Inequalities*, is an emotional and substantive exposition of the disparities that exist in U.S. public schools.

- Make assignments that consider different lifestyles and resources. For example, don't assume that all students traveled or vacationed over summer break—some may have worked or just "hung out."
- Adjust access time to school technology resources so that students without a home computer or on-line service can compete in production quality and depth of information.
- Make an extra effort to meet with lower social class parents and say something positive about their child. Provide low-cost suggestions for help at home. Loan school resources if possible. Reserve some late afternoon or evening conference times, recognizing that parents may not be able to leave work.
- Build classroom esprit-de-corps; use flexible grouping practices and cooperative learning.
- Set high expectations for everyone. Establish a homework support group for students who can't get help at home.
- Establish a climate where the worth of individuals is gauged by more than the brand of clothes they wear. Read and discuss books that portray a variety of family circumstances and occupations.
- Maintain a special reserve of classroom resources such as pencils and paper. Be ready and willing to use school food and clothing supplies in emergency situations, making sure you preserve the privacy and dignity of a child who needs access to such supports. Follow up with parent contact and appropriate referrals if necessary.

We are all, in a sense, captured by our social class. There are burdens and benefits associated with any level of social status—though it would be correct to say that most individuals would choose a higher rather than a lower status if given a choice. Remember, too, that children don't choose their parents or their social class. Ensure that in your classroom they aren't being punished by circumstances beyond their control.

ISSUES IN MULTICULTURAL EDUCATION AND HOW TO HANDLE THEM

Quite a few issues and problems, such as stereotyping and lack of teacher knowledge, emerge when schools attempt to implement multicultural education. Each of the following topics first describes an issue or problem and then offers suggestions on how to handle the situation.

Parent Disapproval

Some parents feel multicultural education is a threat to their view of how America (meaning the United States) "ought to be" and what children should be taught. These individuals worry that we may be loosing track of the "common culture" that binds us as Americans. Sometimes these individuals may have read an article or heard a speech that promoted a view of the correctness of a middle-class, homogenized European-American cultural hegemony (predominance). They may feel the correctness of the European-American "way" is obvious, because of its "success." Given this belief, they feel it is wrong to teach children that other cultural views are equally valid.

Of course, a close inspection of this point of view reveals that it ignores significant differences in the various religions, languages, and lifeways of the diverse European groups that colonized and later immigrated to North America. It also ignores the problems, such as racism, poverty, violence, teenage pregnancy, and drug abuse, that our nation suffers. These critics often evade any responsibility for these problems, shifting blame away from the dominant group to which they belong and laying it squarely on the cultural, ethnic, and racial groups they seek to silence or diminish. They assume the problems of existing or recently arrived racial minorities, ethnic, and cultural groups are evidence of their inferiority.

Experience has shown me that many of these people are not well informed about national and global demographic trends. Because of this, you may want to establish some awareness by giving them a few of the facts quoted on pages 266 and 267. These individuals may also not be thinking clearly about their own ethnic heritage and the conditions that brought their ancestors to the United States. Helping them recall a bit of their own history is often a pleasant diversion. This is especially so if you can slip into a questioning instead of a telling mode. Help these individuals recall the discrimination and other problems that their own immigrant forebearers experienced when they first arrived in the United States. Guiding critics' responses with your well-targeted questions can lead to some powerful analogies with contemporary conditions.

Another solution is including parents from the outset in your multicultural education efforts. Invite parents to share their own family histories, display heirlooms from their ancestors, and demonstrate ethnic cooking and dances. Such visits are a natural time to use a globe or wall map to point out the nation of origin and the route taken to get to the United States. Students also enjoy learning words, expressions, and simple songs in the resource person's native language.

Regardless of the outcome of encounters with skeptical or critical parents, it's important for you to remember that you have a right to exercise professional judgment concerning the content and methods used in your classroom. You have the backing of organizations, such as the National Council for the Social Studies (NCSS), that have recommended guidelines for multicultural education. In addition, your school district will most likely have endorsed or adopted a multicultural education initiative. In many cases the principal or assistant principal may be the most appropriate person to talk with a parent critic. Finally, remember that parents have a right to request that their sons or daughters be provided with alternative instruction. They also have a right to voice criticism of your practices in appropriate forums such as parent-teacher conferences.

Stereotyping

The tendency to stereotype is one of the dangers of teaching about virtually any group. Imagine, for a moment, reading a children's book about a group to which you belong. Surely there would be simplifications that glossed over the differences that exist in individual members of the group. To illustrate our tendency to stereotype, let's consider the common images of a kindergarten teacher and a high-school history teacher. Figure 15-4 gives a series of teacher characteristics. Your job is to check the column that most likely applies to the commonly accepted images of these two types of teachers.

Well, how did you do? Could you find images of your past teachers in the list of characteristics? Do you feel some of the characteristics are unfair—that I chose them to make you select either the kindergarten or the high school teacher? Well, it's true, I did. But consider: Is there any characteristic in the list that you could not assign to *either* type of teacher? No. Could a person who fit characteristics 1, 3, 4, 6, 8, 9, and 10 be a good kindergarten teacher? Yes, with the posible exception of 3.

The point of this exercise is to illustrate that some degree of stereotyping is unavoidable as we think about the world. What is most important is to realize that *all individuals* will fail to meet the stereotype in some ways and that a few may completely defy the popular image of persons occupying that social position.

Stereotyping is useful when it helps us make correct decisions about the actions and thoughts of others. It is harmful when our thinking fails to accommodate exceptions and predisposes us to assumptions and behaviors that turn out to be incorrect or hurtful to others.

CHARACTERISTIC	KINDER-GARTEN TEACHER	HIGH-SCHOOL HISTORY TEACHER
1. Is a middle-aged male		
2. Could be found sitting on the floor		
3. Teaches content, not children		
4. Is a good person to discuss sports with		
5. Bakes banana bread and brings it to school		
6. Uses an overhead projector frequently		
7. Uses simplified vocabulary, even with adults		
8. Was a high-school athlete		
9. Enjoys watching professional wrestling		
10. Overeats and enjoys red meat		

FIGURE 15-4
Stereotypical Teacher Images

Few people object to positive stereotypes, whether applied to their own or other groups. After all, we usually like to be associated with positive characteristics. So, for example, when I say professors are very trustworthy, you probably don't have any real objection to that characterization. (Polls show that they are among the most trusted people in our society.) But even positive stereotypes can have negative consequences and cause hurt to others. Take, for example, the stereotype that Asian Americans are bright and excellent students. I'm sure you can imagine situations where this stereotype didn't fit an individual and much pain and damage resulted from inappropriate comments and actions.

Real problems develop, however, when people feel and express negative stereotypes. For example, many of you might object to my saying that professors are absentminded, out of touch with the real world, elitist, and inept at practical matters. Yet I've heard all of these negative stereotypes expressed about professors. Some of you may have personal anecdotes that illustrate one or more of these negative stereotypes. (I hope that you also have had experiences that illustrate the opposite, too!)

If positive stereotypes can cause pain and damage, just imagine what destruction negative stereotypes cause! As a responsible adult—but more important, as a teacher—you must be on guard constantly to avoid the pitfall of negative stereotyping. This is especially important when learning about ethnic, cultural, or racial groups. Generally speaking, the less you know about a group—the fewer and more limited in range your firsthand experiences—the greater the danger of allowing a negative stereotype to exist unchallenged in your mind.

One technique you can use to become aware of negative stereotyping is to examine, and switch if necessary, the noun referent (for example, substitute a referent to Asian Americans in place of one to African Americans) in spoken or written sentences. This type of substitution can alert you to the fact you've got a negative stereotype because suddenly the statement seems silly, or just doesn't sound right any more. This technique works with all subjects, whether the referent is a group or some other object. For example, the current popular conception of U.S. society is that it is excessively violent and materialistic. This is surely a negative stereotype. Your first reaction is, most likely, to say that this is not true of all people in the United States. So you immediately, and correctly, attempt to differentiate some Americans from others on these two characteristics. You may also have reacted by asking for a comparison group or data from other societies to challenge the claim ("violent or materialistic in comparison to whom?"). Finally, you might have been able to recognize this as a negative stereotype by switching the referent to "Canadians," or "Italians," or "Koreans." Switching the referent may alert you to the negative feelings and implications behind a stereotype.

One final technique to practice is to substitute a different descriptive adjective for the one used in the negative stereotype. For example, we might hear a teenager say "Parents are so nosy!" when it is that person's perception that one too many questions have been asked. So try some synonyms for nosy, like *inquisitive, interested, meddlesome, prying,* or *curious.* Some of these words sound much more positive—and some quite a bit more negative! Anyway, if you really analyzed the thought, you'd probably have to admit that it really meant that "At the moment *my* parents are . . ." (you pick the most accurate ending). Clearly, then, finding good language and qualifying your thoughts are keys to avoiding careless negative stereotypes.

Monocultural Student Population

Authorities agree that homogeneous monocultural classes need multicultural education more than classes composed of a diverse student population. There are several reasons for this assertion, but probably the most important centers on the undeniable fact that we never really come to know ourselves fully unless we can compare our own lives with those of others. The enculturation process is such that we all grow up thinking that whatever we experienced was "normal." People raised in sheltered, monocultural environments are, consequently, in the greatest need of exposure to different lifeways and social realities. Without multicultural contact, people have narrowed conceptions of their own experiences. As a consequence, they are then less able to assess the value of events in their own lives.

Beyond gaining a better view of who we personally are as a result of learning about others, there are other reasons you should be sure that multicultural perspectives are represented in your classroom. One is the expectation that the education you are offering will prepare students for the future. That future, we hope, includes opportunities for travel, either for employment or pleasure. And in tomorrow's world (as in today's) one won't have to go far to encounter different ethnic, cultural, or racial groups. Education should prepare students for what is and what will be, based on the assumption of a full and fruitful life for each and every child in the classroom.

Although there are quite a few other reasons for including multicultural perspectives in a monocultural setting, the final one I want to offer is the necessity of educating future citizens who have the knowledge, attitudes, and skills needed to lead the United States into a prosperous and peaceful future. As our national population grows, the cultural mosaic that spreads across the land is even more in need of the cooperation and understanding that one neighbor lends another. Fostering a climate of acceptance, inclusion, and friendship is a worthy goal that ultimately benefits us all.

Lack of Knowledge

Perhaps you feel uncomfortable teaching about ethnic, cultural, or racial groups with your limited multicultural experience. Several excellent resources make interesting background reading. Patricia G. Ramsey's 1987 book *Teaching and Learning in a Diverse World: Multicultural Education for Young*

Children offers an overview of multicultural education and useful suggestions for implementation in the primary-grade-level classroom. *Multiethnic Education: Theory and Practice*, by James A. Banks (1988), provides a comprehensive design for multicultural education and practical guidelines for the classroom. Eleanor W. Lynch and Marci J. Hanson's 1992 book *Developing Cross-Cultural Competence: A Guide for Working with Young Children and Their Families* contains separate chapters for different ethnic and racial groups that describe geographical and historical origins, religious orientations, family patterns, values, beliefs, child-rearing practices, and significant cultural events and holiday practices. But even a whole lot of "book knowledge" may not be enough to make you feel really comfortable. Here are several suggestions that go beyond the obvious, and absolutely necessary, trip to the library.

- Enlist the help of parents when they are available within your school.
- Make some calls to friends and seek trusted contacts who might be willing to come into your classroom.
- Look for cultural programs that you or your students might attend.
- Get on line and seek a fellow teacher who would be willing to help you identify resources or simply answer questions about customs and beliefs.
- Join civic, service, and recreation groups that have multicultural membership and make contacts that can help out.
- Contact your local college campus and ask for assistance from the speaker's bureau or international student services.
- Attend conferences, such as the one offered by your local social studies council, where multicultural workshops will be offered.
- Enjoy an ethnic or cultural vacation, but learn more than the average tourist!

Putting Minority Students "On the Spot"

One of the pitfalls of having ethnic, cultural, or racial students represented in your class in small numbers is the tendency to put these students "on the spot" to speak for their entire group. This is a very uncomfortable position to be in for anyone, let alone an elementary grade level child.

Remember that each of us is first and foremost an individual, with all of the limitations that come from that singular status. Few among us can speak for any group, regardless of how small.

For these reasons, it's best to include any ethnic, cultural, or racial minority child as you would any other student in the class activities. If a minority student volunteers to speak, help him or her talk about personal experiences and don't expect the child to generalize to others. Parents, if they can take the time to visit your class, may feel more capable of noting their own experiences of the natural differences that exist from person to person, household to household, and group to group.

THE IMPORTANCE OF COMMON GROUND

People who live in the United States share a common bond to the civic culture established by our Constitution and Bill of Rights. These documents established a government that is (1) empowered by the will of the people and (2) limited in its authority. This civic culture includes many citizenship rights, such as freedom of movement, assembly, speech, press, and religion. It includes tax-supported universal education and security that comes from an effective and fair legal system. Citizenship in the United States gives people the right to own property and the opportunity to make a profit.

Because people hold the power and make the decisions in the United States there are many responsibilities that come with citizenship. Foremost is the responsibility to see that the rights extended by our civic culture are not diminished, but strengthened and applied fully to all citizens.

Beyond the bonds created by our civic culture, citizens of the United States share many other manifestations of common culture such as sports, music, theater, and art. We also share a fairly well-standardized system of traffic laws that regulate our prolific use of (and largely peaceful interaction on) roads and highways. We share a nearly ubiquitous commercial culture represented by large businesses such as McDonald's, Kmart, and Apple Computer. In addition, we share our burdens to pay taxes and register for military service. All of these things bind us together as citizens of the United States and remind us of our obligations to one another.

Finally, it is important to stress to children that we are all more similar than we are different. The biological similarities of people are substantial. Anthropologists tell us that the amount of variation within a particular group of people far exceeds the degree of differences between groups. Similar statements can be made about variations in the social and psychological realms. Again, the evidence shows we are more similar in our thinking capacities, emotions, and other social-psychological traits than we are different. Individuals who grow up in a different nation are more culturally like the people they are raised with than those from their native area. This not only reveals the power of culture, but shows how similar we all are in our learning abilities.

Some readers may wonder why I have not mentioned the often used reference to "common Western heritage" employed by commentators, majority-group historians, and many leaders. First, many citizens only recently arrived in the United States, and they do not share our comparatively short history as a nation. Similarly, many new U.S. citizens do not come from a Western cultural tradition.

Of course, the overwhelming influence of our civic, sports, arts, and commercial cultures will "westernize" most, if not all, new members of our nation. This is the "glue" that holds us together, this contemporary manifestation of Western cultural influence, not a shared Western heritage. It is incorrect to say that all Americans share the same Western heritage simply because they are participating successfully in our society.

GUIDELINES FOR TEACHING ABOUT NATIVE AMERICANS

Elementary grade level teachers have taught units about Native Americans for many generations. The content and quality of the instruction offered, as you might suspect, has varied considerably depending upon the historical era, the geographic location, firsthand experiences with Native Americans, and the prevailing political atmosphere. Figure 15-5 identifies a number of typical faults associated with instruction on Native Americans and offers suggested corrections. As you process the information, think about the Native-American-focused instruction you had in elementary school and see if it exhibited some or all of the potential faults.

POTENTIAL FAULTS	POSSIBLE CORRECTIONS
• The instruction treats all "Indians" as the same; it fails to differentiate among different Native-American nations.	• Teach about one or more specific Native-American groups.
• Students are left thinking that Native Americans still live today like they did in the 1700s and 1800s.	• Clearly identify the period of time you are referring to. • Present contemporary images of Native Americans.
• Native-American lifeways and crafts are oversimplified and trivialized as "cute" construction-paper and crayon "art" activities.	• Build full- or reduced-scale models. • Use real materials. • Copy real processes faithfully. • Explore and replicate Native-American art if you want to integrate subject areas
• Native Americans are dehumanized—no real names are used, normal human activities are neglected, and their feelings about invasion, conquest, and removal are ignored.	• Use biographies of real individuals. • Give students imagined Native-American identities with authentic names. • Develop understanding of everyday activities as they actually happened. • Use role play, analogies, and children's literature to activate feelings about invasion, conquest, and removal.

FIGURE 15-5
Guidelines for Teaching about Native Americans

Figure 15-5 sets minimal standards for teaching about Native Americans. You may be able to add other guidelines based on your own knowledge and experience. The sample lesson plan that follows shows how a common elementary social studies lesson may be adapted to better reflect the perspectives of Native Americans. It was adapted from *Teaching about Native Americans*, (Harvey, Harjo, and Jackson, 1990). I selected the plan because it represents a transformation approach to multicultural education. It develops a Native-American perspective on a commonly recognized holiday, Thanksgiving.

EXERCISE 15-1
◆ ◆ ◆ ◆ ◆

1. Now that you have gained the facts and perspectives offered in this chapter, it's time to revisit the opening article. Go back and look at the three statements you wrote. For the statement that you disagreed with, describe why you disagreed and see if you can find any statements in the chapter that support your point of view. Try to find other students in your class who disagreed with the same statement and share your responses. Do you feel your positions are valid? What other evidence could be used to support your point of view? Now repeat this exercise with the statement you agreed with. Again, look for material in the chapter that supports your point of view and share your work with at least one other student.

2. Role play a school board meeting between the people in the article and other citizens who either favor or oppose the point of view represented by Louis Williams and Constance Older. Have Williams and Older attempt to get the school board to end all multicultural education efforts in the school district.

3. Write a letter to the editor in support of multicultural education. Explain the need for multicultural education and the benefits to individual children and our society. Alternatively, write a letter to the editor that condemns either real or imagined excesses of multicultural education. Conclude your letter by telling what limits you believe are appropriate for multicultural education.

A DIFFERENT VIEW OF THANKSGIVING

Grade Level: Primary
Concepts/Vocabulary: Culture and diversity
Main Ideas: Native-American people lived differently in the past from the way they do in the present. Native Americans have varied perspectives on the celebration of Thanksgiving.
Culture Area: Northeast
Time Period: Post-European contact to contemporary time

Teacher Background

This lesson provides an alternative strategy for teaching about Thanksgiving. Many typical Thanksgiving activities perpetuate stereotypes that dehumanize Native Americans. Commonly used songs, activities, and instruction are not accurate and are often considered offensive to Native-American people. For example, the Wampanoag people, who lived where Plymouth Rock stands, did not wear feather headdresses or live in teepees. Native Americans were tribally specific in the past and although they have changed in many ways, still maintain their diverse languages and cultures in modern times.

Objectives: As a result of this lesson, students will:

- identify how the Wampanoags and Pilgrims dressed at the first Thanksgiving and compare this with contemporary dress
- describe differences between present-day and Pilgrim-era cooking techniques

Procedure

1. Read *The First Thanksgiving Feast* (Anderson, 1984) to the students. Allow ample time for looking at the illustrations. Read appropriate sections and show illustrations from *The Folklore of American Holidays* (Cohen and Coffin, 1987), *Squanto and the First Thanksgiving* (Celsi, 1989), *The Pilgrims of Plimoth* (Seawall, 1986), and *Cooking with Spirit: North American Indian Food and Fact* (Williamson and Railsback, 1987). Help the children describe the clothing shown in the photographs, both Pilgrim and Wampanoag. Draw at-

tention to the cooking techniques and foods shown. Make sure the students know whether the food items were obtained from native sources or brought by Pilgrims. Draw analogies with foods and cooking techniques used today.

Here is a listing of the native and imported foods that were available:[14]

NATIVE FOODS

Fruits and Vegetables

black walnuts	pumpkins
hickory nuts	plums
wild cherries	beans
Jerusalem artichokes	onions
crab apples	watercress
grapes	raspberries
squash	chestnuts
currants	gooseberries
strawberries	ground nuts
blueberries	purslane
corn	

Meats

fish	fowl (duck and turkey)
deer	

FOODS BROUGHT BY PILGRIMS

Fruits and Vegetables

parsnips	melons
radishes	turnips
lettuce	beets
carrots	skirrets
cabbages	onions
dried peas and beans	

Meats

salt pork	smoked herring
salt beef	dried tongue
dried salt cod	cheese and pickled eggs

2. Plan an authentic first Thanksgiving feast with accurate costumes and food. Invite parents to help assemble the costumes and prepare the food using original recipes and techniques. For example, grind corn for corn muffins, use fresh

---

[14]Taken from *Coming to America Teacher's Guide*. National Live Stock and Meat Board, Chicago, IL 60611-9909.

wild turkey, and if possible, cook using iron kettles and open fires. On the day of the feast, microwave a frozen TV dinner and have the children compare the flavors and textures of the food.

3. Invite Native-American resource persons to your class and interview them concerning their perceptions of contemporary Thanksgiving Day celebrations. Ask about family traditions that have been handed down. If possible, ask your guests to bring family photographs and seek assistance in assessing the authenticity of the historical illustrations shown in the books you have read.

Evaluation

Involve the children in making a then-and-now mural showing what they believe the first Thanksgiving celebration might have looked like and a composite depiction of the Thanksgiving celebration they are likely to experience. Add cartoon balloons showing what the characters might have been talking about or thinking. Using flipchart paper, have students dictate their own story of Thanksgiving including the Native-American and European-American perspectives of this harvest celebration.

REFERENCES AND SELECTED READINGS

Alleman, J. E., and Rosaen, C. L. 1991. The cognitive, social-emotional, and moral development characteristics of students: Basis for elementary and middle school social studies. In *Handbook of research on social studies teaching and learning*, ed. J. P. Shaver, 121–133. New York: Macmillan.

Anderson, J. 1984. *The first Thanksgiving feast.* New York: Clarion Books.

Angell, A. V. 1991. Democratic climates in elementary classrooms: A review of theory and research. *Theory and Research in Social Education* 19:241–266.

Banks, J. A. 1988. *Multiethnic education: Theory and practice.* 2d ed. Boston: Allyn and Bacon.

————. 1991. *Teaching strategies for ethnic studies.* 5th ed. Boston: Allyn and Bacon.

Celsi, T. N. 1989. *Squanto and the first Thanksgiving.* Milwaukee: Raintree Publishers.

Cohen, H., and Coffin, T. P., eds. 1987. *The folklore of American holidays.* Detroit: Gale Research Co.

Elrich, M. 1994. The stereotype within. *Educational Leadership* 51(8):12–15.

Harvey, K. D., Harjo, L. D., and Jackson, J. K. 1990. *Teaching about Native Americans.* Bulletin no. 84. Washington, D.C.: National Council for the Social Studies.

Kendall, F. E. 1983. *Diversity in the classroom: A multicultural approach to education of young children.* New York: Teacher's College Press.

Kozol, J. 1991. *Savage inequalities.* New York: Crown Publishers.

Lynch, E. W., and Hanson, M. J. 1992. *Developing cross-cultural competence: A guide for working with young children and their families.* Baltimore: Paul H. Brookes.

National Council for the Social Studies. 1992. Curriculum guidelines for multicultural education. *Social Education.* 9:274. (First published, Washington, D.C.: National Council for the Social Studies.)

Pate, G. S. 1981. Research on prejudice reduction. *Educational Leadership* 1:288–291.

Pedersen, P. 1988. *A handbook for developing multicultural awareness.* Alexandria: VA: American Association for Counseling and Development.

Perry, J. A., and Perry, E. K. 1991. *Contemporary society: An introduction to social science.* New York: HarperCollins.

Ramsey, P. G. 1987. *Teaching and learning in a diverse world: Multicultural education for young children.* New York: Teacher's College Press.

Seawall, M. 1986. *The Pilgrims of Plimoth.* New York: Atheneum.

Shapiro, A. L. *We're number one!* 1992. New York: Vintage Books.

Williamson, D., and Railsback, L. 1987. *Cooking with spirit: North American Indian food and fact.* Bend, OR: Maverick Publications.

Wright, J. W., ed. 1994. *The Universal Almanac 1994.* Kansas City, MO: Andrews and McMeel.

Global Education

WORLD TRENDS TIE US TOGETHER
✦ ✦ ✦ ✦ ✦

As the world approaches the third millennium, population growth and advances in communications and transportation have increasingly tied together various nations' worldviews, economic outlooks, and ecological prospects. Population increases alone have resulted in us living closer together with our neighbors. Advances in communications have provided for an ever-improving ability to know the realities of others' experiences. Improved transportation techniques have supported the globalization of international business, opening unprecedented economic opportunities. Amid these truly incredible opportunities fall challenges to world peace and human survival in the areas of food production and distribution, the spread of communicable disease, humiliating poverty, unnecessary ignorance, religious and ethnic conflicts, and willful destruction of the environment.

Consider the implications of the following statements taken from *We're Number One!*[1] The United States is *first*, compared with nineteen other major industrialized nations, in

- single-parent families
- beef consumption per capita
- health-care spending and physicians' salaries
- military aid to developing countries
- failing to vote
- belief in God
- emissions of air pollutants per capita
- forest depletion and junk mail
- nuclear energy and hazardous waste
- the number of AIDS cases
- private spending on education
- ignorance of world geography

At the end of his book, author Andrew Shapiro correctly points out:

Yet international comparisons are anachronistic in this period of rapid globalization. As the boundaries of nations become increasingly permeable to the exchange of people, goods, and ideas, exclaiming "We're Number One!" may be a very backward way of looking at our world. This book was written not only to point out where we really are Number One, but to show how bankrupt the concept of "me-firstism" really is. Ideally, we should be striving not only to make our nation Number One, but working to ensure that all citizens of the world are Number One—in health care, education, housing, environmental protection, security, freedom, and democracy. (pp. 175–176)

---

[1]Shapiro, 1992.

What Is Global Education?

Global education focuses on the world as a complex and fundamentally inter-related system. The global education movement encourages increased study and understanding of other nations, world problems, international processes, and other global phenomena in the K–12 school curriculum. Global education is interdisciplinary, focusing students' attention on processes and phenomena that cut across traditional disciplines and fields of study.

Why Global Education?

Global education is important because (1) national economies have become increasingly international, (2) human activities have placed unprecedented stress on the natural environment, and (3) increasing population pressure amid a base of limited natural resources breeds the conditions under which violent conflicts may erupt and endanger us all. Problems related to the development, distribution, and consumption of energy, the depletion of nonrenewable min-eral resources, overpopulation, immigration, political repression, and sharing the use of both the air and seas confront all nations. It is toward the under-standing of these problems that global education is directed.

Robert G. Hanvey (1982) defined five dimensions of global education that may serve as goal statements for K–12 global education. Figure 16-1 displays Hanvey's five dimensions.

BRINGING GLOBAL EDUCATION INTO YOUR CLASSROOM
♦ ♦ ♦ ♦ ♦

Due to the nature of its complex content and mature-sounding goals, global education efforts initially took place within the middle and high schools. However, attempts to infuse a global perspective into K–6 social studies reach back into the early 1970s, represented most notably in publishers' attempts to include families and communities from other nations in the expanding environ-ments scope and sequence.

Today, global education has secured a place in many K–6 classrooms. Children commonly encounter cultures from around the world in their regular social studies curriculum. Teachers offer activities designed to develop Han-vey's five dimensions of global education. In many situations, classmates may be recent immigrants from other nations around the world.

A sampling of global education activities for primary grade level students follows. These activities are envisioned as an integral part of ongoing inquiry about other countries. As you read the activities, see if you can relate each to one or more of Hanvey's five dimensions of global education. Be prepared to share your analysis of these primary grade level activities.

DIMENSION 1: PERSPECTIVE CONSCIOUSNESS

Perspective consciousness is the recognition or awareness on the part of the individual that he or she has a view of the world that is not universally shared, that this view has been and continues to be shaped by influences that often escape conscious detection, and that others have views of the world that are profoundly different from one's own.

DIMENSION 2: STATE OF THE PLANET AWARENESS

State of the planet awareness involves being aware of prevailing world conditions and developments, including emergent conditions and trends, such as population growth, migrations, economic conditions, resources and physical environment, political developments, science and technology, law, health, and conflicts within and among nations.

DIMENSION 3: CROSS-CULTURAL AWARENESS

Cross-cultural awareness is understanding the diversity of ideas and practices to be found in human societies around the world and how such ideas and practices compare, including some limited recognition of how the ideas and ways of one's own society might be viewed from other vantage points.

DIMENSION 4: KNOWLEDGE OF GLOBAL DYNAMICS

Knowledge of global dynamics involves some modest comprehension of key traits and mechanisms of the world system, with emphasis on theories and concepts that may increase intelligent consciousness of global change. For example, how might a small nation with a relatively low standard of living and few mineral resources increase its standard of living through world trade?

DIMENSION 5: AWARENESS OF HUMAN CHOICES

Awareness of human choices involves showing some understanding of the problems of choice confronting individuals, nations, and the human species as consciousness and knowledge of the global system expand.

FIGURE 16-1

Hanvey's Five Dimensions of Global Education[2]

- Bring in three or four precooked foods from another culture or area of the world. (Invite parents to participate if they are members of the culture or have lived in the country from which the food originates.) Talk about traditional eating customs and preparation of the foods. Allow children to taste the foods. Help the children describe the colors, textures, and tastes of the foods. Write these words on chart paper headed with the names of the foods. Close the activity by asking students to identify foods from their own culture that fit the words they just supplied to describe the foods from another culture. Discuss why different areas and cultures around the world have different foods.

- Visit the produce section of a large supermarket. Arrange to have the produce manager describe some of the imported fruits and vegetables that

[2]Adapted from Hanvey, 1982.

are available there. Keep a list of the fruit and vegetable names and the countries from which they came. Ask the produce manager to tell briefly about a recent import procurement problem he or she experienced due to problems such as drought, health regulations, or political problems. Upon returning to the classroom, allow the children to paint or draw and color images of the different fruits and vegetables. Post these artistic renditions around a world map and run yarn to the countries of origin.

- Dress up in traditional costumes of a culture. Name and describe each piece of clothing. Be sure to point out if the clothing is used only for special occasions or by one particular subgroup. Remind children that people do not dress this way all the time. Discuss some of the customs that go with ceremonies people perform while wearing the clothing. What beliefs and values are represented in these customs and ceremonies? How do they compare with our beliefs and values?

- Learn cultural proverbs, simple greeting and eating phrases, and words for colors and numbers from the culture's main language. Practice saying these words and use them as substitutes for English throughout the lesson or unit. Discuss how the proverbs express a worldview that reflects basic beliefs about human nature.

- Simulate rural or urban living conditions in the country or culture you are investigating. For example, serve a lunch or snack that would be typical for children of that place. Imitate the climate by adjusting the heat or air conditioning, running a humidifier or dehumidifier, or turning on a large fan to simulate a continual breeze. Wear indoor and outdoor clothing like the children there might use. Point out that such food, climate, and clothing feel perfectly normal to children in that country. Discuss why this is so.

- Investigate the connections of our country with others by examining the labels on clothing, foods, and toys that we commonly buy. Using a world map, place pins on the countries of origin and run colored string or yarn back to the mainland of the United States. Extend this activity by categorizing the toys, foods, or clothing. Attempt to discover if certain areas of the world provide certain types of clothing, toys, or foods.

- Simulate a simple chore that a child might perform in the culture such as carrying water, grinding corn into meal, or making woven hats, place mats, and paper-plate holders from dried reeds. Discuss why children would be involved in these activities. Point out that young children used to work in our country and that many children still help out at home with chores. If you feel it is appropriate, discuss examples of the abuse of child labor in the United States and other nations.

- Make globes from balloons and paper maché. Don't be overly concerned about lack of accuracy. Use different-sized balloons to illustrate the consequences of scale on the amount of detail that can be shown. Have each child or team (if you work in small groups) show such features as the major bodies of water, the continents, and the equator. Point out that the earth is our home and that of all other people.

Global education should take place in grades 4 through 6, too. A collection of activities suitable for these grades follows. Many of the activities make use of increasingly popular CD-ROM multimedia databases and Internet resources.

- Bring in a short, videotaped segment of news about some other country in our world community. Use a computer atlas program such as PC Globe® or MacGlobe® to quickly access information about the nation featured in the news.
- Use PC Globe® or MacGlobe® to help students explore relationships among variables across nations and areas of the world. For example, ask students to explore per capita income and educational attainment in several nations from each region of the globe. Post the data on a large world map or an outline of the world projected onto the chalkboard. Discuss the patterns you've detected. Compare your results with data for the United States.
- Use a CD-ROM version of the *CIA Fact Book* (or access this same information through the Internet) to gain more information about any nation you are studying. Compare the *CIA Fact Book* data with other sources. Which is more complete? Which would you trust more? Why? Do you suppose other nations have the equivalent of our *CIA Fact Book*? Why or why not?
- Hook up to the National Geographic Kids Network® and teach one of their social-studies-focused units, such as Too Much Trash or What Are We Eating? Augment the unit by allowing students to conduct independent inquiry projects using the same topic, but focusing on other nations.
- Allow students to use free time to play Where in the World Is Carmen SanDiego? at a center area near the back of the room. Ask advanced students to use the print or computer-based atlases to create a live version (like the television show) of Carmen SanDiego for the class.
- Have children create multimedia reports on nations around the world. Establish a key-pal exchange and send a videotaped or disk-based copy of your report for comments from students in your keyboard-pal country.
- Play a whole-class simulation such as Explosion or Chow from Interact™. Apply the simulation's content focus to the real world by investigating contemporary news articles on population growth or food production.
- Engage your students in Tom Snyder's Mapping the World by Hart, a unit that engages students in in-depth study of places and cultures; The Other Side, a simulation of geopolitics for grades 5 and up; or International Inspirer, a computer-based game that teaches locational geography, decision making, and lots of information about the world.
- Expose your most advanced students to Endangered Species, Garbage, Forests, Population, Immigration, AIDS, Hunger, or other titles in the Opposing Viewpoints® Juniors series from Greenhaven Press.

DISCUSSION QUESTIONS

1. Some individuals have opposed the goals and methods of global education, asserting that children should learn first about their own country and only later be exposed to other nations. Are these individuals correct in holding this view? What might be the basis of their reasoning? What valid arguments can you make against these reasons?

2. How might our nation be different if many more citizens had experienced powerful global education as a part of their school experience?

3. Are some citizens more in need of global education than others? Is high-quality global education a greater imperative for some groups than others? If we could afford only to provide global education for half of our children in public schools, which children should get it?

The following description of a global education unit was sent to me over the Internet by Dick Fuller. I thought what he did with his sixth graders was a good example of what any teacher could do to connect his or her students with the world using a mix of technology and local resources. As you read the unit, note how Fuller involved his students in learning and how he reached out to the global community for help.

I teach "International Cultures" as an exploratory course for sixth graders. The intent of this course is to introduce other cultures to the students and to hopefully spark some interest in other languages. The freedom to explore and create at our school gives us all a wide latitude in pursuing our interests and the interests of the students.

I met with our middle-school facilitator and the principal in the winter of my second year to discuss plans and much to my delight I was told to teach something new. My instructions were simply, "Dick, I want you to teach something different in the spring." That was it. No further guidelines, no suggestions, nothing. Teach something different in the spring.

There is nothing like freedom to spur a person's thinking and there is nothing like thinking and talking to spur the creative energy and synergy to get things moving. I did what any schoolteacher would do in such a case: I went to my mother-in-law, who will be 80 this fall, and said, "Louise, how would you like to team-teach a course in Russian with me to two groups of sixth graders?" Her response was, "Of course I would." Well, it wasn't quite that easy, but almost.

I don't speak Russian, but my mother-in-law, a former schoolteacher, had been to Russia several times and was taking courses in Russian. She agreed to work with me.

Simultaneously, a friend whose daughter attends our school called me over to his house and showed me the wonders of the Internet and what was possible. My imagination went crazy with all the possibilities.

If you are not familiar with the Internet and what the possibilities are for the classroom, you are in for a real treat. My friend showed me how we could scan the library stacks in Australia, download a meteorological program from Germany, and leave a note for a friend in Latin America.

Louise and I set to work to create a curriculum. Now keep in mind, this is an exploratory course. The object is to create a curriculum that will simply let children explore something new. At our school we have them for six weeks, a short 30 days, and then the next group comes in. You can't teach a language in 30 days—you introduce it to your students. Also keep in mind, exploratory courses are truly heterogeneous—your classroom reflects the full range of abilities.

We taught the students the alphabet. The Cyrillic alphabet is so different from anything our students had ever seen, we thought that teaching them the alphabet and the sounds the letters make was a good first step. We made lists of the alphabet, we made flash cards, we reviewed them in sequential order, and we reviewed them in random order. Interestingly enough, almost all the students were able to learn the entire alphabet in less than a week. Learning the alphabet also became the great equalizer with the students. Whether the students were from the enrichment classes or the special education classes, they all seemed to learn the alphabet at the same rate. Of course, we went from letters to words and simple phrases.

We worked on geography trying to give the children an understanding of where the Former Soviet Union (FSU) is and how big it is. We took maps of the U.S. and the FSU of the same scale and ran them off and then simply cut three U.S. maps out and pasted them into the FSU. We looked at the republics, rivers, mountains, and movies about Lake Baikal and Lenin's Tomb.

We went to the library and did small reports on significant historical personalities and events. The children had to look up people like Tschaikovsy, Rachmaninoff, Dostoevsky, Breshnev, and Lenin. They had to be able to label a map with significant cities and rivers, and know the republics. We worked on cartooning and created a zoo of Russian animals with all the beasts being labeled in Cyrillic. We taught them to transliterate their names in Cyrillic. When you are working in the U.S. with our multicultural population, transliteration becomes as much a matter of art as it does of science.

The Internet provided the crowning touch to our unit. I was able to make contact with School 638 in Zelenograd, Russia, through the good graces of Yuriy Sidelnikov. We were able to communicate by leaving e-mail messages with each other. Yuriy is a programmer for the city of Zelenograd and his children, Sasha and Lena, go to school at School 638.

Yuriy and I set to work. He made contact at School 638 and I worked with my students on a letter-writing exercise to students in Russia. My students had the opportunity to have pen pals—actually keyboard pals—in Russia. They were able to write back and forth and it was clear from the first exchange of messages—students around the world are much the same. They were able to experience firsthand what their respective lives were like, what their dreams and their questions were all about. I had the unique experience of making international lesson plans with their teacher Galina Kujava. None of that would have been possible without the Internet. This turned out to be community in the making and it certainly gives me hope for the future.

Our letter exchanges were fun and meaningful. Out of Atlanta, Georgia, the Friendship Force was on its way to Moscow that spring and so we were able to send pictures and books from the library, and Atlanta Braves bumper stickers to our friends in Zelenograd. In return, we were sent pictures, postcards, letters, and books from them. This year we filmed our first videos and exchanged them. It was quite a thrill to put pictures with names. It was sobering to see how much our schools looked alike.

There is so much to this experience that has been great fun. The students have been exposed to a new language and culture. Daily in the hall of Renfroe Middle School, I am greeted with "drasweecha" and "dasvydanya." One student has now learned about Lenin and is fascinated with him. The children have exchanged pictures, letters, books, gifts, and even a video with children their own age from the other side of the world. They now understand just a little bit more about the world we all share.

Dick Fuller
Renfroe Middle School
Decatur, GA[3]

---

[3]Used by permission.

RESOURCES

Several organizations and publishers support global education. Here is a short list.

The Center for Teaching International Relations (CTIR) [University of Denver, Denver, CO 80208, 1-800-967-2847] publishes lesson plans, units, activity cards, and manipulatives for teaching global studies.

The Children's Press publishes an *Enchantment of the World* series that contains sixty-three individual titles. The series seeks to communicate the unique charm and culture of other parts of the world. Included are geography, history, economics, and key attractions, all illustrated with full-color photographs. Each book is approximately 127 pages, 8" x 9¼", with a reference section and an index. The intended grade level is 5 through 9. The Children's Press also publishes the *New True Books* series of 217 books intended for children in grades K through 4. Each 48-page book is designed to help children discover for themselves fascinating facts about the world.

Films for the Humanities and Sciences (P.O. Box 2053, Princeton, NJ 08543-2053) produces a series of seventeen 15-minute videos on nations around the world for grades 4 through 6.

Franklin Watts publishes four series about other nations. At grade levels K through 4, this publisher offers a set of books called the *Take a Trip* series. Each book is thirty-two pages. The *We Live In* series consists of thirty titles. Each book is sixty-four pages. Twelve titles form the *Countries of the World* series for grades 5 through 8. A fourth series available from Franklin Watts is called the *Passport* series.

The Learner Publications Company produces the *Visual Geography* series that currently includes sixty-three titles for students in grades 5 and up. Each book is approximately sixty-four pages and 7" x 10". For children in grades 2 through 5, Learner publishes the thirty-four-volume *Families the World Over* series.

Network of Educators on the Americas (NECA) [1118 22nd Street N.W., Washington, D.C. 20037] publishes units and lesson plans for teaching about minorities and the welfare of peoples in the Americas.

Peace Corps World Wise School Program. For information call 1-800-424-8580 or write World Wise Schools, 1990 K Street, N.W., Washington, D.C. 20526.

Silver Burdett-Ginn publishes the *People and Places* series of twenty-four 48-page books for children in grades 4 through 6.

The Steck-Vaughn company publishes the *My World* series that includes several titles for second- and third-grade readers. Also available for children in grades 2 through 5 is the *Where We Live* series. Presented as a narrative told by children, each thirty-two-page book describes the culture and geography of a country. Children in grades 6 and up may benefit from *World in View*, a series that presents detailed information about other nations.

Thompson Learning publishes a wide variety of books on cultural diversity, nations around the world, world religions, and global issues. Sample titles include: *Birth Customs;* Food Around the World: *A Taste of China; African Stories;* Threatened Cultures: *Kurds; The Alps and Their People; Jewish Migrations;* and Traditions Around the World: *Body Decoration.*

United States Committee for UNICEF Information Center on Children's Cultures. For information call 212-686-5522 or write to the Information Center on Children's Cultures, U.S. Committee for UNICEF, 331 East 38th Street, New York, NY 10016.

The World Bank (Box 7247-8619, Philadelphia, PA 19170-8619, 202-473-1155) publishes reference books, posters, kits, videotapes, and lesson plans for teaching about world conditions and development issues.

REFERENCES AND SELECTED READINGS
◆ ◆ ◆ ◆ ◆

Angell, A. V., and Avery, P. G. 1993. Examining global issues in the elementary classroom. *Social Studies* 83(3):113–117.

Becker, J. M. 1988. Global education: An overview. *Louisiana Social Studies Journal* 15(1):4–8.

Benegar, J., Hursh, H., Johnson, J. S., and Teh-ming, H. 1983. *Changing images of China grades 5–12.* Denver: Center for Teaching International Relations.

Brook, D. L., Field, S. L., and Labbo, L. D. 1995. South Africa's transformation as seen at school. *Social Education* 59(2):82–86.

_____. 1995. The peaceful revolution: Some teaching resources. *Social Education* 59(2):87–89.

Burstein, C. M. 1988. *A kid's catalog of Israel.* New York: The Jewish Publication Society.

Caballero J., and Whordley, D. 1984. *Children around the world.* Atlanta: Humanics Limited.

Carrol, J., and Regan, P. 1983. *World hunger: Learning to meet the challenge.* New York: Impact on Hunger.

Clark, L. E. 1989. Foreign aid: How generous is the United States? *Social Education* 53(4):214–216.

Collins, H. T., and Zakariya, S. B. 1982. *Getting started in global education: A primer for principals and teachers.* ERIC document no. ED215939. Arlington, VA: National Association of Elementary School Principals.

Daley, W. 1987. *The Chinese Americans.* New York: Chelsea House Publishers.

di Franco, J. P. 1988. *The Italian Americans.* New York: Chelsea House Publishers.

Dolan, E. F. 1985. *Anti-Semitism.* New York: Franklin Watts.

Downer, L. 1988. *Japanese food and drink.* New York: The Bookwright Press.

Elder, P., and Carr, M. A. 1987. *Worldways: Bringing the world into the classroom.* Menlo Park, CA: Addison-Wesley.

Fletcher, R. 1986. *Teaching peace.* New York: Harper & Row.

Franz, D. 1987. *Exploring the Third World: Development in Africa, Asia, and Latin America.* New York: Global Perspectives in Education.

Fry-Miller K., and Myers-Walls, J. 1988. *Young peacemakers project book.* Elgin, IL: Brethern Press.

Gross, S. H., and Bingham, M. W. 1985. *Women in Latin America: The 20th century.* vol. II. Saint Louis Park: MN: Glenhurst Publications, Inc.

Hanvey, R. G. 1982. An attainable global perspective. *Theory into Practice* 21(3):162–167.

Johnson, J., and Parisi, L. S. 1987. *Japan in the classroom: Elementary and secondary activities.* Boulder, CO: Social Science Education Consortium Institute.

Lapenkova, V., and Lambton, E. 1988. *Russian food and drink.* Reprint. New York: The Bookwright Press. [1959]

Maloy, P. 1988. *Global issues in the elementary school.* Boulder, CO: Social Science Education Consortium Institute.

Martin, J., ed. 1985. *Global studies: Africa.* Sluice Dock, Guilford, CT: Dushkin Publishing Group, Inc.

Mitsakos, C. L. 1978. A global education program can make a difference. *Theory and Research in Social Education* 6(1):1–15.

O'Neil, J. (1989). Global education: Controversy remains, but support growing. Field strives to better link global studies, civics. *Curriculum Update* n1. Alexandria, VA: Association for Supervision and Curriculum Development.

Ortero, G. G. 1983. *Teaching about population issues.* Denver: Center for Teaching International Relations.

Rutledge, P. 1987. *The Vietnamese in America.* Minneapolis: Lerner Publications.

Sanborn, M., Roe, R., and Hursh, H. 1984. *Teaching about world cultures.* Denver: Center for Teaching International Relations.

Shapiro, A. L. 1992. *We're number one! Where America stands—and falls—in the new world order.* New York: Vintage Books.

Watson, R. L. 1988. *South Africa in pictures.* Minneapolis: Lerner Publications.

Promoting Positive Democratic Values

Today about half the families no longer see it as their duty to pass along values from generation to generation. Unless somebody embraces the agenda of instilling values, children won't have the strength of their values to fall back on. Yes, even when we teach values, children later may abandon them. But you have to give them some values on which to go. It sadly falls on the shoulder of the school. If we don't do this, then just as we have adults who are deficient in writing and science, we will find that adults won't have the character and the values needed to be decent members of the community or decent employees or decent soldiers. (Berreth and Scherer, 1993, 12)

[T]he process of locating and analyzing values is an invigorating first step in establishing a climate for moral education. We teach values and employ values either thoughtfully and deliberately or mindlessly, by default. Both teachers and students need opportunities to analyze their own practices for the values underlying them. Through doing so, they should be in a position to make genuine commitments to deliberately chosen values.
(Noddings, 1991, 322)

If society, parents, and educators are concerned that children are not displaying values such as honesty, respect, care, responsibility, and effective citizenship, then society, parents, and educators must look to themselves. Character education programs, or any other values education program, cannot teach children values in the absence of demonstrations of these values on the part of educators and others in children's lives. (McKay, 1994, 46)

All adults must promote this basic morality by teaching young people, directly and indirectly, core ethical values such as respect, responsibility, trustworthiness, fairness, caring and civic virtue. Good character consists of knowing, caring about and acting upon these core values or virtues.
(Lickona, 1993, 48)

Family disintegration, then drives the character education movement in two ways: schools have to teach the values kids aren't learning at home; and schools, in order to conduct teaching and learning, must become caring moral communities that help children from unhappy homes focus on their work, control their anger, feel cared about, and become responsible students.
(Lickona, 1993, 8)

INTRODUCTION

The topic of values education is indeed exciting. Introductions to values-education programs often leave teachers and parents enthusiastic for launching schoolwide efforts designed to improve the lives of young people and our society. Such enthusiasm is warranted, for there is much that can be done and the work is of great importance.

At the same time, the topic of values education is full of complexity and pitfalls. The nature and outcomes of values education are so complex that research has generally failed to establish its practical effectiveness (Leming, 1993). Similarly, values education is so full of pitfalls that, at different times, various parent groups have strongly exhorted schools to teach children values or to completely remove any mention of values from the curriculum. Particular approaches to values education have been received with great enthusiasm in one decade only to be forced underground by persistent attacks in the next. Under the potential threat of public attack and aware of the uncertainty regarding its effectiveness, more than a few teachers and school districts completely stopped their values-education efforts during the 1980s and early 1990s.[1]

Today, values education is experiencing an unprecedented resurgence. Leaders in the field urge comprehensive approaches that blend the best of established traditions with the newer innovations such as the cooperative and service learning trends (Leming, 1993; Kirschenbaum, 1992; Noddings, 1991). States have mandated that values such as tolerance, courage, civility, honesty, moderation, frugality, and dependability be explicitly taught to all students (Georgia Department of Education, 1991).

Values education is often considered to be essentially the same as character education. Strictly speaking, this is an error, since character education is a broader realm of concern that involves the whole personality of an individual. Character education was traditionally focused on the many tactics adults could use to urge children to practice good habits of conduct as opposed to helping children develop moral reasoning ability or clarify their own conceptions of right and wrong (Wynne, 1985/1986). Thus, while character education was concerned with developing good behavior, it did not offer intellectual, values-education exercises, such as those promoted by values clarification strategies and moral development discussions.

Before we go further, I want to make it clear that values education is normally considered a responsibility of the entire community. Thus, schools play only a partial role in developing students' values. Similarly, social studies plays only a partial—but uniquely important—role within the values (and character) development efforts of the total school experience.

In this chapter you'll improve your conceptualization of values, learn more about the specific role social studies must play in values education, and gain

---

[1]Many schools stopped using the values clarification approach during this period or continued using elements of the approach under labels such as "critical thinking" exercises.

skill in safely implementing three popular approaches to values education appropriate to K–6 classrooms.

THE NATURE OF VALUES

Like most complex social science concepts, values have been variously defined over time by different individuals. Perhaps the most popular conception of values is to define them as standards that people use to guide their lives.[2] Some values deal with proper ways of interacting with others. Examples are people's desire to have relationships with others that are truthful, polite, and cooperative. Other values, instead of defining high standards of interpersonal conduct, describe desirable states of existence to which we all aspire. Examples are people's desire to feel happy, live a comfortable life, or achieve inner peace.

Of course, there are many other ways to subdivide and categorize the myriad values societies use to regulate the affairs of their members. The literature is filled with references to aesthetic, moral, personal, social, civic, family, and conservative values. All of these categories have meaning within the context that they are used. But for our purposes, I believe it is sufficient to talk of values that define desired modes of interpersonal conduct and those that describe desirable states of existence. These two categories incorporate, of course, many examples of values that are primarily moral, those that are social, civic, conservative, and so on.

It has already been stressed that values are standards that define what is desirable. It follows, then, that there are, by definition, no "bad" values. When a person exhibits less than desirable behavior, it is not because he or she has "bad values." Instead, it is more appropriate to say he or she either (1) lacks knowledge of the desired value or (2) is not living up to the value as we might wish. This way of thinking about values leads us to the realization that all behavior is guided by conceptions of what is desirable. This allows us to conceive of misbehavior having its roots in values ignorance, corrupted thinking, or an overemphasis on certain values. This way of thinking about undesirable behavior and values establishes a role for education.

Children learn their values from their parents or guardians (the child's first, and arguably most important "teachers"), the church, the school, the peer group, the media, and the community. If parents fail to impart a full set of values, or if some values taught in the home are corrupted[3] while others are barely present, then the school and other socialization agencies must attempt to

---

[2]The conception of values offered here is based on the work of social psychologist Milton Rokeach.

[3]I've borrowed the conception of a corrupted value from Freeman Butts, who explains that any good thing can be taken too far and thus become destructive. For example, a desire for prosperity is good and there is certainly nothing inherently wrong with wealth. However, when the pursuit of wealth becomes excessive, or when the mere fact of wealth becomes "reason" for all manner of privilege and excess, then this good value has become corrupted.

restore balance or supply the missing instruction. Failure to impart a full and uncorrupted sense of values leaves individuals handicapped in social situations. Significant values-education deficiencies, multiplied over many individuals, threaten the harmony and viability of society.

VALUES EDUCATION IN SOCIAL STUDIES

The school, through its formal and informal curriculum, joins with the family and other agencies of socialization to produce the values learning children need to perform as successful members of our society. Values are evident in the school's handbook and philosophy. Values are taught through science, language arts, and math textbooks and enforced in classroom rules and daily routines. And, as I'm sure you expect, values are taught as an important part of the formal and informal social studies curriculum.

Social studies asserts a special interest in values learning that directly supports citizenship in our democracy. Freeman Butts, in his 1988 book, *The Morality of Democratic Citizenship: Goals for Civic Education in the Republic's Third Century*, identified twelve core values that must be taught as a part of students' preparation for citizenship. The values are divided into two groups: those that deal with the *obligations of citizenship* and those that define the *rights of citizenship*. These values are shown in Figure 17-1.

According to Mr. Butts, we have an important citizenship obligation to support justice for all, equality of opportunity, legitimate authority, participation, truth, and patriotism. Similarly, we have the right to freedom, diversity, privacy, due process, property, and human rights. Mr. Butts believes, too, that we must work to make sure that "corrupted forms" of these twelve civic values

| UNUM VALUES | | PLURIBUS VALUES | |
| The Obligations of Citizenship | | The Rights of Citizenship | |
Corrupted Forms of Unum	True Forms of Unum	True Forms of Pluribus	Corrupted Forms of Pluribus
"Law and order"	**Justice**	**Freedom**	Anarchy
Enforced sameness	**Equality**	**Diversity**	"Unstable pluralism"
Authoritarianism	**Authority**	**Privacy**	Privatism
Majoritarianism	**Participation**	**Due process**	"Soft on criminals"
"Beguiling half-truth"	**Truth**	**Property**	"Property rights superior to human rights
Chauvanism: xenophobia	**Patriotism**	**Human Rights**	"Cultural imperialism"

FIGURE 17-1
Core Values for Democratic Citizenship

are not allowed to prevail in our communities. To avoid this, we must engage students (our future citizen-leaders) in discussions of events that illustrate these values and draw precedents from history to help ground our reasoning. In effect, each generation must engage in a continuing quest to seek appropriate boundaries between the corrupted and true forms of these values. This is the central thrust of the great civic-education/values-education mission of social studies. The strategies for values learning presented later (pp. 306–309) must be applied toward this end.

In practice, social studies does not, however, typically limit its consideration of values to only those twelve defined by Freeman Butts. In fact, it would be safe to say that most of the time and effort spent on values education is devoted to learning other values. Figure 17-2 presents a list of commonly identified values.

I'm sure you are aware of most, if not all, of the values identified in Figure 17-2. The list is not complete, however. Missing, for example, is the value of altruism. You may be able to think of others.

APPROACHES TO VALUES EDUCATION

Approaches to values education in the schools should serve two general aims: (1) to help individuals make the most of their own lives, and (2) to preserve and refine our democratic society. To achieve these two general aims, values education should be implemented in a way that helps students achieve well-defined educational goals. Values education in public schools should help each student:

1. **Become aware of his or her own personal values.** Students enter school with many values, but do not always know the terms commonly applied to these ideals. Schools can help students identify their own family values by involving students in activities that allow them to identify the desirable life standards they have been taught in their homes, churches, and communities.

2. **Learn about the broad array of possible values.** Schools also have a legitimate right to expose students to other, perhaps unknown, values. Teachers can explain why these are desirable values and involve students in exercises designed to foster critical thinking about the desirability of these values.

3. **Learn how to identify values-relevant behavior in oneself and in others.** Beyond helping students learn about values as abstract ideals, schools can help students build skill in identifying values-relevant behavior in themselves and in others. Role playing and many of the strategies associated with values clarification and moral development can serve as vehicles for achieving this skill goal.

4. **Become consistent between professed values and behavior.** Once students have begun to achieve the first three goals of values education, it

A prosperous life/Wealth	A comfortable life
An exciting life	Ambitious/Aspiring
Broad-minded/Open-minded/Tolerant	Beauty/A world of beauty
Caring/Concerned/Compassionate	Capable/Able/Competent
Clean/Neat/Tidy	Cheerful/Happy/Lighthearted
Competitive	Communicative
Cooperative	Conservation
Cultural preservation/Cultural pluralism	Courageous/Brave
Ecological harmony	Dependable
Equality	Energetic
Family security	Ethical/Moral/Virtuous
Forgiving	Flexible/Adaptable
Friendship/Companionship	Freedom/Liberty
Health	Happiness/Contentedness
Honest	Helpful
Humble	Human dignity
Imaginative/Creative/Resourceful	Idealistic
Individuality/Being unique	Independent/Autonomous
Justice	Inner Harmony/Peacefulness
Love/Affection	Knowledgeable/Wise/Having expertise
National security	Modest
Obedient	Nonviolence
Persevering/Persistent	Patriotic
Pleasure/Enjoyment/Gratified	Personal security
Productive	Polite
Respectful	Prudent
Salvation	Rule of law
Self-respect/Self-esteem/Pride	Self-disciplined/Self-controlled
Sincere	Sharing
Social recognition/Honor	Sociable/Gregarious/Affable
Thrifty	Successful
World peace	Truthful

FIGURE 17-2
Commonly Identified Values

is appropriate for schools to ask students to become consistent in practicing the values they profess to hold. Mature and thoughtful people practice living up to their most cherished values.

Values instruction should begin in the earliest years of life and continue throughout the schooling experience. Thus, the values education efforts offered in grades K through 6 cannot be expected to completely achieve the outlined goals. The work of values learning continues throughout life.

The strategies that follow are the primary means of delivering values education. As you learn about the strategies see if you can recall experiencing each approach. Try to recall the feelings particular episodes of values learning created within you.

Inculcation

Values inculcation is the oldest and most prevalent form of values education. Values inculcation assumes that there are certain right or correct values that must be taught to children.

The ways in which values are inculcated are many, including lecturing, story telling, fables, moralistic slogans, the encouragement of hero worship, modeling, offering rewards for desired behavior, punishing undesirable acts, nagging, exhortation, prayer, and providing incomplete and biased information in an effort to influence belief and behavior.

Both parents and schools are accomplished practitioners of values inculcation; after all, it is unavoidable. The only questions are: (1) What values are being inculcated? (2) Which methods are being used? and (3) How often is instruction taking place?

A notable feature of the values inculcation approach is that values are quite often taught as absolutes. Children are taught that it is always good to be honest, always good to be thrifty, always good to be polite, and so on. However, values are often only considered in isolation from other potentially conflicting, simultaneously operating values. Thus, the child is never sensitized to situations in which the behavioral demands of two separate values contend for primacy. Consider the ten-year-old daughter who takes a dollar without permission from her mother's purse to buy some candy for herself and a friend. Once discovered, the child gets a lecture on honesty and is punished. This is clearly a values-inculcation approach.[4] The mother may not even allow the child to explain her action, exclaiming that she doesn't want to hear any excuse for the behavior. There may be no attempt to look at the girl's motivation for taking the dollar, motivation that might come from such values as a desire to be sociable and the need for friendship. These values are either never mentioned, or if they are, they may be disregarded as poor excuses for an unacceptable display of dishonesty.

Values inculcation will happen in your classroom as a result of the hidden and overt curriculum regardless of whether you wish it or not. You cannot avoid being an inculcator of values. I think it is safe to say that, for the most part, parents will support your efforts to inculcate values—especially if your values closely match those of your community. Conflicts may occur if your values—or a parent's—significantly depart from the mainstream.

Beyond Values Clarification and Moral Development

Values clarification became popular in the late 1960s and early 1970s, largely as a result of the publication of *Values and Teaching* by Louis Raths, Merrill Harmin, and Sidney Simon (1966). The character development programs popularized in the 1920s and 1930s (and still functioning, at least partially, in many

---

[4]Kirschenbaum (1995) makes a distinction between values inculcation and values indoctrination. The former is largely positive in its approach; the latter is negative and dehumanizing.

schools as late as the 1950s) had been substantially discredited by the publication of the 1782-page Character Education Inquiry, a multiyear assessment of the character-related behavior of over 10,000 students in twenty-three communities. The Character Education Inquiry had concluded:

> The mere urging of honest behavior by teachers or the discussion of standards and ideals of honesty, no matter how much such general ideals may be "emotionalized," has no necessary relation to conduct. . . . [T]here seems to be evidence that such effects as may result are not generally good and are sometimes unwholesome. . . . [T]he prevailing ways of inculcating ideals probably do little good and do some harm. (Leming, 1993)

The advocates of values clarification asserted that it was time to stop moralizing and manipulating. They proposed an approach to values learning based on a blend of the inquiry model of instruction and decision making. In implementing the model teachers were to relinquish their roles as moral authorities and begin simply to facilitate a process of values clarification that was achieved through more than one hundred different instructional strategies.

Educators quickly took up the approach, perhaps relieved to be removed from the role of moral authority, but more likely attracted by the large collection of easily implemented lessons and the potential for producing important values learning in their students. Kirschenbaum (1992) notes that over forty books were published emphasizing values clarification in the 1970s and that one of them, *Values Clarification: A Handbook of Practical Strategies for Teachers and Students* (Simon, Leland, and Kirschenbaum, 1972), sold over 600,000 copies.

Values clarification was quickly dropped from the roster of acceptable educational practices during the late 1970s and early 1980s. It became a whipping boy of sorts, standing as an emblem of what was wrong with American education in the "hippie-style, free-love 1970s." The mood of the country turned decidedly conservative by the 1980s and considerable efforts were made to return schools "back to basics." In addition, research studies had failed to show that values clarification was having any positive impact on students' morals or conduct. The newspapers were filled with editorial attacks and feature articles centered on the evils of values clarification. School board meetings turned into shouting matches all too frequently when efforts to remove all vestiges of the method were contested.

There is little doubt that values clarification, as originally promoted, contained "a major flaw" (Kirschenbaum, 1992). Namely, the originators held that the process was completely "value free." Critics correctly wondered how a "value free" process could develop values. Reacting to this charge, Kirschenbaum (1977) acknowledged that the values clarification approach, due to its nature, promoted the values of freedom, justice, rationality, equality, and other democratic and civic values. It was "value free" only in that it did not place the teacher in the position of demanding that students ascribe to values such as honesty, friendship, and dependability. Arguments for the acceptance of these values would have to come from the students themselves, or they would not surface at all. This feature was a central point of attack for critics who thought it absurd to allow students to voice and argue for the acceptance of actions that were dishonest, unfriendly, or showed a lack of dependability. Critics did not trust other students to counter such positions, and they thought that removing the teacher's traditional role as moral authority would prove disastrous.

Figure 17-3 presents a modernized, adapted version of the classic values clarification process. The model includes the same steps recommended in the original values clarification model, but (1) adds, in step 4, a conscious consideration of consequences for each alternative in terms of the values that it promotes or neglects; (2) applies, in step 5, the classic ethical tests of reversibility and universality; and (3) asks students, in step 6, to explore their feelings about their decisions.

Lawrence Kohlberg's dilemma discussion approach to the development of moral reasoning became popular in the 1970s. Despite being like values clarification in urging the teacher not to moralize, it continued to be accepted during the conservative swing of the 1980s as a legitimate strategy of values education. Research evidence showed that moral dilemma discussions had a modest

---

1. Identify or develop an open-ended springboard that contains an issue that will enable students to explore their values. (Teacher-created unfinished stories and newspaper articles about unresolved public issues are ideal for this type of lesson, but you may also use role plays, skits, and recent real-life incidents as springboards.)

2. Share the springboard with students and review its key facts and issues. (You may want to list facts, names, and issues on the board.)

3. Frame the central issue(s) that students will explore during the class and state the issue as an open-ended question that invites students to freely choose alternative courses of action. (You may wish to write the question on the board.) As the students identify alternative courses of action, list or record their suggestions without discussion.

4. Help students identify and weigh the possible short-term negative and positive consequences of each alternative course of action. Analyze each alternative for the values that it promotes or neglects. Assess the long-term and/or cumulative consequences of each alternative and identify who benefits and who suffers as a result of the choices.

5. Ask each student to personally endorse an alternative and justify his or her choice. Apply the ethical tests of reversibility and universality (Would it be okay for you, your family, or group, to be treated this way? Would you want all persons to act this way in similar situations?).

6. Help students to explore their feelings about their decisions and generalize about other similar situations.

FIGURE 17-3
Improved Values Exploration and Decision Making

(one-fourth to one-half stage increase) impact on students' moral reasoning when offered over an extended period of time (a semester-long course) in a setting where the teacher-facilitator has been trained to identify each student's stage of moral development and respond, at the next highest stage, to each student's individual moral reasoning statements (Leming, 1993).

I have not recommended this approach to most elementary teachers due to its single-dimension methodology (moral dilemma discussions), focus on stage growth in higher-order moral reasoning, and the demand for considerable teacher expertise in the implementation of the moral dilemma discussions. Experts point out that you can violate some of these demands (such as the demand to always respond at the next highest level of moral development) and still get modest growth in moral reasoning. Nevertheless, Leming (1993, 65) concluded in his review of research, "Thus, even though the moral dilemma approach works, it appears to be of little practical utility in influencing students' behavior."

Social Action and Participation

The social action and participation approach to values education assumes that youngsters learn values best by practicing them. In this approach, students take part, usually voluntarily, in either self-generated or teacher-suggested projects. This participation is often preceded by a thoughtful analysis of the issues involved, a discussion of the values realized by taking action, and an analysis of the facts related to the participation opportunity. In practice, actually doing something is considered more important than being involved in simply thinking about the participation experience.

Examples of social action and participation projects are numerous, including environmental cleanup efforts, adoption of a nursing home, letter writing and poster making designed to prevent drug abuse or rally support for an endangered species, and efforts to influence school authorities or local government to correct some situation such as a dangerous school crosswalk.

The benefits of this approach are many. It is appropriate for all ages. Children like being active and seeing the concrete results of their efforts. Preparing students for the experience, perhaps documenting it with a video camera, and then debriefing the whole activity with a follow-up discussion offers an excellent way to tie abstractions about values to real concrete action.

Potential pitfalls of social action and participation are several. It is possible that children may miss the point of their participation, getting wrapped up in some aspect of the going and doing and not grasping the bigger purpose. It is also possible that the experience may have a negative outcome. If the participation is not voluntary (as I recommend) it is possible that you could have a group of active dissenters tagging along spoiling the quality of the experience for others. Finally, it is possible that parents may react negatively to the extra responsibilities such participation places on them.

DISCUSSION QUESTIONS

1. Based on what you now know, would you be willing to settle for a moral education program that used *only* values-inculcation strategies? Explain your position.

2. What are family values? Who has the authority to define which values qualify and how they should be acted out in daily living?

3. How do you react to the bumper sticker that says, "Hate Is Not a Family Value!"? Do you know at whom or what this bumper sticker is aimed? Hate is most certainly a concept, but is it a values concept like the others displayed in this chapter? Defend your position.

CONCLUSION

It appears the schools have begun a renewed quest for effective moral education. Schoolwide programs that echo 1920s-style character-education efforts are being augmented by renewed and improved versions of values education such as the values exploration and decision-making model offered here. Core values of our democracy have been identified and social studies has been given the task of engaging students in lessons that reestablish the boundaries between the pure and corrupted forms of these ideals. The consideration of other social values has been reestablished as a legitimate concern of K–6 social studies.

WHAT SHOULD TIMOTHY DO?

Grade: Fifth

Objectives: As a result of this lesson, students will:

- describe a similar situation, specifically noting at least two alternative courses of action that were available
- identify the values that were promoted and neglected by each alternative
- take a position regarding appropriate conduct for this type of situation

Materials/Resources Needed: None

Procedure

1. Read the following scenario to your students.

As Timothy rounded the corner of the building he knew it was too late. No teacher was in sight and there was Billy Hudson and his gang of sixth graders.

BILLY: Hey pinhead! Yeah, you beetle breath! Empty your pockets. I need me some spending change.

Timothy's wild turn back toward safety nearly smashed him into the chest of Sylvester.

SYLVESTER: Where you going pipsqueak? Didn't you hear Billy? Empty your pockets!

TIMOTHY: (regaining his balance and composure) I don't have to. You can't make me.

He was getting ready to fight—preparing to aim his first punch at Sylvester's huge nose—when he remembered the new rule on suspension. *Anyone caught fighting will have a mandatory three-day suspension, regardless of who is at fault.* Before he could pick his next strategy he felt Billy's right arm clamp around his throat. From behind a hand thrust roughly down into his left pocket.

BILLY: Got it. Seventy-five cents. Is that all your old man gives you?

TIMOTHY: Hey, wait. That's my lunch money!

BILLY: (over his shoulder as the sixth graders leave) Too bad, chump. You'll have to go hungry.

Walking back toward the swings Timothy felt really angry. He wasn't physically hurt, but felt like crying. He tried to hold back the tears. He thought about telling Ms. Fortson, but that seemed like it might cause even more trouble. He'd get back, he thought, but then he thought about the risks of doing that. Anyway, how was he going to handle lunch. The cashier had said "No more credit" the last time he forgot his money. Maybe Ms. Fortson would help him out, but he'd probably have to lie to keep from telling her what had happened. How was he going to avoid Billy the next time? Could he hide at lunch or play sick in order to avoid having to tell about the incident or keep from making up a story. A hundred thoughts swirled through his head. Suddenly the recess bell rang. Time to go back to class. Let's see, lunch was only 30 minutes away. . . . He had to think fast. What should he do?

2. Tell the class that Timothy has several problems, but that you want to focus on what Timothy can and should do about Billy and his gang. The issue is whether to put up with this type of shakedown or do something about it. Tell the students to suppose, for the purpose of this exercise, that Timothy isn't the only person who is having his money taken and that this is not the last time that he will be victimized.

3. Now have the students suggest alternatives for Timothy, and post them on the chalkboard.

4. Once you have a good selection of alternatives, go back and help the students analyze the short- and long-term consequences of each. Ask questions designed to help them focus on what values are preserved or compromised by each of the alternatives. Consider different people's perspectives on each alternative. For example, how might Timothy's father feel if he does alternative X, Y, or Z? How will Ms. Fortson feel? How will Timothy look in the eyes of his classmates? Accept all plausible answers but don't be afraid to question responses you feel may not be genuine.

5. Ask each student to personally endorse an alternative and justify his or her choice. Apply the ethical tests of reversibility and universality (Would it be okay for you, your family, or group, to be treated this way? Would you want all persons to act this way in similar situations?).

6. Discuss the feelings of the characters involved in the incident and see if the students can identify other situations in which these feelings might arise.

Evaluation

Ask students to write a two-page paper in which they describe a similar situation that they know about or were involved in. In the paper, have them identify two alternative courses of action that were available and the values promoted and neglected by each. Finally, ask students to take a position regarding appropriate conduct for this type of situation in general.

Enrichment

- Role play and videotape the scenario. Take the video to younger students' classrooms and explain the proper course of action.

REFERENCES AND SELECTED READINGS

Berreth, D., and Scherer, M. 1993. On transmitting values: A conversation with Amatai Etzioni. *Educational Leadership* 51(3):12–15.

Brant, R. 1985/1986. *Educational Leadership* 43(4):3.

Burron, A. 1994. Traditionalist Christians and OBE: What's the problem? *Educational Leadership* 51(6):73–75.

Butts, F. R. 1988. *The morality of democratic citizenship: Goals for civic education in the republic's third century.* Calabasas, CA: Center for Civic Education.

Georgia Department of Education. 1991. On board. An unofficial report of state board action. Atlanta: Georgia Department of Education, March 15 news release.

_____. 1991. *Values education implementation guide.* Atlanta: Office of Instructional Services.

Gibbs, L. J., and Earley, E. J. 1994. *Using children's literature to develop core values.* Bloomington, IN: Phi Delta Kappa.

Kirschenbaum, H. 1977. In support of values education. *Social Education* 41(5):398, 401–402.

_____. 1992. A comprehensive model for values education and moral development. *Phi Delta Kappan* 74(10):771–776.

_____. 1995. *100 ways to enhance values and morality in schools and youth settings.* Boston: Allyn and Bacon.

Leming, J. S. 1993. In search of effective character education. *Educational Leadership* 51(3):63–71.

Lickona, T. 1988. How parents and schools can work together to raise moral children. *Educational Leadership* 45(8):36.

_____. 1991. *Educating for character. How our schools can teach respect and responsibility.* New York: Bantam Books.

_____. 1993. Is character education a responsibility of the public schools? Yes. *Momentum* 24(4):48, 50–52.

_____. 1993. The return of character education. *Educational Leadership* 51(3):6–11.

McKay, R. 1994. Character education: A question of character. *Canadian Social Studies* 28(2):46–47.

Noddings, N. 1991. Values by deliberation or default. *The Clearing House* 64(May/June):320–322.

Purple, D. E. 1991. Moral education: An idea whose time has gone. *The Clearing House* 64(May/June):309–312.

Raths, L. E., Harmin, M., and Simon, S. B. 1966. *Values and teaching: Working with values in the classroom.* Columbus, OH: Charles E. Merrill.

Ryan, K. 1993. Mining the values in the curriculum. *Educational Leadership* 51(3):16–18.

Simon, S. B., Leland, W. H., and Kirschenbaum, H. 1972. *Values clarification: A handbook of practical strategies for teachers and students.* New York: Hart Publishing.

Skillen, J. W. 1993. Is character education a responsibility of the public schools? No. *Momentum* 24(4):49, 53–54.

Wynne, E. 1985/1986. The great tradition in education: Transmitting moral values. *Educational Leadership* 43(4):4–9.

CHAPTER 18

Current Events

THE WHAT AND WHY OF CURRENT EVENTS

You may have experienced current events instruction as a part of your middle- or high-school social studies courses. Perhaps your memories of current events are negative because the teacher centered it mainly on reading news clips from the local paper. In some instances the teacher may have done other work during students' presentations, making the assignment seem more like a time killer than anything that might provide meaningful learning.

While current events certainly must include news items from the local paper, for the elementary school it is appropriate to expand the meaning to include, among other things, personal events in the lives of students, holidays, local festivals, visits to the school by resource persons, and even changes in the weather. Once we have expanded the scope of items that may logically be called current events, it's easier to see how it can be included as a part of the early childhood social studies program.

Current events should be an integral part of your social studies program because the citizenship preparation mission of social studies logically requires that teachers help students become aware of and involved in events in their communities. Beyond the important logical need to build community awareness and involvement, you can focus current events instruction on applying and improving students' information-gathering skills, content-area reading skills, and critical-thinking abilities. Current events also offers a way of updating and bringing to life the content of the established social studies curriculum.

Good social studies instruction must connect children with the real world. Social studies isn't fulfilling its purpose if it fails to deal with the known realities of the communities children experience in their daily lives. One way to complete this connection with the real world is through an effective current events program.

CURRENT EVENTS IN THE PRIMARY AND UPPER ELEMENTARY GRADES

Current events in the primary grades presents different challenges and opportunities from those in grades 4 through 6. The most important challenges to K–3 current events stem from children's limited reading abilities, background experiences, and conceptual knowledge. Because of these limitations students cannot be expected to read news articles or write summaries of news events. These limitations should also alert you to the need to very carefully listen to each child's current event report so that you can clarify misconceptions and ask questions that aid understanding.

On the positive side, primary grade level children are profoundly interested in even the most ordinary life events. As a result, you'll have little trouble maintaining interest in current events reports. Encourage these students to give reports on such things as the birth of a new brother or sister, a move to a new house, a birthday celebration, the loss of a tooth, the death of a pet, or a family trip. All qualify as current events news to young children.

Students in grades 4 through 6 generally have the ability to read and write at a level that will allow some exploration of regular news sources. You can still allow them to report personal current events, but increasingly, their reports should deal with a wider sphere of interest. To help make your current events instruction effective, you may want to:

- Enlist the aid of parents in helping children identify appropriate current events and making sure they understand their significance.
- Use praise and encouragement to build your current events program rather than requiring reports.
- Interview children who wish to share an event to see if they understand their event and are capable of sharing their understanding with the class. Have each child identify two to four things that the class should remember.
- Carefully listen to current events presentations and ask questions that help students to draw implications and relationships.
- Stress the relationship between a current events report and the children's lives.

At this point you have some idea of successful current events practices. You may not have realized, however, that there are several ways to implement current events instruction, each with its own benefits and drawbacks.

WAYS TO IMPLEMENT CURRENT EVENTS INSTRUCTION
◆ ◆ ◆ ◆ ◆

One popular way to implement current events instruction in the primary grades is to open the school day with a "calendar activity" and a few minutes of sharing time. The typical calendar activity consists of having a child identify the day of the week and month, using a large-scale calendar displayed on a bulletin board. Teachers often extend and embellish this activity to include using symbols for rain, wind, sun, and snow, and by having students move indicators showing high and low temperatures and/or rain amounts. Teachers sometimes help students to keep track of changes in these events over a period of time using a simple graph to show the data. The calendar activity usually disappears after kindergarten despite the fact that many children still need to learn the months of the year and lack the skills involved in graphing real-world data.

The calendar activity certainly qualifies as a current events report. Time and interest permitting, you can follow it by having students take center stage to give their personal current events reports. It is essential that you give this current events sharing your full attention. Without it, little of significance will be gained. In grades 1 and 2, I've occasionally seen teachers opening their day with a sharing session. The sharing of personal current events seems to disappear by the fourth grade. This is regrettable since teachers lose this vital connection with their students' lives.

The morning opening approach to current events has several benefits. One benefit is that it easily builds interest in what is happening in your school and community. It also ties directly into the realities of your students' lives. In addition, its spontaneous nature requires very little teacher preparation—other than "previewing" each child's contribution.

One drawback of the morning opening approach is that it may be difficult to relate the reported events to the ongoing social studies curriculum. Since one purpose of current events is to help bring the established social studies curriculum to life, this is a serious shortcoming.

An alternative is to organize current events instruction around a specific theme. Teachers often select this theme and coordinate it with the established social studies curriculum. Students then locate and report current events related to the theme. Quite often a bulletin board is used to organize and display shared news reports. Obviously, this approach to current events is more appropriate to grades 4 through 6.

The benefit of this approach is that it ties activities in the real world closely to the ongoing social studies curriculum. In addition, by working within a theme, students more easily gain a coherent picture of real-world events. Relationships among news items abound and can be shown by the way items are grouped on the bulletin board, through systems of color coding, or by connections made with yarn.

A drawback of the thematic approach is that it may be disrupted by an off-theme, but truly big, event. Students may also occasionally have trouble finding current events related to the theme.

A third common method is using a weekly newspaper program, such as *Weekly Reader* or *Scholastic News*. The weekly newspaper program typically picks several important events and provides a simplified coverage of the event targeted for the specific grade level of the children. A weekly news program invites a teacher to save current events instruction until Friday afternoon when the whole class reads the stories and answers the questions provided.

The weekly newspaper approach to current events does offer some benefits. First and foremost, the publishers are experienced at picking age-appropriate material and rewriting the news to fit the intellectual abilities of students. Generally, students find this approach to current events interesting. Parents approve of this approach, not only because it relieves them of the task of going over the news with their children, but also because it eliminates problems with censorship.

A drawback of the weekly newspaper approach is that it ignores local events. In addition, it isn't integrated with the ongoing social studies curriculum. Finally, there is a cost involved in procuring the product.

PROBLEM AREAS IN CURRENT EVENTS INSTRUCTION
◆ ◆ ◆ ◆ ◆

While current events instruction offers many benefits, it does come with a few problem areas that teachers must address. The two most critical are helping students determine what qualifies as news and the related need to censor inappropriate news items. (A quick look at almost any newspaper will reveal just how much inappropriate news for the classroom is reported.)

Determining what qualifies as news is a problem in current events instruction. Quite clearly, not all news events are of equal value. There is a great difference between the news contained on the front page of the *New York Times* and that on the front page of the *National Enquirer*! We already know that virtually any event may qualify as news for very young children. In fact, a large part of your job will be to help draw out the significance of the items children report as news. You can gain some help in determining what events are newsworthy by answering questions such as: (1) How unusual is/was the event? (2) How many people are likely to be affected by the event and will the effect be minor or substantial? (3) Will people be interested in hearing about the event and will they be able to understand it?

Periodically "test" a current event selection for newsworthiness by applying Terry Borton's three-step *What, So What, Now What* teaching model. I have used this aid for years. The child's event report becomes the *what*. It is followed up by asking all students to help tell the *so what* of the event. If there are no so whats, then it is likely that the item wasn't very good news. Finally, I think it's important to prod students into thinking about the future by asking the *now what* question, requiring them to think about what they should do or what will happen in the future given the information just reported. Figure 18-1 presents a sample dialogue illustrating this technique.

Discourage use of trivial news items by asking what concepts, generalizations, and main ideas are illustrated in the event. Extend this test by asking how the news item relates to one of the social science or humanities disciplines. If the event cannot be related to such concepts or subjects, then it is probably of little value to your class.

Sensationalism further clouds the issue of whether an item is newsworthy. A sensationalized account of the news is published or announced in such a way as to draw attention to the lurid details. For example, the amount of time devoted to camera shots of emotionally distraught crime victims is an indication of sensationalism. Asking yourself if the treatment is designed to "whip up" your emotions may be your best protection from sensationalism.

Censorship may prove an even greater problem. News media are full of material that may be inappropriate for children, so some form of censorship is inevitable. Teachers and parents often base their censorship decisions on considerations such as age, experience, maturity, and interest. Without some guidance, teachers tend to censor more news items than necessary. This tendency, while understandable, may inappropriately restrict the kinds of

LAMAR: When I got to school this morning I saw someone had spray painted all over the front doors.

MS. ROWE: I saw that too. What did you think when you saw it?

LAMAR: I thought someone's going to get into trouble over this!

MS. ROWE: Yes, and anything else?

LAMAR: That it was ugly. You're not supposed to use words like that.

MS. ROWE: I agree. Too many places are vandalized with spray paint. What do you suppose will happen now?

LAMAR: Mr. Thompson will probably try to clean it off.

SIDNEY: I think the police will be looking for who did it. The person might come back and do it again.

MS. ROWE: Yes, that's possible. What can we do to help prevent that?

LAMAR: We could try to find out who did it and tell them we don't like it.

SIDNEY: We can never do that kind of thing ourselves.

MS. ROWE: That would help, wouldn't it? Are there other things?

TINA: Maybe we could make it against the law to sell spray paint to teenagers.

MS. ROWE: Now there's an idea. Do you think that would be fair? Would it prevent teenagers from vandalizing things with spray paint?

LAMAR: I don't think so. They'd just steal the paint or get it from some adult.

(Fade . . .)

◆ ◆

FIGURE 18-1
Sample What, So What, Now What Dialogue

topics students are allowed to address as a part of their current events instruction.

Your best protection in regard to censorship is parents. If you can involve them in helping select newsworthy items for their children to share, then you can be much more certain that the reported events are appropriate. Figure 18-2 displays a sample letter to parents requesting help in choosing current events.

TELEVISION NEWS AND SPECIAL PROGRAMS
◆ ◆ ◆ ◆ ◆

The future promises to bring more and more information into the classroom. A large portion of this information will take the form of full-motion video images with sound. Some of this material will be broadcast as part of local television news. Other sources will be cable and satellite feeds from around the nation and world. Networks will quickly prepare and broadcast reports of major news events such as wars, floods, earthquakes, and other disasters. Increasingly, children have access to these news sources and the ability to capture scenes using home VCRs. Using the previously described guidelines

---

Dear Parent:

Next week we are beginning our study of (<u>social studies topic</u>). As a part of this unit, we will be creating a bulletin board of current news items related to (<u>social studies theme related to the topic</u>).

Your son or daughter is being encouraged to bring in news items taped from television or clipped from weekly newsmagazines or newspapers.

Will you please help us stay alert to news items and take the time to help your child understand and share them?

Thank you for your help!

p.s.   To help you with this task, here are some questions you may want to review with your child.

1. What is your news item about?

2. Why is this item news?

3. How might a person react to this news?

4. What are some facts a person might remember from this news piece?

5. What are some main ideas or generalizations that a person might get from this news item?

6. If you had to pick three things for your classmates to remember from your news item, what would they be? Why?

··

FIGURE 18-2
Sample Note to Parents

for determining whether an event is newsworthy, make use of this technology as an integral part of your current events instruction. Preview all video clips brought in by students prior to showing them to the class. Analyze clips for appropriate length, language, and visual content.

Companies are experimenting with specialized video news programs for schoolchildren. CNN Newsroom is an excellent example of a noncommercial product that has been successfully used as early as the fourth grade. Lesson plans for using this half-hour program are available on many computer bulletin boards and several Internet sites.

SPECIALIZED NEWS PUBLICATIONS
·····

There are two major publishers of current events newspapers for elementary school classrooms, Scholastic Magazines, Inc. and Field Publications.

Field Publications is the source of the *Weekly Reader*, a series of K–6 editions published twenty-seven times a year. Each grade-level edition has its own content emphasis. For example, a recent fourth-grade *Weekly Reader* incorporated maps and illustrations with national and international focuses. Field publishes *Current Events* for grades 6 through 12, although most of the use of this publication is in the middle school.

Scholastic publishes the *Scholastic News Series*, which comes in different editions for each grade level K through 6, and is published twenty-six times a year. Like its competitor, each grade level has its own features and content focus. For example, a recent first-grade edition emphasized news about health, safety, and holidays, while the fifth-grade edition emphasized world news.

Scholastic has recently launched its Scholastic Network, an on-line news and information resource targeted for school use. The Network gives students access to global e-mail, Internet newsgroups, WAIS databases, gopher databases, the Library of Congress, National Geographic Online, Reuters Newswires, and CNN Newsroom.

COPYRIGHT GUIDELINES
♦ ♦ ♦ ♦ ♦

Current events teaching benefits from sharing real, up-to-the-minute news with students. Few things add more meaning to the news than some graphic video segments or expert analysis of events. Editorials and in-depth articles serve as a strong support for discussions. Teachers' use of these sources is governed by copyright laws.

Copyright laws are designed to protect the financial interests of the creators of original works. Lawyers build copyright infringement cases on a number of considerations, such as (1) the purpose and character of the use, including whether such use is commercial or nonprofit; (2) the nature of the copyrighted material; (3) the amount and substance of the used portion in relation to the whole; and (4) the effect of the use on the market potential or value of the copyrighted work.

Lawyers have sued schools and school districts for making and storing videotapes of commercial broadcasts for the purposes of offering repeated showings. Copyright law also prohibits the compilation and duplication of anthologies of articles, even when teachers produce them without profit for educational use. Many on-line and CD-ROM-based news sources now warn users not to duplicate or reproduce the material in any form without permission.

I recommend the following procedures as a means of bringing current events news into the classroom without copyright infringement.

- Make an overhead transparency of any news article you wish to share. Project the article and read it out loud. Save the transparency for later use or reference.
- Capture any on-line news articles and use an overhead LCD to share it with the class.
- Observe videotape-showing guidelines. Show the tape once to all classes soon after it has been recorded. Erase the tape following this use. If you feel the program is valuable for future use, write for permission to use it or purchase a copy from the producer.

USING HOLIDAYS AS CURRENT EVENTS

Recognizing holidays can be an important part of your current events program. This is especially true in the primary grades. Children are naturally interested in holidays. They easily get caught up in the symbols, sights, and rituals. Yet they often lack an understanding of the underlying meaning of the holiday, its history, and the values promoted by its celebration. We can use the holidays as a subject of study and achieve many important social studies goals by doing so.

Holidays are important because they have deep social significance. All holidays have a history, and sometimes, as in the case of Halloween, that history is fascinating. Many holidays have significance to a specific religion and may be celebrated by specific denominations within that religion in very different ways. In addition, holidays receive considerable attention in the media and have a large influence on our economy.

Naylor and Smith (1993) point out that holidays serve three important functions for society. The celebration of holidays (1) legitimizes the experiences and perspectives of certain groups, positively sanctioning certain people and events as meriting special attention; (2) helps preserve popular notions of history and perpetuate selected values associated with certain people and events; and (3) serves to bind people together through shared experiences and rituals. They point out that thinking about holidays with these functions in mind may help sensitize teachers to problems such as neglect or misinterpretation of non-Christian holidays, and failure to recognize minority group perspectives on popular, dominant-culture celebrations.

Instead of attempting to ban holidays from the schools, a more productive position is to use them to help achieve legitimate goals of K–6 social studies. Figure 18-3 focuses on how teachers can use Valentine's Day in ways that help children develop skills such as critical thinking and valuing, as well as content knowledge from economics, geography, and history. As you examine this list of activities see if you can imagine similar activities for other common holidays.

DISCUSSION QUESTIONS

1. Not all current events, even those within the child's family or school, are positive. Will you be willing to allow a student to report on an event that is, at best, unpleasant? Give some examples of things you would very likely disallow.

2. What themes might have potential for augmenting a fourth-grade class' study of geographic regions or a third-grade class' study of cities?

3. Which approach to current events seems to make the best sense to you? Do you think it is possible to use more than one approach at a time?

4. Could current events ever completely substitute for the whole social studies program? Explain your position.

- Read and discuss the history of Valentine's Day. Most school media centers contain books on the holidays. Encyclopedias also often contain brief histories of the holidays.

- Investigate money matters related to Valentine's Day. Determine the cost and markup of flowers, candy, jewelry, and other gift items. Chart the amount of money spent on these items by the children's families.

- Have a 1950s Valentine's Day party with committees researching and providing authentic decorations, treats, poetry, and music. Dress like that period on the day of the party.

- Investigate how different cultures celebrate Valentine's Day.

- Use a weeklong Valentine's theme bridging across the entire curriculum based on the study of the Roman Lupercalian festival. This theme week should use poetry, art, and math to support the study of the history of Lupercalia and St. Valentine.

- Write a Valentine to yourself; include all the things that you like about yourself.

- Discuss the underlying meaning of what's printed on candy hearts. For example, locate a heart that says, "Let's Hold Hands" and then discuss the values and feelings associated with such behavior by parents and children, young lovers, good friends, and so on.

- Investigate the history of why chocolate is given and why red is the color often used for Valentine's Day.

- Investigate the mythology and symbolism of Cupid.

- Investigate the history of dating; compare other cultures' practices with ours. Interview parents regarding their own experiences and their present-day wishes concerning dating.

- Play and sing love songs. Discuss the imagery, feelings, and content of the songs. Note changes through time.

- Poll or interview people to find out what they do for Valentine's Day. See if they know its history, can name its symbols, and whether they approve or disapprove of its current celebration.

- Make valentines for the elderly, people with disabilities, or others who might be forgotten.

- Create homemade Valentine's Day cards and value them over store-bought ones. Talk about how people are unique and would appreciate something specially made for them.

- Interview parents and grandparents about their favorite Valentine's Day memories.

- Begin collecting old Valentine's Day cards. Publish an advertisement requesting contributions in the "wanted" column of your local paper.

- Discuss the different appropriate ways to publicly show affection, admiration, and friendship. Try these out to see how they make you feel. Start a campaign to spread the practice if you determine it is valuable.

- Instead of having the traditional Valentine's Day card exchange, have each student write an anonymous Valentine's Day card to his or her favorite person. Post these cards on a bulletin board without revealing to whom they were written. Encourage the class to think of this display as a special statement about what a wonderful group they are.

- Adopt a nursing home and send valentines to the patients. Bake cupcakes and take them to the home on Valentine's Day.

- Study the history of Saint Valentine or some other real, Catholic saint. Invite a priest to come in and talk about the official church process of becoming a saint.

FIGURE 18-3
Sample K–6 Activities Related to Valentine's Day

REFERENCES AND SELECTED READINGS

American Newspaper Publishers Association Foundation. 1991. *Newspaper in education: A guide for weekly newspapers*. ERIC document no. ED333477. Washington, D.C.: American Newspaper Publishers Association Foundation.

Borton, T. 1970. *Reach, touch, and teach; student concerns and process education*. New York: McGraw-Hill.

Floyd, K. L. 1991. Harnessing a hurricane: Social studies in action. *Social Studies and the Young Learner* 3(3):15–17.

Heacock, G. A. 1990. The we-search process: Using the whole language model of writing to learn social studies content and civic competence. *Social Studies and the Young Learner* 2(3):9–11.

Hoge, J. D. 1988. Valuable learning from Halloween fun. *Social Education* 52(6):458–459, 466.

Naylor, D. T., and Smith, B. D. 1993. Holidays, cultural diversity, and public culture. *Social Studies and the Young Learner* 6(2):4–5, 17.

Passe, J. 1991. Citizenship knowledge in young learners. *Social Studies and the Young Learner* 3(4):15–17.

Integrating Other Content Areas

INTRODUCTION

Educators have advocated an integrated approach to instruction for decades. Advocates often view integrated instruction as a naturalistic and child-centered approach to content. At least three meanings of the term *integrated instruction* appear in the literature.

Within social studies, especially elementary social studies, it is common to refer to integrated instruction as teaching that combines the perspectives of the social science and humanities disciplines to focus on a single topic or theme. In fact, this is the way most elementary social studies is taught—integrating the social sciences and humanities, rather than singling out each discipline for separate study.

The second use of the term describes the practice of enhancing instruction in a single subject (such as math) by the use of techniques borrowed from another subject area (for example, music). Elementary teachers often say, "I'm integrating math and music," meaning that they are using a song to help teach math. Or, "I'm integrating language arts and social studies," meaning that they are using a social studies topic to teach language arts.

The third, and most demanding, meaning refers to teachers' attempts to accomplish the goals and objectives of two (or more) subjects simultaneously.

Janet Alleman and Jere Brophy (1991) have investigated attempts to accomplish this third type of integrated instruction, using social studies as one of the subjects. Their research resulted in a series of questions, shown in Figure 19-1, that we can apply to assess the quality of any instruction that attempts to integrate social studies with some other content area.

Just as other subjects use social studies, the intelligent use of reading, math, and other subjects can expand students' appreciation and knowledge of social studies content. The key point in using other subjects is to bring their powers to bear on developing social studies understandings.

---

1. Does the activity have a significant social education objective as a major focus? Is it clear that the instruction will help students achieve this objective?

2. Compared to other potential nonintegrated approaches to the same objectives, does the integrated approach have greater efficiency or does it offer other significant learning advantages that justify its use?

3. Are students relating this integrated instruction to their ongoing social studies curriculum? If you asked them, would they recognize how it fits and would they value what they have learned in the integrated activity?

4. Can students, parents, teachers, and administrators use evidence gained from integrated instruction to gauge progress in social studies learning?

FIGURE 19-1
Questions to Assess Integrated Instruction[1]

---

[1]Adapted from Brophy and Alleman, 1991, and Alleman and Brophy, 1991.

MUSIC ACTIVITIES
◆ ◆ ◆ ◆ ◆

Teachers can use a broad range of music to enhance social studies. Some songs are explicitly written for the purpose of helping students master social studies content. Such songs may help students memorize the states and capitals, develop patriotic feelings toward their state and nation, learn good manners, or recall facts about famous historical personalities such as George Washington. You can find records and tapes of these songs at stores that specialize in selling classroom learning aids. You can also easily locate items by using the topically indexed comprehensive guides to print and audiovisual curriculum materials available in media centers and through on-line database services such as AV-Online.®

Genuine folk songs, music that originated out of the life experiences of common people, offer a perspective on history that is different from songs explicitly designed for instruction. Genuine folk music serves an interpretive function in illustrating what life was like for a particular group of people at a specific place and time. You'll find genuine folk music collections in larger libraries. Figure 19-2 gives the background and words to an old Virginia folk song.

Come all you Virginia girls and listen to my noise,
Don't go with them Tennessee boys,
For if you do, your fortune will be
Hoecake and hominy and sassafras tea.

Thus, the old pioneer song warned the lowland girls to steer clear of the tall young hunters who came down from the Tennessee Gap telling stories of Indian fights and bear hunts across the mountains to the west. These men were hunters and fighters. They left the rest of the work to the women, who chopped wood, carried water and did the ploughing and planting with a rifle handy in case of Indian attacks. Babies came every year. In the family of Jean Ritchie, a fine mountain ballad singer, her great-great-grandmother gave birth to eleven children that lived—her great-grandmother, ten—her grandmother, ten—and her own mother fourteen. My own grandmother bore fourteen babies of her own and raised the eight children of her predecessor, who had died in childbirth.

After years of isolation in the hills, far from stores, the people learned to do without shoes, and often went barefoot even when the snow lay deep in the laurel thickets. Men dressed in buckskin and women in homespun, and the log cabins, built of unfinished green logs were unchinked. A man that would bother to seal up his cabin against the weather would be laughed at for "fussin" around like some ol' granny-woman. The hand-hewed shingles curled after a season or so, so the roofs leaked. The wind blew in through the cracks in the floor in the winter, and the dirt and mud sifted in everywhere, no matter what efforts the housewife made with her little broom of sedge grass.

In time of illness you took strong home remedies and kept your mouth shut about your pain. When babies came, an old midwife might attend who believed that "it would ease your pain, honey, if you lay on your side and holler." No wonder a leather-faced old mountain woman warned her granddaughter against marriage. "Don't do hit, honey, don't do hit." She was thinking of the ways of the mountain men.

(continued on next page)

◆ ◆

FIGURE 19-2
Virginia Folk Song[2]

---

[2]Taken from *The Folk Songs of North America* by Alan Lomax. 1960. New York: Doubleday.

Single Girl

1. When I was single, I went dressed so fine,
   Now I am married, go ragged all the time.
   Chorus: Lord, I wish I was a single girl again.
2. Dishes to wash and spring to go to,
   Now I am married, I've everything to do.
   (Chorus)
3. When I was single, ate biscuits and pie.
   Now I am married, eat cornbread or die.
   (Chorus)
4. When I was single, my shoes they did screak,
   Now that I'm married, my shoes they do leak.
   (Chorus)

5. Two little children, lyin' in the bed, Both of them
   so hungry, Lord, they can't hold up their heads.
   (Chorus)
6. Wash um and dress um and send um to school,
   Long come that drunkard and calls them a fool.
   (Chorus)
7. When I was single, marryin' was my crave,
   Now I am married, I'm troubled to my grave.

FIGURE 19-2, continued
Virginia Folk Song

Popular music, whether rap, country, or rock, often has a message that can be profitably used in social studies. Performers highlight the thoughts and feelings of everyday life, often with a positive message recurring as the theme of the song. When selecting popular music, be extra careful to avoid lyrics that are inappropriate for a school setting.

DISCUSSION QUESTIONS

1. What impressions of early pioneer life are conveyed by *Single Girl*?

2. Is there anything contained in the introduction or song that you consider inappropriate for classroom use? Would it be appropriate to ask fifth-grade students to read this material and describe the images conveyed of pioneer men, women, and children?

3. Is popular music suitable for instructional use in the K–6 classroom? If so, what songs come to mind? If not, give examples of songs that are not appropriate for classroom use.

CREATIVE ART ACTIVITIES

Give students the opportunity to use such art materials as markers, crayons, construction paper, finger paints, and clay as a part of social studies instruction. For example, students might

- use glue, clay, twigs, and split corrugated cardboard to build a model frontier fort after studying several examples
- make a mural of Martin Luther King, Jr.'s life events at the end of a unit while listening to his famous speeches
- paint a storefront on cardboard boxes to create a setting for a classroom store

- make traditional native art objects while studying other cultures
- make a magazine photo collage of city life while listening to sounds on New York's 5th Avenue
- sew a quilt with scenes to dramatize a social problem such as trash disposal or homelessness

When we use such art activities in social studies it is important to remember that the focus is on achieving a deeper understanding and appreciation of social studies content. For example, in sewing a quilt to dramatize the problem of trash disposal or homelessness, students should be well along the way in their learning about the sources and solutions to these problems. Discuss what scenes to show and how to show them. This process is essential if your quilt project is to take on meaning for the students. Remember that you are attempting to give the students something they will recall doing for years to come, something they will look back on with pleasant feelings. The object is not to teach art or to demand highly accomplished craft products. The role of the teacher is to provide materials and support, to answer questions, and to make suggestions when students solicit your opinion.

DRAMATIC ACTIVITIES

Bringing drama into the classroom is within the capability of all teachers. Drama adds much to the emotional involvement of students in their content learning. Emotional experiences are long-remembered and students will appreciate the opportunity to express their feelings in your class. The major forms that drama takes in social studies are dramatic play, skits, role play, dance, and puppetry.

Dramatic Play

Spontaneous dramatic play is a staple of preschool and kindergarten learning. Teachers positively sanction dramatic play in these early learning classrooms, often allocating space and dress-up materials to further the action. Children spontaneously formulate imaginary situations and settings. They take on roles and act out how they've seen parents or other adults, perhaps on television, behave. Wise preschool and kindergarten teachers know that dramatic play is an important opportunity for social learning. They prefer not to interfere with children's dramatic play activities and in my experience, seldom attempt to use them as launching platforms for social learning.

As early as the first grade, many teachers cease encouraging dramatic play, implicitly conveying the message that schooling has now become all business. (As many parents can testify, the transition from a happy kindergarten setting to a worksheet-based first grade often causes more than a few tears.) Yet, children maintain their interest in dramatic play and use elements of it well into the primary and intermediate grades. The closure of the classroom to dramatic play after kindergarten is regrettable. Children will take their natural urge to engage in imaginary adventures outside to the playground.

If you are teaching in a school setting where you think it unwise to allow dramatic play, then skits, puppetry, and role play may be your best alternatives.

Skits and Short Plays

While dramatic play is spontaneous, unstructured, and unscripted, skits and short plays are the opposite; they are teacher-initiated. They have well-defined plots and scripts for their characters. Of course, it's critically important that the skit or play achieve some social studies goal and its related objective(s). Drama for its own sake is drama, and you should not sacrifice social studies time for what can only qualify as a fine-arts learning experience.

Have students perform skits and short plays illustrating aspects of historical or contemporary life. Provide a role for all children when doing skits and plays. If necessary, use two or more casts for skits and plays that do not have many characters. Add to the message and entertainment value of the performance by using props and costumes. Fill an audience with parents or other schoolchildren once the skit or play has been practiced.

Teachers often involve children in creating their own skits and short plays. As an alternative, you may be able to locate an appropriate drama in a source such as *The Handbook of Skits and Stunts* by Helen and Larry Eisenberg or Aileen Fisher's *Year-Round Programs for Young Players: One Hundred Plays, Skits, Poems, Choral Readings, Spelldowns, Recitations, and Pantomines for Celebrating Holidays and Special Occasions.*

Role Playing

Role play is, without a doubt, one of the most effective strategies for learning about feelings and motives for all kinds of interpersonal behavior. Pioneered in the late 1950s, role playing quickly became a part of social studies methods used to promote growth of prosocial attitudes and behaviors. George and Fannie Shaftel (1982) refined the theory and practice of role playing and attempted to expand its use into other areas of the curriculum.

Role playing uses open-ended scenarios. Volunteers for the roles are given a description of their character, the setting, and the subject of the role play, but not much more. Once the action begins, role players must ad-lib and go with the flow of the interaction.

Role playing gives students a detached, reflective view of social issues and problems. Through role playing, students gain a greater understanding of what motivates human behavior, and how their own behavior influences and is perceived by others. Because role playing readily accomplishes these aims, it helps students become more effective social actors. Since role playing helps students develop insight into their own and others' thoughts, feelings, and values, it builds empathy and rationality in human relations—something the world desperately needs.

The first step in using role play as an instructional strategy is to select an appropriate instructional focus. You can conduct role plays on all types of personal and interpersonal problems such as shyness, bossiness, bullying, theft, lying, religious prejudice, sexism, and racism. You can also construct role plays to help children deal with common concerns such as how to deal with annoying younger brothers and sisters, parents who don't want to attend the school's open house, and conflicts that erupt on playgrounds. On the pleasant side, you can devise role plays to help children resolve questions such as who to invite to their birthday party, how to best help a younger brother or sister when he or she feels left out of an older sibling's plans, and many other situations that arise in daily life.

Select or develop role plays based on your own teaching goals and the needs of students. Because role playing is a powerful psycho-social learning tool, it is often best to delay role playing on a specific problem or issue until it has faded from the student's immediate memory. For example, the proper time to role play theft situations is not immediately after a theft occurs. Wait several days and design a role play that is dissimilar from the actual theft incident. Similarly, take care not to allow recent victims or the crime suspect(s) to take parts in the role play. It is better that they simply watch. You are responsible for ensuring the personal security and privacy of each individual when selecting situations.

If you are teaching in grades 4 through 6, and if your students have had little previous experience role playing, you may need to explain it and conduct a warm-up activity to help students relax prior to the first time you do a role play. (Stage fright hang-ups aren't a problem with most younger students!) To warm up older students you might, for example, ask individuals to stand up and wave their arms like they are tree limbs swaying in a gentle breeze. Follow this by asking them to wad up a piece of paper and pretend it is a toy car, driving it about on their desktops. The cars can race and crash with a neighbor's vehicle. Then the paper wads can become imaginary snowballs for a brief and harmless snowball fight. Once students are relaxed, begin your role play following the guidelines shown in Figure 19-3.

Involve the audience in a role play by giving it specific points to look for or suggesting that each person identify with one of the actors. Of course, the audience plays the major part in the debriefing discussion since their perspective was not clouded by direct involvement in the action. Role players, because they were directly involved, can then reflect on the audience's reactions.

Evaluate a role play through discussion or a postsession reaction form. Measure the overall success of role-playing sessions by the degree to which you reached your intended purposes. Note, for example, if the intended purpose was reducing classroom theft, it may take some time to determine your success.

Whether the original role play is brief or extended, it is often beneficial to conduct a reenactment. A reenactment provides a second chance to explore the feelings and issues involved in the role play. The original volunteers may replay their roles improving interpretations in light of the suggestions received,

1. Explain the general situation.

   a. Students should understand the educational purposes of the role play and its relevance to their lives.

   b. The whole class should know the site, central issue, and broad courses of possible action available within the role play.

2. Select volunteers for roles.

   a. Do not allow a child to play his or her usual life role; for example, don't let a bully role play a bully.

   b. Do not allow a child to play opposite his or her usual life role; for example, don't let a child who is a bully play the role of somone being bullied

   c. Role playing must be a volunteer activity. Children should feel free to decline roles without giving explanations. Do not allow peer pressure to force children to role play.

   d. Help each participant determine how to play his or her role.

   e. No actor is expected to present his or her role flawlessly.

   f. Students should understand that the way an actor portrays his or her role has no reflection upon him or her as a person.

3. Conduct the role play.

   a. You start and stop the action. You set the limits for the role-players' behavior, outlawing inappropriate language, hitting, and pushing.

   b. Once the action has started, students should be given enough time to become thoroughly immersed in the role-play situation, taking full advantage of exploring alternative ways of behaving.

   c. Eventually, the director (teacher) will end the role play and bring the actors back into the class group.

4. Hold a debriefing discussion.

   a. Lead the class in reviewing the actions and events of the role play.

   b. Focus on analyzing roles rather than the quality of the role-players' performances.

   c. Encourage students to speculate on alternative behavioral patterns and cause-and-effect relationships.

5. Conduct a reenactment.

   a. Allow individual role players the opportunity to redo the role play to refine their character or explore alternative ways of acting

   b. New volunteers may assume the roles and alter the action.

   c. If desired, replay scenes with additional characters.

6. Debrief the reenactment.

◆ ◆

FIGURE 19-3
The Technique of Role Playing

or new actors may take the roles. Reenactments give students an immediate opportunity to experiment with new and alternative behaviors, adding another perspective to the situation.

Figure 19-4 provides some examples of role plays appropriate for the early primary grades. As you read the role plays, ask yourself if the situations seem realistic, and whether children would benefit by being given such role-playing experiences.

1. Recess time is over and you have forgotten to use the rest room. As the math lesson starts your discomfort gets worse, but the rules are to use the rest room before coming in.

Role play:

- an open-chair interview between the child (represented by three students) and the teacher (represented by the class)
- what you say to your best friend when you are both complaining about things at school that bother you
- what you say to your mother when she hears you had an "accident" at school

2. The work on the math page is too difficult. It doesn't make sense and you can't get the answer. The teacher has already said, "Now work quietly while I check papers."

Role play:

- what you say to your teacher when she calls you up to explain why you are not working
- what you say to your parents when the work folders are sent home
- what your mother might say to your father or to your teacher about the poor work

3. School is over and the teachers are starting to leave. Your mother hasn't shown up and you're starting to get upset.

Role play:

- what you do as it gets later and later
- what you would say to a teacher who walked past or to another parent picking up a child who you know
- what you say to your mother when she finally shows up

4. The principal brings a new child from Haiti into your class. The child can't speak English, but seems friendly. You see him at recess and approach to meet him.

Role play:

- a playground meeting where you try to be friendly
- what you might say to a friend about the new classmate
- what you might say to your mother or father about the child

FIGURE 19-4
Role Plays for the Primary Grades

Dance

Dance has played a role in the expression of all cultures. Dances are a part of celebrations, religious rituals, courting, and even funerals. Modern dance allows an interpretive expression of virtually any experience. Popular dance steps reflect music styles and emotions. Dance styles such as clogging and square dance reflect cultures that students might be studying.

Have students design their own interpretive modern dance designed to illustrate social studies content. Invite in a resource person to demonstrate and teach a dance associated with a group or culture that the students have studied. Have students learn dances that were popular during a particular period of history to develop a greater degree of identification and understanding of that time and place.

Puppetry

Young children love puppetry as an avenue to express their ideas and feelings. A large cardboard box with a rectangular hole cut at shoulder height makes a good stage to stand behind while performing. Children can make tube-sock or paper-sack puppets, sewing or gluing on eyes, using yarn for hair, and scraps of fabric for clothing. Never force children to engage in puppetry. Instead, offer them many opportunities for spontaneous or planned use. Shy individuals may find it attractive to first use the puppetry stage spontaneously and without an audience. Puppetry offers a good nonthreatening avenue for children to act out their social thoughts, attitudes, and values.

Two good sources on puppetry are Tamara Hunt and Nancy Renfro's *Puppetry in Early Childhood Education* and Nancy Renfro's *Puppet Shows Made Easy.*

USING WRITING SKILLS
. . . . .

The purpose of learning to express yourself in writing is to communicate thoughts and feelings to others, a thoroughly social act. Emphasize to students the application of writing skills in real-world situations. Opportunities to write in social studies are abundant; for example, you can ask students to write

- letters to elected officials, editors, businesses, and organizations
- reports on cities, states, countries, national parks, famous people, and so on
- thank-you notes to presenters and resource persons
- summaries of inquiry studies and survey results
- skits and plays to dramatize a historical event
- alternative advertisements for real or imaginary products
- a classroom constitution and a bill of rights
- petitions for change in school policies
- letters to state travel bureaus and chambers of commerce
- travel brochures advertising the places they are studying

When students write in social studies, remember that the purpose is to achieve social studies objectives. Accordingly, such characteristics as grammar, spelling, or other elements of composition should only be a part of the critique you offer. It is more important to focus on content and for the students to offer their own critiques of one another's papers. Approach social studies writing assignments with a writing cycle that involves brainstorming, outlining, writing the first draft, peer review, final draft, and the teacher's evaluation. Feel free to set appropriately high standards for all types of written expression and reserve the right to limit inappropriate or poor-quality writing in letters or other student-composed communications.

USING READING SKILLS

Chapter 4 covered the difficulties students have reading social studies textbooks, made the point that when we read in social studies we read to acquire content knowledge, and offered a variety of strategies for improving students' reading. The reading difficulties and strategies detailed apply to all types of social studies reading including original source materials such as diaries, historic documents, and biographies.

An effective reading program in the elementary school should include the thoughtful, consistent, and pervasive use of children's literature; it should accompany virtually every social studies unit or topic. Ask your media specialist to aid in identifying appropriate titles for your children. This practice is especially important for primary grade level students with their limited ability to locate books, but should not be abandoned with older students. Ask the media specialist to place books on a cart so that they may be brought to the room and set up as part of an attractive display. Call the students' attention to the area and go over some of the titles provided. Ask younger students to help you select one of the titles to read to the whole class during a period of the day reserved for this type of activity. Encourage older students to select their own books for sustained silent pleasure reading and periodically allow them to share what they are learning as the social studies unit unfolds. Of course, children should feel free to interject specialized knowledge they have gained during any phase of your social studies instruction. Also encourage students to use any topically focused, specialized nonfiction works (for example, a book on architecture when you are studying cities) as reference tools during their social studies unit.

As students progress in their reading ability, it is appropriate for teachers to challenge them to read "between the lines." Such reading calls for students to detect the author's point of view; to determine unstated assumptions; and to locate poor logic, name calling, loaded adjectives, and irrelevant facts. Recognizing such characteristics is an important citizenship skill. Armed with it, individuals are better able to determine on their own the truth of public knowledge claims and arguments. Show students how descriptive social studies material may be rewritten to make its subject sound better or worse.

Also, give students opportunities to do their own rewriting. For example, give students a chance to change the slant of a newspaper article or modify a popular television commercial to make the product seem less desirable.

In closing this section, I offer a few words of caution about the use of children's literature. Alleman and Brophy (1994) report that the trend toward using literature to teach social studies may have several negative consequences. While their study focused on the use of children's literature as an aid to social studies textbooks, many of their warnings apply to the use of any literature adopted to teach social studies. They note, for example, that many pages—and much reading effort—may be devoted to a literature selection that focuses on a trivial or narrow aspect of the social studies topic being considered. They question whether this is a wise use of instructional time and whether other, more direct and active means might be used to achieve the desired social studies learning. Alleman and Brophy found that many of the activities suggested for literature selections failed to enhance social studies learning and could only qualify as language arts activities.

They further note that literature selections can lead to stereotyping and misconceptions when students attempt to generalize about entire cultures and places based on a single children's story. For example, the award-winning children's book about a homeless father and son, *Fly Away Home* (Bunting, 1991), does a great job of stirring empathy for the pair, but offers very few insights about homelessness in the United States. Fundamental understandings about homelessness that young children might reasonably acquire are simply not provided by the book. It's up to the teacher to offer high-quality social studies lessons if children are to understand such continuing social problems.

USING MATH SKILLS

Math adds much meaning to social studies, especially when we use it to inspect and illuminate social issues. Numbers take on meaning when compared with other numbers taken from previous times, different locations, or related measures. This means that when, for example, students learn that as of July 1992 the United States' national debt totaled over $3.9 trillion, they can make better sense of this number by stipulating that it amounts to approximately $50,000 for each family living in the United States. This number, in turn, gains meaning when compared with the median 1990 family income of $33,956 and the federally defined 1989 poverty level of $12,675 for a family of four. Another way of grasping the size of our national debt is to explain that from 1940 up until 1978 about $0.10 out of every $1.00 spent by the government went to pay the interest on our national debt. Due to the increases that occurred during the 1980s and early 1990s, today we spend about $0.21 out of every $1.00 to pay the interest on our loans.[3]

---

[3]Data taken from *The Universal Almanac.* 1992, 1994. Kansas City: Andrews and McMeel.

Students of all ages need help in understanding numbers. Pie charts are a particularly good way to visually convey the meaning of proportions. Bar charts easily show the quantity of measured items across discrete categories. Time lines are a useful aid in helping students visualize the amount of time passing between events.

Even very young children can gain an intuitive grasp of numbers by making pictographic bar charts that, for example, show the number of students in class who walk, ride the bus, bike, or come in a car to school (see Figure 19-5).

Graphing experiences such as this one are a real-world use of mathematics that focus on social studies understanding. Help children to understand why people use different modes of transportion and how they influence people's lives. For example, there are different dangers associated with riding a bike to school as opposed to riding the school bus; some families may prefer not to own a car or to use one for transporting a child, and so forth. This type of analysis is clearly focused on social understanding and is not just an exercise in the acquisition of graphing skills.

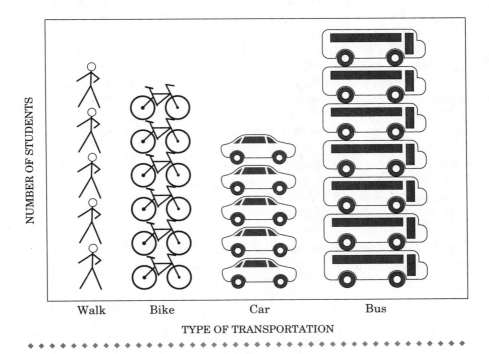

FIGURE 19-5
Sample Pictographic Bar Chart

REFERENCES AND SELECTED READINGS
◆ ◆ ◆ ◆ ◆

Alleman, J., and Brophy, J. 1991. *Is curriculum integration a boon or a threat to social studies?* Research series no. 204: ED337388. East Lansing, MI: Michigan State University, Institute for Research on Teaching.

————. 1993. Is curriculum integration a boon or a threat to social studies? Elementary education. *Social Education* 57(6):287–291.

————. 1994. Trade-offs embedded in the literary approach to early elementary social studies. *Social Studies and the Young Learner* 6(3):6–8.

Barr, I. M., and McGuire, M. E. 1993. Social studies and effective stories. *Social Studies and the Young Learner* 5(3):6–8, 11.

Brophy, J., and Alleman, J. 1991. A caveat: Curriculum integration isn't always a good idea. *Educational Leadership* 49(2).

Bunting, E. 1991. *Fly away home.* New York: Clarion Books.

Drake, J. J., and Drake, F. D. 1990. Using children's literature to teach about the American Revolution. *Social Studies and the Young Learner* 3(2):6–8.

Eisenberg, L., and Eisenberg, H. 1984. *The handbook of skits and stunts.* Martinsville, IN: American Camping Association.

Etchison, C. 1994. Technology plays a leading role in integrating the elementary curriculum. Displaying the states. Technology learning activities. *Technology Teacher* 53(8):31–32.

Farivar, S. 1993. Continuity and change: Planning an integrated history-social science/ English-language arts unit. *Social Studies Review* 32(2):17–24.

Fisher, A. 1985. *Year-round programs for young players: One hundred plays, skits, poems, choral readings, spelldowns, recitations, and pantomimes for celebrating holidays and special occasions.* Boston: Plays, Inc.

Handley, L. M., ed. 1990. Hands-on activities for integrating geography across the curriculum. *Social Studies and the Young Learner* 3(2):24–26.

Hunt, T., and Renfro, N. 1982. *Puppetry in early childhood education.* Austin, TX: Nancy Renfro Studios.

Lombard, R. H., ed. 1994. Social education as the curriculum integrator: The case of the environment. Children's literature. *Social Studies and the Young Learner* 6(3):20–22.

Renfro, N. 1984. *Puppet shows made easy.* Austin, TX: Nancy Renfro Studios.

Schlene, V. J. 1993. Integrated curriculum and instruction: An ERIC/ChESS sample. *Social Studies and the Young Learner* 5(3):15–16.

Shaftel, F. R., and Shaftel, G. 1982. *Role playing in the curriculum.* Englewood Cliffs, NJ: Prentice Hall.

Wall, G. 1992. *"Magic day": Multi-disciplinary, multi-sensory awareness gathered and integrated into the curriculum.* ERIC document no. ED352271. New Albany, IN: Indiana University Southeast.

Whitlow, F. R., and Sidelnick, D. J. 1991. Integrating geography skills and local history: A third grade case study. *Social Studies Journal* 20:33–36.

CHAPTER 20

Resolving Differences of Opinion in the Classroom

(A kindergarten play scene)

TOMMY: *(with authority in his voice)* Girls can't do that. Only boys get to play with the fire engines!

SAMANTHA: *(challenging right back)* My momma told me I can play with anything I want.

TOMMY: Well, my dad's a fireman and he said girls can't play with fire engines.

MS. BELL: *(overhearing exchange)* Tommy, you'll have to share your fire engine with Samantha. Girls can play with fire engines if they want.

TOMMY: *(gripping the fire engine closer to his chest)* My dad said girls can't. Mary couldn't play with my new fire engine.

MS. BELL: *(authority and kindness in her voice)* Well, that's at your house, but now we are here at school. When we are here, you'll have to share the fire engine with all the other children, including girls. Samantha, let Tommy play with the fire engine a few more minutes and then it will be your turn.

SAMANTHA: *(looking up at Ms. Bell)* Momma said I could play with any toy I want. It doesn't have to be just for girls.

MS. BELL: I think your mom is right. You can play with a fire engine or any other toy. That's the rule here at school.

INTRODUCTION
◆ ◆ ◆ ◆ ◆

The opening scenario depicts a situation typical to kindergarten playtime. Both Tommy and Samantha were acting on statements their parents made at home. Tommy's father may have voiced his rule about girls not being allowed to play with fire engines for a variety of reasons. He may have made the comment as an expedient (and thoughtless) way to avoid a conflict between Tommy and Mary. Regardless, Tommy has generalized his father's rule to the kindergarten classroom. Depending on this and other things his father might have said regarding girls, Tommy has probably begun to form opinions about what's right—and wrong—for girls to do.

DISCUSSION QUESTIONS
◆ ◆ ◆ ◆ ◆

1. How would you have handled the situation?

2. Did Ms. Bell do the right thing, telling Samantha that her mother was right?

3. Do you suppose Tommy was hurt to find out that his father's "rule" didn't apply to the school setting?

4. What are the likely consequences of ignoring the situation or refusing to identify which parent's opinion is more acceptable?

I hope the opening scenario has brought back to your consciousness the importance of recognizing and accommodating differences of opinion in your elementary classroom. I believe that even very young children are surrounded by differences of opinion in matters that sometimes dramatically affect their everyday lives. To illustrate this point, and the importance of recognizing differences of opinion as an integral part of the social studies planning process, I offered a chart (p. 64) in Chapter 4, "Planning for Social Studies," that displayed some differences of opinion that might exist regarding the family-life topics of birth, parents' work, leisure, sleep, and eating. I believe children are greatly benefited by an examination of the reasoning behind differences of opinion to which they are exposed. Thoughtful analysis of such differences allows children to begin viewing the rational and moral basis of social behavior.

In this chapter you'll learn more about the nature of differences of opinion,[1] gain information about the full range of areas where differences of opinion may come into play, be introduced to guidelines for selecting and discussing differences of opinion with young children, and see a lesson plan that shows how to resolve differences of opinion that become open conflicts.

---

[1] I have chosen to avoid using the terms *controversy* and *controversial issues* for two reasons. First, these terms are too narrow to include all of the areas where differences of opinion exist. Second, teachers tend to shy away from classroom activities that deal with a controversial issue, thinking that either they or their students lack the ability to thoughtfully inspect the issue, or that parents and administrators will object to such a focus in the classroom.

WHAT IS A DIFFERENCE OF OPINION?
♦ ♦ ♦ ♦ ♦

A difference of opinion exists when two or more individuals' views about what's right or appropriate are dissimilar. Two people might hold differing opinions about what constitutes the quickest route across town during rush hour traffic. Two mothers might hold different opinions regarding what constitutes appropriate future occupations for their sons. Such differences of opinion are based on a variety of factors such as factual knowledge, amount of firsthand experience, assumptions about prevailing conditions, and even personal attitudes and values.

I've occasionally met people who considered matters of opinion differences to be fundamentally unresolvable. These individuals may believe there can be no solution to a problem or issue about which good, concerned, well-informed people disagree. They believe that even if both parties to the difference of opinion had the same information and fully shared their firsthand experiences, they would still choose to disagree. Such individuals may also feel that there is, in actuality, no "best" solution—that all solutions represent compromises that elevate or accentuate certain goals at the expense of other goals and outcomes.

Sometimes individuals who do not wish to examine their opinions simply feel that it would take too much work to explain why they feel like they do. They may also feel that the work involved exceeds the good that might come from reconciling differences of opinion. Finally, they may be fundamentally unwilling to resolve differences of opinion in an open and caring manner.

Occasionally, I've encountered teachers-in-training who have falsely generalized the proposition that "everyone has a right to his or her own opinion" to mean "all opinions are equal." While it is clear that everyone does have a right to his or her own opinion, it is equally evident that all opinions are not of similar value. The latter proposition is not only false, but potentially dangerous to our democracy if thoughtlessly propagated. It should be clear to you that people would seldom give equal weight to the opinions of a novice and an expert in any realm of knowledge or importance. If you wanted to get an opinion about what might be the best configuration of our military in the foreseeable future, you'd be far better off trusting a well-educated, high-ranking army officer who specializes in this topic as opposed to the advice of an eighteen-year-old recruit. Going back to the rush hour traffic question, you'd be far better off trusting the opinion of a person who had lots of knowledge of the local road system and had rich and varied experience driving under time constraints in rush hour traffic than seeking the advice of a person who hadn't driven in the past twenty years.

Harwood and Hahn (1990) state, "The essence of a healthy democracy is open dialogue about issues of public concern." They point out that an integral part of training young citizens includes discussing differences of opinion. Such discussions prepare students for their roles as citizens in our pluralistic democracy, develop essential critical-thinking skills, and improve the interpersonal skills we all need to function effectively in our daily lives as citizens. As the opening scenario demonstrates, even very young children need experiences examining differences of opinion as they arise naturally in their daily lives. Let's inspect the full range of areas where differences of opinion are likely to arise.

EXAMPLES OF OPINION DIFFERENCES
♦ ♦ ♦ ♦ ♦

Differences of opinion exist in virtually all areas of life. People have vastly different opinions about which make and model of car is best, which brand of computer and software they prefer, and what downtown restaurants serve the best Italian food.

Since differences of opinion arise in virtually all areas of life, it is important to have some schema for organizing our thinking about what topics are most appropriate and feasible for grades K through 6. Figure 20-1 displays a selection of topics about which there is likely to be a variety of opinions. As you inspect the list, keep track of whether you believe the topic is (1) more appropriate for older or younger persons, (2) one where there is general agreement about the desirability of the goal within society, and (3) directly impacting the conscious, everyday lives of the children you will most likely teach.

Admittedly, some of the topics are not appropriate for consideration by young children. For example, I hope you thought that abortion was an inappropriate topic for young children. I also hope you were able to identify drug abuse as a topic where there is general agreement about the goal of drug-abuse reduction. Finally, I hope that you were able to identify topics such as homework policy and gender discrimination as having the most direct impact on the conscious everyday lives of children.

Sometimes differences of opinion arise as a result of a tragedy or near tragedy that touches children's lives. Such tragedies often spur expressions of opinions and much speculation. Parents may react strongly to such incidents and say or do things in front of children that heighten fears or foster misunderstanding of the facts of a particular case. Schools commonly call in professional counselors when a tragedy occurs, yet teachers often have to deal with students' comments and fears long after the counselors leave. Following are some examples of tragedies that can happen to young children. As you read the examples, ask yourself if you would be willing to use your developing difference-of-opinion discussion skills to help students resolve questions regarding these incidents.

• **A child is seriously injured while on the playground.** Children are awestruck by the sight of an ambulance and the nearly hysterical teacher's aide. The next day comments begin erupting from students: "My dad says that playground isn't safe." "The teachers should have been more observant." "Why didn't they see what was going on?" "Children are playing too roughly." "We should end recess for a while."

TOPICS	SAMPLE QUESTIONS
Poverty/ Hunger/ Homelessness	Why are some people poor, hungry, or homeless? What kinds and amounts of assistance should the government give to these people—and for how long? How should we pay for and deliver these services?
Foster care/ Adoption	What is foster care and what is it like? Why don't more adults adopt or provide foster care? Should biological parents be shielded from discovery by their offspring? Is the foster care system working?
Immigrants/ Immigration	Is our present system of immigration quotas working well for our own nation and potential immigrants from other nations around the world? Should illegal immigrants receive the same government services as legal citizens?
Family planning/ Overpopulation	Should the U.S. government provide funds to help prevent unwanted pregnancies among women in Third World countries? Should family planning services be allowed to provide information about abortions? Should government offer any financial support for abortions among indigent women?
Recycling/ Waste disposal/ Disposal of hazardous wastes	Should we investigate the issue of whether we need a new sanitary landfill and where to locate it? Should our community continue to support Company X that specializes in processing hazardous waste or is it time to close our doors to this business?
War/ Specific wars	Should we discuss the recent news report Trudy brought in about the children dying in Bosnia?
Drug abuse	Should drug abusers be treated more like criminals or as medical patients?
Child abuse	Do I dare allow the children to discuss the national news story about child abuse in the next-door community?
Religious prejudice	Should we take the time to learn more about Hanukkah or can we omit any mention of this Jewish religious celebration? Do I have to explain what Moslems believe? Should we discuss the reasons why Jehovah Witness children in our class don't say the pledge of allegiance?
Racial prejudice	Was Terrance's fight with Arian just a fight or was it a racially motivated attack? Do we need to include more African-American and Hispanic-American children's stories in our reading center or is our selection just fine?
Gender discrimination	Should I intervene and ask the girls to allow Billy into their play group?
Abortion	Should a sixth-grade girl, raped by her older cousin, be allowed to have an early abortion or be forced to carry the child and give birth? Should a married wealthy woman who has had an undiscovered illicit affair be prevented from flying to Europe for an abortion? Should the government discourage abortion as a matter of general practice?
Gun control	Should parents or people with children around be required to place trigger locks on their weapons? Do we need greater government oversight of gun trading shows and dealers?

(continued on next page)

FIGURE 20-1
Selected Opinion Difference Topics

Use of wilderness areas	Should we allow access to motorcycles on our wilderness park trails? Should hunting parties be allowed to set up camp wherever they wish? Must hunters use logging trails or can they go cross-country in their 4x4s? Should the government preserve and protect wilderness streams for the exclusive use of those who fish?
Air pollution	Is the factory on the outskirts of town emitting too much smoke and noise? Are its air emissions dangerous to our health?
Water pollution	Who or what caused the fish kill in our local river? Should we support or oppose the construction of a new plant that needs our river water for chemical processes in manufacturing?
Downtown development	Would it help our community if we fixed up the downtown? Should we support or oppose further strip-mall development on the outskirts of town?
Educational issues	Is the integrated approach to social studies responsible for children's limited knowledge of geography, history, and civics? Should teachers explicitly inculcate majority culture values? Should we help children think critically about personal and social values even if their parents object?
School bond initiatives	Does the school really need major renovations? Are more special education teachers needed? Is it the right time to make major technology investments?
Use of playground equipment	Are the new swings too dangerous for the children in the lower grades? Do we need a new rule for the slide about going down one at a time?
Classroom or school homework policy	Is homework in more than two subjects too much? Should each child have some homework every school day? Should teachers be forced to grade all homework assignments?
Pet leash/licensing laws	Should dog owners be required to keep their dogs on leashes while using public sidewalks and parks? Should dog owners be fined if their pets are caught roaming the neighborhood? Should cat and dog owners be required to spay or neuter their pets or apply for a breeder's license?
Cultural myths	Is Santa Clause real? Is there an Easter bunny? Did George Washington really chop down a cherry tree?
Getting to school safely: Crosswalks and crossing guards	Do we need a crossing light at 5th Street? Is another crossing guard needed behind the school? Is Mr. Baker still performing his crossing guard job well?
Legitimacy and application of corporal punishment	Was Jeremy paddled illegally last week? What is the proper procedure and who can be paddled? Do parents have a right to paddle their own children?

FIGURE 20-1, continued
Selected Opinion Difference Topics

- **A child is molested while walking home from school.** The news spreads rapidly about the incident though little is known about the perpetrator(s) or circumstances of the crime. "The police aren't doing their job." "No one is safe." "Anyone you see could be a child molester—watch out!" "My dad says he'll shoot anybody that even comes near me."

- **The felony arrest of a teacher, parent, or principal occurs.** A teacher is arrested for shoplifting, when, in fact, she had made a mistake and simply forgotten to pay for the item she had picked up. "They need to do more background checks on teachers!" "She was arrested for shoplifting. Teachers should have higher morals!" "Mom says Ms. T. will lose her license."
- **A parent, teacher, or child dies.** A child's stepfather dies of AIDS. "It was the doctor's fault." "No, I heard that Mike's dad was already sick—he had AIDS." "We should all be checked; any of us could be infected!"

A school or classroom tragedy obviously calls for the presence of professional counselors. But after the counselors leave, how will you address the opinion statements and speculations that children voice? Will you dismiss them, simply saying that you are unwilling to talk about the topic? Will you directly confront statements from students that are based on misinformation? Or will you attempt to help children reason through such statements?

It seems obvious to me that teachers who have experience dealing with differences of opinion will be in a better position to encounter new and more challenging events as they arise. Teachers without such experience may find themselves ill-equipped to address the needs of their students.

WHY DIFFERENCES OF OPINION BELONG IN YOUR ROOM

Classrooms that engage students in meaningful, sustained, periodic discussions of opinion differences have been noted to improve students' tolerance for diverse ideas, increase interest in political and social issues, promote positive civic attitudes, improve attitudes toward social studies in general, and increase students' sense of efficacy, confidence, and trust (Harwood and Hahn, 1990). Most crucial to the attainment of these positive outcomes is the creation of an open, supportive environment where children feel free to express their opinions and ideas.

Beyond these positive outcomes, it is important to note that national standards for social studies instruction call for children in the early grades to practice civic discourse, communicate personal opinions, and address the ethical dimensions of issues (National Council for the Social Studies, 1994). Similarly, the *National Standards for Civics and Government* (Center for Civic Education, 1994) calls for students, by grade 4, to explain that Americans have a right to differ about politics, religion, or any other matter and to express their views without fear. Further, these standards call for the prevention and management of conflicts, specifically stating that students should be able to identify examples of conflicts caused by diversity and act to resolve such conflicts through listening to different points of view, learning about others' beliefs, and working together on school and community problems. Teachers who fail to seize opportunities to discuss naturally arising differences of opinion will not achieve these important standards for social studies instruction.

GUIDELINES FOR DISCUSSING AND RESOLVING DIFFERENCES OF OPINION

As I stated in Chapter 4, I believe you should consciously plan to include the recognition of differences of opinion as a part of your regular social studies instruction. Virtually any topic can serve as a springboard for recognizing such opinion differences; for example, you can encourage children to learn about the various viewpoints of Native-American tribes as they encountered and attempted to cope with the advance of European settlers. Your textbook or curriculum guide may already include resources that can help you recognize differences of opinion. In other cases, however, you may need to look at the way a topic is presented and develop your own entry points for recognizing these differences.

Differences of opinion will also arise naturally in your classroom. Much of the time such differences are expressed without intent to hurt others. Students simply put forth statements that embody a particular point of view. Learning to recognize such opinion-influenced statements takes some practice. You may have to infer that a student is operating with a particular set of assumptions and holds feelings that have influenced his or her view of the topic. It is appropriate to ask students to explain their assumptions and opinions when this opportunity occurs. If necessary, ask questions designed to solicit this information.

Occasionally, students may get into arguments or even open conflicts based on their differing views. When this happens it is important to stop the argument or open, physical conflict and establish the kind of civilized and thoughtful exchange that can resolve matters peacefully.

Figure 20-2 presents a list of guidelines that may be used to help you conduct productive classroom discussions on issues where students are likely to hold differing points of view.

Harwood and Hahn (1990) offer two sets of recommendations regarding issue discussions that may prove helpful. First, they recommend giving each

---

- Select issues that fit your students' maturity, life experiences, and interests.

- Make sure the issue has significance to society and fits with the ongoing social studies program.

- Provide additional information on the issue if students have not already gained sufficient background.

- Make sure all viewpoints are presented as fairly as possible. Support students who need help presenting their point of view.

- Reveal your own position only toward the end of the discussion and, preferably, only if invited to by students.

FIGURE 20-2
Issue Discussion Guidelines

student a few tokens that he or she "spends" as discussion contributions are made. When a student runs out of tokens, he or she must wait until more tokens are distributed. All students are encouraged to spend their tokens during the discussion.[2] Collect unspent tokens and redistribute them at the next discussion occasion. Second, Harwood and Hahn believe that posting an agenda for the discussion may help students stay on track. An issue or opinion discussion agenda might consist of:

- stating your point of view
- clarifying your terminology—telling what you mean by the words and phrases you have used
- presenting any firsthand or other evidence you might have to support your point of view
- attempting to draw conclusions or state consequences that would result if your opinion or viewpoint were acted upon

Here is an imagined sample dialogue showing how the suggested discussion agenda might work as it is applied to a student's early morning comment about bus drivers.

STEP 1 State your point of view.

(*Angela storms into the room, throwing her books on the desk.*)

ANGELA: "Boy, those bus drivers are stupid!"

(*Overhearing this, Mr. Simms, the teacher, recognizes that a strong opinion has been stated and proceeds to the second step of the suggested discussion agenda.*)

Step 2 Clarify your terminology.

MR. SIMMS: Angela, that's a pretty strong statement. Do you mean all bus drivers or just the one who drives your bus?

ANGELA: I mean all bus drivers!

MR. SIMMS: Even those who drive city buses?

ANGELA: No, just the school bus drivers.

MR. SIMMS: So you think all of our school bus drivers are stupid?

ANGELA: Yeah. Really stupid. They won't even let us get out of our seats!

MR. SIMMS: Once you get on you can't move?

ANGELA: That's right! Not even to across the aisle. Deborah's been put on bus suspension for three days for moving from her seat to mine.

---

[2]You may want to experiment with allowing students to silently pass tokens to individuals who have run out. This is a way of supporting a point of view that a classmate has adopted. If you are concerned about shy students never speaking for themselves, set some limit on the number of tokens that may be silently given away.

MR. SIMMS: I thought you were claiming that bus drivers were not very smart. This sounds more like you're angry because they have been enforcing a rule about bus behavior.

ANGELA: I think it's a stupid rule! Stupid people make stupid rules.

MR. SIMMS: Can you rephrase your original statement so that it more accurately reflects what you wanted to say?

ANGELA: I think the rule about not being able to move from one seat to another is stupid.

Step 3 Present any firsthand or other evidence to support your point of view.

MR. SIMMS: That's better. Now what kind of evidence would you need to prove your point?

ANGELA: Well, I could get other kids to tell me how they feel about the rule. I bet they hate it as much as I do.

MR. SIMMS: Okay, and that would prove that it was a stupid rule?

ANGELA: No. I guess you'd need to show that it prevents injuries or bus accidents. Donna told me that was why the principal said we had the rule.

MR. SIMMS: Okay. Maybe someone's done a study. Or maybe it's just common sense.

ANGELA: I could try to find out. Maybe the bus drivers don't even like the rule.

MR. SIMMS: You could contact the transportation director and we can request an interview regarding the bus rules. Maybe he would even come to the classroom.

Step 4 Attempt to draw conclusions or state consequences that would result if your opinion or viewpoint were acted upon.

MR. SIMMS: What will happen if you find out that there have been studies done and the data support requiring children to stay in their seats while the bus is moving?

ANGELA: I suppose I'd feel different about the rule.

MR. SIMMS: So would I if I thought it would help me have a safer bus ride.

(*Fade . . .*)

CONCLUDING THOUGHTS

Social studies addresses many areas of learning in attempting to achieve its citizenship aim. The discussion of differences of opinion deserves to hold an important place in your regular ongoing social studies program. It is a basic skill of democracy that schools are best positioned to address.

As you begin your teaching career you'll have plenty of opportunity to practice recognizing and resolving differences of opinion. Depending upon your grade level and the nature of the instructional opportunity, you may wish to follow initial discussions of opinion differences with small-group research assignments, additional readings, presentations from resource persons, or creative role playing.

Social studies lessons that tap into students' beliefs, feelings, and opinions are powerful motivators of intellect and emotion. Because of this you'll have to be judicious in your implementation of activities designed to help young children achieve the confidence and skills needed to thoughtfully consider their own and others' opinions. Following the suggestions and guidelines offered in this chapter should help you address this important area of the curriculum in a safe and productive manner.

SAMPLE CONFLICT RESOLUTION LESSON PLAN

MS. MEDIATOR, THE PUPPET[3]

Grade Level: K–1
Time Required: Two class periods
Concepts/Vocabulary: Mediator, mediation, conflict, compromise, dispute, disagreement

Main Ideas

a. Mediation is a good way to peacefully resolve conflicts because each party helps to work out a satisfactory solution.

b. Mediation is a technique students can use to resolve disputes inside or outside the classroom.

Objectives: As a result of this lesson, students will:

- learn the steps in the mediation process
- apply the steps in the mediation process to resolve realistic classroom conflicts

Instructional Strategies

Playing "musical chairs" as a springboard to conflict mediation

Teacher-led introduction to the mediation process

Role-playing conflict resolution with Ms. Mediator puppet

Teacher Background

Mediation is one way of resolving a dispute. In mediation, the disputing parties go to a third party to help them settle their disagreement. The mediator does not make a decision as a trial judge does. Rather, the mediator helps the parties work out their own solution.

The process used in this lesson is a simplified version of mediation. Interestingly, mediation is being used more and more as a means of settling adult disputes. It is increasingly used to work out divorce and child-custody settlements. Proponents contend that mediation, because it results in solutions to which each party contributes and in which each side "wins," can achieve more long-lasting and satisfactory resolutions to disputes than formal litigation.

One way to help your students understand mediation is to give them a chance to experiment with the mediation process. The goals of mediation are different from those of a trial. Mediators do not try to decide who is right and who is wrong; nor do they call witnesses, present evidence, or crossexamine people under oath. Mediators do not take sides, and they do not tell people what they ought to do. The mediation process involves (1) determining exactly what has happened, (2) fully hearing what each person's problems are with the disagreement, (3) listening how each person wants the disagreement resolved, (4) determining several fair ways of resolving the disagreement, and (5) agreeing on one of the ways—making sure that each side is happy.

Materials/Resources Needed: Paper sack or sock puppet (Ms. Mediator), means for music or drumbeat, chart-paper display of "Ms. Mediator's Questions for Solving Disagreements" (see handout at end of lesson)

Procedure

Period One

1. Tell students that you want to play musical chairs and set up the room to begin the game. (You will need music or a drumbeat, and one less chair than the number of students in the class.)

Have students march around the chairs with the music. When the music stops, the students must find chairs in which to sit. The student without a chair is eliminated and another chair is removed. (You can speed up this game by removing more than one chair at a time.) Continue playing until two students get into a dispute over who got to a chair first. Then stop the game and review the problem: Both student one (Jessica) and student two (Antonio) think they got to the chair at the same time.

2. Introduce Ms. Mediator puppet.

TEACHER: Class, this is Ms. Mediator. (Write the name on the board.) She is going to have a very special role in our class; she will help us solve

[3]Adapted from a lesson by Janice Habersham, published as a part of the Georgia Elementary Law-Related Education Curriculum Supplements (GELRECS). ERIC document no. ED352293.

some problems if we disagree with one another. To disagree is to differ with one another. Ms. Mediator will show us one way to settle disagreements. The name for this way to settle disagreements is *mediation* (write the word on the board).

Right now, Jessica feels she has a right to have the chair, while Antonio feels he has a right to the same chair. We would say that they have a conflict or disagreement and they need to settle this disagreement. (Look at the puppet.) Ms. Mediator can you help us?

MS. MEDIATOR: Hey, I sure can. That's why they call me Ms. Mediator!

(Say, with rhythm.)

When people are angry or having some trouble
I come to their aid giving help on the double.
My skills are so keen—I'm a real peace creator
So take all your disputes to Ms. Mediator!

TEACHER: Thanks, Ms. Mediator. As you have already heard, we do indeed have a problem. While we were playing musical chairs, Antonio and Jessica reached the chair at exactly the same time. Can you help us?

MS. MEDIATOR: Yes, I have a set of questions that I'll ask Antonio and Jessica. Their answers should help us reach a solution to their disagreement.

3. The mediation process is demonstrated in the following dialogue.

MS. MEDIATOR: Jessica, tell us what happened. ("Jessica" responds to the puppet.)

Now, Antonio, tell us what happened. ("Antonio" responds to the puppet.)

(to each child in turn) What is the problem? (Each child responds.)

(to each child in turn): How do you think we should solve this problem?

(*Encourage each child to respond. The class may also contribute solutions to the disagreement. Some potential solutions are to (1) replay the round, (2) toss a coin to determine whether Jessica or Antonio will stay, and (3) ask both Jessica and Antonio to sit down. The teacher writes their recommended "fair" solutions on the board.*)

MS. MEDIATOR: (to one child) Which of the solutions would be okay with you? (Child responds.)

(*If one solution is all right with Jessica, Ms. Mediator checks to see if it is all right with Antonio. Make adjustments to the solution if needed. The important thing is that they both be happy with the solution.*)

4. Discuss and review the process used by Ms. Mediator. To review, display a chart paper showing "Ms. Mediator's Questions for Solving Disagreements." Stress that these questions each have to be answered by both sides, and that both sides should be happy with the solution.

Period Two

1. Use the following scenario (or make one up from a classroom incident) to practice another mediation.

Jane and Rob are playing in a big sandbox. Jane has been playing with a large dump truck for a long time. She has been bringing sand to a place where she is building a big tower and dumping it. She needs five more loads. Rob has wanted the truck for some time. He asked Jane twice and she said no both times. Finally, he grabs the truck. Jane tries to hit him.

Select one student to be Jane (who wants to keep the truck longer to finish her task) and one to be Rob (who thinks it should be his turn and wants the truck now). They should act out the scenario with Ms. Mediator watching.

2. Using the Ms. Mediator puppet, repeat the mediation dialogue and process used during Period One.

3. Discuss the mediation process. Review what happened, the questions asked by Ms. Mediator, and the responses of the children. Ask, Was Jane happy with the solution? Was Rob happy with solution?

Suppose they had fought and Jane had gone away crying: Would Jane have been happy? Would Rob have been happy? (Maybe, but he might feel bad inside.)

Suppose Jane had taken the truck and run away: Would Rob have been happy? Would Jane have been happy? (Maybe, but she might feel bad inside, too!)

Help students to see that Ms. Mediator enabled the children to talk out the argument and decide on a solution they both agreed with.

This way both were happy. Ask, Is this a good way to solve arguments?

4. Review by asking students to help you list the questions Ms. Mediator uses at each step of the mediation process.

Evaluation

- Place the Ms. Mediator puppet at a table in the back of the room. Invite students to come to the table three at a time to act out the mediation process using real-life conflicts from the classroom or playground. Place the chart-paper process near the table and observe the action from a distance.

Enrichment

- Develop a series of dispute scenarios to provide regular weekly or biweekly practice in mediation.
- Encourage students to share this procedure with their families or friends.
- Let students make Ms. Mediator puppets of their own to use at home.

H A N D O U T   **Ms. Mediator's Questions for Solving Disagreements**

Ask *each* person:

1. What has happened?

2. What is your problem or disagreement about?

3. How do you want the disagreement solved?

4. What would be some fair ways of resolving the disagreement? (These should be fair to each side.)

5. What way of resolving the disagreement can we agree on? (Be sure each side is happy.)

◆ ◆

REFERENCES AND SELECTED READINGS

Braun, J. A., Jr. 1992. Social technology in the elementary social studies curriculum. *Social Education* 56(7):389–392.

Center for Civic Education. 1994. *National standards for civics and government.* Calabasas, CA: Center for Civic Education.

Charney, R. S. 1993. *Teaching children to care: Management in the responsive classroom.* ERIC document no. ED369531. Greenfield, MA: Northeast Foundation for Children.

Cramer, R. H. 1988. Clear the air with class meetings. *Learning* 17(1):58–61.

Ensley, M. L., ed. 1993. Making our school a peaceful community: A curriculum guide on conflict resolution for classroom guidance in grades

Hahn, C. L. 1991. Teaching controversial economics issues. *Georgia Social Science Journal* 22(2):7–13.

Harwood, A. M., and Hahn, C. L. 1990. *Controversial issues in the classroom.* ERIC document no. ED327453. Bloomington, IN: ERIC Clearinghouse for Social Studies/ Social Science Education.

Holmes, E. E. 1991. Democracy in elementary school classes. *Social Education* 55(3):176–178.

Kreidler, W. J. 1990. Elementary perspectives 1: Teaching concepts of peace and conflict. ERIC document no. ED370873. Cambridge, MA: Educators for Social Responsibility.

Landfried, S. E. 1988. Talking to kids about things that matter. *Educational Leadership* 45(8):32–35.

Lane, P. S., and McWhirter, J. J. 1992. A peer mediation model: Conflict resolution for elementary and middle school children. *Elementary School Guidance and Counseling* 27(1):15–23.

Love, M. J., and Baer, D. 1991. Classroom management. Tired of tattlers? Then teach your students to stand up for themselves. *Learning* 19(7):74–76.

National Council for the Social Studies. 1994. *Expectations of excellence: Curriculum standards for social studies.* Bulletin no. 89. Washington, D.C.: National Council for the Social Studies.

O'Donnell, C. 1991. Rights and the "common good." *Update on Law-Related Education* (15)2:21.

Schmidt, F., Friedman, A., and Abrams, G. C. 1991. Creative conflict solving for kids: Grades 3–4. ERIC document no. ED363850. Miami Beach, FL: Peace Education Foundation, Inc.

_____. 1993. Enriching classroom diversity with books for children, in-depth discussion of them, and story-extension activities. *Young Children* 48(3):10–12.

Shatles, D. 1992. Conflict resolution through children's literature: Impact II. ERIC document no. ED344976. New York: New York City Board of Education.

A P P E N D I X

A Sample Social Studies Unit

I've developed this two-week unit to show you how the various topics included in this book can be integrated to form high-quality social studies instruction for children in grades 4 through 6. As you examine the activities and other parts of the unit, you'll see how elements of history, geography, political science, economics, sociology, anthropology, and religion form the core disciplinary content of this learning experience. You'll also see how inquiry instruction, multicultural education, values education, and differences of opinion may be easily incorporated into regular classroom instruction.

In developing this unit, I followed the guidelines and planning suggestions provided in Chapter 4. The specific components of the unit are those typically found in teacher-directed instruction. Activity ideas have been substituted for traditional lesson plans in order to demonstrate the flexibility of this approach for instruction.

The twelve activities identified should take a little over two weeks to complete. Many other activities could have been specified and added to this unit. The activities I've described here can be modified and improved. Due to space limitations and production constraints, I did not include samples of photographs and resources such as commercial maps and brochures.

THE AMISH

Rationale

The United States is a diverse, multicultural society. We are a mosaic of different peoples functioning in a common, shared culture, but often maintaining distinct cultural and religious practices associated with our origins.

The Amish were one of the first groups to immigrate to the United States. They came in the early 1700s, seeking freedom from religious persecution and good farmland. A product of the tumultuous Protestant Reformation, the Amish interpret many passages of the Bible literally.

The story of the Amish offers important lessons about our nation. Foremost among these is the importance of religious freedom. Lessons may also be learned about the importance of the nuclear and extended family, the benefits of nonviolence, deep care for nature and the environment, fellowship and affiliation, and the benefits of simplicity in living. Activities centered on these topics offer insights into life and the nature of our democratic society that will help children grow into the kinds of adults needed to sustain our freedoms in the future.

Content Outline

I. History of the Amish
   A. Persecution in Europe
   B. Immigration to North America
   C. Early Years in Pennsylvania
II. The Amish of Today
   A. Religious Beliefs and Practices
   B. Family Life
   C. Dress
   D. Work
   E. Schooling
   F. Food
   G. Language
   H. Conflicts with Outsiders and Government
   I.   Population Growth and Geographic Dispersion
III. The Amish and the Future
   A. Rising Costs of Farmland
   B. Commercial Exploitation/Tourism

Unit Goals

As a result of participating in the activities offered in this unit, students will accomplish the following goals.

Knowledge and Information Goals   Students will:

1. learn about the origin and history of the Amish
2. gain an understanding of the Amish culture and religion
3. become acquainted with social problems in the Amish experience
4. speculate about how probable future developments in American society may impact the Amish

Attitude and Value Goals   Students will:

5. learn about the values of tolerance, nonviolence, parsimony, and fellowship
6. develop positive attitudes toward the Amish

Skill Goals   Students will:

7. practice and improve their map-reading, discussion, critical-thinking, valuing, and inquiry learning skills

Social Action and Participation Goals   Students will:

8. practice taking actions designed to influence others

Introductory Activities

Here are some high-involvement ways to start your Amish unit. Consider your resources and the nature of your students as you examine these ideas; then feel free to adapt and improve them.

Activity 1 What We Want to Know about the Amish

Objective(s)   As a result of this activity, students will:

- become aware of the ways in which a group of people can distinguish themselves from others in the larger society (unit goal 5)
- identify questions they would like to have answered about the Amish (unit goal 2)

Gather the class near you on the floor and select five volunteers who are willing to be separated, temporarily, into a "special society." Ask the whole group to help suggest ways that the special society members could be made to look different. Lead the students to suggest things like rolling up pant legs to the knees, wearing construction-paper armbands, parting their hair down the middle, and so on. Encourage the group of volunteers to adopt the suggested modifications and to act as though they are proud of these changes. (Point out to the rest of the group that these changes in appearance are only superficial; the students are still the same. Stress, too, that differences in appearance are interesting and should never be used as the focus of jokes or the target of ridicule.)

Now brainstorm other ways, such as food, housing, customs, and behavior, that the "special society" could further distinguish itself from others. List these on the board, asking questions designed to elicit how each difference might be shown ("How could they make their food different?").

Tell the class they are about to learn about a special society called the Amish. The Amish have separated themselves from others in real life. Ask students to tell you (1) things they may already know about the Amish and (2) things they would like to know about the Amish. Accept reasonable answers and list these on chart paper or enter them into a computer with an LCD panel. (Save these statements and questions for later reference.) Close this activity by briefly showing students some of the resources (books, photographs, videos) that you have gathered. Give students one more opportunity to add to their list of questions. Then see if they can predict which questions will be easiest to answer and what sources are most likely to give the needed information. If some students are anxious to research specific questions, make assignments and challenge them to get to work as soon as possible.

Activity Analysis   This activity primarily addresses topic II in the content outline. Elements of multicultural education, sociology, and anthropology are likely to be involved in students' questions. Since the activity uses a springboard to capture students' interest and then involves them in stating their own interests, it leans toward an inquiry approach to instruction.

Activity 2 Photo Contact with the Amish

Objective(s)   As a result of this activity, students will:

- describe five distinctive features of contemporary Amish life (unit goal 2)
- state tentative generalizations about Amish life (unit goal 2)

Show the class a variety of photographs depicting contemporary Amish men, women, and children in the surroundings of their preferred home and work environments. (About thirty suitable photographs appear in the three children's books listed in the Selected Readings at the end of the unit.) Ask the students to remain silent during this exposition of photos, using only their eyes to catalog the things they see that look different from what they might expect to see in one of their own homes. Following the viewing, use chart paper or the chalk-board to make a list of the students' observations. Note that you may have to prompt students with questions like, "What did you notice about the men's clothing?"

Once each student has had an opportunity to contribute to the list, ask if any of the items are similar and can logically be grouped together. Identify pairs of items with a symbol or numeral and ask students to provide their reasons for grouping the items. Once most or all of the items have been grouped, ask the students to state generalizations about Amish life. For example, several state-ments made about Amish dress might be used to support a generalization such as "Amish women wear long dresses and bonnets when they leave their homes for trips to the city."

Writing Enrichment   Ask students to use what they have just seen as the basis for writing descriptive sentences about Amish life. Allow ample time for independent or paired work. Then, using a large-screen monitor or LCD, transcribe selected sentences into the computer in front of the whole group. Add a story line or plot to show how the descriptive sentences may be used as a part of a story about Amish life.

Activity Analysis   This activity will most likely focus on topic II, elements C through F, in the content outline. Students' statements are likely to involve understandings from multicultural education, sociology, anthropology, and economics. This activity blends elements of the Taba concept development and the generalization teaching strategies.

Activity 3 Mystery Phrase Mix-Up

Objective(s)   As a result of this activity, students will:

- learn the meaning of at least five Pennsylvania Dutch phrases that might be used by Amish children (unit goals 1 and 2)

Fill a shoe box with enough English and Pennsylvania Dutch phrases for each student to have one. Once all of the phrases have been drawn, have the students read their phrases out loud. See if students who have Pennsylvania Dutch phrases can guess what they mean. Now allow the students to mingle and attempt to find the matching pairs. When a match is found, have the students come and write the Pennsylvania Dutch phrase and its translation on the chalkboard, chart paper, or a computer hooked to a large-screen monitor. (Save the phrases and translations to add to them as the unit develops.)

Practice reading the phrases and their translations. Cover the phrases and translations and read ten Pennsylvania Dutch phrases aloud. Ask students to write the English translations. Check to see if each student can write at least five.

Close this activity by asking students to think about the phrases they just learned. See if they can detect that there are many animals mentioned and that this might suggest a rural, farming lifestyle. Also note that the phrases do not mention cars, computers, guns, money, or television.

Activity Analysis   This activity addresses content outline topic II.G. and the linguistic branch of anthropology. The instruction initially takes the form of a card-sort activity, then turns to traditional recitation strategies and finally ends with a higher-order thinking focus.

Some Pennsylvania Dutch phrases and their English translations follow:

PENNSYLVANIA DUTCH PHRASE	ENGLISH TRANSLATION
Schten uff!	Get up!
Geb acht!	Watch out!
Guck, guck!	Look, look!
Redd-up your room.	Straighten up your room.
Baa! baa! schwarz schof	Baa! baa! black sheep
Buwe, geh naus!	Boys, go outside!
Was hoscht du?	What do you have?
Daat	Dad
Gut himmel!	Good heavens!
Ich hop der gross fisch.	I have a big fish.
Des macht mich bees!	That makes me mad!
Gut marriye	Good morning
Sell iss gut!	That is good!
Die gens	The geese
Outen the light.	Turn off the light
Mache schnelle!	Hurry up!
Haufa mischt	Horse manure
Net so hatt	Not so hard
Guck datt hie!	Look there!
Rum springa	Running around

Activity 4 Five-Questions Mystery Quiz

Objective(s)   As a result of this activity, students will:

- learn at least ten facts about Amish history and contemporary life (unit goals 1, 2, and 7)

Ask students if they have ever played Twenty Questions. Briefly review the rules, and state the modification for this game—a limit of five questions before play passes to the other side. Divide the class into two teams.

Tell the class that you are thinking about a particular group of people and they have to guess who this group is. Begin with five questions from the first side. (You may want to pick a captain for each side and allow that person to select different students to ask each question.) Remind students that if they listen to the questions and answers they will be able to narrow down the possible answers and therefore ask better questions.

If students have too much difficulty, begin dropping a few hints, such as "These people do not use electricity." "They don't drive cars." "Women from this group never cut their hair." "Married men wear beards, but no mustache." "Many of these people are farmers." "These people are Anabaptist Christians." "These people came to North America in the early 1700s." "They live primarily in the Northeast and Midwest." "Jacob Amman was their founder." "These people came to Pennsylvania to escape religious persecution in Bern, Switzerland."

Appoint an official note taker on each team to post the "known facts" as they are revealed, then you can review these lists to help close this activity.)

Activity Analysis   This activity can address virtually any topic in the content outline depending upon the clues you use. All disciplines of the social sciences, except psychology and social psychology, are likely to be involved. History and religion are the principle humanities that will be used. Because this activity attempts to create a mystery that students desire to solve, and because that mystery is solved through their own brain work, I believe this activity is directly related to the philosophy of inquiry instruction.

Developmental Activities

These activities are designed to help students fully achieve the goals of this unit on the Amish. You probably won't need to implement every activity described, but if you skip too many or concentrate only in one area, students may not be able to achieve all of the unit goals. As in the introductory activities, consider your resources and the nature of your students to determine which activities seem best—and feel free to adapt and improve these ideas.

Activity 5 Amish Dress

Objective(s)   As a result of this activity, students will:

• state at least two observations about how Amish men, women, and children dress (unit goal 2)

Display new pictures of Amish men, women, and children around the room so that each is grouped separately. Ask students to use notepaper to write down hypotheses about the rules that these three groups observe in their dress. Gather back into a large group and share some of the hypotheses. Then share the following generalizations about rules of dress for Amish men, women, and children.

Men

Amish men wear dark black or blue jackets that have no pockets or lapels.

Loose fitting, pocketless pants are held up by suspenders.

No zippers, belts, or buttons are used, only hooks and eyes.

Shirts are often white, though other solid colors (except red) are allowed.

Amish men wear a broad-brimmed black felt hat when outdoors in the cold.

During summer they wear straw hats with a black band.

No jewelry is allowed.

Unmarried men are clean shaven.

Married men wear beards but no mustache.

Women

Amish women wear long, full dresses, all of the same style.

An apron is worn over the dress, white if the woman is unmarried, otherwise dark.

Only solid colors are permitted.

A white cap is worn over the back of the head and tied under the chin.

No jewelry is allowed.

In cold weather women wear heavy, dark-colored shawls.

No zippers, belts, or buttons are used, only hooks and eyes.

Women part their hair down the middle and roll it into buns. They never cut their hair.

Children

Amish children dress like their adult counterparts.

Multicultural Enrichment   In some areas it may be possible to arrange a visit by an Amish family or a person who has firsthand knowledge of the Amish. Tell your guest in advance that your children are interested in the customs of Amish dress.

Activity Analysis   This activity addresses topic II.C. and aspects of religion, anthropology, sociology, and history. The instructional strategies used are observation and straightforward teacher exposition of content. The enrichment activity will provide an opportunity for a true multicultural learning experience and perhaps some values education.

Activity 6 Amish History

Objective(s)   As a result of this activity, students will:

- correctly identify factual statements about the origin and history of the Amish (unit goal 1)
- be able to write a short paragraph that describes some of the core religious beliefs and practices of the Amish (unit goal 2)

Begin this activity by asking students if they know what the word *persecution* means. Accept reasonable guesses and, if necessary, have a student look up the word. (Persecute means harass with ill-treatment or annoy, but during the Reformation it included physical attacks, the burning of homes, arrest, torture, and execution.) Tell the students that the Amish came to North America to escape persecution due to their religious beliefs.

Explain that the group of people known as the Amish originated during the Protestant Reformation of the sixteenth and seventeenth centuries. During this time many groups of Christian people in Europe broke away from the practices of the Roman Catholic Church and formed their own congregations. A German priest named Martin Luther (1483–1546) was a leading figure in this revolt away from Catholic authority. In Switzerland, a priest named Huldrych Zwingli (1484–1531) led another revolt against the Roman Catholic Church. From his pulpit Zwingli demanded immediate religious reform. He asserted the sole and absolute authority of the Bible and affirmed the doctrine of salvation by faith and faith alone.

> Soon, under Zwingli's influence, the city of Zurich abolished the Mass. Religious statues, pictures, crucifixes, altars, and candles were removed from the churches. Relics were destroyed. Holy water was done away with, and even church frescoes were covered with whitewash. To Zwingli, since none of these practices could be found in the Bible, they were evil and detracted from the true spirit of Christian belief. (Israel, 1986, 12)

Martin Luther's work led to the establishment of the Lutheran Church. Huldrych Zwingli's work led to the development of the Reformed Church, which eventually split into dozens of smaller groups. One group that formed under Konrad Grebel (c. 1498–1526) did not believe in the baptism of infants, contending that only adults could declare their faith in Christ and promise to follow his ways. Grebel's followers came to be known as the Anabaptists and they were severely persecuted for their beliefs. The Anabaptists eventually came to be known as Mennonites, named after Menno Simons (1496–1561), one of their most influential leaders. Zwingli attacked this group and forced them to flee from Zurich. Under continued persecution, many Mennonites immigrated to North America and settled in what is now the state of Pennsylvania.

In 1693 a Swiss Mennonite elder, Jacob Amman (1644–1730), broke with his church because he felt the Mennonite religion had lost its purity. In particular, Amman felt that church members who violated the teachings of their faith should be shunned or barred from all religious, social, and economic contact. Amman insisted that shunning be total, even demanding that the wife and children of an excommunicated member be prohibited from eating at the same table with the sinner until proper penitence had been made. He also favored nearly complete uniformity in dress. Amman's followers became known as the Amish.

People in Europe continued to persecute the Amish for their religious beliefs. Hearing of the religious freedom Mennonites had found in Pennsylvania, the Amish followed them to North America.

Today there are no Amish left in Europe. They have, however, spread and prospered in the United States. They live on farmland around small rural communities throughout the Northeast and Midwest. A few have moved to Canada.

Using a question-and-answer format, review the following with the students.

Question

What does the word *persecution* mean?

When did the Amish originate?

Where did the Amish live in Europe?

Who was Huldrych Zwingli and what did he do?

What did Zwingli and his followers believe?

What happened in the Roman Catholic churches in Zurich during Zwingli's revolt?

Konrad Grebel broke away from the Reformed Church and formed a group that came to be known as the Anabaptists. What does the word *Anabaptist* mean?

Who was Menno Simons?

What happened to the Mennonites in Europe?

Where did the Mennonites go?

Who was Jacob Amman and what did he believe?

What is *shunning* and how did it figure in the formation of the Amish?

Why did the Amish come to Pennsylvania?

Where do the Amish live today?

Ask students to write a short paragraph that describes some of the religious beliefs of the Amish. To help students with this assignment, write some of the terms and names associated with Amish history on the chalkboard.

Examine students' work and share the best paragraphs.

Activity Analysis   This activity develops students' understanding of topics I.A., I.B., and II.A. in the content outline. History and religion are the principle disciplines featured. The instructional strategy used is a lecture with follow-up questions and answers. The writing assignment gives students an opportunity to put this newly acquired information into their own words.

Activity 7. Locating the Amish

Objective(s)   As a result of this activity, students will:

• correctly identify the states where the Amish currently live (unit goal 7)

Using a large wall map of the United States, have students identify New York, Pennsylvania, Ohio, Indiana, Illinois, Wisconsin, Minnesota, Kentucky, Tennessee, Arkansas, Oklahoma, and Kansas. Tell them that these are the states where most Amish live. The Amish usually live on farms near small towns. Make an overhead of the map on page 4 of Israel's 1986 book, *Meet the Amish*, and project it onto a screen near the U.S. map. Have students attempt to locate towns near Amish settlements.

Enrichment Obtain maps of the states where Amish live and attempt to pinpoint Amish communities. Write or call each state's tourism department and request information about Amish settlements.

Activity Analysis This activity gives students practice in using map skills and addresses outline topic topic II.I. The instructional strategy used could be characterized as traditional teacher-led map work. Using three different views of the same area and attempting to locate and describe the surroundings of Amish communities helps make this an interesting and challenging activity. If the tourist bureaus supply large-scale maps of counties where Amish live, this activity will gain added meaning and interest for students.

Activity 8 Amish Family Life

Objective(s) As a result of this activity, students will:

- become aware of the attitudes and values that unite Amish families and demonstrate this awareness by helping to create a short skit centered on some aspect of home life (unit goals 2 and 5)
- show their understanding of social problems the Amish experience by writing a one-page paper that shows the lure of the dominant culture for youth and/or conflicts that sometimes erupt between Amish adults and their children (unit goal 3)

Tell students that you want them to learn more about Amish families and how they live. Read Chapter 1, "Samuel Beiler and His Kin," from *Amish People. Plain Living In a Complex World* (Meyer, 1976). These twenty-three pages cover some of the temptations of the outside world and the feelings and practices that surround internal family relationships. Stop at appropriate places and invite students to react to the story. Note especially how the values of tolerance, parsimony, and fellowship are drawn out in the story.

Involve students in creating short skits that mimic some of the situations portrayed in the story. Ask the skit writers to rehearse their skit for you to help make sure the actions and words seem realistic. Once skits are ready, perform them for the whole group.

Ask students to write a one-page paper about the temptations of the dominant culture and the conflicts that can occur between Amish adults and their children.

Activity Analysis This activity uses literature to connect students to the world of the Amish family. Sociology, social psychology, and religion are the main disciplines that offer concepts and generalizations for thinking about the content of this activity. Many of the areas of topic II will be captured in the story listening, writing, and skits.

Activity 9   Video Field Trip

Objective(s)   As a result of this activity, students will:

- demonstrate positive attitudes toward the Amish by taking a stand that defends their right to live life as they do (unit goals 6 and 8)
- gain additional information about the Amish and demonstrate this learning by writing three sentences that communicate it (unit goals 1, 2, and 3)

Tell students that now that they know something about the Amish you think it would be nice to take a field trip to Lancaster, Pennsylvania, to actually visit some Amish. Point out, however, that many tourists make this trip and don't get to see or meet the Amish because the Amish want to be left alone. So instead of going to visit the Amish, the class is going to take a video field trip. Engage the class in naming some of the things they would like to see and learn on their video field trip, and then show the video, *The Amish: A People of Preservation.*

Debrief the video by asking students to reveal the information they sought and learned. Focus also on the Amish's right to use the roads with their horses and buggies, and their right not to wear certain clothes, or drive cars, or watch television. Ask the students to take a stand regarding these rights.

Conclude this activity by having students write three sentences each about new information they learned from the video. (Have them leave two blank spaces between each sentence so they can be cut apart.) Share these statements and place them on a bulletin board. Try to group the statements. Analyze why some things were mentioned more often than others.

Activity Analysis   Because of the broad scope of the 54-minute video, this activity helps students learn about virtually all topics in the content outline. The primary disciplines involved are history, sociology, and religion. Since the preparation for the video attempts to turn students into knowledge detectives, and since the ending asks students to take an evaluative stance regarding the rights of the Amish, this activity is a blend of direct instruction and inquiry techniques.

Activity 10   Amish in the News

Objective(s)   As a result of this activity, students will:

- develop an understanding of how the social problems and pressures of contemporary society impact the lives of the Amish by publishing a classroom newspaper featuring stories like the ones in real newspapers (unit goals 3 and 4)

Tap into on-line newspaper databases and search for stories about the Amish. For example, the *Columbus Dispatch* published twenty-six news stories between February 1988 and December 1994 that dealt with how laws and legal proceedings are affecting the Amish. Some of the titles follow: "Game Officials Take Aim at Amish Hunters Who Won't Wear Orange"; "New Amish Residents Put Lights on Buggies"; "Old-Line Amish Buck Buggy Safety Law"; "Chick Farm Idea Opposed"; "Officials Are Wary of Bill to Free Amish from Workers' Compensation"; "Jailed Man's Faith Clashes with Law"; "Amish Deaths May Alter State Law"; and "Amish Families Issue Plea to Respect Privacy."

Distribute the stories and have students read them in small groups. Once the stories have been shared, tape them to the wall and attempt to categorize them. Note if some topics appear more frequently than others and speculate why.

Using a desktop publishing program, engage students in publishing the front page of a fictitious *Amish Times* newspaper that covers the same issues, topics, and problems found in the real news. Display this work as a part of a bulletin board about the Amish.

Activity Analysis   This activity helps students gain an understanding of topics II.H., III.A., and III.B. The disciplines involved will most likely be sociology, social psychology, and economics. The use of newspaper articles as data sources, and attempts to categorize and explain these articles reminds me most of the generalization teaching strategy. The publication of the paper gives students an opportunity to demonstrate their learning in a creative manner.

Activity 11 Comparing the Amish with Our Own Culture

Objective(s)   As a result of this activity, students will:

- demonstrate their knowledge of how the Amish are similar and different from their own culture by completing a data collection chart (unit goal 2)

Show the video *The Amish: A People of Preservation*, stopping it frequently to point out how similar and different the lives of the Amish are from our own. For example, when the video first shows a horse and buggy, pause the tape and ask students to tell how this means of conveyance is similar to the cars that we use. (It has four wheels, seats, doors, and so on. It takes you where you want to go. It has a license plate and electric taillights, and so on.) Now have the students tell you how it is different. (It doesn't use gas. It's slower. It doesn't have chrome or bright paint. It lacks a horn and turn signals. It doesn't have a radio or power steering.) Repeat this process for ten other manifestations of Amish culture such as a barn raising, a scene from an Amish kitchen, a view of a horse-drawn harvester, Amish dress, and so on.

Once you've stopped the video for ten points of contrast, stop and ask students to complete a blank data collection chart about at least five of the similarities and differences.

Activity Analysis   This activity helps students gain a deeper understanding of the elements shown in topic II. Information will be brought out from economics, sociology, anthropology, religion, and social psychology. This activity takes a direct instruction format, but students are involved in generating the similarities and differences rather than having to listen to the teacher point these out.

Activity 12 Future Problems for the Amish

Objective(s)   As a result of this activity, students will:

• write a short story that describes how future developments may impact the Amish

Begin this activity by reading the following story reprinted, with permission, from *The Columbus* (Ohio) *Dispatch.*

CHICK-FARM IDEA OPPOSED
◆ ◆ ◆ ◆

Columbus Dispatch (CD) - WEDNESDAY, November 2, 1994
By: Donna Glenn, Dispatch Staff Reporter
Edition: Home Final Section: NEWS LOCAL & NATIONAL Page: 06B

MOUNT VICTORY, Ohio - A proposed chicken farm in southeastern Hardin County that would raise as many as 925,000 pullets would cause considerable air and water pollution, residents told an official of the Ohio Environmental Protection Agency at a public hearing last night.

The pullet farm would be built 5 miles northwest of LaRue, which is in Marion County. It would supply laying hens for a 2.5 million egg farm, which is under construction 12 miles northwest of LaRue, says a proposal to the EPA by the Agri-General Co.

Agri-General has applied to the EPA for a livestock waste management plan to store, handle and dispose of dead chickens and manure.

"These chickens will produce approximately 66 tons of manure per day, the equivalent to human waste produced by a city of 253,000 people," tree farmer Mike Hardin said.

Residents called on the EPA to reject the proposed operation based on owner Anton Pohlmann's farming record in Germany. In September, the German government banned Pohlmann for life from raising poultry in that country.

"Anton Pohlmann's record of compliance with or defiance of German law relates to how he will conduct a multimillion-hen operation in Ohio," said John Guendelsberg, attorney for the Hale Township Site Opposition Group.

Residents told the EPA that manure from both operations spread on the soil of nearby farms would leach into the Scioto River and Tymochtee Creek. In a letter submitted last night by the opposition group, Amish Bishop Levi Petersheim said Agri-General trucks likely would use Township Rt. 250, a thoroughfare for 79 Amish families.

"We feel this would create a dangerous situation . . . and humbly ask that you choose an alternative route for the safety of our children," Petersheim wrote. The

Amish also worry that Agri-General wells would affect the water supply, chicken diseases would transfer to smaller flocks and flies would annoy horses working fields. EPA will receive written testimony concerning the pullet farm until Nov. 18.

Help students recall the main ideas and facts in the article, and then point out to them that the Agri-General Company is seeking to fill a demand for chicken. This demand is a result of increased population and changing tastes for meat products. This is a manifestation of population growth and large-scale production facilities for raising chickens represent progress in agricultural technology. (Chickens are fed a precise diet that produces maximum growth; they live in a highly controlled environment; they are processed in large numbers; and so on.)

Now help students understand the reasons why Amish Bishop Petersheim felt this chicken farm would be a danger (road hazard to buggies from large trucks, pollution of well water, threat of poultry diseases, and flies that would annoy Amish workhorses).

Point out that this is just one example of how progress can threaten the lifeways of the Amish. Help students imagine other forms of progress that might threaten the Amish and list their suggestions on the board. Some examples are: (1) the growth of tourism making it difficult for the Amish to maintain their privacy; (2) increases in land prices making it more difficult for the Amish to own farmland, make a living from their produce, and pay their taxes; and (3) the development of industries that cause noise, air, and water pollution making it more difficult for the Amish to lead peaceful lives close to nature. Other manifestations of progress also intrude on the Amish way of life. Examples are such things as when a small road becomes a four-lane highway; when large power lines are run past or through Amish property; and even smaller things like merchants no longer stocking basic food supplies as demand for microwavable dinners and other fast foods increases.

Ask students to select one form of progress and write a one-page essay that describes how the Amish are likely to react to and cope with the progress. Challenge students to come up with solutions that do not require the Amish to forsake their way of life.

Activity Analysis   This activity is designed to help students focus on topic III in the content outline. Virtually all of the social science and humanities disciplines offer conceptual tools and understandings for examining these conflicts. The instruction starts off with an inquirylike springboard, but never moves students farther into the inquiry process. Instead students are teacher-led through an examination of the springboard and then called upon to generate a list of similar topics to use as the topics of essays. Students have some freedom to be creative in their thinking and writing process, so this activity moves beyond the recall level of learning.

Concluding Activities

The two activities that follow offer ways to finish your Amish unit. As with other activities, you'll need to consider the amount of time and other resources you can devote to them. Adaptations for your individual circumstances may be necessary.

Activity 13 Amish Food Festival

Objective(s)   As a result of this activity, students will:

- demonstrate their knowledge of Amish cuisine culture as they prepare Amish foods and serve them to their guests (unit goals 6 and 8)

Use the information already gained about the Amish culture and sections from Israel's 1986 book, *Meet the Amish,* to draw out ideas about what foods the students might prepare for an Amish food festival. If possible, bring in a copy of Good's 1988 book, *The Best of Amish Cooking: Traditional and Contemporary Recipes Adapted from the Kitchens and Pantries of Old,* and select authentic recipes that are easy to prepare. Ask parent volunteers to participate and support the food festival by preparing dishes that the students can't handle in the school environment.

On the day of the food festival, ask students to wear plain clothes. Allow the girls to part their hair in the middle. Make Amish-style construction-paper caps and hats for the girls and boys to wear, respectively. Encourage students to serve any guests that come to the festival and share what they've learned about Amish culture. Display products of students' work on the Amish unit around the room.

Activity Analysis   This activity allows students to review and present many aspects of their knowledge and, therefore touches on virtually all topics in the content outline. Similarly, all disciplines of the social sciences and humanities will be involved. If students are involved in evaluating ideas for the festival, this activity will reach into the higher levels of thought, while presentations to guests will involve the recall and interpretation of knowledge. Opportunities to infuse math exist in preparing and increasing the sizes of recipes. Writing skills can be exercised meaningfully in issuing invitations and writing thank-you notes to parents who support this activity.

Activity 14 Living Diorama: Amish Culture on View

Objective(s)   As a result of this activity, students will:

- demonstrate their knowledge of Amish culture as they prepare a life-size Amish diorama (unit goals 1, 2, 5, 7, and 8)

Tell students that as a way of culminating their unit on the Amish they are going to build a life-sized diorama of Amish life that can be put in the entry way of the school for others to enjoy. Review the concept of dioramas and help students recall museum displays that they have witnessed.

Engage students in selecting the scenes from Amish life that they would most like to portray. (Allow them to look at the photos contained in the three children's books if they have trouble deciding.) Stress that the scene should allow viewers to gain a lot of information about Amish culture, so a picture of a solitary woman walking down a road would probably not be as effective as a picture of the inside of an Amish schoolhouse or kitchen.

Once students have decided on one or more scenes, help them determine what would go into the scenes and how they might be made. (Large refrigerator boxes can serve well as the backdrop and side walls. Borrowed or donated items can be used as props.)

As the diorama is built, help students assess the quality of their work. Write viewer posters that describe the contents of the diorama. Ask some students to play the role of interpreters for the diorama and bring the diorama to life with real characters for at least one full school day. (Have several different students take the same roles at different points during the day.) Invite parents, school officials, and the media during the live diorama day.

Activity Analysis   This activity addresses mainly topic II of the content outline. The disciplines involved in producing the living diorama include most of the social sciences and humanities. This construction project is run democratically and involves higher-order thinking.

Unit Evaluation Plan

Students will be evaluated on meeting the goals and objectives of this unit by a variety of means. Collect students' work at the end of activities and use it to assess whether objectives have been met. Involve students in self-evaluation, helping judge how well they performed the learning tasks offered in the unit. Compose an end-of-unit test consisting of true-false, multiple-choice, matching, fill-in-the blank, listing, and essay items. Samples of each type of item follow.

TRUE-FALSE

1. Amish men wear mustaches.   T   F

2. The Amish are Anabaptist Christians.   T   F

MULTIPLE CHOICE

3. The Amish live in several different states. Which of the following is one of them?

   a. Oregon

   b. Texas

c. Florida

d. North Dakota

e. Pennsylvania

4. Which of the following men is recognized as the founder of the Amish religion?

a. Martin Luther

b. Huldryich Zwingli

c. Gut Himmel

d. Jacob Amman

e. Menno Simons

M A T C H I N G

5. Match the following words and phrases by drawing a line to connect the matching terms.

Baa! baa! schwarz schof	I have a big fish.
Geb acht!	Dad
Schten uff!	Good heavens!
Gut himmel!	Straighten up your room.
Ich hop der gross fisch.	Baa! baa! black sheep
Guck, guck!	Get up!
Redd-up your room.	Look, look!
Des macht mich bees!	That makes me mad!
Daat	What do you have?
Was hoscht du?	Watch out!

F I L L   I N   T H E   B L A N K

6. Long ago, the Amish lived in _____.

7. The Amish don't use any _____ or zippers to secure their clothes.

E S S A Y

8. Write a one-page essay that describes the clothing of Amish men and women.

9. Describe three potential conflicts the Amish might have with the dominant society in the future. Explain why the Amish might have a problem with this situation and how society might accommodate the Amish way of life.

SELECTED READINGS

For Children

Ammon, R. 1989. *Growing up Amish.* New York: Atheneum. Well illustrated with black and white photographs of children and youth, this book describes different facets of growing up Amish.

Israel, F. L. 1986. *Meet the Amish.* New York: Chelsea House. One of a series of books on the peoples of North America, this book offers eighty pages of information and photographs suitable for fifth-grade readers. Covered are the history, practices and beliefs, home and farm, and education of the Amish.

Meyer, C. 1976. *Amish people. Plain living in a complex world.* New York: Atheneum. Told from the perspective of individuals within the Amish Beiler family, this book presents many of the thoughts and feelings experienced by the Amish as they encounter outsiders and function within their own communities.

The Amish: A people of preservation. 1991. Worcester, PA: Gateway Films/Vision Video, Inc. 54 minutes. Color. Filmed in Lancaster County, PA, this video features authentic scenes of farm life, childhood, school, worship, recreation, and courtship.

For Teachers

Good, P. P. 1988. *The best of Amish cooking: Traditional and contemporary recipes adapted from the kitchens and pantries of old.* Intercourse, PA: Good Books.

Guilty plea offered in death of 5 Amish children on road (19-year-old Eric Bache pleads guilty to aggravated vehicular homicide in Wooster, Ohio). 1993. *New York Times,* 9 Sept. 1993, v142, pA18(L), col 6.

Hostetler, J. A. 1992. *Amish children: Education in the family, school, and community.* Fort Worth, TX: Harcourt Brace Jovanovich.

_____. 1993. *Amish society.* Baltimore: Johns Hopkins University Press.

_____, ed. 1989. *Amish roots: A treasury of history, wisdom, and lore.* Baltimore: Johns Hopkins University Press.

Keim, A. N., ed. 1975. *Compulsory education and the Amish: The right not to be.* Boston: Beacon Press.

Kraybill, D. B. 1989. *The riddle of Amish culture.* Baltimore: Johns Hopkins University Press.

_____. 1993. *The Amish and the state.* Baltimore: Johns Hopkins University Press.

Kraybill, D. B., and Olshan M. A., eds. 1994. *The Amish struggle with modernity.* Hanover, NH: University Press of New England.

McLary, K. 1993. *Amish style: Clothing, home furnishing, toys, dolls, and quilts.* Bloomington, IN: Indiana University Press.

Nagata, J. A. 1989. *Continuity and change among the old order Amish of Illinois.* New York: AMS Press.

Nolt, S. M. 1992. *A history of the Amish.* Intercourse, PA: Good Books.

Redekop, C. W. 1989. *Mennonite society*. Baltimore: Johns Hopkins University Press.

Ruth, J. L., Miller, I., and Good, M. 1990. America's Anabaptists: Who are they? *Christianity Today* 34(15):25–30.

Schreiber, W. I. 1962. *Our Amish neighbors*. Chicago: University of Chicago Press.

Stone, P. 1989. The Amish answer: An ecological, spiritual small-farm subculture is thriving in the heartland of America. *Mother Earth News* 56–61, 118.

Wave goodbye to the Amish? (prosperity threatens their way of life). 1989. *The Economist* 312(7612):28.